Susan Rosenfeld Falb
6017 Onondaga Rd
Washington. D.C. 20016

D0891500

Jonathan Boucher

Loyalist in Exile

Daniel Gardner. Jonathan Boucher. *Ca. 1782.*
Yale University Art Gallery, Mabel Brady Garvan Collection.

Jonathan Boucher

Loyalist in Exile

by Anne Y. Zimmer
Wayne State University

Wayne State University Press
Detroit, 1978

Library of Congress Cataloging in Publication Data
Zimmer, Anne Y., 1920-
    Jonathan Boucher, loyalist in exile.

    Bibliography: p.
    Includes index.
    1. Boucher, Jonathan, 1738-1804.   2. American
loyalists—Biography.   3.   United States—History—
Revolution, 1775-1783.   I.   Title.
E277.B753Z55   973.3'14'0924 [B]   77-29257
ISBN 0-8143-1592-5

This volume is published with the support of a grant from the American Council of Learned Societies for publication of first books by scholars in the fields of the humanities.

To Arnold Zimmer
and Robert Arthur Stewart Zimmer,
and in memory of Kathleen Anne

～Contents～

Illustrations 8
Preface 9
Note to the Text 14

ILLUSTRATIONS

⮡ Preface ⮠

Scholars have only recently begun to recognize that Jonathan Boucher was a significant figure in the history of eighteenth-century American thought. In terms of intellectual capacity and ability to philosophize, he was perhaps the leading Tory figure, one of the very few men on either side of the American Revolution who developed a complete system of conservative political thought about it and about government in general. Of all the American refugees in England, only six men achieved the distinction of having private conversations with members of the British administration; two of them were Thomas Hutchinson and Jonathan Boucher. Among his clerical colleagues in exile, Thomas Bradbury Chandler chose Boucher as most worthy of his esteem and as the friend in whom he had the greatest confidence. He preferred his letters to those of any other man. In the nineteenth century, Moss Coit Tyler in his literary history commended Boucher for his able presentation of the deeper principles and motives of the American Loyalists, while another writer called him a formidable opponent in intellect. Andrew Scott, in *Political Thought in America* (1959), described him as the most talented if not the most influential of Tory spokesmen.

Boucher was considered one of Maryland's best preachers, with the most exemplary of characters, and one who therefore stood in sharp contrast to many of his contemporaries. He was also the leading spokesman for the Anglican church in the South, and the strongest advocate of a resident bishop for America. A nineteenth-century writer complimented him as the most erudite and eloquent of Maryland churchmen. More recently Wallace Brown included him as one of five of Maryland's outstanding men, and Ronald Hoffman in *A Spirit of Dissension* (1973) declared

9

that Boucher was the leading and most powerful American church-man in Maryland before the war.

Boucher's ideas received some acceptance in England during his lifetime, but it was along party lines from those who detested the French Revolution. In America, however, Tories were accorded short shrift after hostilities began. The best treatment which men of Boucher's principles could expect was oblivion; at worst they were denounced as traitors, as materialists following their pay-checks, or as mindless sycophants. Boucher was declared the worst of traitors, while his book was consigned to near oblivion. A partial rehabilitation occurred in 1897, one hundred years after the ap-pearance of his book of sermons dealing with the causes of the American Revolution. A full renaissance waited for another hun-dred years.

1997 ?

No one would have been more surprised than Boucher at the attention he was given during the extended bicentennial cele-bration of the Declaration of Independence. The commemoration resulted in symposia from coast to coast and a flood of publica-tions, and provided the most full and varied discussion of Loyalist principles and their spokesmen since Revolutionary War days. Boucher would have appreciated the irony in that. But he would also have been pleased that Americans could now take a com-prehensive historical view of the "other side," without partisan-ship and with room for some sympathy. He knew that day could not come in his own lifetime, although he wistfully hoped it might, but his book of sermons has served his purpose: to prove that many like himself who became Loyalists were not "fools or knaves." Perhaps America has come of age.

Nonetheless, in spite of Boucher's increasing popularity as a source of conservative thought, no book-length biography exists. There has never been an adequate exposition of his ideas; most of what has been written by scholars has been essentially a Patriot view of him as a hopeless reactionary and a defender of Filmer and the divine right of kings. The exceptions are brief encomiums in English publications and complimentary articles in church-oriented volumes. It is less well known that Boucher's life con-sisted of three distinct careers, marked off by radical alterations in his social position, economic interests, and friendships, which paralleled substantial changes in his political thinking. He took the path leading to high toryism with reluctance in 1775, but his

10

advance along it was fostered slowly but certainly by personal and historical events throughout the last quarter of the eighteenth century.

Little has been known of Boucher's life in England after 1775, of his two schools, first at Paddington and then at Epsom, of his concern for Samuel Seabury and the health of the newly established Protestant Episcopal church of the United States, and of his clerical and personal interest in the Scottish churches. Few American historians have known of the narrow margins by which Boucher twice missed becoming a bishop, and why. His writing in local history and his sweeping program for voluntary social welfare programs and projects for the development of natural resources in Cumberland had a limited audience, largely because his work was published anonymously. Even his most ambitious work, a lexicon intended to correct the errors and omissions of Samuel Johnson, slipped into obscurity.

Boucher's life has significance beyond the merely personal, although the complexity of his mind, the venturesomeness of his spirit, and the mixture of practicality, imagination, romanticism, and determination in his personality made his life colorful. He was a fascinating individual. More importantly, he was representative of the heavy losers in the American Revolution, many of whose lives were endangered, whose property was confiscated, and whose family ties were disrupted and divided between the opposing sides in this essentially civil war. Boucher's story reminds us that there was an articulate body of citizens with logical and reasoned arguments on the British side of the war. His experiences as a Loyalist serve to press the point that individualism has been so much a part of the American national character that it has been accepted almost as an absolute. Boucher understood the threat to an orderly society implicit in the ultimate development of individualism, reminding us that there may be other values to consider in order to preserve the fabric of society. Although it has not always been the dominant theme, a stream of conservatism has always existed in America. Jeffersonian philosophy has frequently overshadowed Boucher's brand of conservatism, but has never caused it to sink without a trace. Much of Boucher's thought was good fundamental Whig philosophy, shared by John Adams, Andrew Hamilton, Fisher Ames, and other Federalists who participated in the foundation of the new nation.

In drawing together the threads of Boucher's long and full life, I have necessarily avoided extensive treatment of local history. I have tried to keep in mind James Reston's thought that the whole of a life can be given a sense of reality by the use of the "creative fact." If I have given Boucher's life a touch of reality, and a shape that he would have recognized, I will be pleased. The American Revolution was a tragedy in his life, and throughout it he could never see "an inch before me" in a war that seemed to him wholly unnecessary. For a man of his temperament, being a pawn of history was particularly hard to bear. However, unlike the passive chessman, he never ceased to struggle, and as one of his close friends remarked to him, "If fortune has sported with you, she has likewise sported for you and upon the whole I think you may be said to have had pretty good sport."

In preparing this biography I have incurred numerous debts to various individuals, societies, and institutions. I am much indebted to Jonathan Locker-Lampson, Boucher's literary heir, for his permission to use many Boucher-related letters, and for many courteous replies to queries at various times. I am also grateful to Arthur C. Young of Russell Sage College, for advice and encouragement at every point of difficulty, and to Paul Mattheisen of the State University of New York at Binghamton for directing me to little-known letters at Rowfant Hall. Among my colleagues at Wayne State University, I am particularly indebted to Richard D. Miles, Goldwin Smith, and to the late Alfred H. Kelly.

Many individuals on the other side of the Atlantic aided my research in a variety of ways, among them John Syrad, Mavis Mackinnon, Alan Murphy, and F. W. Cranmer, the last two of the *Croydon Times*. H. Hale Bellot, Emeritus Professor of American History at the University of London, gave me valuable information, as did Brig. C. E. F. Turner, Sir Michael Heathcote, Sir John Gutch, Kenneth Smith, Henry Hodgson, Margaret Brander, J.P., A.L.A., reference librarian of the Cumbria County Library, and B. C. Jones and Jeremy Godwin of the Record Office in Carlisle Castle.

I also wish to thank the staff members of various American and British institutions, too numerous to record here, who rendered service beyond the necessities of their offices. However, the following individuals deserve particular mention: Denis H. Merry of the Bodleian Library, J. L. Burgess of the *Cumberland News,* E. G. W. Bill of the Lambeth Palace Library, Veronica Mathew of Sotheby's, Patricia Barnden of the Paul Mellon Centre, Jacqueline Meredith of the National Portrait Gallery, Ann Goring and H. Powell of the Queen's College library, and Veronica Brinton of the Courtauld Institute.

In America, Marjorie G. Wynne and Bonnie Collier of the Sterling Memorial Library of Yale University, John Knowlton and Carolyn Sung of the Library of Congress, and F. Garner Ranney, historiographer of the Maryland diocese, all gave generously of their time and expertise. John Kilbourne rendered valuable assistance over a period of years at the Maryland Historical Society, the Annapolis Hall of Records, and the Historical Society of Pennsylvania, institutions at which other staff members went out of their way to be helpful. I wish to thank the staff of the Purdy Memorial Library at Wayne State University for a variety of services, but especially for the personal interest in the book which Donald E. Ewing and Gladys Hogland expressed through service well beyond what was required of them. The reference librarians of the William Clements Library and of the Graduate Library of the University of Michigan rendered superior service, as did the staff of the Burton Historical Collection of the Detroit Public Library, particularly Irene Dudley, Bernice Sprenger, Alice Dalligan, and Gloria Birkenmeier. I am also grateful to Sherwyn T. Carr of the Wayne State University Press for her expert editorial counsel during the publication process, and to Jean Osborn for preparation of the index.

To the American Association of University Women I acknowledge my sincere appreciation for a fellowship which provided critical financial support for extensive research both in the United States and in England and a year of free time in which to work; my thanks are due also to the Zonta Club of Detroit for its generous fellowship, which supported my initial graduate work and made all the rest possible. I am deeply grateful to the following women who helped to prepare the manuscript at various stages with patience and care: Clare McKnight, Lillian Motis, Kathleen Taylor, Kathryn McNulty, Marjorie Miles, Jeanine Head, and Nancy Zindler. Finally, my fullest gratitude is reserved for my family for their encouragement and understanding.

◝ Note to the Text ◜

The letters written by Jonathan Boucher to the Reverend John James began in 1759 with Boucher's arrival in America, and ended twenty-six years later with James's death in January 1785. The bulk of the letters was published between 1912 and 1915 in the Maryland Historical Magazine. *Additional unpublished letters were discovered in 1960 at Rowfant Hall, the family residence of a Boucher descendant, and made available to me through the courtesy of Jonathan Locker-Lampson. They have now been transferred to the East Sussex Record Office, Lewes. Another series of letters between Boucher, the senior James, and his son John were edited by Margaret Evans and published as* Letters of Richard Radcliffe and John James of Queen's College, Oxford *(Oxford: Clarendon Press, 1888). Evans did not use all of John James, Sr.'s letters, according to a note in her edition. Some of them may have been the counterparts of the 1759-85 series upon which my biography is largely based. However, a survey of potential sources, including Queen's College, the East Sussex Record Office, the Bodleian Library, Cumberland County respositories, and Arthuret Parish failed to reveal any trace of them.*

When I quote from unpublished material, I have modernized Boucher's spelling and punctuation, and silently corrected obvious errors. I have not modified his grammar, and missing words supplied from the context of a manuscript appear in square brackets. I have also silently modernized eighteenth-century typography in some quotations from published sources. Full references to all sources can be found in the bibliography and notes, but the three most important and frequently quoted are cited within the text. Boucher's Reminiscences of an American Loyalist *is cited as* Rem.; *his 1797 book of sermons is cited as* A View; *the letters published in the* Maryland Historical Magazine *are cited as* MHM, *followed by the appropriate volume and page numbers.*

The
American
Years

Chapter 1

Early Years in Cumberland

Cumberland County, in the northwestern corner of England, forms a part of the beautiful English Lake District which inspired many of the thoughts and images of its native romantic poet, William Wordsworth. The county's mountainous southern portion, deeply dissected by lake-filled valleys, has craggy volcanic rock formations which give way in the north to the softer scenery of the slate mountain region. In the northern coastal strip, some ten miles from the Solway Firth and the Irish Sea, Jonathan Boucher was born in the family home of James and Anne Boucher in Blencogo, a quiet hamlet of Bromfield Parish, on 12 March 1738.[1]

The parish in 1738 was thoroughly undistinguished and undeveloped, and remained so throughout Boucher's lifetime. There were no great estates, no manufactures, and no mines. Living conditions were nearly primitive; the houses were constructed primarily of mud or clay, with thatched roofs, while roads and bridges were exceedingly poor. In the whole of Cumberland County there were no public libraries, hospitals, infirmaries, poorhouses, or workhouses, nor did Bromfield's social and cultural amenities extend beyond a parish church, a small free school, and the usual alehouse.

Yet in spite of the mean surroundings, the Boucher family took pride in its land, and cherished a long Cumberland heritage. As a child, tales were told to Jonathan of ancestors who had acquired an extensive Cumberland estate for border duty in the service of William the Conqueror against the encroaching Scots.

17

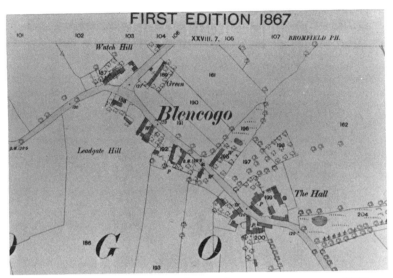

Blencogo, Cumberland, detail of ordnance survey map. 1867.
Archives Department, Record Office, Castle Carlisle.

Artist unknown. Blencogo Hall, Cumberland. *Ca. 1860.*
Cumbria County Library, Carlisle.

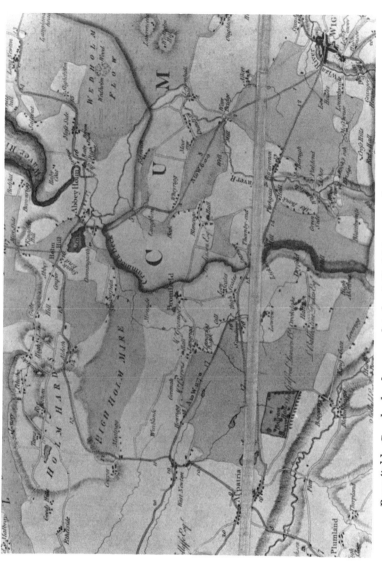

*Bromfield, Cumberland area; detail of Hodskinson and
Donald's Map of the County of Cumberland. 1774.*

Daniel Gardner. Dr. John James.
Queen's College, Oxford.

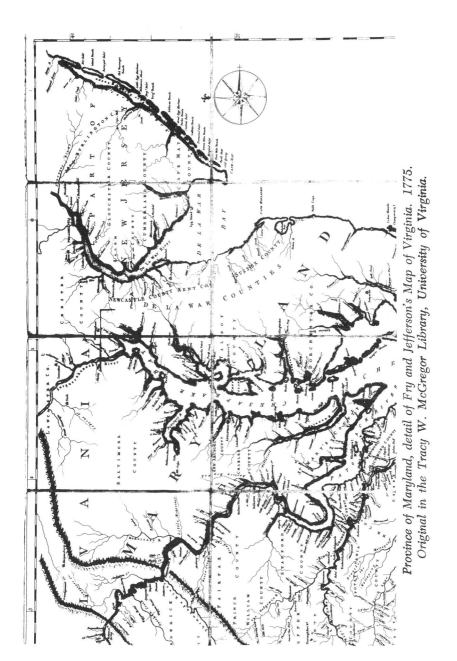

Province of Maryland, detail of Fry and Jefferson's Map of Virginia. 1775. Original in the Tracy W. McGregor Library, University of Virginia.

Daniel Gardner. Mrs. Jonathan Boucher *[Eleanor Addison]. Ca. 1782.*
Yale University Art Gallery, Mabel Brady Garvan Collection.
Photo Joseph Szaszfai, 1972.

I Thomas Brooke Hodgkin Clerk of the General Court of the Western
Shore of the State of Maryland do hereby Certify and Attest that at a
General Court held at the City of Annapolis on the second Tuesday of
May Anno Domini 1781, Indictments were found by the Grand
Jury against the several following Persons following late Inhabit=
ants of Maryland for adhering to the Enemy, to wit.

" Jonathan Boucher, late of Prince Georges County Clerk.
" Henry Addison ————— Ditto.
" Daniel Addison ————— of Prince Georges County.
" Daniel Stevenson ————— Ditto.
" Charles Gordon ————— Kent County.
" John Montgomery ————— Ditto.
" Daniel Dulany (of Walter) Ann Arundel County.
" Daniel Dulany (of Dan.l) Ditto.
" Lloyd Dulany ————— Ditto.
" Walter Dulany ————— Ditto.
" Nathaniel Richardson ————— Ditto
" Anthony Stewart ————— Ditto
" George Howard ————— Saint Maries
" Henry Riddle ————— Charles.
" Philip Key ————— Frederick.
" Leigh Master ————— Ditto.
" Bennett Allen ————— Washington
" David Carcaud ————— Calvert
" Thomas French ————— Baltimore

Indictment for treason by the grand jury of Maryland. 15 July 1781.
Hall of Records of Maryland.

Daniel Gardner. Jonathan and Eleanor Addison Boucher. *Ca. 1782.*

James Cranke. Thomas James. *Ca. 1780.*

James Cranke. John James, Jr. *Ca. 1780*.

Daniel Gardner. John James, Jr. *Ca. 1784*.

Artist unknown. Portrait of Mrs. Elizabeth Boucher *[Elizabeth Hodgson].*
Gellatly Collection, courtesy of National Collection of Fine Arts,
Smithsonian Institution.

A Chapter from the Secret History of Hutchinson's Cumberland.

It is much to the Credit of the present Age, as it will be to the benefit of those that succeed it, that County Histories have, of late met with, all due Encouragement & Patronage from an indulgent Public. Many Facts of great Moment to History, but which have hitherto been suffered to pass un-noticed, among the ordinary Events of the passing Day, are there arrested, as it were, in their Flight; & recorded for the Consideration of Future Ages. And how great soever the other Disadvantages may be, under which this, the most Northern & the remotest of the Counties of England, still labours, we have not to lament the Want of a County History. Besides the many curious & valuable Accounts of Cumberland contained in Camden & other general Histories, We have the learned Work of Horsley on our Roman Antiquities; the Scientific Natural History of Wr Robinson; & the elaborate & very useful Compilation of Burn & Nicholson To all these another new History is

Page one of Boucher's "A Chapter from the Secret History of Hutchinson's Cumberland." Ca. 1793. Cumbria County Library, Carlisle.

Coledale Hall, Cumberland.

Boucher's bookplate and coat of arms, from a silver cup.
Courtesy of Henry Hodgson, Cumbria County Library, Carlisle.
The arms are argent, a cross engrailed gules, between four
bougets, or bougers. A bouger was a purse or water bag,
and signified one who was rich, a keeper of the treasury,
or a purser. The crest displays a Saracen's head rising out
of a crest coronet. The motto reads Non Vi Sed Voluntate
("Not by force, but by goodwill").

JONATHAN BOUCHER, M.A.

W. J. Thompson. Steel engraving.

Saint Martin's Church, Epsom Parish.

Memorial bust in Saint Martin's Church, Epsom Parish.
Photo John Syrad, Epsom.

JONATHAN BOUCHER, M.A.

W. J. Thompson. Steel engraving.

Saint Martin's Church, Epsom Parish.

Memorial bust in Saint Martin's Church, Epsom Parish.
Photo John Syrad, Epsom.

From the reign of Edward I to the establishment of the Commonwealth, few families equalled the Bouchers (originally known as the Bourchiers) in prominence, wealth, or political power. Intermarrying with the sovereign house of Lovaine and with the Plantagenet princesses of England, they distinguished themselves in military service, in the council chamber, at court, and in letters.[2]

All of this glory was now past. Some of the family's lands and prestige had been lost during the Puritan Revolution, when Sir John Bourchier had supported the Roundheads. He sat on the tribunal that ordered the execution of Charles I, and as a consequence some of the family's lands were taken by Charles II after the Restoration. Poor management in the course of the eighteenth century contributed further to the decline of the family. When Boucher's grandfather John (1677-1702) inherited the estate, probably in the 1690s, it was worth about sixty pounds a year. "In that age and that country this was a handsome property" (*Rem.*, p. 3), Jonathan wrote later, and enough to entitle his grandfather to marry one of the three coheiresses to a modest local fortune at Dryam in nearby Abbey Holm. With this marriage, he doubled his estate. John did not live long enough to enjoy it, for he died before the age of twenty-five, leaving behind a young widow and four small children: James, John, Jonathan, and Catherine.

In the next several years, the Bouchers lost all pretensions to membership in the gentry. The young widow soon remarried, this time to a cabinetmaker who took the family off to Dublin. It was not a happy match and the family did so poorly that it became necessary to apprentice two of the sons, James and Jonathan, to a shoemaker, while the daughter married a hosier. James, who inherited the remnants of the family estate, prospered at first, but all too soon he also experienced financial difficulties. When very young, he had married Eleanor Walker, a widow who had "good connections" (*Rem.*, p. 5) and a small fortune in Kilkenny. For some years the young shoemaker carried on a thriving trade in Dublin—later he often spoke of having had thirty men in his employ. After a time, however, his business declined and James finally had to close out his shop, avoiding bankruptcy only by dipping into his modest English estate. His straitened circumstances now forced him to leave Ireland and return to Blencogo.

For a man of James's temperament, all of this was disastrous. He was gregarious, with a great love of life, and Blencogo, a "thoroughly obscure and unpolished village" (*Rem.*, p. 5), promised to be very nearly intolerable, particularly without an adequate income. James's wife hated the place; she became fretful and quarrelsome; eventually she lost her spirits, her health, and finally her life. She confessed on her deathbed that she had planned and hoped to speed her husband's ruin, calculating that he would then of necessity return to Ireland, where she longed to be. James drank heavily, and his little estate began "mouldering away" (*Rem.*, p. 6).

With the death of Eleanor the family circumstances became even more straitened. The two daughters, Sally and Kitty, the only offspring of the first marriage, were summarily disposed of by packing them off to distant relatives, virtually to become domestic servants. Sally went to remote cousins in Ireland where she lived the life of an orphan, and Kitty to the family of the Reverend Thomas Thomlinson, rector of Glenfield in Leicestershire, who spent the summers at his manor in Blencogo. This arrangement later was to make it possible for Jonathan, a child of James's second marriage, to see his half-sister occasionally.

James had been unhappy in his marriage and was not visibly affected by the death of his wife. Soon he met and married Anne Barnes, daughter of a weaver, who was the housekeeper in the home of one of his uncles. At the time of the marriage, James's circumstances were at their nadir; his estate now would hardly have sold for the mortgages on it. Anne was apparently a rather coarse woman of low taste, but she was an energetic housewife, and she soon persuaded her husband to become the village schoolmaster. The pair also opened an alehouse, hoping to maintain the family as the successive children arrived. John, the eldest son, was born in 1734, to be followed by Mary in 1736, and by a second son, Jonathan, in 1738.[3] The youngest, Jane, whom the family nicknamed Jinny, was born in 1741. Of the four children, Jonathan and Jane were to live most of their lives together.

The early childhood years at Blencogo were wretched for Jonathan. His father was his own best customer at the alehouse, which yielded only a pittance. He used a small legacy left to him by a friend who had died in Jamaica to repurchase a modest portion of the former family lands, but this little windfall produced no more than five pounds annually. In all, the family income scarcely amounted to more than ten pounds a year. Fortunately, Boucher's wife practiced a rigid system of household economy, so that a regimen of painful frugality enabled the pair to bring up four children successfully with some new pretensions to middle-class status.

Long afterward, Jonathan Boucher vividly recalled these years as "a state of penury and hardship as I have never since seen equalled, no, not even in parish almshouses" (*Rem.*, p. 9). James's sense of mortification and deep sorrow that the patrimony which had long been in the hands of a Boucher had been allowed to melt away through his own improvidence communicated itself to his young son. The father's nostalgia for the past also moved him to inspire in the youth a respect for family tradition that was in sharp contrast with the terrible monetary insecurity of the present. Jonathan could remember years later with what fervor his father had instilled in him an attachment to the land. "A thousand and a thousand times he charged both my brother and myself with an earnestness hardly inferior to that with which Hamilcar is said to have enjoined his son Hannibal never to be at peace with the Romans, never to suffer the estate to go out of the name of Boucher" (*Rem.*, p. 33).

The sense of belonging to these few acres remained with Boucher for a lifetime. He inherited the property at the death of his father, since his oldest brother had died in 1765. Although Boucher was often in debt, he never considered for a moment disposing of the property. Something "attaches me" to its "miry plains and rugged hills," he explained in a letter written on 18 June 1766, which was independent of "relations and friendships" (*MHM* 7:302). At the same time, Boucher considered his father's injunction so sacred that "a curse would overtake me if I violated it" (*Rem.*, p. 33).

Along with a profound sense of loyalty to the land, Boucher grew up with the tradition of loyalty to the Crown. The Carlisle area, county seat of Cumberland, had been loyal to the Stuart cause in the Puritan Revolution. Boucher always thought that his ancestors who had joined the Roundheads had well deserved to lose their land. The price of disloyalty was firmly impressed on his mind when as a child of eight he was allowed to watch the host of the Young Pretender march through the country on its way to battle. After their defeat the following year, the impressionable boy was taken to Carlisle to see the executions of the Young Pretender's followers, and to gaze with fascination and revulsion at the severed heads mounted on pikes along the way. Experiences of this kind doubtless played a substantial part in shaping the mind and spirit of the boy toward conservatism and loyalty to established order.

In spite of James's fondness for drinking, he found time to teach Jonathan to read "almost before I could speak" (*Rem.*, p. 9). When the boy at age six entered the small free school at Bromfield, he could already read and spell very well. There he studied Latin with a dedicated teacher, a Mr. Lowther, who apparently was a man of some ability. Boucher later recalled that he loved the man who gave him his first sense of the joy of learning. All too soon Lowther disappeared, to be replaced by a series of mediocre pedagogues who provided only an indifferent schooling at best. Poor teaching and Jonathan's own frequent absences, caused by the family's need for his labor, resulted in a hit-or-miss education. The family's modest circumstances required him to perform his share of hard, grinding labor around the tavern and in the fields. He carted "coals, turf, and peat" (*Rem.*, p. 10), handled a heavy plow in the spring planting, and labored until exhausted in the harvest season. Later as a young scholar he was to be found deplorably weak in grammar.

Jonathan's first glimpse of a better way of life came when the Thomlinson family, in whose home Boucher's half sister Kitty had been a domestic servant for some time, took an interest in the boy. For a time the Bouchers relished the expectation that the Thomlinsons would make Jonathan their heir, a hope that was presently frustrated when Mrs. Thomlinson bore her husband a son after sixteen years of childless marriage. Still, the attachment persisted, with numerous small advantages for the eight-year-old Jonathan. He picked up useful cast-off clothing, while Mrs. Thomlinson from time to time presented him with small sums of cash for his services in acting as a companion and playmate for her little son. It was enough to keep him in school books and a pittance of pocket money.

More importantly, the Thomlinson family was considerably more genteel than young Jonathan's, and conversation with its members softened his manners and taught him the elements of courtesy, a process which rendered him, in his own words, "not quite so awkward and uncouth" as formerly. The lad was now almost self-supporting; later he would recall his experiences with the Thomlinson family as a time when he learned how to manage his finances, to budget his time, and generally to plan his life, an experience which he considered "fairly worth all the rest of [my] education." All in all, he was gaining a notion of a way of life superior to that of his own family, so that by the age of twelve he was thoroughly discontented and on the alert for any possibility or opportunity for self-improvement. He was determined that he "would not pass through life like the boors around me" (*Rem.*, p. 12).

A new opportunity soon came Jonathan's way. At nearby Wigton, a town of some size, there was a school which prepared students for teaching, and Jonathan presently prevailed upon his father to allow him to attend classes there. His father, in making this concession, insisted that in addition to his other studies the boy spend at least a half-day in learning writing and arithmetic, in order that he might qualify the sooner for his new goal. For some time, Jonathan walked the four miles to and from Wigton, morning and evening, "carrying my morsel of dinner in a satchel" (*Rem.*, p. 14), in order to study under Rev. Joseph Blaine.

In 1754 Jonathan, just turned sixteen, qualified as a school teacher. He refused masterships at Crookdale and Raughtonhead for eight and twelve pounds respectively, and instead accepted an offer at Wigton where he soon acquired thirty-two boys as pupils, for each of whom he received ten shillings annually. He also opened an evening school where he undertook to teach writing and arithmetic to a number of young men and women in the community, thus adding a couple of guineas to his income. Industry and enterprise on this scale, unusually imaginative for a small-town teacher in eighteenth-century England, yielded a measure of prosperity. Life, Jonathan felt, consisted mainly of dull, hard work, but he was now sending money home regularly to his father—about a fourth of his total wages.

Jonathan soon found some pleasure in life. He fell in and out of love with two young ladies in rapid succession. Later he became acquainted with three navy lieutenants, whose ideas concerning recreation were decidedly more sophisticated than his own. Enough wild oats were sown to persuade Boucher or someone in his family later carefully to tear out two pages of Boucher's *Reminiscences* in which he referred to his social life in Wigton.

Jonathan's life was now moving smoothly enough, but he had

little taste for monotonous routine, and he soon became restless. In 1755 he left his school to learn mathematics, navigation, and land surveying under one Isaac Ritson at Workington, a town some twenty miles distant on the seacoast. A shoemaker by trade, Ritson was a self-taught mathematician of surprising talent who at the age of forty had gone into orders and now also served as both the town schoolmaster and the local surveyor. If Boucher had not as yet learned self-discipline and frugality, he had an excellent model in Ritson. Incredible as it seems, Ritson had brought up his family and contrived to save a thousand pounds, on an income of only fifty pounds a year. Ritson and Boucher carried on their surveying duties from sunup to sundown without stopping for either food or drink, often in very severe weather. For this opportunity to learn Boucher paid the family one guinea a month, which included his room and board. The daily diet was singularly monotonous, consisting solely of locally abundant salmon and potatoes.

Jonathan was determined that he would become a professional literary man. For a time he entertained the idea of going to Ireland, a notion which his father promptly quashed by ordering him instead to offer himself for an ushership at Saint Bees. Saint Bees, the birthplace of Sir Edwin Sandys of the old Virginia Company, was situated in a narrow dell with low and marshy lands to the east and exposure to the storms from the Irish Channel to the west. As usher, Jonathan would assist the schoolmaster and board with the family. One day in 1756 he reluctantly walked the ten miles from Workington to Saint Bees, put in his application, and was accepted.

His initial disappointment at being obliged to abandon his Irish plans soon turned to pleasure. John James, rector at Saint Bees and the master of the boys' free grammar school there, was shocked at Boucher's lack of grammar, but apparently recognized his potential and agreed to give the boy the post. Jonathan moved in with James, who soon thereafter married Ann Grayson (nicknamed Nancy). Jonathan found himself sharing in the warmth and pleasure of an affectionate and closely knit family. Of all the men Boucher was to know in his lifetime, James undoubtedly exercised the most influence on him.[4]

Life at Saint Bees was hard but rewarding. James had taken over the school only recently and both James and Boucher wanted very much to make a success of the once declining and mismanaged institution. They rose at six in the morning and ended their labors only when it was too dark to see. The strenuous effort produced results. Within two years the enrollment had increased to eighty boys, and thereafter the school continued to grow. Boucher earned ten pounds a year, for example, but "entrances and cockpennies amounted to as much more," he wrote. In the second year he had thirty pounds (*Rem.*, p. 21).

But Boucher benefited more than financially. Each day James first went over the lesson with him, and he in turn taught the boys assigned to him. Friday was "repetition day," and James obligingly changed places with his usher in order that Boucher might hear all the higher classes recite. On Thursday nights, James listened to Boucher read through the entire week's assignment. Boucher thought that he had learned more at this time than in all of his previous schooling.

Jonathan basked in the genuine affection which John and Nancy James bestowed upon him. He developed a tremendous respect for James and thought him the best schoolmaster he had ever known. In turn, James became a second father to the young man and Jonathan began to turn to him for advice whenever he was puzzled, a relationship which lasted until the death of James. Years later, Boucher reciprocated by adopting a similar role with respect to James's son John, whom he eventually took as an usher in his own school at Paddington.

In 1759, the satisfying life at Saint Bees came to an abrupt end. Suddenly an opportunity appeared for the twenty-one-year-old Jonathan. A Whitehaven merchant, John Younger, acting as an agent for his factor in Virginia, was seeking a young man to go out to the colony as a private tutor. The pay was sixty pounds a year plus board for teaching four boys, with freedom to take on four additional students under whatever terms the tutor might arrange. The passage to distant America was to be paid by Younger. Much as James disliked losing his usher, it was too promising an opportunity for Boucher to pass up, and the older man encouraged his protégé to take it, knowing that Boucher still cherished the idea of going abroad.

Boucher borrowed thirty pounds to buy a wardrobe, with his own bond as security. In March 1759, he set sail from Whitehaven on the *Rose,* bound for Virginia. It was typical of Boucher that

37

he charted the entire voyage day by day, drawing on his navigation studies to do so, and presented the result to Captain Rothery, the master of the *Rose*, upon their arrival in America. It was a dangerous passage because of the war between France and England and the presence of privateers. On one occasion their ship was chased by a vessel from which they escaped with difficulty under cover of night.

On 12 April 1759, Boucher stepped ashore on the banks of the Rappahannock River at Urbanna, a port of custom, and then proceeded to travel the eighty miles up river to Port Royal, to the home of Capt. Edward Dixon, father of his prospective pupils and the man for whom Younger had been acting. Jonathan Boucher was twenty-one years old, in debt, and very much alone; he found himself a stranger among a people alien to him in manners and way of life.

ᗒ Chapter 2 ᗕ

Virginia Schoolmaster and Planter

Boucher found a cordial reception at Dixon's home. Port Royal, a seaport with a population of about 300, was inhabited primarily by factors from Scotland. Dixon had long commanded a ship "in the service of Mr. Howe" (probably Admiral Richard Lord Howe). and had earned a reputation for valor and skill against superior forces. Dixon acquired wealth in land and slaves by means of a fortunate marriage in Virginia and thereupon quit the sea. He opened a large store at Port Royal, became a successful factor for Younger at Whitehaven, and shipped two or three cargoes of tobacco to England each year.

At first Boucher was depressed both by the physical environment and by the society in which he found himself. The climate, he thought, was nothing short of frightful. "The hotness of the weather," he wrote James on 19 August 1759, has "so prodigious an influence on the constitution that it fevers the blood and sets all the animal spirits in an uproar." In the "violent mid-day heats," he complained, one became "all unhinged and save some few intervals" a man "can scarce boast of one sedate thought" (*MHM* 7:8-9). He was also shocked by the style of life he found around him. Dixon, stout, fifty-six, and widowed, often filled his house with "toddy-drinking company," as Boucher expressed it (*Rem.,* p. 26). His coarse talk and rough manners at first dismayed the rustic lad from Cumberland—this was not the genteel way of life he had observed at Thomlinson's manor in Blencogo, nor at James's in Saint Bees. "Libertinism," Boucher continued in his 19 August letter, was the "reigning topic" of conversation; in a letter written on 7 August he had complained that "social chatter," instead of dwelling upon "manly, instructive discourse," turned invariably to gaiety mixed with a humor too broad for his taste, and even with obscenity, from which "no sex, no rank, no conduct" was exempted (*MHM* 7:4-5). Even the clergy attempted "by specious sophistry to justify their compliance" with the prevailing loose standards of morality (*MHM* 7:9).

Not all Boucher's comments were critical. He readily admitted that Americans were of a livelier and quicker wit than the English. The colonials in general he thought were "eminently endowed with a knack of talking; they seem to be born orators" (*Rem.,* p. 61). Naively, he was unsure whether to credit this to the climate or to the Virginians' manner of education—their "being early introduced into company and soon commencing ripe." The Virginians were also the "most hospitable, generous people I ever saw," once a stranger had given them an opportunity to show a kindness (*MHM* 7:4-5).

The wealth and luxury all around him astonished him. Virginians lived well and dressed well, seemingly "without any labor and almost without any concern of their own." "The common planter's daughters here," he assured the Jameses, "go every day in finer clothes than I have seen content you for a summer's Sunday." His own garb seemed modest by contrast with that of the well-to-do colonials. "You thought ... my satin waistcoat was a fine best," he told Mrs. James, but "Lord help you, I'm nothing among the lace and laced fellows that are here." One could see more "brilliant assemblies" in a corner of Virginia than a modest Englishman could ever find, except for royalty, in the whole of the mother country (*MHM* 7:5).

The horse races which usually came each fall in the first week in October presented Boucher with a unique opportunity to see society at its best. Boucher was something of a social climber and he was frankly delighted when he made the acquaintance of several Virginia grandees whose attentions flattered him. He wrote James on 14 October 1759 that in the evening there were dances and balls, "which I am confident for their splendor and brilliancy exceeded anything I can make you believe." Boucher was impressed and also a bit worried; he was hard put to it to win any notice from the elegantly gowned ladies who swirled around him. He was, he told James sadly, what Shakespeare called "*a man of no likelihood*" in this kind of company (*MHM* 7:13).

Although the new style of living was sharply at odds with his recent experience, Boucher soon accommodated himself to the "idle customs of the country" (*Rem.*, p. 27) and joined the round of balls and parties with "a set of gay, rackety good-natured mortals" with an ease that alarmed him (*MHM* 7:9). The American manners and conversation, which had earlier "stunned and stupefied" him, no longer made him feel "sheepish" nor like a "stingy milksop." Presently he lost the label "parson," which his earlier innocence had earned him (*MHM* 7:23).

In spite of his acceptance among Virginians, Boucher failed to find intellectual companionship. He genuinely missed the good company of James at Saint Bees, which he remembered as that "golden portion of my age" (*MHM* 7:10). There were no literary men nearer than in England, he concluded, nor were literary attainments other than mere reading or writing "in vogue" in America. His new friends were interested only in pleasure and practical pursuits, having little concern for what Boucher called "a generous mind." Virginians believed that if a man corresponded merely to preserve a friendship, he lacked "good sense" (*MHM* 7:11). Later, when Boucher reflected upon his years at Port Royal, he could not recall a single close friendship that meant anything to him.

Almost as quickly as Boucher adjusted to the manners and mores of the country, he acquired the spirit of aspiration that was so much a part of Americans. Boucher saw many easy opportunities for gain, and began to think of ways to improve his own fortunes. He had never cared deeply about school teaching, although it was satisfactory enough as a career in England. However, he was becoming disenchanted with teaching in Virginia. "Children I have seen here," he confided to James on 14 October 1759, "are not...of a very amiable disposition and seem not formed for being easily made so" (*MHM* 7:12).

Accordingly, Boucher now began looking about for a chance

to enter a new and more profitable livelihood, preferably one "most in request in the country in which my lot seemed to be cast" (*Rem.*, p. 27). He was intrigued by the thought of becoming a planter, and to that end he studied a bit of "physic and law" (*Rem.*, p. 27), both of which he knew to be valuable skills for a Virginia tobacco farmer, and he also sought to learn something about the actual techniques of tobacco cultivation. But he lacked the all-important capital to buy land, and reluctantly he abandoned for the moment his agrarian dream. It was trade that seemed to offer the best possibilities for gain, and he soon turned his attention increasingly to mercantile activities.

Before Boucher had left Whitehaven, John Younger had suggested that he think about trade as a career, and had sold him goods at wholesale cost to take with him. "A pedagogue," Boucher wrote optimistically, might "make no contemptible merchant" (*MHM* 7:22). In the autumn of 1761, Boucher ordered another cargo of goods from Younger and took a house in Falmouth, about twenty miles up the Rappahannock River, intent upon operating a store. His prospects seemed good and he wrote James on 31 January 1760 with pleasurable anticipation that he was about to be "struck off the list of the venerable society of the birch" (*MHM* 7:16).

Unfortunately for Boucher's innocent mercantile ambitions, he was about to receive his first lesson in vengeful duplicity. Dixon recently had been negotiating a financially advantageous match with Mrs. Dorcas Washington, a widow from nearby Machotac Creek, and Boucher by his own account had been "serviceable to him" in the courtship (*Rem.*, pp. 28-29). The question of the paternity of a certain neighborhood child had come to the widow's attention, and the embarrassing matter soon threatened the projected marital alliance. Dixon thereupon approached Boucher with the blunt suggestion that the young schoolteacher solve his problem by marrying the child's mother, or at least by acknowledging paternity. The quid pro quo Dixon offered was a tempting trade arrangement with a nice prospect for profit. But Boucher resented the overture and scornfully rejected the suggestion. He thereby incurred Dixon's lasting enmity.

Dixon, disappointed, ashamed, and vengeful, now deliberately ruined Boucher's budding mercantile career. He wrote Younger that circumstances had changed and that there was now no advantage in attempting to enlarge his trade with Virginia. Younger thereupon cancelled his expansion arrangements for the present. Boucher did not know of Dixon's vindictive intervention until some time later; even then, out of a sense of honor, he never informed Younger of Dixon's real motive.

The Dixon incident marked a turning point in Boucher's life. Never again did he entertain seriously the idea of becoming a merchant. At the same time, his refusal to go along with the Dixon paternity suggestion may well have made possible the opportunity for a vastly different career as a cleric. Had Boucher sacrificed his integrity for a trade concession, thereby calling his character into question, the invitation to consider ordination might not have been offered to him. For some time James apparently had been pressing his young friend in America with the idea of entering the clergy, but at first Boucher was altogether unresponsive. He had no sense of vocation for the clergy, and even less sense of religous fervor. He had seldom thought about God except during the perils of his sea voyage, while the great questions of immortality and salvation interested him little, if at all. (Later, after his ordination, he was to have trouble even in accepting the idea of the Trinity.)

Boucher knew also that the clergy occupied a comparatively low position in the Virginia social order. With a few exceptions, the colony's clerics were a worthless lot, "the most despised and neglected body in the colony." They were inclined to complain of poor treatment and lack of respect by the colonists, but Boucher commented with some asperity that "none have less reason than they to complain of injustices" (*MHM* 7:16-17). "You would blush to hear the character of some of our brethren," he wrote James on 9 March 1767. In his opinion too many Scotsmen, "rigid true-blue Presbyterians," had been converted by the "convincing argument" of a fat stipend only to become "ignorant and debauched episcopal pastors" (*MHM* 7:340).

Nevertheless, when in 1761 Boucher was approached on the subject of becoming a minister, he found the prospect of becoming a man of the cloth irresistible. Boucher had lately struck up a friendship with the Reverend Isaac William Giberne, rector of Hanover Parish, whom he considered to be the most admired and popular parson in Virginia. Giberne, whose parish lay directly across the river from Port Royal in King George County, had preached before the House of Burgesses, and had the additional prestige of being the nephew of the bishop of Durham in England. Boucher himself was less than impressed with Giberne's ability, finding him "a companionable man, nothing more," who like most Virginia clerics was more than a little addicted to "high life," and to gambling in particular (*Rem.*, p. 30). Boucher had good reason to be aware of his friend's weakness; on one occasion he relieved him of more than a hundred pounds in this fashion.

Giberne, soon to be married to a rich widow in Richmond County, was about to resign his parish. Apparently at Giberne's suggestion, the vestry of Hanover Parish recommended Boucher to the bishop of London for ordination, with the expectation that the young teacher then would be assigned to the vacated parish post, an arrangement to which Boucher had agreed.[1] Somewhat defensively, Boucher later admitted that his thoughts long had been "withdrawn" from the church. On the other hand, he insisted, he had agreed not so much "because of not knowing what else to do with myself, but because of the suddenness of the offer and a deep sense of their kindness" (*Rem.*, pp. 29-30).

Ordination, Boucher was aware, meant a voyage to England. Because of the Anglican doctrine of Apostolic Succession, the sacrament of ordination could be performed only by a bishop. There was no Anglican bishop resident in colonial America; instead the bishop of London had jurisdiction over all activities of the church in the colonies. Hanover Parish, Boucher learned to his astonishment, expected him to sail for England within a week. A precipitous return home suddenly loomed as an imperative necessity.

Arranging for this unexpected voyage was not as difficult as Boucher at first supposed. Captain Stanley of the ship *Christian* gave him a round-trip passage, as was customary for ordination voyages. Although Boucher was apparently unaware of it, his prospective parish reimbursed the shipowner. And Dixon, although not on good terms with Boucher, was nonetheless willing to give Boucher letters of credit of £100, upon Boucher's insuring his life for £200. Dixon knew that the voyage entailed considerable risk, and he recognized a good business venture when he saw it. In addition to the letters of credit, Boucher was already in debt to Dixon for £100.

Boucher sailed for England about 15 December 1761. His departure was somewhat complicated by the fact that his sister

Jinny, having tried her fortune in London, had decided to come out to Virginia without waiting for his approval, and he had been expecting her arrival any day. He therefore arranged for her to board on credit with a local family until his return. As the *Christian* dropped anchor down the harbor, it passed within hailing distance of Jinny's inbound vessel, and Boucher managed to catch a glimpse of his sister. On 17 January 1762, after a rapid but rough and stormy passage on the tempestuous North Atlantic, the *Christian* arrived in England. Once ashore, Boucher purchased a horse and set out for London.

Although the prospective cleric had not anticipated a lengthy stay in England, he remained for several months. On 26 March, after some considerable delay, the Right Reverend Richard Osbaldeston, bishop of London, duly inducted Boucher into Anglican orders as a deacon. Five days later, he was ordained a priest. But Boucher's own experience made clear the ease with which one might become an Anglican cleric in America. Ordination rested upon a few letters of recommendation, and required no university degree and no particular preparation. It was essentially a political affair. The greatest hazard in the venture lay in the ocean travel, for some eleven ministers destined for American parishes lost their lives in the passage during the colonial period. Once ordained, Boucher's personal embarrassment over lack of funds evaporated. He now found it easy to arrange for credit from shopkeepers, from whom he purchased furniture and a quantity of books for his new parsonage.

Before embarking for America, Boucher made a sentimental journey to Blencogo to bid his family farewell. It was to be his last visit with his parents, both of whom were to die in the next few years, well before Boucher's next return in 1775.[2] In May he sailed for America, and on 12 July 1762, the Reverend Jonathan Boucher landed once more at Urbanna on the Rappahannock River, three years and three months to the day since he had first set foot in Virginia.

Boucher had no more than taken up his new clerical duties at Hanover when he found himself involved in an unhappy brawl, this time with both Dixon and Giberne. Boucher unwittingly had triggered this contretemps by making some highly indiscreet disparaging remarks about Giberne's literary ability, particularly about his lack of knowledge of Greek. Dixon, still smarting from Boucher's rebuff in the proposed paternity scheme, promptly passed on this gossip to Giberne, who was outraged and swore that he would have his revenge. Giberne first told Dixon that Boucher had betrayed his secret, and then wrote letters both to Captain Stanley and to Younger in England, accusing Boucher of duplicity. Next Giberne personally called on all of the principal families in Hanover Parish, alerting them to Boucher's "treachery," and finally incorporated the story in several of his sermons.

Boucher's handling of this new crisis in his personal affairs showed something of the contentious temperament frequently demonstrated when thoroughly aroused. His first move was to preach a sermon at his new parish asking his parishioners to suspend their judgment on the "cruel treatment" he had received at Dixon's and Giberne's hands, at least until he had a chance to disprove the "vile calumnies" directed against him. Boucher then accepted one Colonel Thornton's offer to mitigate matters. Thornton, a witness during Boucher's imprudent conversation about Dixon, supported Boucher by explaining that Boucher had meant no harm; he had been defending Dixon at the time, but had inadvertently "told too much of the truth" (*Rem.*, p. 36). Boucher apologized to Dixon privately, admitting his unintended indiscretion.

The strategy which Boucher chose to employ with Giberne was recklessly bold. He challenged Giberne's scholarly abilities to his face, handed him a Greek Testament, and dared him to translate it into English. Giberne backed down, protesting that Boucher's demand was childish and beneath him. Boucher, he said, was a "bully in small learning" (*Rem.*, p. 38). With little charity, Boucher warned his colleague that if ever again he "ill-used" him behind his back, he would wipe him down "with an oaken towel." With one of his rare attempts at humor, the arrogant Boucher described himself to James as having become for the moment, at least, a "member of the Church Militant" (*MHM* 7:152).

With all of this bluster and righteousness, Boucher had managed to conceal the fact that he in all probability knew little Greek himself at this time. Not until much later, after he had returned to England, did he begin a serious study of the language, admitting then that he "hardly knew the Greek alphabet" (*Rem.*, p. 150). In short, Boucher was himself an outrageous fraud in his pretension to scholarship, and only good fortune protected him against humiliating exposure. On the other hand, Boucher's handling of the situation was typical of his reaction to trouble. If he believed that he was right, his first inclination was always to risk a confrontation, whether the encounter involved a battle of words or a physical assault. Whatever the merits of his position, the quarrel and his course of action had one happy consequence: Boucher stood completely vindicated in the eyes of his new parishioners. "I even became popular," he exulted. People suddenly vied with one another to be kind to him, his financial standing rose abruptly, and "whatever I wanted, I could easily get on credit" (*Rem.*, p. 38).

After this unpromising beginning in Hanover Parish, the new minister then settled down into the routine of his daily duties. He had found a house at Smith's Mount, a hamlet near Leedstown in his parish, established Jinny as his housekeeper, and took in six boys to board and tutor as a means of supplementing his income. Clearly, affairs were looking up for Boucher.

Yet life was not altogether pleasant. For one thing, Boucher, like most Virginians, was plagued by recurrent bouts of bad health. As a youth in England he had suffered from what he called an "hectical complaint," apparently some kind of respiratory disorder, which he had hoped the Virginia climate would meliorate. Instead, once in America, he promptly acquired an intermittent light fever (probably malaria) which aggravated his health problem, and from which he never recovered completely. His ordination visit to England gave Boucher some relief, but upon his return to Virginia the fever recurred—this time in violent form. In the summer of 1764 he had an attack so severe that by 2 September he could describe himself to James as no more than "a poor, emaciated, half-animated skeleton," unable to "walk across the room without a support" (*MHM* 7:286). His sister Jinny thought it a "miracle" that he recovered at all, while Boucher himself believed the illness had seriously damaged his eyesight and his constitution (*MHM* 7:347). "Heartsickening fevers," as he put it, continued to plague him thereafter during the hot summer months; indeed he was not completely free of fever well into the fall (*MHM* 7:286).[3]

Nor did Boucher find Hanover Parish a particularly attractive place. He was popular with his congregation, but there was little opportunity for him to satisfy his ambition to become a tobacco planter. His house was not well suited for boarding boys, and he was unable to find a better one. The parish had no glebe, "but paid 4,000 pounds of tobacco in lieu of it, enough to pay the rent of almost any house in the parish, had there been one available" (*Rem.*, p. 40). In November 1763, Boucher had a chance to move to a better position, and he eagerly seized upon it. Rev. Musgrave Dawson of Saint Mary's Parish in Caroline County died and the post was offered to Boucher. Port Royal was in this parish and he still had many friends there, several of whom urged him to accept the new position. After some delay to put his affairs at Hanover in order, Boucher left for his new parish in December 1764. He departed with the good will of his old congregation, which voted to continue his salary for three months after his departure.

Boucher was not altogether happy even at Saint Mary's, but his circumstances there were unquestionably much improved. The glebe house which he now acquired near New Post, about six miles from Fredericksburg, was large and commodious, while he was able to remodel a second dwelling nearby to suit the needs of his school. Boucher's school flourished here; soon he had some thirty boys, all he could conveniently handle.

The years at Saint Mary's involved Boucher in a daily routine of almost incredible activity. He now plunged into three simultaneous careers—those of parish clergyman, schoolmaster, and planter. The pace of daily life might have broken a lesser man, but Boucher was driven by a loathing for indolence (although he thought of himself as a man with an inclination to be lazy) and an almost psychopathic fear of poverty, which he viewed as "next to sickness . . . the most desperate of human plagues" (*MHM* 7:347). He labored constantly to acquire wealth, status, and social position. It was a combination of motives, talent, and energy which within ten years would lift the young man from the status of barely established immigrant to membership in the prosperous and powerful elite both in Virginia and Maryland.

Of his three concurrent careers, Boucher found school teaching "the most irksome and thankless of all employments" (*MHM* 7:301). His pupils were youngsters of some considerable social position. Among them at various times were Washington's stepson, John Parke Custis (Jacky), the younger son of the celebrated Maryland pamphleteer Daniel Dulany, Benjamin Tasker Dulany, Walter Dulany's two sons, Walter, Jr. and Grafton, and Benedict Calvert. But Boucher thought the school "an inconceivable trouble and expense and hardly an adequate profit" (*MHM* 7:160). His friends, he complained, seemed to think they did him a special favor by sending their children to him. Not impressed with favors of this sort, Boucher responded by charging the highest fees of any schoolmaster in Virginia: twenty pounds per year per student for "board and education" (*MHM* 7:339). Boucher rather expected that attendance at his school would fall off as a consequence of the high fees he charged, but it never did.

Boucher had already developed considerable confidence in his ability as a schoolmaster, although he candidly admitted that many of his rivals who were from the North were "infinitely my masters in Latin and Greek." On the other hand, he found it easy to meet their competition because in other respects he found them "such *illiterate* dunces" (*MHM* 7:339). In 1765, with the school now numbering fifteen boys, Boucher hired two assistants to relieve the burden. One was a Mr. Lewis, son of a gentleman from Augusta County, and the second the "pert and petulant" James Madison, cousin of the future president James Madison, who would one day become the first bishop of the Protestant Episcopal church in Virginia and president of William and Mary College. Still the school prospered; by 1768 Boucher had thirty boys, all boarding with him.

Meanwhile, Boucher was attempting to establish himself as a planter. A Virginia law of 1695 entitled ministers in the colony to a glebe of at least 200 acres; Boucher's at Saint Mary's was apparently somewhat larger than that. Delighted with his new opportunity, Boucher deliberately ran himself into debt to the extent of five or six hundred pounds, for cattle, horses, and slaves. "We live here chiefly by credit," he wrote James on 10 September 1763, hinting that he believed that going into debt actually would improve his credit (*MHM* 7:158). Boucher's complacent attitude toward indebtedness was in fact that of a typically socially ambitious Virginian. Acknowledging frankly that he had not "the patience to wait for the slow savings of a humble station," he sought deliberately to cultivate a prosperous appearance, under the conviction that he could gain a better position more quickly "only by my being taken notice of by people of condition" (*Rem.*, p. 31). However, Boucher abided by one important resolution, which but for one brief lapse he steadfastly kept: never to owe more than his estate could pay off should he die.

In addition to purchasing slaves, Boucher took on an overseer and at least one or two white indentured servants, one of whom was a convict from his native district of Cumberland. However, the overseer proved to be disappointing, and Boucher soon had to part with him and undertake to manage the plantation himself. Good fortune attended his efforts; his first tobacco crop was a large one and yielded him a fine return. Scientific agriculture was in its infancy, but Boucher, apparently already aware of the value of crop diversity, also was experimenting with a variety of plantation staples.

Meanwhile, Boucher was gradually acquiring a convivial circle of friends. For a time following his arrival in Virginia he had suffered from loneliness, feeling keenly the absence both of adequate intellectual companionship and of intimate friendship and affection. The death of his brother in 1765, who had only recently been ordained and whom he dearly loved, was a particularly cruel shock. For solace Boucher soon turned to a heavy round of parties, involving by his own admission a not inconsiderable amount of hard drinking. "There was hardly a day," he later recalled, "in which I did not have company" (*Rem.*, pp. 27, 48). Boucher might have degenerated into a typical carousing, gambling Virginia parson of the more dissolute sort, but he had too much intellect, self-discipline, and ambition to allow it to happen.

To his delight, nonetheless, he found himself attractive to women. He had a "natural gallantry and attachment to the sex," he wrote later, "which made them secure of my good will and friendship." But not all his female friendships, apparently, were platonic or even very discreet. Long afterward Boucher confessed that in his relationships with women, "no man knew the sex better; yet no man who was not quite a fool had so often . . . been made a fool of by them" (*Rem.*, pp. 80-81). When Boucher wrote this he may well have been thinking of Judith Chase. Mrs. Chase was a young Maryland widow who had been married at sixteen to a prominent lawyer, only to have her husband poisoned by a slave a month later. Boucher first met her at a ball at Port Tobacco, and it was not long before he had fallen deeply in love.

A younger brother of Mrs. Chase was a student at Boucher's school, which led Boucher to a holiday visit with her family at Christmas 1765. He saw Judith only a few times in the next year, but they soon fell into a regular correspondence, and Boucher discovered to his delight that she wrote charming letters. By the spring of 1767, now thoroughly captivated, Boucher was entertaining thoughts of marriage. He wrote James on 9 March 1767 thanking him profusely for the good advice his friend had given him in persuading "this lovely nymph to listen to my addresses." In his "all-perfect fair one," he exclaimed, "the fire of wit is tempered and chastened by a happy judgment and the purest benevolence" (*MHM* 7:341-42). And in a decidedly cooler mood, he observed that Judith had a sizable estate, which although it had been badly managed was still worth about £1,500. Together with the £500 he had saved, he thought it quite enough to get married.

Unhappily for Boucher, his idyllic matrimonial dream was soon shattered; Mrs. Chase rejected his proposal, apparently out of hand. Heartbroken, he wrote to James on 22 June 1767 that his charming Judith had explained frankly that he was said to be so "unsettled, so giddy and fickle," that she dared not enter into an engagement with him (*MHM* 7:348).

However, his affair with Mrs. Chase by no means ended there. Although the subsequent record is not explicit, it appears highly probable that Boucher and his beloved became the parents of illegitimate twin girls, for whose welfare Boucher assumed at least some responsibility. Judith Chase also apparently contributed to the children's support (*MHM* 7:347-48).[4] Boucher did not forget Judith; even years after his first and happy marriage he wrote of her very fondly and with traces of charity in his heart. By then he would be in possession of more information about Judith which would permit him to excuse her behavior. He was to learn that she had been manipulated by her "'first ruiner," William Smallwood, "a fool as well as a knave," Boucher would declare, who had persuaded Judith to "use me ill." Because Judith relied too little on her own judgment, Boucher had been used "egregiously ill" (*MHM* 9:59).

But Judith remained something of an enigma to Boucher. In 1776 he was to analyze the charm, virtues, and shortcomings of an unknown woman, undoubtedly Judith Chase, entitling it, "A Character from Real Life:—in the Manner of Swift, on Stella." In truth, the character study was to be a pensive love letter. Although Judith was past the period of mere youth in the 1760s, and was perhaps not "handsome," Boucher was to recall that "men (the only proper judges of female beauty)" neglected beautiful women and were attracted to her. He was also to recall with admiration her ability to "think as a man," yet with quickness of perception, brilliance, warmth and imagination—all qualities which made her a good companion. Judith had "fire and vivacity," but he would remember with pleasure her "gentleness" and "delicateness." She was "truly feminine," and unforgettable.[5]

In spite of his frustration in the Chase marital adventure, Boucher soon cast his eyes about once more. One of his neighbors, he presently discovered, was a woman of very considerable wealth and social position, who it was said planned to leave her fortune to her granddaughter. This young lady's father was Col. Henry Fitzhugh, of the illustrious Fitzhugh family. Deckar Thompson, one of Boucher's friends, urged him to seek permission to court the Fitzhugh girl, to which suggestion Boucher somewhat incautiously agreed. But the colonel, to whom both the young woman and her grandmother referred him, cut Boucher off short with the terse comment that while he had no objection to him personally, he would of course expect Boucher to make a very substantial marriage settlement on his daughter—obviously one quite beyond the young parson's means. In short, as Boucher later put it, the colonel "knocked the whole project on its head."

Sometime later, the same young woman "fell down in a fit in a public room" (*Rem.*, p. 64), and a medical friend, Dr. Hugh Mercer, confided to Boucher that she had been subject to such seizures all of her life and congratulated Boucher on his escape. Although both the colonel and his daughter later made overtures in the direction of a courtship, Boucher now coyly declined, and turned his attention instead to his obligations to his church.

⌒ Chapter 3 ⌒

Tidewater Minister

The years at Saint Mary's were fruitful ones for Boucher. The unsophisticated and inexperienced youth became a man with some charm and with a striking personality. His last six years in Virginia, between his twenty-fifth and his thirty-first birthday, brought him a measure of respect and prestige that earlier he had not thought possible. Saint Mary's Parish was large, a strip of land twelve miles wide extending twenty-five miles along the Rappahannock to the outskirts of Fredericksburg. Keeping in touch with all parts of this region involved an almost inordinate amount of travel on horseback, but Boucher was a conscientious minister and he made his rounds regularly, visiting the sick and comforting the dying.

The church itself was located some eleven miles up the river from Boucher's home, and two miles inland from the Rappahannock. Unlike most Virginia churches of the day, which as a rule were constructed of wood and lacked spires, towers, steeples, and bells, Boucher's was a substantial brick structure with three galleries, reflecting a membership of prosperous planters, merchants, and county officials.[1] Boucher had no stock of sermons to draw upon in 1763, and a considerable portion of his time had to be spent in composition. Fortunately, his friend James had furnished him with several sermons which he could use as models. Later, when he had had a chance to prepare some of his own, he sometimes sent copies of his sermons to James, carefully written in a precise shorthand.

In 1764 Boucher was flattered and delighted by the offer of a post at William and Mary College, that of grammar master at a salary of £200 sterling a year. The offer, which undoubtedly reflected his growing reputation as a sound schoolmaster and a man of some intellect, appealed to Boucher, who yearned for the more intellectual life which William and Mary promised to offer. Even more attractive was the prospect of a prestigious position, particularly for a man without a university background and with a marked ambition to succeed. After much reflection, however, Boucher's sense of honesty prevailed and he regretfully declined (*MHM* 7:299).

Other honors were not long in coming. In 1768 Boucher accepted a post as a trustee for the newly organized Fund for the Relief of Widows and Orphans of Clergymen. Of the six trustees, Boucher already knew John Camm, Cambridge graduate and professor of divinity at the College of William and Mary, and Rev. Joseph Tickell of Trinity Parish, Louisa County, with whom he felt a sense of kinship since both Camm and Tickell had come from the Wigton area. According to the *Virginia Gazette*, the trustees met at William and Mary, raised a collection at church in the amount of £1 15s. 1½ d., and appointed officers for the following year.[2]

A warm, generous-spirited man, Boucher often found himself involved in extensive personal assistance to friends and clerical colleagues, although it sometimes cost him a great deal of trouble. This was the case with his friend Joseph Tickell, with whom he had already corresponded for some time, offering him gratuitous medical advice. Both men expected to have short lives, and they arranged a pact whereby the survivor should handle the affairs of whoever died first. Tickell died in 1769, leaving Boucher to settle his small estate. Boucher presently sent £300 to Tickell's Wigton relatives, advancing them £40 of his own, which he expected to collect later out of debts owed to Tickell. He never did. The grateful relatives, impoverished though they were, arranged for a silver cup which, Boucher recalled, cost fourteen guineas and which had his name inscribed (*Rem.*, p. 63).

On another occasion Boucher befriended a Mrs. Campbell, whose first husband had been the late Colonel Spotswood, son of the former governor of Virginia and a general under the duke of Marlborough. The widow then married Campbell, a native of

Jamaica who owned extensive property there. The Campbells lived close to Boucher and were "good neighbors." Boucher thought Campbell "a sensible and agreeable man" (*Rem.*, p. 63). Unfortunately, the couple lived expensively and ran into debt, and Campbell followed the route of many another bankrupt mainland planter. He escaped to Jamaica, deserting his wife permanently and leaving her to face his creditors. After two or three years, the Virginia creditors grew impatient and attached not only his property but also that which belonged solely to Mrs. Campbell and consisted primarily of slaves. Boucher felt sorry for the woman, particularly since her uncharitable former friends had abandoned her, and contrived to ease her predicament. Borrowing £300 from Tickell's estate (he had not yet sent it on to the relatives), Boucher added £200 of his own, and bought the woman's slaves at the forced sale of her estate. The slaves were then legally his, but Boucher granted Mrs. Campbell the sole use and benefit of them.

Boucher's resources were now great enough to allow him to indulge in generosity of this sort without too much difficulty. By a law of 1697 which remained in force until the Revolution, a Virginia cleric was entitled to a minimum salary of 16,000 pounds of tobacco, while a 1748 law had granted an additional allowance of 4 percent for shrinkage. Since tobacco sold at prices varying from two to six pence a pound, Boucher had an assured basic salary of approximately one to three hundred pounds. In addition, like other parish clergymen, he had a steady income from a variety of small fees. Twenty shillings was the customary fee for a marriage in which he both published banns and performed the ceremony, while a funeral ceremony commonly netted him forty shillings.

Boucher's feelings about his congregation were somewhat mixed. Occasionally he grumbled about his members, complaining that "people here pretend to like good sermons," yet "here as elsewhere, those I should think the best, half of them hardly understand." Like any Virginia parson, Boucher had to be content with a large reservoir of indifference in his congregation. "It was a melancholy truth," he had written while still at Hanover, that too many "respectable characters, think themselves at liberty to live totally negligent of either of the Sacraments."[3] The situation at Saint Mary's was much the same. On one occasion twenty-nine members of his new parish were fined five shillings or fifty pounds of tobacco by the vestry for being absent from services without excuse for at least two months running.[4]

Heresy was also a problem. Of the Dissenters, Baptists were the most numerous, but many were Methodists, Quakers, or Presbyterians.[5] Boucher considered it his duty to recover as many of these people as possible for the Anglican church. Although later he comforted himself with the thought that there were no Dissenters in his parish (*Rem.*, p. 47), the truth is that three Saint Mary's parishioners were reprimanded for allowing their homes to be used for "unauthorized services," while thirteen others were charged with attending the services, although the charges were later dismissed.[6] Boucher adopted a twofold stance toward Dissenters. On the one hand he avoided disputes with their ministers, treating them with "well-judged ridicule and contempt," because of what he considered to be their ignorance and impudence (*Rem.*, p. 48). At the same time he treated the lay Dissenters with "gentleness, persuasion, and attention." On one occasion, a dissenting minister attempted to draw Boucher into a public debate, but the latter refused firmly to become involved. Instead, he arranged for Daniel Barksdale, a carpenter of Saint Mary's Parish, to go in his place. Barksdale was a highly articulate man, and Boucher had only to coach him in argument to assure him an easy victory. Even so, Boucher occasionally befriended those whom he found so "contemptible." Once when several Baptist leaders were jailed for preaching without a license, Boucher visited them and provided bail to secure their release.[7]

On the whole, Boucher's relations with his congregation were excellent. In an optimistic moment he could boast to James on 10 September 1763 that he had "several more intelligent hearers than the best in your flock" (*MHM* 7:157). Certainly, as at Hanover, he was popular enough. His fame soon spread, and as a consequence, he received repeated invitations to preach before other congregations in the Tidewater, and far up in the back country as well. He delivered sermons in two forest parishes of Caroline and Spotsylvania in 1769, and on one occasion he preached without benefit of a church in the backwoods near the Blue Ridge area, a section "overrun," as he described it, with Dissenters. Long afterward, Bishop William Meade, third bishop of the Protestant Episcopal church in the diocese of Virginia, would recall that Boucher had become justly famous for winning the "love and confidence" of his people, and that he was "one of the best preachers in Virginia."[8]

Unlike most Virginia clerics, Boucher's concern for the spiritual welfare of his parishioners also extended to his Negro flock. His predecessors at Saint Mary's had considered the slaves to be too ignorant and irresponsible for induction into the church, but Boucher, taking as his model Saint Thomas's work among the natives of Africa, deliberately set out to bring religious instruction and even baptism to his slave parishioners. On 24 November 1765 he baptized 115 Negro adults and on Easter Monday of the following year he baptized 313 more. He preached to more than 1,000 Negroes following the baptismal ceremony (*Rem.*, pp. 57-58).

Most of the baptized Negroes were illiterate, but Boucher noted in his parish records that there were twenty or thirty of them who could read their prayer books, while thirteen of these he could count as communicants who participated regularly in the Eucharist. Boucher also attempted to spread some degree of literacy among his remaining Negro parishioners. While still at Hanover he had corresponded with Rev. John Waring of the Society for the Propagation of the Gospel (SPG) on a plan for free books to that end. Unfortunately, Boucher's white parishioners had interposed with such a number of objections that he had become completely discouraged and had abandoned his Negro free school plan.

At Saint Mary's he was more cautious. Nonetheless, he trained two or three of his more intelligent Negroes as schoolteachers, hoping that they in turn could spread some literacy among their fellows. Boucher hoped these efforts would make some amends for the drudgery of the slaves' daily lives, "unfetter them from the chains of ignorance," and "emancipate them from the bondage of sin, the worst slavery to which they can be subjected."[9] Too optimistically he expressed the hope that these bonds, in a spiritual sense at least, might be broken. Boucher was later to describe his effort to educate his slaves, and his ideas seem to have resembled the Sunday school concept which was not to emerge in England until 1780.[10]

Boucher's busy schedule left him but few idle moments for abstract theological speculation, but he was a man who relished ideas, and he presently found himself in what amounted to a crisis of faith. From 1763 on, he had found time occasionally to puzzle in some disquiet over the doctrine of the Trinity. He had read avidly on the subject, including articles in the *Monthly Review*, a journal for which Boucher had great respect. His faith for a time was shaken to the point where he "had well nigh made shipwreck" of his orthodoxy. Yet he did not know what it was he wanted to reject, or what faith to put in its place. For a time Boucher became a sort of bewildered skeptic. He confessed to James on 28 November 1767 that he had not read the Athanasian Creed, required regularly of all Anglican clergy, more than two or three time in the five years he had been an officiating minister in America (*MHM* 7:352).

With his customary thorough approach, Boucher read with care what had been written in defense of the Trinity by Daniel Waterland (1682-1740), archdeacon of Middlesex, and by George Bull (1694-1710), bishop of Saint David's in Wales. In the process of inquiry, Boucher came to believe that he had lost himself by attempting to stick to the "expressions and definitions of our Creed" (*Rem.*, p. 44), and he finally decided that it was necessary to search the Scriptures themselves. Boucher ultimately gave up his attempt to account philosophically for the mystery of the Trinity, concluding simply that it was "beyond the reach of human faculties" (*Rem.*, p. 45). Thereafter he contented himself with reading the New Testament in the original language. He then accepted the orthodox Anglican doctrine as revealed truth, and as such not a subject for philosophical disquisition, which he regarded as no more than a kind of intellectual exercise.

For Boucher thus to subordinate his powers of reason "to the obedience of faith" required some considerable discipline and intellectual "self-denial" (*Rem.*, p. 45). He was convinced that man was intended to use his intelligence and that he was allowed and required to examine both nature and faith with all possible care. In the final analysis, however, he thought caution and reverence necessary in any such speculative process, "because there are infinite particulars in both that lie beyond the reach of our abilities" (*Rem.*, p. 46).

Boucher's crisis of faith was no doubt the more severe because of his growing interest in contemporary science. He wrote James on 29 September 1769 about the appearance near the Pleiades of a comet whose tail extended to fifty degrees—some thought to seventy-five degrees. This was the largest comet that had been seen since Halley's comet was first observed in England in 1682, and whose reappearance in 1758 had occasioned great excitement both in Britain and in the colonies. Boucher asked James if this newest comet had been visible in England. He also noted that on 7 September, when the comet was calculated to be nearest the earth, Virginia and the continent in general had had the "most violent hurricane for upwards of twelve hours ever known in the memory of man." He wondered if a causal relationship existed, but was quick to anticipate charges from James of "credulity, ignorance and superstition." He reminded James that Whisten's theory of the Deluge considered a comet to be a natural cause of the flood, and was not sure that this hypothesis had yet been "exploded." For the time being, Boucher thought it "temerity and presumption" completely to rule it out (*MHM* 8:47).

In spite of the poor reputation of most of the Anglican clergy in Virginia, Boucher managed to find a few congenial spirits in the religious community, such as Joseph Tickell and James Maury, rector of Fredericksburg Parish in Albemarle County. Boucher had first met Maury in 1763 and soon the two men became firm friends. Maury was born in Ireland of French parents who emigrated to Virginia when he was less than a year old. He later attended William and Mary College and married a "blithe and buxom lass" who was to bear him thirteen children (*MHM* 7:344). Like Boucher, Maury operated a boarding school for boys. Boucher thought himself fortunate to have found the "sensible, generous, elegant, and agreeable" Maury, and as he wrote to Tickell on 13 January 1764, he "set no ordinary price" upon the friendship of his "most worthy and ingenious" friend (*MHM* 7:164). In spite of the fifty or sixty miles that separated their parishes, the two clerics saw each other often, corresponded constantly, and formed a deep friendship which lasted until 1769, when a grieving Boucher administered the last rites to his dying friend and made a deathbed promise to oversee the education in England of one of his favorite sons.[11]

Under Maury's tutelage, Boucher took his first hesitant steps toward involvement in Virginia politics. His initial efforts were some unsigned verses intended to support the Anglican clergy in the current controversy over the so-called Twopenny Act, a subject of dispute in Virginia since its enactment in 1754. This measure, later renewed on several occasions, permitted the payment of all public levies including clerical salaries, excepting only quitrents, in either tobacco or money. This had been no hardship when the market price for tobacco was two pence a pound, but with the failure of a series of crops owing to the drought, the price of tobacco had risen and most parishioners chose to pay in cash. The clerics, who obviously would have preferred payment of salaries in tobacco which could be sold at two or three times the value of a cash salary payment, entered a spirited protest. When the legislature in 1758 renewed the Twopenny Act, the clergy drafted a variety of memorials and petitions and hurried them off to the bishop of London and to the Privy Council. The protest was successful. On 10 August 1759 the Crown disallowed the act. A number of clergymen, including James Maury, thereupon sued for back salary. Thus began the celebrated Parsons' Cause.

The clergymen's suit almost at once precipitated a vigorous little pamphleteering war. Col. Landon Carter, one of the wealthiest landed planters in the colony, and Col. Richard Bland, already an influential political figure whom the Stamp Act controversy was to make famous, fired off a series of pamphlets in defense of the legislature's position. In reply, John Camm took up the argument for the clerics. At this point, Boucher entered the fray, intending to offset the "overbearing colonels" who had "published and abused us." Boucher's role was modest enough; in addition to writing verses, he revised a number of Maury's essays on the subject and dared even to publish an essay or two of his own, taking care meanwhile to preserve his own anonymity. Only Maury and Camm were "in on the secret." His effort, Boucher thought, had "had some weight here" (*MHM* 7:161).

Boucher's first venture into Virginia politics thus had conservative political overtones. Self-interest and his obvious sympathy for the position of the Anglican clergy had drawn him toward a political stance which emphasized the right of the Crown to interfere in Virginia's internal legislative sovereignty. Later historians would identify Patrick Henry's subsequent successful defense of the popular position in the Parsons' Cause as one of the earliest manifestations of the revolutionary Patriot sentiment in the colony, and in fact James Maury's case was the one in which Henry established himself as a master of rhetoric by persuading the jury into an unsympathetic award of one penny to the plaintiff.[12]

In spite of this apparent early conservative alignment, however, Boucher was for the most part at this time identified with the group which would emerge eventually as the Patriot party. By 1768 he had developed a personal acquaintance with Col. George Washington and thereafter they were guests in each other's homes. Washington and other Virginians with similar ideas introduced Boucher to contemporary Virginia thought and almost inevitably most of his political reactions at this time were very close to good Patriot orthodoxy.

Boucher, like most Virginians, was severely critical of the Proclamation of 1763, which had barred colonial settlement and land sales west of the Appalachian ridge. The policy involved was one he considered to be, as he told James on 9 March 1767, "very impolitic as well as unjust." Boucher's indignation was inspired at least in part by personal circumstances. His friend Maury, who, like many others had taken up large tracts of land in the fertile Ohio and Mississippi valleys "for the sake of his children," had now found himself frustrated in his desire to live there (*MHM* 7:344).

Boucher's reaction to the Stamp Act two years later was even more pronounced. The new tax measure had produced tremendous excitement in Virginia. A few days after news of the obnoxious law reached the colony, Patrick Henry in introducing his famous resolves had compared George III to a Caesar or a Charles I, insinuating that he wished another Cromwell would arise.[13] The colony boiled with talk of the rights of Englishmen, and the philosophies of Locke, Vattel, Sidney, and Lord Coke were all used to refute the assertion that Parliament had any such power of taxation. Boucher shared fully the sense of outrage and indignation abroad in the colony. In a letter to James written on 9 December 1765, he railed against the Stamp Act, saying it constituted a merciless invasion by Parliament of the rights of the colonists. No one, he continued, "whose understanding is not totally blind, and whose heart is still undepraved, can help seeing and owning that the Act in question is, in every sense, oppressive, impolitic and illegal." Boucher suggested that even if Parliament had a right to impose such an internal tax, it ought not to have done so because James would "hardly believe how unaccountably ignorant [Parliament members] are of the present state of the colonies." One had only to read the debates in the House of Commons, Boucher pointed out, for evidence that members firmly believed in "the opulence of the Americans"; whereas the truth was that "they are immersed over head and ears in debt." His opinion here had a sharply personal note; he was himself deeply in debt in spite of the general improvement in his circumstances, and would remain so for years (*MHM* 7:295-96).

Englishmen were incredibly ignorant on matters other than American prosperity. For example, Lord George Beauclerk, a man "of no inferior rank" in the military, sent between four and five hundred Highlanders to be quartered in James City. No one in England seemed to know that there was but one house in the entire city, and that a private one, Boucher remarked. Boucher attributed such abysmal lack of knowledge on the part of the British to poor communication, observing that "nobody of consequence comes amongst us to get any personal information of our affairs, and those entrusted to communicate such intelligence are themselves either too ignorant or too knavish to give any to be depended upon." Under such circumstances, Boucher concluded, Parliament was in no position to levy taxes on the colonies, any more than it was to "prescribe an assessment for the inhabitants of Kamchatka" (*MHM* 7:295-96).

In the summer of 1766, a celebrated murder soon commanded Boucher's attention. Col. John Chiswell, the father-in-law of the powerful and prestigious Landon Carter, killed Robert Routledge. Routledge, a popular merchant of some standing, on the occasion of the Cumberland court session, had spent the day carousing at Mosby's Tavern, and by evening he apparently began talking in an overbearing manner, his language peppered with oaths. A brawl ensued in which words led to weapons—both men using first wine glasses, then candlesticks and tongs. At the climax of the quarrel, Chiswell ran Routledge through the body with his sword. A local justice of the peace promptly committed Chiswell to the county jail, refused to grant bail, and ordered him bound over to be tried for murder.

The Routledge-Chiswell affair spilled over into the pages of the *Virginia Gazette* and soon became something of a cause célèbre.[14] It was apparent enough that Chiswell was too powerful and influential to be dealt with as a commonplace criminal. The authorities, under extremely heavy pressure, handled Chiswell's case in a highly questionable manner. Even before the prisoner could be delivered to the county jail for safekeeping, as the law provided, the judges of the General Court, although that honorable body was not then even in session, took Chiswell from the sheriff and admitted him to bail without seeing the record of his preliminary examination and without examining any of the eyewitnesses. Two of the three judges were Chiswell's personal friends. William Byrd was a partner in Chiswell's lead mines, while Presley Thornton had extensive business dealings with him and would become Chiswell's executor.

All of this was irregular in the extreme. Under Virginia law at the time, a defendant in a capital case ordinarily would not have been bailable. A writer in the *Gazette* presently suggested that what had happened was in fact a "rescue" under the flimsiest pretext of law. Not even the letter which John Blair, the third judge, wrote to the *Gazette* on 3 July 1766 served to quiet the growing sense of public indignation. Blair insisted that Chiswell had not been admitted to bail until the court had been advised by three eminent lawyers that such a procedure was indeed lawful. He further argued that although the murder had resulted from "a most unhappy drunken affair, and very culpable," yet there had been no malice in the killing. The two men, Blair pointed out, had enjoyed "a long intimate friendship." Furthermore, Routledge had been the original offender; "the first assault" had been from "the deceased," who "threw a glass of wine in Chiswell's face, both much in liquor." There was some evidence also, Blair added, that Chiswell had not even thrust his sword at his victim; although Chiswell had drawn his weapon, his arm had been restrained by alarmed witnesses, at which point Routledge himself had broken loose from restraining hands and rushed forward to be impaled. Thus Blair attempted to pass the whole matter off as self-defense, or at worst manslaughter.

At this point, Boucher injected himself into the controversy with an anonymous letter to the *Gazette* addressed to Blair. Although the murdered man was an entire stranger to him, Boucher observed later, the case interested him. As he saw it, Chiswell had "in a strange fit of aristocratic insolence" killed Routledge. Although Chiswell had been arrested, he had been "bailed in a very extraordinary manner; and in a still more extraordinary manner was found dead, it was never known how, the night before the trial," as Boucher put it. What bothered Boucher were the "efforts made in behalf of his murderer," which Boucher considered "such an outrage on common sense as well as on humanity" that he could not help "drawing up some answers to these vindications" (*Rem.*, p. 111).

Boucher's letter of 25 July censured Blair, Byrd, and Thornton for altering the constitutional relationship between the county court and the General Court. The sheriff had an absolute authority for conducting Chiswell to prison; he had a legal warrant, which superseded the authority of any of the judges. In fact, had the sheriff commanded the judges to assist him in getting the prisoner jailed, they would have been obliged to do so and fined if they had refused. Furthermore, taking the prisoner from the sheriff was a rescue, if not by violence then by artifice, for the judges had no authority to issue bail in a capital case of this kind. Blair's excuse that three eminent lawyers had advised the bail would not satisfy the intelligent public, Boucher wrote, since his legal advisors were all friends of Chiswell and *ex parte*. The depositions taken in the case also drew Boucher's fire; he found several aspects questionable. The Crown was a party in the case, but no one, not even the attorney general, appeared on behalf of the king. Unfortunately, the attorney general had gone out of town without providing for a substitute in his absence. Furthermore, the judges had used hearsay witnesses, ignoring available eyewitnesses. Neither the undersheriff Jeffe Thomas nor John Wayles, attorney for Chiswell, deponents, had been at the scene of the killing, although they had been present at the examination.

Boucher's letter to the *Virginia Gazette* is a reflection of his emerging social consciousness. He now had a feeling for the country as his own, with a sense of responsibility to protect the constitution and the rights of the people. The sense of being an equal in an open society is strong. He felt no qualms about addressing Blair, although as president of the Maryland Privy Council, Blair held one of the highest posts in the colony. Boucher aimed an arrow at Blair for his seeming arrogance in explaining that he was waiving the dignity of his station to set forth the position of the judges. "Is there a dignity in this land which exempts any person whatever from a duty to satisfy, if possible, a people which conceives itself injured?" Boucher thought not, since "men of equal

64

merit have (while you are not dispensing justice in the General Court) a right to an equal dignity with yourself." Blair, he said, was in an indefensible position, one "subversive of that constitution of which he hath so long been the support," even if his predicament was inadvertent.

Boucher's sense of concern for the commonweal was in part a revelation of his new self-confidence. The gauche and uncomfortable immigrant of seven years before had disappeared with the acquisition of a certain amount of prestige as the rector of Saint Mary's and as an effective schoolmaster. With some justification he considered himself a member of the "intelligent public" which he felt had a right to resent the feeble attempts of the three judges to exonerate themselves. Although the letter addressed to Blair is not necessarily the work of a lawyer, it is well-written, informed, and analytical. Boucher raised pertinent questions about the case which had not been dealt with in the press earlier, and he was correct about the legal aspect of bail granting in murder cases.[15]

The newspaper controversy went on through the summer and fall of 1766. The inquest was held on 15 August 1766, and letters to the *Gazette* continued to appear through October while Chiswell awaited trial. The Virginia government, considerably upset by the newspaper exposure and by the public furor, sued the *Virginia Gazette* for libel.

John Chiswell was never tried; he died the night before the case was to be heard. A one-paragraph item in the 17 October 1766 *Gazette* newspaper noted briefly Chiswell's passing: "On Wednesday last at 11:00 in the afternoon, at his house in this city [Williamsburg] . . . after a short illness. The cause of death, by physician upon oath, nervous fits, owing to a constant uneasiness of the mind."

Unfortunately, Boucher's identity as the writer of the 25 July letter became known. Col. Landon Carter could not forgive him and the incident became the basis of a private grudge. Boucher's sense of justice, which had impelled him to put his thoughts into print, thus had earned him the enmity of one of Virginia's foremost planters and a leader of the ardent nascent Patriots. Although Boucher supported the American cause in the recent Stamp Act controversy in his letters to James, his position may not have been known publicly, and he had now placed himself in a position where any prominent political association with the Virginia Whigs would be extremely difficult. Without intending any political move, Boucher had taken a first step, perhaps an irrevocable one, away from the tightly knit community of opinion of Virginia's foremost planters. Before long, Boucher would reap a bitter harvest from Carter's enmity.

The next two or three years brought a period of relative quiet in the internal affairs of the colony and in British-American concerns, despite the announcement of the Townshend Acts in the summer of 1767. Compared with the New Englanders, Virginians reacted mildly. Massachusetts drew up the famous *Circular Letter* (1768) requesting support from the other colonies, and then refused to rescind it. The Virginia Resolves, averring that Virginians could be taxed only by their own representatives, that the trials of Americans in England would violate British rights, and that it was "lawful and expedient" for the colony to unite with other provinces against unconstitutional actions of Parliament, were not adopted until 1 May 1769.

Lord Botetourt, the first resident governor in many years in Virginia and an extremely popular one, nevertheless considered the resolves sufficient cause to dissolve the House of Burgesses for its insolence. The leaders of the House thereupon met in special convention, and endorsed a Nonimportation Agreement drafted by George Mason. Under this arrangement, no dutiable goods were to be used except cheap paper, no luxuries were to be imported, and no slaves brought into Virginia after 1 November 1769. Most of the planters signed it, although only a few of the merchants did so. The Virginia Nonimportation Agreement soon gained general approval in the rest of the South.

In this crisis of 1769 Boucher's sympathies still were firmly with the Americans. In a letter to James 25 July 1769 he denounced the Townshend Acts as victimizing the "poor, persecuted Americans." American opposition he commended in the most glowing of terms, describing it to James as "the most warrantable, generous, and manly that history can produce." Although Boucher did not admire individual members of the House of Burgesses, thinking them "almost" deserving of "the contempt with which our Lords and Masters the Parliament treat them," nevertheless he conceded that collectively they had gained much honor for their eloquence for their resolves and petitions to the king. Boucher thought the Americans had a "virtuous" cause, which "will certainly in the end be successful" (*MHM* 8:44). Boucher's sister Jinny was also convinced of the justice of the cause, and promptly canceled a short vacation at the Frederick Warm Springs with the Washingtons because she thought it inconsistent with the Nonimportation Agreement's principles of austerity.[16]

In the same letter, Boucher criticized the British for misunderstanding what he considered to be so "plain a question," as they had at the time of the Stamp Act. At least part of the trouble was that "the people of England never read the American publications," although they mistakenly believed "the villainous reasonings" of hirelings bent on disgracing the American cause. By now Boucher had identified himself closely with the Americans, believed that the cause would succeed, and worried about "the consequences of this to the Parent State" (*MHM* 8:44-45). Except for the smoldering problem with Landon Carter, Boucher was for the moment completely identified with the nascent Patriot faction, as were many of the Virginia clergy.[17]

In 1769 Boucher celebrated his tenth anniversary in America. Looking back at the past decade, he was obliged to recognize that he had made a few injudicious decisions, but he had also matured and was a man of some substance and stature in Virginia. He now was increasingly concerned with public affairs and had become acquainted with some of Virginia's leading political personalities. But Boucher's thoughts strayed more and more to Maryland, where one of America's choicest clerical posts and prime tobacco lands lay.

Chapter 4

Church Politics in Maryland

It was Boucher's acquaintance with the Reverend Henry Addison of Barnabas's Manor in Prince George's County which had first aroused his interest in the colony to the north. The two men had met when Addison visited Boucher's school to "see and judge for himself" its suitability for his two sons, who were ready for training in grammar, mathematics, and the Latin classics (*Rem.*, p. 51). Addison was satisfied with his investigation, and in July 1765 he determined to send them to join the four Maryland youths and a number of Virginians who were already enrolled. The acquaintance between the clerics ripened into friendship when the two men discovered a common tie in their Cumberland County ancestry and a mutual interest in books and serious conversation.

Unlike Boucher, whose origins were in the impoverished yeomanry, Henry Addison was born in 1717 into a prominent Maryland family of impeccable Cumberland antecedents. Oxon Hill, the Addison estate and the most desirable Boucher "had ever seen in any part of the world," was located in Prince George's County on the Potomac a few miles below present-day Washington (*Rem.*, p. 51). Like many another prosperous colonial, Henry Addison had gone abroad for his education. He matriculated March 1734 at Queen's College, Oxford, at the age of sixteen, earning his A.B. in 1738 and his A.M. three years later. After ordination in England in 1742, he returned to his native county in Maryland, taking up his duties as rector of Saint John's Church at Broad Creek in King George's Parish, commonly known as Piscataway Parish.[1] Addison's marriage to Rachel Dulany Knight, the widowed daughter of the elder Daniel Dulany of Annapolis, further enhanced his prestige.[2] One of Rachel's brothers, Daniel Dulany the younger, was secretary general to the province and a leader of the Maryland bar. Another brother, Walter Dulany, was mayor of Annapolis in 1765 and was appointed commissary general in 1767. Both brothers were also on the Provincial Council. Marylanders generally considered them to be men of first-rate ability, a judgment in which Boucher concurred.

The friendship between Boucher and Addison deepened rapidly. Boucher thought he had never met a better scholar, reflecting ruefully that Addison's education "had been as good as mine had been bad" (*Rem.* pp. 52-53). Addison reminded him of James in many respects, although unlike his English friend, Addison was "keen, shrewd, active, and busy" in public affairs (*MHM* 7:354). The two men entertained a high regard for each other, although each also recognized the other's shortcomings. Boucher admired Addison's "cool, orderly and cautious" manner, but did not fail to observe that Addison was already confirmed in his habits of indolence and was "degenerating fast into a mere humdrum country parson." Furthermore, although his new friend was a wealthy man, he was also stingy and "tenacious of money" (*Rem.,* pp. 52-53).

Addison, although he sympathized with and encouraged his young colleague, also disapproved of his "hasty, rash, inconsiderate, flighty, and fickle" moments, a criticism which Boucher relayed to James on 28 November 1767. Boucher allowed himself too often to be guided "by imagination and the first impulses of passion" (*MHM* 7:354). Interestingly, this description was curiously similar to Boucher's own self-evaluation when he had written on 25 November 1763 of his "too sanguine temper" (*MHM* 7:160). It also resembled a characterization Boucher gave of himself some years later as a happy but "rash, sanguine, indiscreet man" in whose "motley character" romanticism was "a most material ingredient" (*MHM* 8:185; *MHM* 7:348). But in spite of occasional criticism of each other, the friendship became "most intimate and cordial" (*Rem.*, p. 52), and Boucher could write James that he had found "my James in America" (*MHM* 7:353).

Addison's impact on Boucher's intellectual development was nothing short of remarkable. Boucher began to build up a serious library and to develop his interest in American geography and history, in English history and the history of "civil society," in penology and criminology, in diseases endemic to the American continent, and in etymology. He wrote James on 29 September 1769, asking him to find a copy of Franciscus Junius's *Etymologicum Anglicanum*, which had been edited by Edward Lye, an Oxford graduate of 1743, confessing as he did so that he had developed "a mighty inclination for antiquarian knowledge" (*MHM* 8:48, 49-50).[3] Other requests for etymological material included studies of the ancient Caledonians, Picts, and Europeans, books on the origin and the structure of the Greek tongue, and a number of works on grammar and the structure of language. Later this interest was to lead to his pastoral poem "Absence," and would eventually serve as the foundation for his lexical work.

Wide-ranging conversations with Addison also led Boucher into new enthusiasm on diverse topics. In 1769, for example, he bought Charles Beatty's *Journals of a Two Months Tour Among the Indians to the Westward of the Aleghanny Mountains,* Costard's *History of Astronomy,* Dilly Chalmer's *Essay on Fevers,* Cesare Beccaria's celebrated treatise *Crimes and Punishments;* and the *Essay on the History of Civil Society* by Adam Ferguson, the Edinburgh philosopher-historian. In his letter requesting this last Boucher also asked James whether any additional volumes of Catherine Macaulay's *History of England from the Accession of James I to that of the Brunswick Line* had been published lately. Boucher explained that his own three volumes did not yet bring the history down to the "Elevation of the House of Hanover, as is promised on the title page, but [instead] end with Charles the First." Boucher apparently wanted to create a handsome library, for in the same letter he wrote James "let these books be bound etc. (not in the manner of Whitehaven) but elegantly, and lettered and some of them gilt" (*MHM* 8:50).[4] From time to time, Boucher asked James to send him newspapers, magazines, reviews, pamphlets, and any other materials that he thought worthwhile, and he also arranged to have the students whom James recruited for tutoring posts in America bring copies of the *Annual Register,* the

Monthly Review, and occasionally other periodicals.

As Boucher and Addison discoursed amiably on books, philosophy, and religion during many a long evening, the Virginia cleric's thoughts turned increasingly to a possibility that Addison had occasionally mentioned in their conversations—a prosperous parish in Maryland. He was already well aware that ministerial salaries in the proprietary colony north of the Potomac were for the most part far more generous than those in Virginia. Thomas Bacon of All Saints' Parish, he had learned, had an income averaging some 100,000 pounds of tobacco annually, a sum equivalent to £600 or £700 sterling (*MHM* 7:340). In fact, Boucher's estimate was conservative. According to William Eddis, the surveyor of customs at Annapolis, All Saints' was worth no less than £1,000 sterling annually, and was easily the most lucrative of the forty-five clerical livings in Maryland.[5] Even allowing for the fact that there was often a great difference between the sum nominally due to a cleric from his parishioners and the amount actually received, and that the tobacco might well be in poor condition and thus command a low market price, the Maryland salary situation was decidedly superior. It appeared that an Anglican minister in Maryland might aspire to an income approaching that of an attorney with a moderate practice.[6]

Addison's own income also impressed Boucher. King George's Parish, Boucher estimated in a letter to James on 9 March 1767, yielded an annual income of six or seven hundred pounds (*MHM* 7:340). Hence when Addison proposed in 1766 that the powerful influence of his wife Rachel's Dulany family relatives be enlisted to find Boucher a Maryland living, he accepted the offer with enthusiasm and was soon filled with optimism over his Maryland prospects and the assurances Addison was giving him. As it happened, Addison was as good as his word. He prevailed upon Walter Dulany, a vestryman of Saint Anne's Parish in Annapolis, to ask Gov. Horatio Sharpe of Maryland to use his influence with the proprietor to obtain a Maryland benefice for Boucher. Sharpe agreed readily enough to recommend Boucher to Lord Baltimore for the rectory at Saint Anne's as soon as it should fall vacant. Boucher preferred a country living and Saint Anne's was not a large parish, but he saw immediately that it was a step in the right direction. Annapolis rectors had been promoted to better benefices so often that the parish was called the *Gradus ad Par-*

nassum. Boucher now expected that there would be only a short wait for a call to a Maryland post. Instead, he soon encountered the intrigues and politics of the Church of England in Maryland.

By Christmas 1766, the living at Annapolis had fallen vacant. Boucher, together with Addison and the Dulanys, assumed that he would shortly receive his appointment. Instead, he suffered the first of a long series of setbacks to his plans. In January 1767, a gentleman arrived in Maryland from England carrying "very extraordinary recommendations" from Lord Baltimore, which amounted virtually to an express order to Governor Sharpe to give him the first vacant parish acceptable to him.[7] The new arrival was the Reverend Bennet Allen, on occasion known also as Benedict Allen, a fellow of Wadham College, Oxford, and a companion of the dissolute Baltimore. Although Boucher could not have known it, letters in advance of Allen had arrived for Sharpe both from Lord Baltimore and from his secretary, Hugh Hamersley, ordering Sharpe to give Allen the best church living available in Maryland. The letter which Allen brought with him stipulated further that he was to have two livings if necessary to produce the income he desired. But Sharpe balked at this instruction, since such pluralism ran counter to both local law and local feeling. Sharpe told Allen he would rather pay him fifty pounds annually out of his own pocket than provide him with two parishes. The benefice of Saint Luke's was open, the governor suggested, and he would be glad to name Allen to it forthwith.

To the chagrin of Boucher and his wellwishers, Allen rejected the offer of Saint Luke's and insisted instead on having the vacant parish at Annapolis. Saint Luke's paid more, but was located on the Eastern Shore, away from the center of affairs in the colony. Allen preferred to be in Annapolis where an ambitious cleric could more readily court provincial officialdom. Reluctantly, Sharpe acceded to Allen's demand. Disappointed and frustrated, Boucher considered his alternatives, and asked James for advice. Should he patiently wait in Virginia for a benefice, leaving his future to chance? On the other hand, he could return to England with the hope of enjoying once more the company of James. On second thought, leaving America meant relinquishing "elegance and plenty, in exchange for contempt and poverty" in England (*MHM* 7:351).

While Boucher still pondered his prospects, the parish of Saint James at Herring Bay, not far from Annapolis, became vacant and

Boucher's hopes rose once more. Herring Bay, Boucher told James on 28 November 1767, looked like a "charming situation" (*MHM* 7:355). Addison, well aware of Boucher's interest in the Herring Bay living, determined to press the matter. The day after the vacancy occurred, he rode fifty miles to dine with Governor Sharpe and to remind him of his earlier promises. With some disgust, Addison learned that Allen's greed was about to frustrate Boucher once more. Allen, Sharpe informed Addison, had unabashedly demanded the Herring Bay living also, boldly proposing thereby to increase his income by another £300 a year. Yielding to pressure, Sharpe surrendered his earlier objections to double livings and issued a license for Saint James's, subject to the approval of the vestries both of Saint Anne's and Herring Bay.

Thus for a second time Boucher's plans came to nothing. One faint possibility of thwarting Allen remained; the two vestries might not grant their approval. Walter Dulany determined to make the most of this opportunity. From the beginning he had wanted Boucher to have Saint Anne's, and he was now more than ever reluctant to see both Saint Anne's and Saint James's fall to Allen. He shrewdly enlisted the support of two distinguished fellow vestrymen of his own parish, Thomas Johnson and Brice Worthington. Both lawyers and assemblymen, they also were violently opposed to pluralism. In spite of Dulany's efforts, the vestry at Saint James early consented to the double appointment, but with the all-important reservation that Saint Anne's Parish also approve the arrangements. Thus the vote of Saint Anne's Parish now became critical.

This situation presently led to a bitter quarrel between Allen and the Dulanys, who were still pressing the interests of Boucher. Allen, desperately determined to have both parishes, now brazenly courted votes from various vestrymen at Saint Anne's. One of these was Samuel Chew, a lawyer who apparently viewed Allen's case with a cold and disinterested eye. In spite of an earlier quasi commitment to the ambitious cleric, Chew shortly refused to cast his vote in favor of the plural living. Allen thereupon accused him of being influenced by Walter Dulany. Chew denied the charge, swearing on a Bible that he had had nothing to do with the Dulanys. When Allen persisted, Chew called him a scoundrel, dragged him to the door, and struck at him with his cane, barely missing the greedy cleric's bald head. Allen thereupon challenged Chew to a duel. However, Chew went to the dueling ground with a blunderbuss, and Allen, hearing of the weapon, failed to keep the appointment.[8]

Infuriated that his own earlier efforts to ingratiate himself with the Dulany family had not been successful, Allen now took his argument into the pages of the *Maryland Gazette*. Writing under the pseudonym "Bystander," Allen accused Dulany of manipulating the Saint Anne's vote. Dulany defended his integrity with a series of letters which Boucher described as "admirably well written." Boucher also replied to Allen in verse and prose. But other writers presently joined the fray with crude satire and scurrilous doggerel verse, and after some four months Jonas Green, the printer, shut off the debate. Naturally the controversy did nothing to dispel the animosity between Allen and Dulany. Allen met Dulany on the street one day and struck at him with a light rapier which he carried hidden in his cane. In spite of the surprise attack, and notwithstanding the fact that Dulany was "a heavy, gouty and clumsy man," Dulany "thrashed him soundly" (*Rem.*, p. 56).

The newspaper controversy gave Boucher an opportunity to express his own frustration and anger anonymously in his verse and prose.[9] He reflected later that he had "had the luck at length to get the laugh of the public against [Allen] so that he was completely worsted" (*Rem.*, p. 56). But the impasse over Allen's demand for a double living remained unresolved. Allen, denied the plurality, continued to pressure Sharpe. At this point, Sharpe received new instructions from Baltimore that provided another approach to the problem of Allen's demands. Allen, the proprietor wrote, was to receive a high office, one having to do with fiscal matters in the Proprietary's bureaucracy, so that he would no longer be obliged to push for a double clerical appointment. Sharpe obliged by making Allen the provincial escheater, a plum worth some £300 a year. Allen thereupon retained Saint James's Parish and gave up Saint Anne's.

To his disgust, Boucher did not benefit even now from this latest development. Instead the vacated parish went to Allen's friend and curate, one Mr. Edmiston, who apparently had carried strong recommendations from Lord and Lady Essex, relatives of Lord Baltimore (*Rem.*, p. 54). The situation now had become so embarrassing to both Sharpe and the Dulanys that the governor saw fit to explain his difficult position to them. Reluctantly, the Dulanys agreed to set Boucher's claims aside once more, explaining in turn to the unhappy cleric that one post or another would soon fall vacant. Addison comforted Boucher as well as he could, cheering his friend with the reassurance that Allen was by now in poor grace in several quarters and could hardly claim further official favors. Sharpe had commented that there was no restraint or decency in the man. Stories were now flying about the colony which sought to explain the interloper's extraordinary influence; he was, rumormongers had it, an illegitimate son of the late Lord Baltimore. Boucher's friends even insinuated that the lady Allen had brought with him to Maryland, whom he called his sister, was "a sister to him as Sarah was to Abraham" (*MHM* 7:341).[10]

Boucher himself importuned James, on behalf of his friends in America as well as himself, to make discreet inquiries about Allen back in England, apparently in the hope of turning up something sufficiently scandalous to ruin him. This approach, however, failed to uncover anything of importance. An attempt to confirm the suspected "Sarah and Abraham" relationship between Allen and his supposed sister also ended in failure. James's inquiries further made clear that Allen, in spite of his pretensions, came from humble enough origins, but that he was unquestionably in Baltimore's favor. Baltimore, who in fact enjoyed a thoroughly bad moral reputation, had just been tried and acquitted on the charge of rape brought by a Miss Woodcock (*Rem.*, p. 55).[11]

As one disappointment followed another, Boucher's spirits sank and he indulged himself with wistful thoughts of a return to a quiet living in England. Thoroughly discouraged with his Maryland prospects, he asked James about the possibility of purchasing a living in Cumberland. He thought he could raise a thousand pounds if necessary and hoped that he might borrow the rest. James apparently reminded Boucher about the question of simony involved. Boucher replied on 28 November 1767 that he saw "no moral turpitude in this terrible crime of simony," and that in any event he thought it "infinitely more venial than the thousand dirty finesses and unworthy condescensions daily imposed upon the candidates for preferment" here in America. He told James bitterly that he might as well at once avail himself of the expedient of kissing "my thumbs instead of the Book; or, like Captains of ships

at the Custom House, take a previous oath that all I swear...
should go for nothing" (*MHM* 7:352).

These thoughts were of short duration, for Boucher's common
sense told him that such a course of action was foolhardy and
against his own best interests. In the same letter he admitted to
James, "America is doubtless...the country for me." Soberly he
remembered the indignities he had suffered in his native country
and contrasted with them the self-sufficiency and respect he enjoyed in Virginia. Even in his clerical role he exercised a degree
of autonomy which was not possible in England. He doubted that
his "pride would suffer him" at this point in his life "to act in a
subordinate capacity to any man whatever—scarcely perhaps to
Mr. James himself" (*MHM* 7:352-53). He concluded on 9 March
1767 that "the advantages of staying where I am are so infinitely
superior to anything I could expect in a change, that I hardly
dare hope I shall ever have virtue enough seriously to resolve
upon [leaving America]" (*MHM* 7:338). Even if he remained in
Virginia his salary would exceed what he could expect in England,
where benefices were poorly paid, for his present salary far exceeded the seventy pounds earned by James.

Although Boucher decided to remain in America, he doubted
that he should ever make a fortune in the colonies, believing that
his "own heart (or perhaps it is indolence or vanity) perpetually
suggests...that I have *too much virtue* to do it." He reminded
James that the principles of the "art of thriving" were the same
everywhere, and that there were those "of your acquaintance and
mine who would make fortunes on the barrenest Caledonian Hills,
whilst others would still be poor, though in partnership with Clive
himself." It seemed to Boucher that a "peculiar temper" was necessary to effect "this mighty business," and he hoped that he possessed as much of it as James thought necessary. "All things considered," he wrote, "I have no reason to complain of my fortune
in the world" (*MHM* 7:338-39). In any event, Addison was still
determined to see his young friend comfortably established in
Maryland. Although Boucher was distinctly embarrassed by the
continuing scramble for "places and preferments," Addison had
no such inhibitions. "To his friendship I owe all my hopes of
advancement," Boucher confided to James on 28 November 1767
(*MHM* 7:353-55). Both men hoped for better results in 1768.

Bennett Allen, however, was still not satisfied with his income.

He had long envied Thomas Bacon, the rector of All Saints' Parish in Frederick County, who held the richest glebe in Maryland. Bacon was dying, and Allen was hopeful. Meanwhile, however, Maryland voters were intent upon petitioning the Assembly to pass an act dividing the parish as soon as Bacon died, something they had long wanted accomplished. Even Bacon thought the parish too large, and Boucher shared his opinion. But the greedy Allen did not wish to see his coveted parish salary cut in half. Governor Sharpe obliged him once more by anticpating Bacon's death and giving Allen the induction on 15 May 1768. The result was still another vacancy at Herring Bay. Once again, Boucher's expectations soared.

Bitter disappointment awaited him once more. It soon became clear that he could not even have what Allen no longer wanted. The parish now went to Walter Magowan, a Virginia cleric whom Boucher earlier had recommended for ordination.[12] Boucher noted sourly in a letter to James on 25 July 1769 that this "raw Scotsman, whom I alone got recommended and into orders," had been inducted at Herring Bay (*MHM* 8:39). Boucher's anguished inquiry to Sharpe elicted only the response that he had promised him Saint Anne's, and that parish was not vacant (*Rem.*, p. 57).

By 1768 Boucher was thoroughly disgusted with the whole project. "My Maryland projects have been ill-fated and unlucky from the beginning; and now they are almost totally ruined," he wrote James on 26 November. The newest problem was a change of administration. Governor Sharpe, on whom he had founded his hopes, was being superseded by Robert Eden, brother of Sir William Eden of Durham, by direction of "that creature-led Lord, the Proprietary" (*MHM* 8:34). It had become painfully clear to Boucher that proprietary prerogative left little discretion to any governor, and much less to one without a stong personality. It was obvious also that the church in Maryland was weakened shamefully in the eyes of the public by the prevailing system of political appointments to benefices without regard to competence or character. It appeared that the groundwork of several years, so carefully laid to secure an appointment for Boucher, might well come to nothing.

Meanwhile, in late spring 1768, Boucher had made the acquaintance of George Washington and his fourteen-year-old ward, John Parke Custis. Upon marrying the widow Martha Custis, Washington had assumed responsibility for her children Jacky and Patsy, looking after their education and estates. In May 1768 Washington wrote to Boucher, asking if he would be willing to take Master Custis as a pupil. "He is a boy of good genius . . . untainted in his morals and of innocent manners," Washington told Boucher. The future American commander assured Boucher that the youth had been reading Virgil for two years and had already "entered upon the Greek Testament." Washington proposed that Jacky have a body servant and two horses with him, for which he would "cheerfully pay ten or twelve pounds a year extraordinary to engage your peculiar care of and a watchful eye to him." He added that Master Custis was "a promising boy, the last of his family," who would one day possess "a very large fortune." For that reason he was anxious to make the boy "fit for more useful purposes than horse racer."[13]

Boucher, flattered at the preference extended to him, assured Washington of his interest, but felt obliged to explain that he had "for some time been endeavoring to establish an interest in Maryland," and hoped that this anticipated move would not deprive him of the "opportunity of obtaining some credit" by tutoring Jacky. There would be no use in Custis coming to Virginia in the face of an incipient move, unless Washington agreed to the boy's accompanying Boucher to Maryland, whenever that might be. Reassuringly, Boucher wrote Washington that the situation at Annapolis would be better than that at Saint Mary's, and also more convenient for Washington to receive letters every week "if necessary," since Annapolis was a post town. He promised that if Master Custis were entrusted to his care he would do his best to help the boy meet his family's expectations. Boucher suggested that Jacky be sent down to Saint Mary's for a trial period, after which Washington could decide about Annapolis. Although Washington had named a specific fee, Boucher chose to sidestep the financial question, suggesting that they might discuss the terms later.[14]

Washington agreed to the arrangement almost immediately. He rode with Jacky on 30 June 1768 to the Boucher plantation, dined there, and left the lad with Boucher. The Washingtons had wanted "peculiar care" for Jacky, but Boucher chose to construe this in his own way. He was unwilling to make any great exceptions for Custis, candidly telling Washington that he was not about to give the lad "particular attention" on "trifling circumstances of his diet or other accommodations"; any such arrangements, Boucher considered, would not be in the boy's interest. He was prepared, however, to give Custis "vigilant attention" on questions of "propriety and decorum," and proposed to restrain him from "many indulgences which I should willingly allow perhaps to another boy." Boucher also assured Washington that Jacky would be allowed "more frequently to sit in my company."[15] Washington soon was satisfied with the trial arrangement, and Jacky remained with Boucher.

It was necessary that Boucher give careful thought to his school in relationship to his contemplated move to Maryland. Should he continue his large boarding school, or drop it in favor of keeping just one or two students? The school had been decidedly successful and it was a source of pride to Boucher that he had attracted several sons of men prominent in Virginia and Maryland. As early as 1765, he had taken satisfaction in the knowledge that he had already educated three or four scholars who could give him "some tolerable credit" (*MHM* 7:299). One of these had already spent a successful year at William and Mary College. Billy Jackson, another student and son of a respected Fredericksburg factor, had been sent to James in England to continue his education. Boucher counted it a compliment to his own earlier efforts with the boy when James sent back good accounts of Jackson's progress.

The responsibilities of operating a boarding school were numerous; they presented burdens that were particularly onerous to a man with "no chick nor child" of his own, although he was fully aware that Jinny bore the brunt of the household management (*MHM* 7:301). Caring for the health and well-being of the boys in his charge presented challenges that might well have puzzled an older, more experienced man, even one with medical training. Boucher had to determine whether a pain in the stomach was "colic" or "worms," requiring his own dosing of the ailing boy with two or three concoctions, or whether it was serious enough to require a doctor. In general, he did not immediately resort to a physician (usually Dr. Hugh Mercer), believing firmly that to do so tended to make children timorous and cowardly. Boucher did not make exceptions, even when Jack Custis met with an accident. Although his charge expected the services of a doctor, Boucher reserved the right to make the decision, commenting later to Washington that the boy's own indiscretion had been responsible for the accident and "as I saw there was no danger, I thought it not amiss not to indulge him." The malarial climate insured perennial "fevers" every year, some "sickly seasons" being worse than others.[16] One trying summer both Jinny and Boucher's assistant were ill, and Boucher dismissed the boys early to lighten the burden and to enable him to leave and spare his own good health. Instead, parents and friends neglected to send for the students and the household got completely out of hand.

In addition to medical responsibilities, Boucher took seriously the task of teaching his students self-reliance, the manners of gentlemen, and morality. In the free and easy society of the wealthy planters, this was no simple task. In dealing with the indiscretions of his charges, Boucher had to weigh the delicate question of how much, or how little, to tell the parents of those in violation of the standards Boucher set.

Of all the burdens of the school, Boucher thought the financial ones the most irksome, in part because of his own distaste and considerable ineptitude for keeping accounts. The expenses of the school required large outlays of Boucher's own funds, for which he often had to wait too long for reimbursement. He was certain that over the years in Virginia he had lost money on the students' room and board.

As Boucher contemplated the future of his school, he gave considerable weight to his own dislike for teaching, particularly on a large scale. The truth was, he had been teaching by necessity and not by choice. "I have often found myself so ill-required," he confessed, and the position of schoolmaster considered so low, that he often felt that he had added little to his fortune and reputation after more than seven years of labor.[17] Unfortunately, too many of his colleagues were unworthy of scholarly respect. With some relief, Boucher decided to close the large school if and when he moved to Maryland. With the prospect of an improved income in a Maryland post, he could manage in spite of the loss of tuition income. However, his desire to accommodate Washington and the Calverts of Maryland officialdom prompted him to decide to keep Custis and Benedict Calvert with him in the hoped-for Maryland benefice. Later he was to agree to have Overton Carr as well.

Boucher had had Master Custis under his care for only a brief time when he was forced to the conclusion that Jacky was "far from being a brilliant genius." The boy was hardly a scholar at all, and disliked books. For the benefit of the Washingtons, however, Boucher softened his words, telling them that he could honestly say that he had "not seen a youth that I think promises fairer to be a good and useful man than John Custis." Jack's laziness had caught Boucher's attention early, but he thought it not an incurable problem when he discovered that Jacky would "bear driving," with respect to his studies.[18] Boucher persisted in his efforts with Jacky, in spite of the academic odds, and stoutly maintained later that there were few masters under whom Jacky would have learned more than under himself.

Boucher was as good as his word in attempting to make a gentleman out of Jacky. He had agreed to let Jacky "sit in" his company, and so he did, also providing the boy with additional opportunities for conversation with him by taking him along on various trips into the countryside. He was acutely aware that Jacky's role as a prominent planter's son required some amenities that he himself could not provide. When the opportunity arose, Boucher recommended that Washington permit Jacky to enroll in a Mr. Newman's "floating" dancing school, which had just begun to hold sessions in various private homes. Boucher also exercised his own brand of discipline to encourage a sense of responsibility and self-reliance in the lad. On one occasion, Jacky had lost his watch through his own carelessness. Boucher dutifully reported the incident to the Washingtons, noting that the young man deserved a reprimand and explaining that although the watch was now in Boucher's possession, he "did not care soon to put [Jacky] out of pain."[19]

Boucher was eventually to charge Washington more for his services to Custis than the colonel had expected to pay. If Washington was surprised at the charges, he may well have been doubly alarmed at Boucher's accompanying letter which advised that he would no longer take any boys for less than twenty-five pounds a year. He told Washington that he now had four boys with him on these new terms and expected more soon. "Unless, therefore, you object to it in time," he stated, "you must expect next year to find your son charged so too."[20]

Apparently their mild difference of opinion over the bill for educating Custis did not interfere with the developing friendship between the Washington and Boucher families. Mount Vernon was not an impossibly long journey from Annapolis, and it was often convenient for Washington to dine with the Bouchers and to stay overnight with them. The Washingtons in turn invited Boucher to Mount Vernon in the recess of the Whitsun holidays, April 1769, and again for the holiday festivities at the end of that year. Boucher forwarded letters and packages to and from the Washingtons, occasionally noting "another large cargo of physic" for the ailing Patsy Custis, who suffered from what we know today as epilepsy, or advising Washington of the dispatch of a whaleboat or two cases of excellent claret wine. The Washingtons, in turn, were helpful when they could be. When Jinny needed a music book she was assisted by Washington, who arranged to have his printer rule a notebook for her. Martha Washington sent remembrances from her garden to the Bouchers, for which Boucher thanked her with affection.

Boucher's friendship with the Washingtons provided one of the few pleasures which marked an otherwise frustrating year, as Maryland church politics continued to thwart his ambitions for a living in that colony. The new governor, Robert Eden, had been appointed in the summer of 1768, but he had not been expected to arrive in Maryland until the following winter. Addison and the Dulanys prepared to make another "push," as Boucher termed it. On balance, Boucher thought that Allen's abuse had "really rendered me popular," and would perhaps do him no harm with Eden (*MHM* 8:36). Addison and Dulany suggested that Boucher obtain a letter of recommendation addressed to Eden on his behalf, hoping thereby to prevent the governor from making a commitment to any rival candidate before his arrival in Maryland. Accordingly, Boucher appealed to James, asking that he write to Dr. L. Fothergill of Queen's College, Oxford, requesting a letter recommending Boucher to Eden (*MHM* 8:34). James obliged by applying to several acquaintances in Oxford. However, Boucher's copies of the letters arrived too late to be useful, and indeed, as it developed, would have made no difference anyway.

Boucher had not seen the Dulanys, who represented his interest with the governor for almost a year by July 1769, and he felt out of touch. To renew his contact with them, he and Henry Addison "stepped over" to visit with the Dulanys, Addison's relatives by marriage, hoping meanwhile that the new governor would arrive. After three weeks of waiting for Eden, Boucher and Addison gave up and departed. Eden arrived a day or two later, but Boucher heard nothing from him. It was clear to Boucher that the new governor was under no obligation to fulfill any commitment made by his predecessor. He now found the waiting intolerable, and only with some difficulty was Addison able to persuade Boucher to a course of patience. Boucher was disenchanted with "this dangling after great men," denouncing it as "a dirty trade," and confessing to James that he was "ashamed and sick of it (*MHM* 8:40). Boucher wanted to take his case to the public, which Addison counseled against. But presently Boucher informed James that he had written to Eden, complaining of the treatment which he had received and using the opportunity to forward some verses he had written on the subject. If Eden and the Dulanys thought them passable, they were to be printed (*MHM* 8:39).

The whole Maryland business was mortifying, and he could scarcely forbear wishing that he had never seen that colony, "having there met with little else but vexations and disappointments." He now had almost decided that it would be better not to move from Virginia at all, if it meant accepting "a mean place" in Maryland. "I am now 31 and fully satiated with strolling," he wrote James. Addison disagreed with him on this point, believing that Boucher ought to take whatever he could get in Maryland and hope for a better post later. But Boucher's self-confidence now was shaken; he wondered whether Addison and Dulany had not over-estimated his capabilities. It occurred to him that it might be "fairer and really honester" to lay out his money and purchase a living in England (*MHM* 8:40).

Another winter went by, and with the spring of 1770 the appointment at Saint Anne's at long last became a reality. On 10 May Governor Eden wrote the Honorable Walter Dulany, asking him to inform Boucher that the promise of a living was to be fulfilled without further delay. Soon after Eden wrote again to get Boucher's Christian name, in order to hasten the induction.[21] On 12 June 1770, after four years of waiting, Boucher was formally inducted at Saint Anne's Parish.

But the years of waiting had tempered Boucher's enthusiasm. Assuaging his own wounded ego, he informed James on 8 June 1770 that he had hesitated long about accepting the appointment at all. He even persuaded himself that material advantage had not affected his decision. Instead, he thought, it was a "meaner motive, resentful pride" that had determined his move. He had wanted to convince Allen that he was not so insignificant as the latter had supposed him to be. Boucher was now basking in his belated recognition and Governor Eden's attention. With evident self-satisfaction he assured James that his appointment was, at last, a matter solely of the governor's own "mere will and pleasure"— a questionable conclusion. Delightedly, he recounted how Governor Eden had sent a messenger to fetch him and had made out the induction papers before he arrived. Proudly he informed his friend that he had dined two or three times a week with Eden, who had bestowed on him "many marks of civility and politeness." All this was some considerable compensation for the earlier shabby treatment he had received (*MHM* 8:169).

In anticipation of his induction, Boucher had arrived in Annapolis about the first of June 1770, and had immediately sought living accommodations. For the time being he agreed to board with a local family, an arrangement which soon proved to be both expensive and unsatisfactory in many respects. But he was not yet in a position to settle down completely in Annapolis, since much unfinished business remained to be dealt with in Virginia. The major problem confronting him there was the disposition of his plantation. Although Boucher was in Annapolis in June 1770, he told James that he expected to return to Virginia within two weeks to harvest a good crop and to settle his affairs. He did not expect to complete the move to Annapolis before December of that year. With disarming candor, he told James that he had more than one motive for the delay, intending "by this means, to retain both parishes; though they are above 100 miles distant, and I have five navigable rivers to cross in traveling from one to the other" (*MHM* 8:169).

Within the next few months, Boucher sold his crops of corn and tobacco, his cattle and horses, and some of his furniture. Much of the latter would no longer be necessary when boarding only two boys. He gave his slaves the option of going with him to Maryland or choosing themselves masters in Virginia. All of the unmarried ones went with Boucher, while the rest were sold "by their own desire" to gentlemen who had been former pupils. After the sale of the plantation, Boucher cheerfully estimated his worth at £700 sterling, knowing that the uncertainty of the past years had blunted his plantation effort considerably and had probably reduced his profit (*Rem.*, p. 60). However, he could still reflect with some satisfaction that his economic status was much better than when he had arrived in Virginia completely penniless and in debt.

Resignation from his parish at Saint Mary's was the easiest part of Boucher's move. The vestry had had ample warning of Boucher's impending departure and the problem of his replacement had been resolved months ago. Boucher had earned the respect of the vestry and of his parishioners, and on his recommendation they elected Abner Waugh, a native of Orange County, Virginia, who had studied at William and Mary between 1765 and 1768. In fact the long wait for the Maryland parish had been advantageous for Saint Mary's, for Boucher had had ample time to train his successor. The vestry, grateful for his services, wrote him a complimentary farewell letter when he was ready to depart for his new post, which pleased Boucher immensely. In addition, Boucher recalled later, they generously "overpaid me half a year's salary" (*Rem.*, p. 59).

Closing the school was not a difficult problem, for the decision had been made long before, and for some time Boucher had been refusing to take on any new students. In accordance with his agreement with the Washingtons, Custis was to accompany Boucher to Annapolis, along with Overton Carr, his only other student until Benedict Calvert joined him. Carr, who was soon to marry into the Addison family, was a steady and competent scholar whom Boucher considered trustworthy and close to the family. Indeed, in a few years Boucher was to give Carr a general power of attorney and to entrust to his care all of his plantation affairs.

Boucher did not regret the years at Saint Mary's. He had had many hospitable and friendly neighbors, and he had been able to indulge in many plantation improvements. They had been busy and bustling years, not without profit to himself and he hoped to others. But he regretted that it had not been a literary life and for that reason he looked optimistically toward the future. In the late fall of 1770, Boucher preached his final sermon in Saint Mary's Parish, recrossed the five rivers to the north, and took up residence in Annapolis.

⌒ Chapter 5 ⌒

Annapolis: "The Genteelist Town in America"

The years 1770-71 in Annapolis marked the beginning of a new life for Boucher. The town, he later wrote, was "the genteelist town in North America," and in it he grew more expansive, gave expression to his literary abilities in a variety of ways, and enlarged his social horizons. In spite of his great desire for a country living, he was captivated by the city's charm. Annapolis, the county seat of Anne Arundel County and the capital of Maryland, was the residence of the governor and of all the great officers of state. Lloyd Dulany and Samuel Chase were building mansions in the city, while the Carrolls, Taskers, Bordleys, and Stewarts were already established there. The town afforded opportunities to meet "the most eminent lawyers, physicians, and families of opulence and note" (*Rem.*, p. 65). The circumstances were propitious for an aspiring young man.

Annapolis was "nearly encompassed by the river Severn," and commanded a view of the mouth of the river, of the majestic Chesapeake Bay, and of the eastern shore of Maryland. The town was settled in 1649 by Puritans fleeing from Virginia; first called Providence, it was later named Anne Arundel Town after the wife of the third Lord Baltimore. In 1694, it was renamed Annapolis in honor of Princess Anne of Denmark, and soon after replaced Baltimore's first capital, Saint Mary's, as the seat of the new royal government. The site of Annapolis suggested a great port city potential, but the harbor was more picturesque than useful. Shallow water prohibited the passage and anchorage of large ships, while ice sealed off the waterway for several months in winter. However, the city on the Severn enjoyed a certain commercial prosperity in 1770, which was to last until the superior harbor facilities of Baltimore resulted in its designation as an entrepôt in 1780. In 1770, the little city boasted a population approaching 1,400.[1]

English gentlemen in laying out the early town had patterned it on two circles; the larger one was reserved for the seat of government.[2] Here stood the building erected late in the seventeenth century to house the courts and other public offices. Never elegant, by 1769 the capital had fallen into such disrepair that a contemporary described it as "being both without and within, an emblem of public poverty."[3] Two years later, a stately new pillared and domed building would begin to rise to become the focal point of the government circle. West of the larger circle, a smaller one was set aside for Saint Anne's. Streets radiated from both circles, many of them with gracious Georgian town houses. Well-stocked gardens, often surrounded with high brick walls and terraced box hedges, contributed to a pleasing appearance. Westward lay the highroad, with shops and homes of tradespeople; to the east lay storehouses and long wharves sloping down to the harbor.

Late eighteenth-century Annapolis was noted for its cultivated society, and Annapolitans prided themselves on being residents of the "Bath of America," the home "of fashion, of wit, and of the art of living."[4] The cultural opportunities far outweighed anything that Saint Mary's Parish had offered. "I hardly know a town in England so desirable to live in as Annapolis," Boucher declared (*Rem.*, p. 65). In part the city's charm lay in its style of living, which was similar to that of the squirearchy of upper and middle class England. The aristocratic ideal was deeply imbedded in Maryland life; its origins lay in the early manors which the first Lord Baltimore had established on a feudal basis.[5] As great wealth in land developed out of tobacco production based on slavery and the plantation system, the genteel way of life had continued to thrive. There were numerous great estates, varying from twenty

87

thousand to forty thousand acres, among them Rousby Hall, Colonel Fitzhugh's handsome country home, and former governor Horatio Sharpe's villa, Whitehall.[6]

Maryland aristocrats had great respect for knowledge of the law, interest in it being wider than the circle of those who were formally trained in the profession. Some degree of legal knowledge was taken for granted among the wealthy. The large landholders dominated the provincial offices, and most justices of the peace were laymen; in this respect Maryland was typically English. Boucher was like the Marylanders in his interest in law, and he was not at all diffident about his knowledge of it. After his arrival in Maryland, he once found it necessary to write to James concerning some family business in which a power of attorney for James was involved. James had questioned the validity of a power of attorney which Boucher had had drawn up in America, and Boucher countered with the comment that his friend's "sneers at my civatlanticque law may have wit, but they want solidity; and I will not yet yield to you in jurisprudence." He informed James that a power of attorney from America, even on unstamped paper, would be "deemed legal in any court in England." To back up his statement, he told James that he might read so in "old Coke, *Qui facit quod potest, facit quod debet*" (*MHM* 8:170). Along with interest in the law, Marylanders concerned themselves with classical and secular knowledge. The spirit of reason and liberty was pervasive in Maryland, as it was quite generally in the colonies and in England in this period. The pages of the *Gazette* and the *Maryland Almanack*, which imitated Addison and Steele, reflected this spirit.

In addition to its cultural assets, Annapolis was a magnet for social life and for the horse-racing set. The racing season began when the hot weather abated in late September or early October, and attracted patrons of great distinction from long distances. George Washington regularly made the journey from Mount Vernon to watch the thoroughbreds perform and to bet on his favorites. The big races, held at the mile straightaway just outside the city gates, involved sizable purses. The rush of visitors each fall stretched the public accommodations of the little city to the limit. Mean and inadequate as the crowded inns were, the beds were taken up almost entirely by regular customers, so that guest rooms in private homes were much in demand. With this situation in mind, Boucher invited Washington to stay with him during the fall festivities. Not surprisingly, Washington gratefully accepted the offer of privacy and clean linen, amenities not to be expected in the inns of that day.

Hospitality in Annapolis and in the country houses nearby was lavish and social life was sparkling. Daylight hours were devoted to the races; after dark the activities gave way to theater parties, dining, and dances. The Maryland elite customarily attended a round of dinners; Washington, for example, in the fall of 1771 dined at the homes of Daniel and Lloyd Dulany, Governor Eden, Samuel Galloway, and Boucher himself. Dinners of this sort were elaborate affairs. The tables were laden with fish, oysters, and terrapin, and with the wild game which abounded in the Maryland countryside, while a host prided himself on the great variety of choice Madeiras, champagnes, sherries, and ports with which he plied his guests. The numerous courses were broken at intervals by toasts which the guests were obliged to drink. At the close of festivities gentlemen were on occasion quietly carted off to their homes by their servants. It was no disgrace to succumb to a twenty-one glass "salute," which was no mean test of capacity.

At the height of the social season it was fashionable to attend the theater after dinner, often three times in the week, as Washington did in the season of 1771. That year marked the opening of a new and elegant theater whose stage was outlined in soft light and whose sets had been designed and painted by the popular local artist Charles Willson Peale. The galleries and boxes were regularly filled with the local "tobacco princes" and distinguished visitors. Beautifully gowned women and their escorts often arrived by coach-and-four, or coach-and-six, sometimes with outriders. Liveried servants were not unusual. At the peak of the season the theater performance customarily was followed by a grand ball held in the assembly room. The balls were brilliant affairs, and probably no London event of the day turned out more lovely women brocaded and velveted in the latest fashion.[7] Colonel Washington attended three such assemblies in a single week in the fall of 1771.

However, all was not pleasure and elegance in Princess Anne's town. Annapolitans and their visitors alike were consumers of their own major product, tobacco, and they spattered their streets, pews, fences, and doorsteps liberally with the juice of the sotweed.

89

There were no sidewalks; rows of posts separated the pedestrians from the passing vehicles, while slops and kitchen water flowed in the streets. Another liability of colonial life which town living accentuated was the generally poor state of health of the people. Smallpox, which the aristocrats suffered along with everybody else, was a scourge, although inoculation, still in a primitive state with the use of live virus, was beginning to win acceptance. Washington himself bore the scars of the disease, and Boucher had lately been shocked at the hideous ravages it had inflicted on a promising young son of James Maury. Sore throat and appendicitis, the latter generally undiagnosed, were also prevalent. The mortality rate was high. Abysmal dental health was another commonplace affliction. As elsewhere in America, decayed teeth and barren gums were to be seen everywhere.

In spite of the negative aspects of city living, its advantages far outweighed its liabilities, and Boucher resolved to make the most of the months in Annapolis while he waited for the next appointment to a coveted rural parish with plantation opportunities. The governor had made him welcome and Walter Dulany was his benefactor. With this backing and his cleric's position, he was virtually assured entry into polite society, and the connection with Washington could hardly fail to bolster his social acceptance. Unfortunately, Boucher's behavior in the first months after his arrival in Annapolis jeopardized his initial acceptance in the community. Two incidents, both of them related to Boucher's clerical role, precipitated trouble. One was relatively minor, and the other had implications of major significance.

The less important incident arose out of Boucher's service as chaplain to the House of Delegates, an official duty incident to his position as the rector of Saint Anne's. The salary for this service was about ten pounds a session, which was less than that paid the doorkeeper or the macebearer. It seemed clear to Boucher that the House operated on the assumption that pastors and schoolteachers should be properly humble, an idea to which he did not subscribe. With typical directness, Boucher wrote a letter to the Assembly, "in as handsome terms as I could, that I would, if they so pleased, serve them for nothing, but that if I was paid at all I would be paid as a gentleman."[8] The letter caused a good deal of talk, gaining him "some friends and more enemies" (*Rem.*, p. 66).

The second action, which seriously antagonized Eden and the Dulanys, was Boucher's too enthusiastic espousal of the cause of an American resident bishop. Again Boucher's action arose out of his conception of his role as a cleric. As a leading minister, Boucher perceived himself as a guardian of the general welfare of the Church of England, with an obligation to promote its interests in America. He wrote James on 25 August 1770 that he heartily prayed to God "to defend this our Established Church, which, with all her imperfections I will still maintain it, is the glory of the Reformation" (*MHM* 8:174). Acting from these convictions, Boucher met with a group of Maryland clergymen who assembled in Annapolis to form a Society for the Relief of Widows and Orphans of the Episcopal Clergy, an organization similar to that with which Boucher had been associated as a trustee in Virginia. Under normal circumstances a meeting of the clergy of the Anglican church was forbidden, but it had been determined earlier that Lord Baltimore would approve the foundation of such a society, and a charter for that purpose was expected daily. It was slow in arriving and the group remained together for a time awaiting it. Boucher seized the opportunity to propose that the assembled clerics discuss the controversial subject of an American episcopate, with a view toward drafting a petition to that end. It was a step which would cause him no little immediate embarrassment, while it had unfortunate long-term consequences for him as well.

The issue of a resident bishop for America was long explosive throughout the colonies. The Church of England was the established religion, yet there was no resident Anglican bishop anywhere in America. Instead, the bishop of London had jurisdiction over all Church of England activities.[9] The bishop's authority in America was more theoretical than real, however, because of the vast distance and poor communication between England and her colonies. The lack of a resident bishop posed several problems, two major ones being the difficulty of supplying American pulpits and the lack of discipline over personnel. Boucher saw a pressing need for a resident bishop to provide the means for the ordination in America of a colonial clergy. The hazardous ordination journey to London tended to keep native clergymen in short supply, while at the same time academically well-qualified men in England seldom volunteered for colonial posts. Thus qualified Anglican clerics of good character were scarce. Furthermore, many clerics and laymen agreed that some better means of disciplinary control over Anglican ministers was necessary. Even the most profligate behavior often went unnoticed in England.

In spite of the evident advantages of a resident bishop, low church people and non-Anglicans generally were violently opposed. Although the English establishment had always considered that a bishop in America would be a "primitive bishop" with only those powers necessary to preserve the church through ordination of ministers and supervison of personnel, it appears that few in England's provinces believed the statements. The majority of people in Maryland rejected the concept even of a primitive bishop, fearing a hierarchy that would require financial support, that might interfere with local civil government, and that could be used as an instrument of political control by England. Indeed, they seemed to picture another Archbishop Laud. Public opinion in Maryland was no different from that elsewhere, and Lord Baltimore's position had been made clear—a resident bishop would run counter to Maryland's first charter. The governor had been so instructed. In this respect at least Marylanders were in accord with the proprietor's position, if for different reasons.

Boucher was well aware of the negative feelings of the colonists toward such an episcopate. While still in Virginia he had explained the situation to James on the occasion of Myles Cooper's visit to the southern colonies in 1767. Cooper, president of King's College in New York, had made the journey with two other northern Anglican ministers in order to estimate the support that might be mustered for the cause of a resident bishop. He had found many Anglican ministers both in Virginia and Maryland opposed to the idea, and he failed to convert them. Boucher's use of the Widows and Orphans Relief Society meeting to advance the cause of a resident bishop made him twice vulnerable in the eyes of Eden and Dulany, and if his role were to become generally known he would be in great danger of acquiring a sudden unpopularity. None of these considerations deterred Boucher, who believed the matter too important to drop (*Rem.*, p. 65).[10]

Boucher and seven other clerics assembled in early summer 1770, and resolved unanimously to address petitions for a bishop to the king, the archbishop of Canterbury, the bishop of London, and Lord Baltimore. Governor Eden was also presented with a similar petition, and in reply he in effect rejected it; he denied that the petition represented the will of the whole clergy of Maryland. A petition on a matter of such great importance, he informed Boucher and his colleagues, must come from a more representative body of clergymen if it were to be given serious consideration. The eight clerics thereupon sent a circular letter to the other clergy of the province, requesting permission to add their names to the petitions. The Connecticut Congregational clergy, ever watchful for such attempts, learned about the letter and complained that the additional signatures had been solicited without proper explanations of the document involved.[11]

The repercussions from the petitions were swift and severe. The Dulanys and Eden were greatly offended, and Boucher recalled later that "for some months neither the Governor, nor any of the Dulanys, even so much as spoke to me." But Boucher, firm in his belief that his duty to the Anglican church was his primary moral charge and that his role had been a correct one, refused to apologize. He remained convinced that he had done "no more than my duty," and that conscience would allow him to "make no concessions" (*Rem.*, p. 65).[12] So sure was he of his rectitude that when one Mr. Wormley of Virginia, a friend of Washington, volunteered his services as an intermediary between Boucher and his estranged Maryland benefactors, he rejected the overture. I "had more reason to be offended" than Eden or Dulany, he insisted later, explaining that "in matters of duty whatever deference I owed to their opinions, or however much I was bound to them in gratitude for past favors, or by interest in the prospect of future ones, I could allow no man to dictate to me" (*Rem.*, p. 66).

Nothing constructive came of Boucher's efforts with respect to the petition, other than that King's College in New York conferred a master's degree upon him in 1774. Boucher continued to work for an American episcopate, although he knew that "unhappily for us" the issue was "exceedingly unpopular" and was made more so by "a banditti of furious Dissenters in yonder mischief-making Northern governments." He urged James to talk and correspond with anyone in England who would "stand forth in our cause—or, at least counsel us how to conduct it." He counted "Oxford and its Bishop" among the cause's "staunchest friends," but mistrusted her sister university "Cambridge, and our present Diocesan, the Bishop of London," both being "suspected of being less warm in it than we think it becomes them." Could a resident bishop be established, however, "it were a glorious achievement" (*MHM* 8:177-78). He may well have envisioned himself as the first resident bishop in the South.[13] But in Maryland, Boucher reaped only a harvest of ill will. He was now a visible target for the opponents of the church on the episcopacy question and upon other church-related issues.

Public hostility toward the Anglican church deepened when it became known that the "Address to the Bishop of London" contained some unflattering remarks concerning the House of Delegates. The clerics of course had not anticipated that the contents of their petitions would be disclosed in Maryland. In some unhappy fashion, however, the remarks leaked back and fell into the hands of a group of members who constituted the core of the nascent Country party, very soon to become the nucleus of the Whig or Patriot party in the colony. For the time being, Boucher was spared the knowledge of how serious his involvement in church politics might become. Yet the whole incident was significant in moving him from his relatively liberal position in public affairs in Virginia to a more conservative one in Maryland. He hardly perceived his stance on the resident bishop issue as a plunge into Maryland politics; in fact, however, it was very nearly that.

That first summer and fall in Annapolis provided Boucher with more leisure than he had ever before known, and he savored it. Although the first few months involved many trips back to Virginia to see to his harvest there and to settle plantation affairs, still the duties at Saint Anne's with its city parish were less time-consuming than those of his far-flung parish at Saint Mary's. And during the months when he boarded, he had not even the numerous and petty demands upon his time encountered by a householder. Now at last he was free to enjoy the cultural opportunities of Annapolis, and to indulge his old desire to be a literary man.

The theater attracted him immediately. The opportunity to be a playgoer, and in excellent company, was a new experience for Boucher and he made the most of it. Soon he ventured into writing for the theater, producing a prologue for a play. He was an enthusiastic admirer of various leading ladies who came to town. On at least one occasion he was moved to write some verses to the talented Nancy Hallam, whose performances captivated him during two of her appearances with the American Company in Annapolis. Boucher was more than a little pleased when the

Maryland Gazette printed his verses (*Rem.*, p. 66).[14] Annapolitans apparently took more pride in their theater than in their Anglican church. The handsome theater dwarfed neighboring old and ordinary Saint Anne's, whose shabby appearance had little to recommend it.[15] The contrast moved Boucher to contribute some light-hearted verses to the 5 September 1771 *Maryland Gazette:*

To the Very Worthy and
Respectable Inhabitants of Annapolis,
the Humble Petition
of the Church Showeth:

That late in century the last,
By private bounty, here were placed
My sacred walls, and tho' in truth
Their style and manner be uncouth.
Yet whilst no structure met mine eye
That even with myself could vie,
A goodly edifice, I seemed,
And pride of all St. Anne's was deemed.
How changed the times! for now all round
Unnumbered stately piles abound,
All better built and looking down
On one quite antiquated grown:
Left unrepaired, to time a prey,
I feel my vitals fast decay;
And often have I heard it said
That some good people are afraid
Lest I should tumble, on their head,
Of which, indeed, this seems a proof,
They seldom come beneath my roof.

.   .   .   .   .

Here in Annapolis, alone,
God has the meanest house in town.
The premises considered, I,
With humble confidence, rely,
That Phoenix like, I soon shall rise,
From my own ashes, to the skies;
Your mite, at least, that you will pay,
And your petitioner shall pray.

95

Although Boucher's literary aspiration led him down diverse avenues, his most serious scholarly pursuit was the study of language. He had been intrigued with the origin and development of words and with the structure of language since his friendship with Addison. At first his attention was focused on the languages of the ancient Greeks, Europeans, Picts, and English. However, the language of the Americans soon engrossed him. The Americans, in his opinion, spoke with the purest pronunciation of English tone that one could find anywhere. He was impressed with its "perfect uniformity," and he noted that there were no dialects in America comparable to those of England. Boucher did observe that there were substantial differences between the speech of northerners and southerners; the tempo and accent of soft southern speech was markedly unlike the harsh nasal twangs heard in the North. Local differences in vocabulary and idiom also attracted Boucher's attention, particularly after he moved to Annapolis. He soon concluded that the common expressions of Potomac upperclass planters were as close to dialect as one would find in America, and he began to keep careful notes of words peculiar to his new neighbors. Later he was to incorporate them into a poem he titled "Absence, a Pastoral." Boucher thus became the first commentator of any importance on the English language in the colonies.[16] The following lines from "Absence" illustrate the variety of dialectical words and expressions he collected.

> In *twist-bud, thick joint, bull-face, leather-coat,*
> I'd toil all day; or *fall,* and *mall,* and *tote*
> Brown linen shorts, and cotton jackets wear,
> Or only *wring-jaw* drink, and *'simmon* beer;
> My *pone,* or *hoe-cake,* without salt, would eat,
> And taste but once a week a bit of meat;
> Could my *old woman,* whilst I labored thus
> At night reward me with a *smouch,* or buss.
>
> . . . . .
>
> Strolling, last *fall,* by yon *pacosen* side,
> Coil'd in a heap, a rattle-snake I spied:
> Was it for me a *rompus* then to make?
> I'm *mad* to see some people dread a snake:

96

Instant I caught a *chunk,* and, at a blow
To pieces *smash'd* my notice-giving foe,
For this, if merit's aught, to go no higher
I look to be a col'nel, or a 'squire
But what are titles to a swain forlorn?
My Mollsey's gone, and I all honors scorn.

Many years later H. L. Mencken gave Boucher credit for producing the first glossary of American usage of the English language.[17] Boucher's interest in the American idiom was to lead to his own major work in etymology and philology.

Boucher's facile pen soon won him attention in the Annapolis newspaper, and by the winter of 1770-71 his growing literary reputation had aided him in bridging the gap between Eden and himself. He now was in sufficient favor with the elite of the town to become one of the first members of the Homony Club, a new social and literary venture of the local gentry. Several such clubs, essentially literary and social in purpose and expressly disavowing any political allegiance, were already in existence in Annapolis. Established between the opening of the eighteenth century and the Revolution, the most sophisticated elements in the social life of the upper class of Maryland flourished within them.[18] The Homony Club was intended "to promote innocent mirth and ingenious humor." An important regulation forbade the discussion of local politics. Its members amused themselves with satire, puns, conundrums, speech making, and particularly with mock trials which elaborately caricatured the procedures of the law. Drinking presumably was incidental, but the real situation may well have been somewhat like that in the more famous Tuesday Club, pen-and-ink sketches of which show a group of members seated around a table smoking and drinking, while one member has slipped beneath the board.

Established 22 December 1770, the Homony Club soon attained such fame "that the Governor and all the principal people of the country ambitiously solicited the honor of being members or honorary visitants." For the three years of the club's existence, its officers kept records replete with clever references to Greek and Roman history and mythology, and the club "archives soon swelled to two or three folios" (*Rem.,* p. 67).[19] According to its surviving records, the club had several officers who were elected monthly: president, secretary, advocate general, master of ceremonies, poet laureate, and a secretary for foreign affairs. Its stated purpose was to "promote the ends of society—and furnish a rational amusement for the length of one winter's evening a week."[20] The club convened annually at a coffeehouse on the first Saturday in November, and thereafter met every Saturday sometime between five and six in the evening for several hours of drinking and camaraderie. Whist and backgammon were allowed before supper, to be played for any sum not exceeding half a crown. The first toast was to the prosperity of the Homony Club, the last to wives and sweethearts. Bills and a last bottle were called for at half after ten, at the option of the president. The club year closed in March.

Membership was limited to seventeen, a sponsor was required, and three negative votes could exclude a prospective member. Any married man resident in Annapolis was potentially eligible for membership; candidates were required to be forty or older if not married. In addition, the club might designate eight nonresident honorary members. However, each member was entitled to bring a guest on any evening.

Boucher, who was only thirty-two in 1770 and unmarried, required a waiver of the age rule. The record of the club's exception in his favor is amusing for its lighthearted remarks on the relationship between church and state. Admittance in his case was on the presumption that "the sanctity of his character would supply a fund of discretion not otherwise to be expected from his tender years," and on a second assumption "adopted by all wise States, that no government can be complete without an alliance with the Church." One member insisted that a caveat be entered, that "we should be upon our guard against the exorbitant influence of Church Power which, without a watchful eye, may too much encroach upon the liberties of this Club." William Stewart, commissioner of the Land Office, wished to enter on the record that he would raise his hand against the introduction "of any more priestly power into this club, unless it comes from the pure Kirk of Scotland, and then we should be safe enough, for we never heard that Kirk and Church ever entered plots or combinations against the States, no no, they love one another too well for that."[21]

The first president was John Lookup; the first secretary was William Deards. Boucher was admitted to membership on 29 December 1770, along with William Stewart and Reuben Meriweather. Soon three additional members were accepted: William Eddis, Thomas Johnson (later governor of Maryland), and William Paca. Lloyd Dulany, lord mayor of Annapolis, and Thomas Jenings, alderman, applied for membership in the club, which they said was becoming more famous than the *convivium* of the Romans. Boucher penned some verses in answer to the petition of these last two, granting both the right to visit, but for no more than one meeting.[22] Sharpe, the former governor, presently was admitted to honorary membership, as was the present governor, Eden. However, when Samuel Chase applied he was blackballed. No explanation was recorded. Thus William Paca became a member of the select group, while Samuel Chase was excluded. The two men were soon to become strong political allies and bitter enemies of Boucher.

On 19 January 1771, Boucher was elected president for the month, being chosen over Dennis Dulany.[23] He also presided at the club's first mock trial, that of William Stewart, for a "toast of evil tendency and ambiguous in meaning," making "a very capital figure" as he did so. On another occasion, Boucher was referred to as a member "whose judgment has generally great weight with the Society."[24] It was also he who prepared an amusing "Remonstrance" intended to settle a disagreement over the origins of the club's name.[25] The debate began at an early meeting when William Stewart and Dennis Dulany suggested that the name signified a group of men of like age. Boucher objected to that explanation. "Homony," he insisted, was derived from the Greek word *omonoia*, and more correctly described "a club of men of like minds."[26]

Boucher served as poet laureate throughout most of January 1772, and during that time composed a song for the club.[27] But it was Thomas Jenings who wrote some verses describing the Homony Club members. Even after one makes allowances for exaggeration, Jenings's doggerel indicates that Boucher had ingratiated himself with his fellows:

How oft do I admire with fond delight
Great Boucher's works, and wish like him to write,
Alas! Vain Hope that might as well aspire
To copy Virgil's song, or Homer's fire.

Who can like him with ease and sweetness join,
The mild companion, and the grave divine.
Sure of all vices which mankind have cursed
That of hypocrisy is still the worst
Then learn ye sons of superstitious gloom
To act like Boucher in the festal room.[28]

On one occasion the Homony Club invited Charles Willson Peale, the distinguished Maryland portraitist, to make sketches of the members.[29] Whether Peale obliged or not is uncertain, but soon Boucher knew Peale well enough to ask for his opinion on some drawings made by the young son of John James in England. Apparently Boucher was no stranger in the Peale home, for he observed Mrs. Peale nursing her child, and was so touched by the tenderness and warmth of the scene that he suggested to the artist that he capture its appeal on canvas. By April 1770 Peale had completed a picture which he entitled *Mrs. Peale and Child: an attempt of a Tender Sentiment*, showing his wife Rachel with her sleeping infant, just lifted naked from its bath. A similar Peale work completed a year later moved an anonymous author, possibly Boucher, to write some tender verses entitled "On a Picture of Mrs. Peale."[30]

These early years in Maryland were busy and productive ones for Boucher. He now had a wider scope for his far-ranging interests than he had had in Virginia, and he was on the inside at long last. Through his acquaintance with men of importance, he soon acquired a considerable knowledge of colonial affairs. He no longer thought of himself as a foreigner, as he had occasionally described himself in Virginia.

Like most Americans, Boucher had an avid interest in western lands. In the summer of 1770, Dr. David Ross showed him a letter he had received from George Croghan, the Indian trader and land speculator who was at Fort Pitt, informing him of the probability that London would soon organize a new government for the upper Ohio valley. Croghan predicted that either Col. George Mercer, son of the secretary of the Ohio Company, or Samuel Wharton, prime land speculator of the Indiana Company, would be appointed governor. Boucher passed along this bit of gossip to Washington, asking him if he had yet heard the news, and if so, whether he had any further particulars. Boucher thought such a development in the west would result in "an immense acquisition, if not immediately to the wealth, certainly to the strength of these governments—and a fine field for a projecting spirit to adventure in."[31]

It thus appears that Boucher was privy at an early date to the initial venture of what might have become the greatest speculative coup of the eighteenth century. Samuel Wharton had maneuvered for the Indiana Company to absorb rival land companies in America, and then turned his attention to marshaling political support in England to acquire the entire Fort Stanwix cession of land. Soon the venture was expanded once more, taking advantage of a suggestion by Colonial Secretary Hillsborough that Wharton's group try to acquire an even larger tract of twenty million acres, a request he himself deemed so outrageous that he expected it to be rejected by England out of hand. In December 1769, the Grand Ohio Company, meeting in London, petitioned the crown for twenty million acres to establish a proprietary colony, Vandalia, in the area extending from the forks of the Ohio south to the Greenbrier River and west to the mouth of the Scioto. Although the Walpole Company, as the venture became known in England, for a time seemed certain of success (to the astonishment of Hillsborough), a combination of political circumstances in the end prevented the issuance of the necessary charter.[32]

Boucher's keen interest in western lands kept him alert for new maps of the "back parts of America," and he shared information about subscriptions for good ones with Colonel Washington.[33] This same concern for the development of the back country led him to share Washington's interest in improving the navigation of the Potomac in order to provide easier access to western markets. Transportation by freight wagon to the shipping point at Baltimore was expensive; farm produce and iron products were heavy cargo. Thus it was natural enough that the earliest interest in a canal would develop in the west. Early in the 1760s interested parties at Fredericksburg, the site of a foundry and a thriving center for the grain trade, were beginning to talk of a company to improve navigation of the Potomac.[34] Opening of the west via the Potomac had a certain appeal for land speculators, as well as for producers of grain and iron products, since their land hold-

101

ings would become more valuable with increased accessibility and consequent heightened demand.

Washington was one of those who fully appreciated the great potential for the Tidewater area if the resources of the Great Lakes region could be channeled by rivers and canals to the Chesapeake and on into the Atlantic trade. A Tidewater route, he recognized, would be about 168 miles shorter overall than a Saint Lawrence River valley route to the seaboard. He also knew that other areas threatened to be competitors for the vast commerce from the interior. Robert Morris of Philadelphia had published a scheme in 1764 for utilizing the Schuylkill and Susquehanna rivers to reach the upper Allegheny. Once such a route was established, Washington knew, it would be difficult to divert trade to his own region.

By 1770 Washington was convinced that the time was right for serious consideration of a Potomac project. However, he recognized that the odds were against public financing of the venture by Viriginians alone. Interests in Virginia were divided, opinions were too often parochial, and capital was scarce. At a comparatively small expense, Maryland and Virginia could act together in making the Potomac the channel of commerce between Great Britain and the immense western territory. In order to succeed, the plan had to be presented on a broad and practical basis as a trade route beyond the fall line of the Potomac to Fort Cumberland, and westward from that point to the waters of the Ohio. At the same time, Washington was afraid that through ill-timed parsimony trade would be diverted from the Tidewater and conducted through other channels, such as the Susquehanna and the Great Lakes-Saint Lawrence route.

Washington and Boucher talked of the practical difficulties of navigation on the Potomac, the former confessing his meager knowledge about locks, canal engineering, and the like. Boucher appeared to be somewhat better informed on the subject, principally because of his reading about such operations in England.[35] However, their conversations dealt primarily with the problem of financing the project, and 2 April 1770 Boucher wrote to Washington outlining a solution, apparently in continuation of an earlier conversation. He urged that an act of Assembly be passed setting up a commission empowered to borrow the necessary capital at an interest rate, possibly 10 percent, high enough to attract investors. The debt would be retired from funds "raised from a tax proportioned thereto, on all the vessels making use of said navigation." Furthermore, if the navigation would eventually bear the cost, then the tax could "be rated so as to produce a considerable surplus, enough not only to sink the original loan, but to raise a fund for still farther improvements."[36]

Again, Boucher was drawing on his knowledge of the financing of similar public improvements in England. He asked Washington: "Are not some of the canals in England and the turnpikes on this system?" He thought that the "very grand canal" currently under construction in Scotland was being financed in this fashion also. It seemed like a reasonable plan, but he agreed with Washington's opinion that the Virginia Assembly "would not easily be persuaded to advance any cash towards the scheme." It was a pity, he thought. Although he commented that he himself could have no immediate interest in it (he had no crops to transport nor had he much capital to invest), he would "be grieved so beneficial a project should be dropped."[37]

Washington incorporated the substance of Boucher's ideas in a letter he wrote to Thomas Johnson in July 1770. The colonel feared that few persons would be likely to contribute anything to the project unless they could immediately benefit by it, thus dampening the prospect for private subscriptions. Washington recommended as an alternative that the subscriptions be vested by the Maryland and Virginia legislatures, "with a kind of property in the navigation under certain restrictions and limitations and to be reimbursed their first advances with a high interest thereon."[38] Funds to repay the two colonies would be raised by reasonable tolls levied on ships using the canal. Rates would be based on a scale "proportionate to their respective burthens." Following Boucher's suggestion, Washington pointed out the practical advantage of attracting "the monied gentry" who would be "tempted by lucrative views" of the high interest rates, even if they had no other personal or economic purpose which a canal might serve.

The effort to enlist public support for the venture failed. Although Washington had written to Eden asking him to lend his influence in obtaining the necessary enabling legislation in Maryland, no amount of pressure from any direction altered the Maryland House of Delegates' refusal to act. Since the Virginia House of Burgesses also denied support for the proposal, the plan publicly to finance a canal died. Boucher and Washington, however, did not lose faith in the idea of a Potomac canal to the Ohio Valley interior. Instead they shifted their attention to the prospects for private backing. Both were aware of the efforts of Thomas Johnson and Lancelot Jacques, who were in Annapolis selling subscriptions of stock in a canal company. Interest in the plan was keen, and the pair had reported subscriptions totaling £400. Bolstered by the enthusiasm of Annapolitans, Johnson and Jacques left for Frederick Town to enlist further support for the project.

Nevertheless, another quarter-century and the Revolutionary War were to intervene before ships would bypass the Potomac Falls in 1802 on their way up the Potomac under the auspices of the Potomac Canal Company. Interestingly enough, it did not occur in 1770 to Boucher nor to the other colonials involved that a venture of this magnitude required any consultation with authorities in England. The sense of autonomy, which Boucher so much enjoyed as a cleric, already had become pervasive in America.

In addition to his growing involvement in intercolonial enterprise, Boucher was making rapid progress in Maryland political affairs. The early breach with Governor Eden had been bridged rather quickly, aided on Eden's part by his respect for Boucher's sincerity and conviction and by Boucher's growing reputation as a writer of some wit. Boucher's repaired friendship with the Walter Dulanys and Addisons, his connection with the Washington family, and his membership in the Homony Club made it relatively easy for a warm friendship between Eden and Boucher to develop. Boucher was drawn to Eden in part for the same reason that other Marylanders had quickly accepted the new governor. Eden (1741-84), the second son of Robert, third baronet of West Auckland, and brother of William, had the open graciousness of the best type of English aristocrat.[39] He represented a class of Englishmen with which Boucher had had little or no social contact in the past. Such an association held considerable promise, enhanced by Eden's ability to reel off lines from Horace from memory, which delighted Boucher and led him to consider Eden "a bit of a scholar." Although Eden's tenure in office was concurrent with a particularly stormy time in Maryland history, biographers in general credit him with ruling with tact and wisdom until he was forced to leave in 1776.

As the second son in a titled family, young Robert Eden had

embarked on an army career in 1757, saw active service in the Coldstream Guards in Germany in 1760, and retired from the army with the rank of captain in 1768 in order to accept the post of governor of Maryland. Eden's marriage in 1765 to Caroline Calvert, sister of the sixth Lord Baltimore, the profligate proprietor of Maryland, had prepared the way for this appointment. Eden and his wife believed that inheritance of the province on the death of the present Lord Baltimore was implicit in the appointment; the lure induced them to brave the rigors of Maryland.

When Eden arrived in Maryland he had been separated only recently from army life, and still seemed to Boucher to be a "hearty, rattling, wild young dog of an officer." Describing his new friend to James on 25 August 1770, Boucher paid Eden a distinctly left-handed compliment. "As was said of poor Charles," Boucher wrote, "were he anything but a Governor, he would be a very clever fellow." Boucher anticipated that Eden would suffer some handicaps in office with "a set of the arrantest rascals around him for his court I have ever met with," adding that he hoped that "these were palmed upon him by the Idiot Lord, his brother-in-law, and not of his own choosing" (*MHM* 8:173). As the two men became firm friends, however, Boucher somewhat revised his estimate of Eden. He was soon describing him as handsome, lively, and sensible; in short, he was a good companion. At the same time, he was fully aware of Eden's alcoholic dissipation and propensity for gambling, which would one day be fatal to his fortunes. In spite of his income of three or four thousand pounds, he was chronically in debt and on at least one occasion he asked for Boucher's signature as security on a loan of £1,200 from Henry Harford, the acknowledged illegitimate son of the sixth and last Lord Baltimore. Much to Boucher's chagrin and financial loss, Eden never repaid it.[40]

In spite of Eden's shortcomings, the bond between the two men grew steadily stronger. Years later Boucher wrote of his friend as a man of warmth and affection whom it was impossible not to love. "With no other man," he reflected, "did I ever live half so long in such habits of the most unreserved friendship and confidence." The two "were constantly together," and when they could not be, they "constantly wrote to each other" (*Rem.*, pp. 67-68). Boucher thought few men equalled Eden in his talent for letter writing. Even after Boucher moved from Annapolis to a country

105

living, the two managed to dine together often, and Eden's coach was frequently at Boucher's door. In the five years between 1770 and 1775, the foundation was laid for an intimate family relationship that was to extend beyond Eden's death and into the next generation, for Boucher and Eden's eldest son, Frederick Morton Eden, were to become lifelong friends.[41]

For Boucher, the friendship with Eden meant more than simply the personal pleasure of congenial company. Boucher had always been determined to improve his status in the world and he believed that social connections could aid him in his objective (*Rem.,* p. 31). His approach had been successful in Virginia, and now in Maryland he had succeeded in attracting the attention of a man of the first "condition." Eden's goodwill and conviviality enhanced Boucher's social prestige in Tidewater society, gave him propinquity to the source of ecclesiastical patronage, and furnished him with the opportunity to be an insider, albeit an unofficial one, in Maryland politics. Eden soon came to trust Boucher completely and made him a kind of "confidential secretary."[42] He recalled later aiding Eden in drafting legislation, writing speeches and messages, and drawing up important council papers. For a time, even the management of the House of Delegates was left to him. He remembered that "hardly a Bill was brought in, which I did not either draw or at least revise, and either got it passed or rejected." Boucher considered it unnecessary to "set down how such things are done; ... I have not a doubt but that they are done in the same manner and by the same means in the British Parliament" (*Rem.,* p. 92).

Eden was no less confidential about personal matters. When his hopes of inheriting the province of Maryland were blasted in 1771 with the announcement that it had been bequeathed to Henry Harford, Eden turned to Boucher in his bitterness, determined to attempt to break the will.[43] With the death of Frederick Calvert in Naples in 1771, it became apparent that Harford's inheritance was open to some doubt. A primary question was whether the province was willable; the second question involved the validity of the will itself. Two wills existed in England, but it was discovered that Calvert had executed a third one in Venice fifteen months before his death. One of the earlier wills had bequeathed Mrs. Eden one-half of the estate. The last will bequeathed the entire province to Harford, whose mother Baltimore had long since dis-

106

carded in favor of his current paramour and travelling companion. Eden's share, under the terms of the last will, was a mere £1,500 and an additional £100 a year. In spite of Eden's plans to break the will, Harford ultimately succeeded in enforcing his claim to the proprietorship.

In just two years in Annapolis, Boucher had secured a comfortable niche for himself. The close tie with Eden advertised to any who would see that Boucher was a "government man" in Maryland politics. Rumors of his unofficial power were soon commonplace. Assessing his new position with some complacency, Boucher thought it not unreasonable that a lucrative country parish in the best tobacco-growing district in America might soon be his, unless Eden's desire to assist him should be thwarted by Lord Baltimore's own patronage plans. Meanwhile, as he waited for the next step up, he considered that town life had many compensations and only one liability, his difficulty in fulfilling his obligation to tutor Jack Custis.

The Custis problem was one which Boucher had not foreseen, and when it became obvious he avoided dealing with it squarely. His absorption with literary, cultural, social, and political affairs left him little time for Jack, yet he disliked terminating the arrangement with the Washingtons. For one thing, he was genuinely fond of the boy. Also, he felt that he had accomplished enough as the lad's tutor so that he was reluctant to see another succeed him and thus reap any credit that might be forthcoming. Finally, Boucher was not a man to overlook the pleasure as well as the prestige of the connection with the Washington family.

Early in 1770, the Washingtons had considered entering Jack in a college in order to give the boy the advantage of a larger school than Boucher's. In an effort to cooperate with the family, Boucher investigated the possibility of enrolling Jack at King's College in New York, and requested information from President Myles Cooper to that end. Cooper answered on 22 March 1770, advising Boucher that the expense at the college was not "half as much as at others" such as the College of New Jersey or the colleges in New England. "Tuition is £5 (on the basis of one dollar passing for 8 shillings) New York currency," Cooper wrote, to which must be added the rental of a room and board. Firewood, candles, and washing would also be extra. The plan of education, Cooper explained, "copies in most material parts from Queen's College,

Oxford," which was quite familiar to Cooper who for many years had been both a scholar and a teacher at that institution. Boucher had had the temerity to ask for special attention for Washington's ward, which Cooper politely declined to give. He assured Boucher that he would extend "every mark of care and attention" and would see that "his other teachers shall do the same," but "as to my turning private tutor as it were . . . I must beg to be excused."[44] Boucher relayed the information to the family. However, Jack's college enrollment was deferred for the time being.

Meanwhile, Boucher presented Jack's family with an alternative to college for the boy—a tour of Europe for Custis in company with himself. The Grand Tour was a tantalizingly attractive idea, "a bait there is no resisting," which Boucher cherished second only to his desire for a country parish (*MHM* 8:177). He envisioned an extensive itinerary lasting perhaps two years, to be undertaken in 1772. Boucher wished to revisit his native country, and to increase his "slender stock of knowledge" by a tour through "those countries where the Arts and Sciences have been most successfully cultivated." As for Jack, Boucher assured Washington that such a tour could "stimulate him to pursue his studies with greater earnestness" in order to avoid appearing illiterate among men of letters into whose company he would fall while traveling.[45]

The proposed tour was intended to benefit Jack, who was provincial in his outlook. At home Jack had little opportunity to observe the manners of any but Virginians and Marylanders, seeing only "here and there a needy immigrant from Great Britain, an illiterate captain of a ship, or a sub-altern merchant." Lest the prospect of a more sophisticated view of men and foreign countries carry less weight with the Washingtons than he hoped, Boucher pointed out a highly utilitarian reason why all Virginians should "be taught to open their eyes and extend them beyond their own foggy air and dirty acres." A man of capacity could be "eminently useful by promoting and encouraging the arts" in Virginia, a colony whose planters were hardly in the avant-garde among the world's agricultural people. Boucher observed that "till very lately you could hardly anywhere see a piece of land tolerably plowed, or a person who could be persuaded that plowing made any difference." Even those who had made the greatest improvements in their agricultural pursuits "fall infinitely short of some other countries." Thus, Boucher suggested, a man who traveled and observed other techniques "may . . . learn to double the value of his estate."[46]

Boucher also offered a more specific argument why Jack in particular would benefit by a European experience. It might curb the youth's chief failings, indolence and voluptuousness. Jack was still young and these propensities were yet in embryo, but if they were not checked Jack might yet become "sunk in unmanly sloth," leaving his estate to the management of "some worthless overseer" while he himself might become entangled in some matrimonial adventure in which "passion will have much to say," while "it is not very likely reason will be much listened to." He reminded Washington that this last statement could be "sadly verified by many living instances" which had already come to Washington's attention. Boucher added one final note of caution. Jack must be inoculated against smallpox. "I can never consent to his leaving Virginia unless he is first inoculated," he wrote, and he recommended that it be done as soon as a good opportunity presented itself.[47]

In May 1770, Boucher was encouraged in his European venture with Jack when Washington pressed him for more specific information about his itinerary. By now Boucher had included a tour of North America, wishing to avoid "the absurdity" of taking Jack abroad when he knew nothing about his own country. After a winter or so in England, Boucher planned to conduct Jack "through the principal counties and towns of the three kingdoms," which he estimated would take nearly a year. Following this, he recommended spending six months in the "metropolis," after which they would set out on a tour through some of the principal countries on the continent.[48]

At Washington's request, Boucher submitted a budget, estimating his own and Jack's expenses at £1,000 per year. Bearing in mind Washington's admonition that Jack's estate was "a good one, but not profitable," Boucher accompanied his budget with the suggestion that he would render accountings during the trip and would adjust expenses along the way if Jack's income made it necessary. Although Boucher included in his estimate £250 per year in lieu of his ministerial salary, he generously agreed not to take into account in his charge for services any injury he might be doing to his "future prospects in life," suggesting that this ought to be charged "to the pleasure I propose to myself from the scheme."[49] Clearly, Boucher did not intend to seem too eager, and certainly his prospects for a rural parish were now excellent with Eden on his side.

No decison was made about the tour for some time, for it was still under discussion in summer 1770 after Boucher had moved to Annapolis. Boucher had the project much in mind, and when an opportunity for smallpox inoculation presented itself in October 1770, he urged the Washingtons to take advantage of it and send Jack to one Dr. Stephenson at Baltimore the following spring. Washington agreed to the inoculation, "whether he travels or not," citing the increasing exposure in Virginia. In April 1771 Boucher took the boy to Baltimore, had him inoculated immediately "for fear of his possibly catching it in the natural way," and left him in residence with the doctor to await the reaction.[50] He returned to Annapolis, but promised Jack that he would be with him when the fever was expected and eruptions were likely.

To the relief of Boucher and Washington, Custis was out of danger by 19 April 1771, and Jack had eight pockmarks to attest to his newly acquired immunity. To the relief of Martha Washington, Boucher reported none was on his face. However, Jack was to remain in Baltimore for several days until there were no obvious symptoms to create a smallpox scare in Annapolis. Meanwhile, Jack was feeling well, and upon his discharge by the doctor he took an unscheduled holiday for himself, with no notice to anyone. By the third of May, neither Boucher nor the Washingtons had heard from Custis, which prompted Boucher to make discreet inquiries in Baltimore. It appeared that Jack attended the wedding of a friend, and then made the most of the opportunity and dropped out of sight, causing much concern on the part of Boucher and the Washingtons.[51]

The incident served to focus attention on the pleasure-loving Jack once again. Boucher had to admit that the responsibility for the boy was a burden and that living in Annapolis exaggerated the difficulties of the relationship. Jack's interest in women left Boucher at a loss. His concern was shared by Washington, and Washington was having doubts about his ability to control Jack. Boucher insisted that the situation was aggravated because so much notice was taken of Jack everywhere. Although Boucher conceded that he was often pleased with the attention bestowed on Jack, still it was "the source of infinite disquietude" to him. Jack "seldom or never goes abroad without learning something

I could have wished him not to have learned," he lamented, while the excessive socializing caused the boy's schoolwork to suffer.[52]

Boucher was in part responsible for Jack's academic deficiencies. The first six months in Annapolis had been comparatively unsettled. Boucher made frequent trips back to Virginia in order to close out the Virginia plantation, leaving Jack too much alone. Jack, on the other hand, spent a considerable amount of time back home at Mount Vernon away from his books. Moreover, Boucher's own new and varied life detracted from his competence as a tutor. In spite of his earlier assurances to Washington, Jack did not make any headway with his studies and Washington was increasingly aware of it. The colonel raised the question with Boucher in July and in November 1771, complaining about Jack's deficiencies in mathematics and his lack of progress since 1768. Boucher could only insist in his own defense that at least Jack now understood the concepts involved in what his former tutor Magowan had taught him "by rote only."[53]

Feeling under attack, Boucher rendered no charge for Jack's education during the year and a half in Annapolis. He was forced to admit that his attention to Jack had "not been so regular and constant as that I could conscientiously make a charge of it." Although it hurt his pride and his pocketbook to admit it, he did so out of principle. Lest Washington should conclude that Boucher was being abjectly humble about his teaching services, he made it clear immediately that his neglect had been only in the more formal aspects of the boy's education. He pointed out that he had faithfully done his duty in seeing Jack through some "pretty trying and perilous scenes" with "tolerable safety." "The truth was," Boucher told the Washingtons, he loved the lad and had not wanted to part with him unless it were absolutely necessary. He was certain that Jack had a "very affectionate regard" for him, and was equally certain that no other person had as much influence over the boy as he himself had. Unsatisfactory as the Annapolis experience had been, Boucher still hoped that the Washingtons would think it "proper to try me a little longer." He added that he no longer needed to teach for a livelihood and would never again "take charge of another youth" other than those now with him.[54] For the time being, Jack was allowed to remain with Boucher.

In the meantime, a rural parish in Maryland fell vacant in

111

1771 and offered the prospect of an improved environment for Jack. There were many parishes that did not interest Boucher; "nothing should tempt me to go," he wrote on 25 July 1769; "the mosquitoes of one summer would kill me" (*MHM* 8:40). But a healthy parish now seemed within his grasp, and he hoped to be appointed to it immediately. However, his "fair prospects" of the parish "not twenty miles from Mt. Vernon" were dimmed when he was told by Eden that a "schoolfellow and a relation of his own" from England was expected soon to fill the post. Some hope remained; Boucher was told that if the gentleman did not choose to come, he might then be appointed to the parish. Unfortunately, the outcome lay several months in the future and the uncertainty posed a dilemma. The Washingtons had not yet come to a final decision with respect to Jack and the tour. Although Boucher still desperately wanted that jaunt, he felt constrained to warn Washington that his own affairs were so unsettled that he was not certain that he would be free to accompany Jack. He thought it would be highly indiscreet to turn himself once more adrift "into the wide world" without first securing to himself "a comfortable retreat." He could hardly afford to ask for a leave of absence while the question of a country post remained in doubt. He was acutely aware of the "silent lapse of time" and that he had "already trifled away but too great a part of it."[55]

Boucher's friends and advisors, Addison included, thought it his best course not to breathe a word of his hoped-for leave of absence until he could be installed in a parish of his choice. Mindful of his earlier problem in Virginia when he had abided by the advice of his "timorous" friends, Boucher mulled over the best approach to Eden. He decided to be straightforward with the governor, discounting the counsel of his friends. Without doubt he relied on the connection with Washington to aid his cause and on his established friendship with Eden. He was successful. On 4 July 1771 Boucher was able to write Washington that he had "the very high pleasure to inform" him that with respect to himself, "things are much altered and if you [will] make it suitable in other respects, I am willing and ready to accompany Mr. Custis on the proposed tour." He expressed one condition, that the two set out within the next year. Eden, pleased with Boucher's candid statement of his problem, had promised him the parish as soon as it was within his power to bestow and agreed to the necessary leave. The technique was to grant but one year's leave at a time, but renewable, an expedient which Eden was obliged to resort to "through a fear of giving cause of offense" to the Marylanders, who were "so unreasonably jealous of any extension prerogative." Boucher had thoroughly discussed the projected tour with Eden and so could advise Washington that the governor wished to oblige both Master Custis and his guardian.[56]

With Boucher's affairs now in the clear, the decision rested again with Washington. The colonel took another hard look at the project. It is clear that his obligations as a guardian weighed heavily on him, and serious doubts occurred to him. An expensive chancery suit had lately been entered against Jack's estate, the lands were exhausted, crops were "short," and although a number of slaves appeared to be assets, in reality they added to the expense. There were also family circumstances to consider. Patsy's health was deteriorating and the prognosis was poor. This sad fact influenced Martha. She was willing to go along with the idea, but she had "pangs" about parting with Jack for two years.[57] The European tour collapsed. Boucher's hopes for a subsidized trip back to Cumberland and for a Grand Tour were crushed. Many years lay between him and the realization of his great dream; he was never to travel through North America.

This disappointment was less painful than it might have been, however, for it was offset by Eden's offer of Queen Anne's Parish in Prince George's County in fall 1771. The parish was particularly valuable because the tobacco, "of the yellow or kite-foot sort," which could be cultivated there was the best in the province. Estimating that the parish, with between 1,200 and 1,300 taxable persons, was worth three or four hundred pounds per year, Boucher gratefully accepted the offer and prepared to leave Saint Anne's and Annapolis. He was inducted at Queen Anne's Parish on 11 November 1771 and was then in "very nearly as good a church preferment as America has to give." Boucher thought of the sharp contrast between himself and his friend James in England, whose annual salary was still approximately seventy pounds (*MHM* 8:176).

The church, Saint Barnabas, was a new one provided for by the Assembly in 1770.[58] Unfortunately the parish had no glebe and Boucher had to rent a house. He found one called Mount Lubentia, on the Patuxent River, which was "quiet and comfortable."[59] With his sister Jinny, Jacky, Overton Carr, and Benedict Calvert, Boucher moved in December 1771. The boys promptly dubbed the place "Castle Magruder," after one Captain Magruder who owned it. On 10 July 1772 Boucher wrote James a jubilant letter about the parish itself, assuring his friend that he was "quite contented that this should be my *Ne plus ultra*" (*MHM* 8:180). But he yearned to possess a house. "I am now resolving in good earnest to become frugal," he wrote Washington, adding that he comforted himself with the hope that he would soon be "in a capacity to get one of my own."[60] Fulfillment of that desire waited upon an accumulation of funds, which a fortunate marriage was soon to provide.

In 1771, during the theater and racing season in Annapolis, Boucher had met Eleanor Addison—"Nelly," as her family called her. She and her sister Ann, the Reverend Henry Addison's nieces, were house guests of the Walter Dulanys. Boucher saw them there often and was attracted to Nelly. He remembered that he had seen her before, in Virginia at a ball in Port Tobacco which he had attended with Judith Chase. Nelly, having seen little of Boucher on that occasion, did not remember him at all. Boucher had noted then that Nelly was "handsome, sprightly, and a general toast," but in the intervening years he had seen her only once and both were attached to other persons. Now in 1771, Boucher's romantic alliance with Judith Chase had long been broken, and Nelly had remained unmarried. Nelly's excellent principles, Boucher thought, had prevented her from finding among her admirers one whom she could thoroughly like, so that she had "rejected them all" (*Rem.*, p. 72).

By the time the vacant parish at Queen Anne's was offered to Boucher he had renewed his acquaintance with Nelly, and since he had already determined to court her he was delighted at the prospect of living in the same county. He said nothing of his intentions regarding Nelly to anyone while he waited for his circumstances to improve and thus to make his plan less presumptuous. No doubt Boucher remembered ruefully his rebuff at the hands of blunt old Col. Henry Fitzhugh some few years before. With his prospects more promising, Boucher was determined to put his plan into action as soon as he moved to Prince George's County. By January he was reasonably settled at Castle Magruder and ready for his first step, a consultation with Henry

114

Addison. In this maneuver he was thwarted for some days by an unprecedentedly heavy fall of snow which isolated the household for three weeks. But as soon as the ground was passable, he set out to see Addison. Addison discouraged him, assuring him that the lady would not have him. No man to be dissuaded so easily, Boucher ignored the advice of his friend and wrote directly to Nelly, who agreed to see him. Boucher was much encouraged by her "frank, honest, and generous" response. He recalled years later that he had told Nelly quite candidly "everything that made against as well as for me." The day was won, "with a generous contempt of all the little idle tricks of teasing" (*Rem.*, pp. 75-76).

Fortunately for Boucher, Nelly "possessed an uncommonly independent mind," and was prepared to marry in spite of objections raised by both Addison and her mother. Addison's true reason, it developed, was a desire to see his niece married to a "near and opulent" Dulany relative on his wife's side of the family (*Rem.*, p. 73). From Addison's point of view Boucher was not a good catch for his niece. Boucher estimated his own assets at this time at £1,000 sterling (excluding his income from Queen Anne's Parish), while Nelly's dowry consisted of currency and sundry slaves, together totaling £2,500 sterling. The other objection Nelly faced was that posed by her mother, who Boucher thought wished her daughter not wed at all.[61] A few months passed "in courtship and preparations" which Boucher was to remember as "by far the happiest in my life" (*Rem.*, p. 76). Nelly had just celebrated her thirty-third birthday and Boucher was thirty-four when they were married in an evening ceremony, according to the custom of the country, at Oxon Hill, the great Addison family home on the Potomac. Robert Eden issued the license and Rev. Henry Addison read the service. After refreshments Boucher took his bride to Castle Magruder, some twenty miles away.

The new Mrs. Boucher had once been "exquisitely handsome," Boucher was to write in the seventh year of their marriage, but a long series of illnesses had much impaired her beauty. Yet in his eyes Nelly, a woman of middling stature with jet black hair and lustrous eyes, was even yet a "neat, elegant, and lovely" person. Boucher attributed her loss of good health (and later her life) to the "ingenious mismanagement" and "ill-judged tampering" on the part of her relative, Dr. Ricard Brooke, whose "worth and abilities" had not been demonstrated in his care of Nelly (*Rem.*, pp.

77-78). Her health was further jeopardized three months later by a miscarriage following a minor accident in their home. She was never able to bear children. Although Boucher wrote nothing of his disappointment at the time, as the years went by his great yearning for a son and his sense of frustration at being childless were apparent enough. Nelly never regained good health. Of the eleven years they were married, only three were years in which she enjoyed even a modicum of well-being.

In spite of her aristocratic family connections, Nelly had virtually no formal education, yet she possessed considerable social grace. Boucher found her "well-bred, of a liberal turn of mind, and possessed of an uncommonly good understanding." She amazed and amused him in turn. "I never in my life knew a person who had seen so little of the world that knew so much of it," he wrote. "She is artless, blushing, bashful," as a mere country wench might be, yet she dressed with good taste, conversed with ease, and acted with all "the propriety and dignity of a woman of fashion." Boucher also admired her "native good sense and solid virtue," which he thought "by far the most useful qualities a woman can possess." He believed she had a mind with a "capacity for any extension" and had the potential to be a great woman, although he also knew that she was content to be merely "a good one." She bore her infirmities with patience and dignity, shielding him from the knowledge of her great discomfort on occasion in order to remain a good companion. Boucher respected her fortitude, for "no sickness, sorrow, nor any other calamity ... has yet been able to subdue her." With her habits of industry, frugality, and easy contentment, she was indeed a good wife to him, and much beloved (*Rem.*, pp. 78-79).

Absorbed with settling into the new parish, with his happiness in Nelly's company, and with his search for an available plantation, Boucher for a time neglected his correspondence. Myles Cooper, concerned about Boucher's long silence, inquired of Jack Custis about his friend.[62] Even his correspondence with James suffered. The letters to James show a gap between 4 April 1771 and 10 July 1772. However, Boucher specifically stated in the latter that he had written a letter to James in August and another in November of 1771. Either the letters failed to reach James, or they have not been preserved with the others.

Although Boucher and his wife found Mount Lubentia comfortable enough, the marriage had enhanced Boucher's social and economic position considerably, and it was now feasible to think about a home of their own. With much pleasure, he wrote James on 10 July 1772 that he was looking around for a plantation, "which when I have purchased, as I am now enabled to do, I flatter myself I may repose myself for the remainder of my life, under my own vine, blessed with that ease, competence and independence, which I have so long been in search of." "Very little is wanting to fill up the measure of my happiness," he told James. After long years of hard work and ambitious striving, he felt a sense of security that he thoroughly enjoyed. As he told James, "I really have so long been a child of fortune, so unsettled and undetermined a projector about ways and means of living, that I feel my heart glow with gratitude to the author and giver of every good gift, that he hath at length conducted me to where I would be" (*MHM* 8:180-81).

With a deep sense of gratitude to the long-time friend and advisor who had given him his first great assistance on the way to a career, he poured out his feelings. "My dearest friend, you know not how it is this heart of mine clings to you and yours: it is not an attachment of esteem, gratitude and love only, but (if I may be pardoned the expression) partakes something of that regard which I feel for the Deity. To him I owe it that I am— to you almost alone, next to Him, that I am (if I am) virtuous and consequently happy" (*MHM* 8:180). Significantly, Boucher failed to mention a sharp and thorny issue that threatened already to eat away mercilessly at his new-found contentment. Maryland's established church now was coming under serious attack by a group of able lawyers in the House of Delegates who formed the nucleus of the Country party. Boucher's own parish, in the heart of Prince George's County, was a focal point of antiproprietary and antichurch activity.

✑ Chapter 6 ✑

Controversy in
Prince George's County

Boucher met with a cold reception at Saint Barnabas's. On his first Sunday in his new parish the church doors were locked against him, and some Sundays later a "turbulent fellow" paid eight dollars for wagon loads of stones to throw in an attempt to drive Boucher and his friends from the church (*Rem.*, p. 74). Many of his parishioners were outraged by his appointment; they had wanted the post to go to a native son of Queen Anne's, Rev. Edward Gantt.[1] Others disliked Boucher's politics, regarding him as too closely connected with the establishment. Although most clerics were "under the patronage of government," as he expressed it, and thus on the side of the political establishment, Boucher's friendship with Eden made his position even more pronounced (*Rem.*, pp. 68, 74). As a consequence he felt himself to be a marked man from the moment of his arrival in Prince George's County, whose residents were to become ardent supporters of the Patriot cause (*Rem.*, p. 93).

But a more fundamental reason underlay objections to Boucher himself. Church affairs were completely entangled in the increasingly turbulent politics of the province. Politics in Maryland had long been a three-cornered power struggle between the Crown, the Proprietary, and the Assembly, marked by parallel commercial aggressiveness against British merchants. From the time of the Stamp Act, the Assembly's resistance to both the Crown and the Proprietary had been increasing. The colony had solidly opposed the Stamp Act, citing its charter guarantees, the laws of England and Maryland. In the process it had demonstrated how much resistance to authority could be mustered for a popular cause.[2] The spirit of opposition had seriously weakened the proprietary government, and very early Boucher observed that the populace was divided into two parties, with "placemen and their dependents" coalescing into a Court party on the side of government, and a Country party developing under the leadership of a group of capable lawyers in the House of Delegates (*Rem.*, p. 68).

Two of the most able lawyers in the Country party were William Paca and Samuel Chase, both members of the Anglican church. The latter was presently to earn for himself the title "the Torch of the Revolution."[3] Boucher took a dim view of these men, believing as he did that they were motivated by no more than a selfish desire to obtain offices for themselves (*Rem.*, p. 68). In autumn 1770, the conflict between the Court and Country parties involved three issues: renewal of the statute covering tobacco inspection, fees for the proprietary officers of the colony, and salaries for Anglican clerics. In this last issue, Boucher soon became conspicuously involved.

The conflict had begun quietly enough in 1770 in a quarrel over renewal of the Tobacco Inspection Act which had expired on 20 October. This law, enacted in 1747, had placed Maryland tobacco under inspection requirements similar to those of Virginia by providing for a system of eighty public warehouses under the charge of official inspectors. Inspectors gave notes for tobacco of sound quality, well and uniformly packed; the rest had to be repacked or burned. Overproduction of tobacco and the serious competition with Virginia for markets made such a law essential, and no one in the legislature questioned the need for its renewal. However, a quarrel broke out between the House of Delegates, the Provincial Council, and the governor over the fees to be paid the tobacco inspectors. The result was a deadlock and a failure to renew the law; Eden thereupon prorogued the Assembly. He then sought to resolve the stalemate by issuing a proclamation on 26 November 1770 authorizing a collection of fees based on the schedule outlined in the earlier inspection law. To Eden's credit, he used tactful language, defining his proclamation in terms of defending the people against exorbitant fees, and his decree was later confirmed by his superiors in England. But the Country party reacted negatively to the proclamation, denouncing it as a usurpation of legislative power.

With the question of the tobacco inspectors' fees still unresolved, an even more inflammatory quarrel arose in the next session over fees for the colony's principal proprietary officers. The upper house proposed that all fees and emoluments incident to the most lucrative proprietary appointive posts of the colony, those of secretary, commissary general, and judge of the Land Office, be abolished and that instead salaries of £600 sterling be substituted. The lower house, after investigation by one of its own committees, rejected this measure in favor of its own projected table of fees. Shrewdly, the delegates arranged to have the fees of the top provincial office holders printed, which revealed payments unlikely to quiet the public mind. The provincial secretary, for example, received tobacco fees worth from £1,000 to £1,500 annually, while the clerk of the Land Office, William Stewart annually received more than £1,800 in fees.

In 1771, with the deadlock over fees incident to public office still unbroken, Eden again prorogued the Assembly. Thereafter the death of Lord Baltimore and the succession of Henry Harford to the proprietorship precluded the assembling of another House of Delegates until 1773. As Boucher recalled later, it was a time when public issues occupied and agitated the minds of the people beyond measure, keeping them "restless and dissatisfied, forever discontented and grumbling . . . and forever projecting reformations." The "fierceness in opposition" seemed to him unusual (*Rem.*, pp. 68-69).

While the row over the fee issue continued, another quarrel broke out over the salaries of the Anglican clergy which soon involved the establishment of the church itself. When the Church of England had been permanently established in Maryland in 1702, clergymen were assured incomes from a poll tax. This tax was originally set at forty pounds of tobacco per head, or "per poll," as it was commonly expressed, based on the parish population. Although the tax was later reduced by an act of 1747 to thirty pounds per poll, most rectors enjoyed steadily increasing salaries as the colonial population expanded at the rate of 20 percent.[4] Parishes were typically large, an area of from four to eight hundred square miles being not unusual. Maryland clergymen were better off than their counterparts in England in that the poll tax system of collection, handled through the local sheriff's office, freed them from the difficulties encountered in the collecting of tithes. But when the Inspection Act lapsed, leaving the fee schedule question open, the Anglican ministers promptly maintained that they had legal basis for a one-third increase in income. The House of Delegates disagreed. With a singular disregard for the appearance of greed and with no political sense, the clerics sued.

Unfortunately for the clerics, the public was less than sympathetic to their cause. Even before the onset of the fee controversy the colony's clergy had enjoyed a very bad general reputation, a consequence in large part of the Proprietary's system of clerical patronage, which sacrificed the church to politics through the appointment to benefices of incompetent or immoral men. Commissary Jacob Henderson, the bishop of London's Maryland agent, had described one clergyman as an "idiot" and a second as a "rake."[5] Another had fallen into the fire while drunk and burned to death, while yet another had murdered his wife. Many of the clergy were notorious drunks who "had to hold on to both sides of the pulpit even while exhorting the faithful" in order to avoid falling flat on their faces. Even Boucher conceded that "some individuals" were "irregular, licentious and profligate" (*Rem.*, p. 69). It was no wonder that a widespread belief prevailed that Maryland's clergy already were overpaid.

Boucher could not restrain himself from entering the fray, and he boldly plunged into a written battle in the *Maryland Gazette* with Paca and Chase, a contest which a contemporary Marylander would later describe as one of "great acrimony."[6] As the opponents in the paper war warmed to their tasks, the controversy became more and more emotional, and soon developed into a bitter exchange, highlighted by mutual character assassination, extending over a period of some four months. Boucher, like other honest clerics, had to admit that some individuals deserved public censure. But he, unlike the Country party, considered the root of the problem to be the lack of a resident bishop; no supervision or discipline by the church existed. The resulting anarchy provided an opportunity for the lawmakers to interfere with the constitutional pre-

121

rogative of the church, which disciplined its own everywhere but in the American colonies.

For some time certain members of the House of Delegates had made overtures toward creation of a civil body to oversee the clergy. The colony's churchmen successfully fended off these moves until 1770, when the Assembly passed a law requiring every Anglican clergyman to swear an oath of loyalty to the government and to provide a sworn statement that his benefice had not been purchased. The law also established a special court consisting of three clergymen and three laymen, all appointed by the governor, to handle complaints against ministers. The court was given the power to rebuke the defendant, to suspend him, or to relieve him of his parish. Boucher thought it a sad state of affairs that he and his colleagues now were subjected to a "novel jurisdicton . . . of a novel Court" (*Rem.*, p. 69).

Although the assumption by the legislature of the church's disciplinary power disturbed him, Boucher was even more exercised over the salary issue, which touched him personally. The existing salary arrangement, he thought, was fundamentally inequitable. Payment was in tobacco, but for the convenience of those who did not plant that crop, the poll tax might be paid off at twelve shillings and six pence per hundred pounds, the highest market price quoted for tobacco at the time the 1747 law was written. However, for several years since that time the crop had been selling at a price between twenty and forty shillings per hundredweight. Boucher thought it probable that the price would never be much lower again, and therefore two clergymen who rendered essentially the same services were being compensated very differently, depending upon whether one received his payment in tobacco or in cash.

To make matters worse, the Assembly now was proposing that a law be passed enabling all parishioners, whether or not they grew tobacco, to pay off their church obligations at twelve shillings and six pence. Boucher knew that it would be hard on the clergy; in his particular parish he stood to lose between fifty and one hundred pounds annually. Clerical opposition to such an act compelling acceptance of a money payment in lieu of tobacco had for a long time prevented such legislation by the Maryland Assembly. In Boucher's opinion this failure had much disappointed the lawyers, who now "in a sort of frenzy" pretended that the "law by which the clergy claimed the forty per poll was null and void." It seemed to Boucher that the lawyers aimed at a "total renversement," and were prepared to "stick at nothing to attain their end" (*Rem.*, p. 69).

A far more fundamental argument against the church establishment had developed as early as 1770, with the publication of a handbill signed "The Church of England Planter," in which the anonymous author complained that the clergy rode him "like an ass."[7] The writer advanced an argument which struck at the vitals of the church; he attempted to prove that the Act of Establishment of 1702 itself had no constitutional validity. The argument as to the unconstitutionality of the 1702 law rested on the highly technical point that the governor who signed the act had done so some weeks after the death of King William III, under whose sovereignty he held his commission. To be valid, the argument ran, the law should have been reenacted and signed under a commission from Queen Anne, the new sovereign.

Boucher thought this argument ignored both practicality and common sense. The governor in 1702 could not have known of the death of King William at the time he signed the law. Moreover, Boucher pointed out, "the law had been in force, and observed as a law for upwards of seventy years, had been recognized by many subsequent laws, and had been ratified by the succeeding sovereigns as well as by succeeding Assemblies" (*Rem.*, p. 70).[8] The only previous objection to the law had been to the definition of salaries. In Boucher's opinion it was at least possible that the attack on the Act of Establishment was a deliberate political move to enhance the position of the more radical delegates. "Great placemen," he thought, "had cunningly contrived to place our Order in the front of the battle," so that they "might take shelter behind us" (*Rem.*, p. 69).[9]

Unfortunately for the church, subsequent newspaper contributors continued to advance the argument raised by the Church of England Planter. On 6 August 1772 Samuel Chase published a legal opinion in the *Maryland Gazette* which followed the Planter in expressing doubt about the validity of the church establishment, although the stand he took was decidedly equivocal. On 10 September 1772 Willam Paca published another letter in the *Gazette* subjecting the Act of Establishment to a radically anticlerical argument. Chase had conceded that King William's death did not abrogate the proceedings in the courts or suspend the powers of the commissioners in the province, although he held that the Assembly had been dissolved. But now Paca contended not only that the Assembly was dissolved but that "the assembly which afterwards met and enacted the contested forty per poll law, being called without a fresh *writ of summons*," was *illegally and unconstitutionally convened*." Paca concluded that "no obligation can result from said forty per poll act as law."

Paca's opinion, coming as it did from a leader of the Country party in the lower house, appalled Boucher. Even more disgusting to him was the offer of Paca, Chase, and Thomas Johnson to defend gratis the people who in consequence of the Paca-Chase legal stance refused to pay their poll tax to the clergy (*Rem.*, pp. 69-70).[10] The result of all this was that many people stopped paying church taxes. Boucher, whose salary in Annapolis had already been somewhat affected, found his salary grossly reduced.

In December 1772, Boucher thought he saw an opportunity to embarrass Paca and Chase on a charge of inconsistency and challenged them in the pages of the *Maryland Gazette*. Thus began an exchange of letters far more frank and insulting than those commonly published today. Boucher was aware that were he to enter the controversy he would involve himself in a great amount of time and work, but he did not anticipate adequately the depth and breadth of the controversy that now loomed. Nor could Boucher have anticipated the deep and long-lasting political consequences both for him and for Maryland.

In his letter dated 31 December, Boucher openly identified himself, bluntly attacking Paca and Chase for their blatant inconsistency in collecting and dispensing taxes for a church they had declared unconstitutional. "I have been informed you still continue to act as vestrymen of St. Anne's Parish," he chided, referring to the vestry's recent petition to the county court for an assessment of five pounds of tobacco per poll for repairs to the church and chapel. This was extraordinary behavior, he thought, for two men who flatly denied the constitutionality of the Act of Establishment. Dramatically Boucher charged the pair with being "the immediate agents of fixing on the necks of a free people that odious badge of slavery, *taxation without their consent, taxation without the least pretense of law*." How could it be otherwise, he reminded them, when "*your* tax on the people cannot be justi-

124

fied" by a law of the province which the pair denied. How unlike the great Hampden in England in 1637 these two lawyers were, Boucher sneered, reminding them that Hampden had chosen "to be confined to a loathsome jail" rather than pay a single shilling "without authority of Parliament."

Boucher did not have long to wait for an answer. On 14 January 1773 Paca and Chase counterattacked in a letter in the *Maryland Gazette* which raised once more the inflammatory issue of an American bishop. Observing that "an offended priest is a most revengeful and unplacable enemy," they demanded that Boucher produce forthwith a list naming the clerics who had prepared the 1770 "Address to the Bishop of London." In what kind of "Tremendous Court," they inquired further, would the prospective bishop of America exercise his powers, and what would prevent him from fastening a "multiplication of offices and powers upon the people?" "The Lord have mercy upon us!," they exclaimed, for if the invidious plan came to fruition, "Heaven and our prayers must be our only attendance."

Turning to the church tax question, they defended their vestrymen's right under common law as elected representatives of the people to protect the members of their parishes from unjust and illegal taxation. And they ended with scorn, "Your genius and erudition," they assured Boucher, "may be respectable," but on the complicated legal question at hand "we can only consider you as a mere echo." This last jibe was a conjecture that Boucher was writing with the guidance or consultation of Daniel Dulany or Thomas Jenings, the attorney general of the province.

In a sharp political move, Paca and Chase shortly afterwards arranged to have the 1770 "Address" reprinted. Their evident purpose was to accuse its authors of fraud in implying that it represented the will of the people. Obviously Paca and Chase had come to see the episcopacy issue as one finely calculated to keep popular opinion in a state of ferment and they did not intend to let the issue die.

The argument rapidly degenerated into an interminable legal argument and personal attacks in which both sides drew some support in letters to the printer of the *Gazette*. On 1 April 1773 an "Eastern Shore Clergyman" deplored the "scurrilous" treatment which Boucher had received, then volunteered his own opinion that an act which had been acknowledged for more than seventy years by some "of our ablest lawyers," and which lately had been determined to be valid "by a Dulany," could not lightly be set aside. He also took the occasion to charge Paca with the use of delaying tactics to impede the progress of a lawsuit by which the clerics intended to test in the courts the validity of the Act of Establishment. "Patuxent" had also risen to the Paca-Chase bait to draw the argument to the old episcopal question. He wrote in the *Gazette* on 5 April 1773 that he had favored Boucher until he learned of his position on the resident American bishop issue.

In a lengthy reply on 15 April 1773 to a series of charges and innuendoes by Paca, Boucher hotly denied that he had solicited a better parish (although he had), insisting that there were more effective means of recommending one's self than by direct solicitation and that Paca himself had used such means to obtain the governor's favors.[11] To the charge that Boucher had written his letters to the *Gazette* merely in search of publicity, the cleric replied that he could gain no fame by "a trial of skill with a penman [Paca] who cannot even spell." His sole purpose, Boucher said, was to show the people of Maryland that Paca and Chase were not the "sound lawyers, sensible politicians, or consistent patriots" which they represented themselves to be. He also cautioned the pair that much as he disliked "the dirty business of tearing and worrying private character," he would engage in it if necessary.

Boucher attempted to concentrate on the question of law involved in the controversy, and had gone to some trouble to check on legal sources for his argument. First he questioned the Paca-Chase interpretation of the common law with respect to vestry authority, carefully distinguishing between parishioners and freeholders. In Boucher's opinion, Paca and Chase were wrong about the common law; their power as vestrymen derived from Maryland's legislature. In marshaling evidence to support his contention Boucher first cited the election process, reminding Chase that in his own recent election a controversy had developed when a number of parishioners who tried to vote had been challenged and sent away. Unless the elections which had put Chase and Paca in office had been "unfair and therefore illegal," they had been elected by freeholders as part of the Maryland legislative process, and not "by authority founded upon common law, and common right."

The two lawyers were in error because they misunderstood the vestry as a body politic. In English common law a vestry was "properly speaking" the assembly of the whole parish. Every parishioner who paid the church rate had a right to come to the vestry, or meeting, and public notice was required of such assemblies. Historically the meeting was called the vestry, but not all persons entitled to participate were called vestrymen. For the purpose of levying the rates to defray all parochial expense, the parishioners were a corporate body capable of making bylaws. All of these rights were by the common law of England.

Paca and Chase were mistaken in drawing a parallel between the relationship of English common law to English vestries and that of English common law to Maryland vestries. English common law knew no such delegation of powers permitting parishioners at large to elect a chosen few to serve as "a *select vestry*" as was the practice in America. The vestry of Saint Anne's in Maryland was certainly a select vestry; therefore, according to Boucher, it could not exist on the principles of the common law of England. Boucher supported his argument with references to Blackstone, Burne, Parson's *Law*, Wood's *Institutes*, Shaw's *Parish Law*, Godolphin, and Gibson, "the most respectable authors on this subject," while he charged the two lawyers with incorrectly quoting Blackstone on the applicability of English common law to Maryland by omitting the "very many and very great restrictions" which the eminent barrister imposed.

The cleric contended that the case of the vestries in America was sufficiently different to warrant the deviation from English common law on the subject. The lack of ecclesiastical courts alone proved his point, he thought. In England, if any parishioners refused "to pay the church-rates, or tax, demanded by the church-wardens, they were to be sued in the ecclesiastical court, and not elsewhere." Since there were no such courts in Maryland, how could the tax be collected from those who refused to pay? Boucher believed that here lay "the true reason why the common law of England, relating to vestries, never prevailed" in Maryland or in any other colony in America. Rather Maryland's legislature, along with other colonial assemblies, had been forced to enact laws "empowering vestrymen to assess the parishioners," and to perform the usual additional duties. An act of 1700 in Maryland had established select vestries, a "system of parochial polity totally different from that of the common law," and intended for the purpose of "incorporating a political body," capable in law of acting in all cases for the parish or church. Furthermore, Boucher pointed out, every act of the legislature providing for new parishes since then had contained a clause empowering the freeholders of the several new parishes "to choose and nominate vestrymen and other officers." Vestries in Maryland owed their existence to acts of the Assembly and to nothing else.

But Paca and Chase were arguing from "higher law"; from a "law of right founded upon reason and ripened into perfection by the wisdom of ages: a system of jurisprudence adored by Englishmen, as the *palladium* of their rights, liberties and properties," as they wrote in their letter of 18 March 1773. Paca and Chase cited common law and common right as the basis of the authority "of the whole" which the parish could delegate into the hands of vestrymen and churchwardens, arguing the "self-evident proposition" that "what a man may do *by himself* he may do by *another*." In the process they quoted, then directly challenged, the opinion of Thomas Jenings, Maryland's attorney general, which stated that a parish was a creation of prescription charter or act of Parliament. Paca and Chase said their power as vestrymen depended on a church compact, not the statutes of Maryland.

In addition to challenging the interpretation of the attorney general, Paca and Chase questioned the whole issue of tithes in terms of taxation without representation. They summed up their argument: "The lands we have purchased are our property; as such they cannot be burthened or charged without our assent; the common law shields us from such an evil; the eternal laws of nature and reason are invincible bars to it.", Ironically, by the eve of the American Revolution, the idea of natural right upon which Paca and Chase leaned so heavily had already been abandoned in English law.[12]

In the politics of confrontation in Maryland, Paca and Chase were conducting the controversy with Boucher in the same terms as all issues contested by the Proprietary and the representative elements in Maryland. The liberal thought which the lawyers espoused gave little ground to those who opposed it, while it put those who used these intellectual arguments far outside the laws and establishments of colonial Maryland. Boucher concluded that in part Paca and Chase were able to persuade Marylanders to their point of view by writing with such obscurity that they were often misunderstood. "Like the loligo, or ink fish," he told the pair, "you have the art of rendering dark" any subject by couching it in "loose and indeterminate" terms. He deplored their habit of shifting their position frequently in argument, like "true French generals" who beaten out of one ground "instantly take possession of another." But even more frustrating to Boucher was the way in which they ignored logic by failing to see the incongruity of an established church without an establishment for the minister. Paca and Chase earlier had remarked that the clergy ought to be reduced to the simplicity of the Apostles; it now appeared to Boucher that their present arguments squared with their "ultimate aim" to "reduce us all to a staff and a pair of shoes." In the course of the newspaper controversy Boucher had despaired of persuading "the good people of this province" to listen "to the *still, small voice of reason*," particularly after his opponents had painted a picture of him as an "oppressor," "a plunderer," and "an obnoxious person." But he had persisted, convinced that any diminution of the church's patrimony was "*sacrilege* and likewise contrary to my coronation oath."

The dispute finally ended in April 1773. Boucher acknowledged that he was "generally allowed to have the better of the argument, but they carried their point" (*Rem.*, p. 71). The most enthusiastic response he received came from Myles Cooper in New York. Cooper told him he had been in Philadelphia and had "heard so much of your prowess" that he wanted to see the whole controversy in print if it could be arranged. "Every soul who spoke of the controversy declared loudly in favor of your superiority," he assured Boucher.[13]

In spite of Cooper's words of praise, Boucher did not feel elated. The matter had cost him much time and thought, yet he had gained little or nothing. Indeed, he had very likely lost ground for the church and for himself. Boucher wrote James on 16 November 1773 that he had not received one penny for the two years he had been the incumbent of Queen Anne's Parish. It was a hardship for a man "whose daily bread depends on his yearly, if not daily, income." His estimate of the plight of the church itself was little better. "Church affairs in this part of the world continue, in a regular progression, to deteriorate; and, if they go on as they have for some months past, I think twelve months from this time is the longest period it can be possible for our Church to exist" (*MHM* 8:183).

The clergy meanwhile continued to strive to prevent Assembly action of a radical nature. On 8 December 1773 Eden read to the Assembly an address from the Maryland clergy which suggested a salary compromise. Whenever the solvent taxable persons in a parish exceeded 2,200, the excess could be appropriated to the service of the church through the foundation of a fund for religous instruction. This proposal was intended to answer the charge that clerical salaries were too large in some parishes. The Assembly, however, refused to consider it, which was hardly surprising since in the June session of 1773 the delegates had quickly adopted the position of Paca and Chase and declared the Act of Establishment unconstitutional and therefore void. In its place, the delegates framed a bill to pay all ministers equally, as was the custom in Virginia. In the November sesson, the lower house had proposed a bill which provided thirty pounds of tobacco or four shillings per poll for the clergymen, the taxpayer to have the option of paying either tobacco or money. Chase and Paca had won out; the bill was passed. Ironically, Chase had just cut his father's salary in half.

Boucher explained their success in terms of pressure from the Provincial Council. "After I left Annapolis [removing to Prince George's County] the Governor, beset and worried by his Council to give us up for the sake of peace as it was called, in evil hour passed the law." Boucher did Eden the justice to say that when the governor found he could no longer resist the "importunities with which he was urged," he had sent for Boucher, pressing him to come to him at Annapolis, and assuring him "that if I still stood out he also would." Unfortunately Boucher was absent on a journey and did not get the message from Eden in time. "The deed was done," he wrote, "before my return and irrevocable" (*Rem.*, p. 71). Boucher reflected that on occasion history hinged on small personal things. No doubt he always felt that his absence at that time was a misfortune, and that he might have influenced Eden to veto the measure. By his failure to do so he had sacrificed the clergy. Although the bishop of London and Secretary of State Dartmouth disapproved, the act remained on the books.

Meantime the case earlier begun on behalf of the clergy over the salary differential had finally been prepared for trial after numerous troubles and delays. But as public opinion crystallized on the side of Paca and Chase during the newpaper battle, lawyers had second thoughts about being involved in the case (*Rem.*, p. 71).[14] Boucher had done everything he could to prevent the events that Paca and Chase had worked equally hard to bring about. He continued to feel obligated to do what he could to "check the immense mischief," but his stand on the whole issue had made him more enemies than friends. Some lines of verse had even appeared in the 18 March 1773 *Maryland Gazette* suggesting that the cleric "stick to souls."

The altercation with Paca had been particularly personal and abrasive. At one point Paca was so incensed with some of Boucher's jibes that he tendered him a formal challenge to a duel. Oddly enough, Paca requested Robert Smith, the secretary to the governor, to be his second. Smith, "with great readiness of mind and adroitness," Boucher recalled, "told him that I had foreseen long ago how our dispute would terminate, and accordingly had actually engaged him to attend me as my second" (*Rem.*, pp. 115-16). Apparently Smith also embroidered a few instances of Boucher's bravery and prowess. In the end Paca was dissuaded from pursuing the matter. Although the challenge to a duel was set aside, the personal enmity was less easily dissipated. The newspaper quarrel had embroiled Boucher with the sharpest exponents of Whig politics. His political philosophy had not yet been called into question, but his opposition to the measures being taken against the church, his advocacy of an American bishop, and his intimacy with Governor Eden already had marked him as persona non grata with those in whom the Whig spirit was developing.

Boucher had long since been "applied to by my brethren of the clergy, chiefly of Virginia," to devise "ways and means of forming something like some general and uniform line of conduct for the whole body of the clergy of the Church of England throughout the continent" (*Rem.*, p. 100). The Paca-Chase dispute had pushed Boucher unexpectedly far into the limelight, and had brought him even more attention from Myles Cooper. Cooper considered him a key man in the South from whom he might expect leadership of the clergy, and he determined to pay him a visit in late October 1773. Cooper's plans for a conference with Boucher and others materialized, and in an attempt to implement plans made during their conversations, Cooper persuaded both Boucher and

Rev. Henry Addison to accompany him to Philadelphia, where Boucher spent a week lodging with Dr. William Smith, provost of the College of Philadelphia. A general plan was worked out to concert efforts for an American bishop and to unify the church against "republican" activities such as those of Paca and Chase. Unfortunately, the plan developed in Philadelphia failed. Boucher reflected ruefully later that it was "too well known how little the clergy of Philadelphia regarded this agreement, how generally they went into the views of Congress, and what dreadfully bad consequences" their defection had "on the country in general or on the well-affected clergy in particular" (*Rem.*, p. 100). As for Smith, his personal convictions appeared to Boucher to be unsettled, and he was to learn later that Smith would resolve his indecision in favor of the American cause. It is clear that Boucher's understanding of the Philadelphia agreement differed substantially from that of the other parties to it, especially with respect to the meaning of the term "republican activities" against which they were to stand together. Boucher came to believe that the violent actions of the emerging committees of enforcement of the Continental Association of September 1774 were subject to the agreement, an opinion which his confreres obviously did not necessarily share.

Although the visit to Philadelphia was destined to fall short of its desired results with respect to both church and state, it did provide Boucher with his only opportunity to see something of North America other than the Virginia-Maryland Tidewater region. "I cannot describe to you the surprise it gave me to see so rich, so cultivated a country, so large, so busy a city," he wrote James on 16 November 1773. It appeared to him there were not five cities in England which exceeded Philadelphia either in size or commerce, and yet the city was the product of less than one century. It was in fact second only to Bristol and London in the British empire. Philadelphia, Boucher thought, might well become "the London of America." His experience exclusively in the tobacco colonies had not prepared him for the "vast progress" he observed in Pennsylvania, where many farmers and few slaves met his eye, but where improvements in agriculture exceeded anything he had seen in the Tidewater or indeed in most of his native Cumberland. "Upon my word," he said, "the daughter here treads very close on the heels of the mother" (*MHM* 8:184).

This glimpse of the prosperous Pennsylvania colony whetted his appetite to see more of America, and he promised Cooper that he would accompany him on a tour of the whole continent and certainly of the northern parts of it, "if ever I am able." He longed to view "those vast lakes and hills" he had read about, for he was by now familiar with "almost every book of any character" that had been printed concerning America. He also thought them deficient, and planned to write a better one some day himself (*MHM* 8:185).

Many years later, when Boucher recalled this visit to Philadelphia, his revolutionary experience had altered his old feelings, and his earlier enthusiasm for the city had dimmed. He would then think of its disgusting uniformity and sameness, its dull appearance without green squares, and its lack of public edifices of any size or dignity. Boucher's memories had been transformed along with the modification of his politics; he now thought of Philadelphia's "Republican aspect." "The people, too, are like their town, all very well, but nothing more. One is as good as another." Even their conversation irked him in retrospect, for "the almost universal topic of conversation among them" was the "superiority of Philadelphia" over every other place on earth, and "all their geese are swans" (*Rem.*, p. 101).

But in 1773, pleased with the results of his brief trip to Pennsylvania, Boucher settled back comfortably into his plantation life. In spite of his general feeling of unease in the parish and his early nonacceptance by the nascent Whig Patriots, Boucher did not feel isolated from the provincial affairs of either Virginia or Maryland. His residence at Mount Lubentia was easily accessible by the Patuxent River, although on occasion spring freshets made ferrying difficult. The roads were passable between Annapolis and Queen Anne's Parish except during unusual winter snows. Eden was a frequent guest and continued to regard Boucher as a confidant. Calvert, Dulany, and the chief justice, among other prominent Maryland officials, were also guests, and thus Boucher was privy to Maryland's internal affairs. Washington kept him informed on much of the business of the Virginia House of Burgesses, either by means of the frequent visits the two men paid each other or by letter. Jack and school matters necessitated much correspondence, and Boucher often received letters requesting assistance in expediting sundry other matters.[15] Thus Boucher was in touch in informal ways with a man prominent in Virginia affairs, and little of importance in Tidewater politics escaped his attention. He subscribed to the *Virginia Gazette* and kept abreast of the published news in spite of the somewhat erratic delivery of the paper.

Washington had expressed the hope that Mount Vernon would often have the pleasure of the company of Boucher and his wife, and accordingly he extended an invitation to them two months after their wedding to be guests, along with Robert Eden, at the plantation on the Potomac. A month later, on 4-5 September, Boucher and Nelly entertained George and Martha Washington and Benedict Calvert, a member of the Maryland Provincial Council and a relative of the proprietor's family. Calvert's second daughter Nelly was also a house guest. Hospitable occasions of this kind provided opportunities for Jack Custis to see Nelly Calvert, whose charms had not escaped his notice. Young Benedict Calvert also was a student member of Boucher's household, a situation which provided further opportunities for the romance between Nelly and Jack to blossom. However, Jack was careful for the moment not to make his interest in the young lady too obvious. Instead, he nicely deceived Boucher by deliberately cultivating Betsy Calvert, Nelly's older sister.

As the Christmas season of 1772 approached, Washington sent his carriage for Boucher, his wife Nelly, and Jinny to celebrate the holiday at Mount Vernon. The occasion gave Washington the opportunity to discuss with Boucher a tentative plan to enroll Jack in college. For some time Washington had been turning over this idea in his mind, for he was still dissatisfied with Jack's academic performance. In his opinion, Jack knew "little arithmetic," was still "ignorant of Greek," was "little farther in Latin," "knew no French," and in general gave "poor attention to studies."[16] Washington now determined to act, and consulted Boucher about a suitable college.

Boucher first recommended William and Mary College for its Anglican background and its proximity to home. However, both men had heard rumors about the lowered standards of that institution and it was agreed that Washington would make discreet inquiries at Williamsburg. In early January 1773 Washington reported regretfully to Boucher that the rumors of mismanagement of the college (inattention of the masters and too many holidays) were true.[17] Washington now asked Boucher what he thought of the College of New Jersey, but Boucher's caustic criticism of it quickly persuaded Washington to drop that idea. The two men next weighed the merits of the College of Philadelphia, but again Boucher found himself opposed. Instead he suggested King's College in New York. Philadelphia, Boucher suggested, was a "large, populous, thriving, commercial city," but nothing more, whereas New York was all of those things and offered other attractions as well. The city had a substantial aristocracy of wealth and influence; it was a magnet for strangers of distinction and the headquarters of the military. In Boucher's opinion, Manhattan was "the most fashionable and polite place on the continent," and it would provide the best substitute for the Grand Tour which had once been projected.[18]

Boucher took the moment to deliver himself of some frank ideas about American education in general. Too many colleges, he complained, seemed to produce young gentlemen educated with a kind of "smattering of every thing" who were "with very few exceptions, arrant coxcombs." The College of Philadelphia in particular seemed to foster this spirit, while King's College, Boucher thought, was less vulnerable to criticism on this account. The Dulanys and Henry Addison were thinking seriously of sending their sons to the college in New York.[19] In a spirit of helpfulness, Boucher offered to write a letter of introduction either to Smith or to Cooper at New York. He also expressed an interest in accompanying Washington and Jack on the prospective trip north in order that Boucher might seek treatment for an indisposition of one of his eyes. In a short time the Washingtons decided in favor of New York and plans were made accordingly for Washington to accompany Jack to New York about the first of May.

Early in April, the Washington family was completely surprised to learn that Jack and Nelly Calvert were engaged. Boucher had been caught wholly off guard and had known nothing of the affair until he was informed by Governor Eden. In some embarrassment, he wrote to Washington explaining, "On my word and honor . . . never till that moment had I the most distant suspicion of any such things being in agitation." He had repeatedly warned Jack, he assured Washington, "of the hazard every man must necessarily run who precipitates himself into so important an attachment, ere the judgment be fully matured." In an attempt to soothe Washington, Boucher suggested that rash though the en-

135

gagement might be in some respects, it might provide some advantage to Jack's morals, and enable him "to collect the dissipated powers of his mind" and apply himself once again to his studies. Jack had admitted to Boucher that he had been unable to concentrate for nearly a year because of the "impression of this passion." Boucher was not particularly pleased that Jack had not taken him into his confidence, for he thought that their friendship should have entitled him to that. However, he decided not to make a great point of the matter, reminding Washington that Jack had also neglected to inform his own family. If Washington appeared to be forgiving of a "breach of duty," then Boucher could forbear "murmurings" about a breach of friendship.[20]

Meanwhile an amiable but cautious Washington had written to Benedict Calvert, the young lady's father. After turning the matter over in his mind, Washington evidently thought there might be advantages in the union, for he wrote, "an alliance with your family will be pleasing to his." But he added the warning that Jack's youth and inexperience would be an insuperable obstacle to a happy marriage. He suggested that the wedding ought to be postponed until some time in the future. With some bluntness, Washington then raised the question of Nelly's dowry. Jack was a wealthy man. His estate consisted of about 15,000 acres of land in and around Williamsburg, between two and three hundred Negro slaves, and about eight or ten thousand pounds loaned out to merchants. In addition, Washington informed Calvert coolly, Jack would fall heir to his mother's estate at her death. "You will readily acknowledge," he concluded, that such an estate "ought to entitle him to a handsome portion in a wife." Washington added that he "should never require a child of my own to make a sacrifice of himself to interest, so neither do I think it incumbent on me to recommend it as a guardian." He hoped that at the proper time Calvert "would also be willing to do something genteel" with respect to a dower for his daughter.[21]

Washington insisted that the youth enter King's College despite his engagement. The pair left for New York in May, arriving on the twenty-sixth. Custis took up residence in the college and arrangements were made for him to dine in the college hall with the professors and President Cooper. In July Jack wrote his guardian that he was settled and dutifully attending classes in mathematics, languages, and moral and experimental philosophy. He hoped his progress would do credit to Washington for "the parental care and attention" which the colonel had always shown him. Jack added condolences for the recent death of his sister Patsy, which had occurred on 19 June 1773 in the midst of "one of her usual fits." He had been "too much agitated" to write any "comfort to my distressed parent" at the time, and had by his own account given himself up "entirely to melancholy for several days." He urged that Washington bring his mother to New York in order to remove her from the scene of Patsy's death, where everything "must put her in mind of her late loss."[22] The projected visit did not materialize.

To Boucher's surprise, Jack at first devoted himself seriously to his studies. Perhaps there were fewer distractions in New York. John Vardill of the college wrote the Washingtons in September 1773, complimenting them on the boy's conduct. Somewhat astonishingly, he wrote that Jack seemed to have espoused "remarkable purity of morals" and had eschewed pleasure for constancy to his studies.[23] The Washingtons must have wondered if Vardill had been carried away by his desire for a good relationship with the Virginia squire, or if he had confused Jack with some other student. Possibly Jack's engagement inspired him to apply himself and to prove his worth.

One thing is certain; Jack received special attention at the college at the behest of Boucher. He was exempted from the strict academic discipline applied to other boys because he was so unlike the others and had "been so much in company." He was allowed to attend any lectures he wished to hear, "without regard to *classes*," and Cooper assured Boucher that he would have private instruction from himself and the other professors. Cooper also arranged to get a private room for Jack. Cooper admitted that all of this was "an indulgence we have never yet shewn," but he thought Jack seemed deserving. Although he also said he wanted to please Boucher, another factor may have influenced him to do so much more for Jack than he had earlier been willing to concede at Boucher's request. Washington was already a figure of some prominence and undoubtedly his stepson benefited.[24]

In spite of this promising beginning, Custis's formal education came to an abrupt end three months later when he dropped out of King's College to marry Nelly Calvert. Washington informed Cooper in December 1773 that he had yielded to Jack much against his own judgment. The colonel could no longer hold out in the face of Jack's "inclination, the desires of his mother and the acquiescence of almost all his relatives."[25] By January Jack was back in Virginia, and on 3 February 1774 Boucher's socially prominent but difficult student married Eleanor Calvert.

Meanwhile, Boucher's relationship with his neighbors in Prince George's County continued much as they had begun. Boucher had taken "the more pains" to minimize the difficulties he had experienced on his arrival, but he would not make the "least concession" in his principles. Slowly he had "made a little party" among his parishioners and was now able to get through the months with "tolerable quiet, though never with much comfort." He thought it impossible to become popular in such times with neighbors who were a "singularly violent, purse-proud, and factious people" (*Rem.*, p. 74). The lack of popularity might have worried a lesser man than Boucher, but he was no ordinary one. Those who knew him well recognized that he was "possessed of a strong mind;" he formed his opinions "calmly, and expressed them frankly and fearlessly." He was a "thoroughly honest" individual, and never one to sacrifice his convictions.[26]

In spite of less than affable personal relationships, Boucher had managed his financial affairs rather well. Although he still owed money to James, he told him on 16 November 1773 that he was "fairly worth £3,000." Like most planters in the South, he lacked liquid assets. "This is a terrible country for matters of this sort," he asserted. "The property one gets in it" is no more use in "cases of exigency" than were the property to consist of "the golden sheep of El Dorado." The lack of cash often made his situation "distressful" (*MHM* 8:182).

When Boucher was not worrying about disagreeable neighbors or wishing for more liquid assets, he fretted about the numerous Dissenters "of the true, Puritan, or rather independent republican spirit" who posed what he believed to be a serious threat. These Dissenters had planted schools, colleges, and churches "in every corner" and openly taught principles subversive of "good government," he told James. He disapproved of a commencement oration recently given at the College of New Jersey by a student who denounced the king for consenting to laws so oppressive to America that he put himself in violation of the compact between monarch and subjects. The result, the student pointed out, was that the king had thus forfeited "all title to allegiance." The compact was void. It seemed incongruous to Boucher that such statements were being made openly while yet the "poor Church of England, loyally and truly teaching" obedience to the state, was being "cruelly kept under by withholding from her an episcopate" which would give her "consequence and stability." The Anglican church, in Boucher's opinion, was no longer suffering merely from the minor ailments of a chronically fevered body politic; she was acutely ill. He feared for the very life of the church (*MHM* 8:183-84).

Boucher was enjoying his final days of peace in America, although he was on the edge of trouble as the political situation grew more ominous. He had had no wish to engage himself in politics per se. He had embroiled himself in the newspaper battle with Paca and Chase for what seemed to him to be nonpolitical reasons; his opposition to the measures being taken against the church and his advocacy of an American bishop. His political philosophy had not yet been called into question, although it is clear that Boucher was becoming more and more concerned about the tenor of the political theories being expressed so freely in America. Once a liberal and nascent Patriot in Virginia, Boucher's latent conservatism had been bolstered by the economic and social developments in his life and by his close relationship with the establishment in Maryland. His position in Maryland was conservative in relationship to Maryland's internal politics, but had not yet been called into sharp focus with respect to transatlantic affairs.

The encounter with the two chief Whig lawyers of Maryland may well have initiated the crystallization of Boucher's political thought. His defense of the church irretrievably committed him to the defense of royal authority, precisely at a time when such a position was under attack. It required him to think carefully about the resistance to the constitution of the church and about its implications as a training ground for civil resistance. The groundwork was now laid for an even more searching examination later of the problem of liberty versus licentiousness. Whatever might have been the political road for Boucher before 1773, the events of that year had both triggered his political thinking and narrowed his choices.

⌒ Chapter 7 ⌒
Year of Crisis: 1774

The year of decision for the colonies was 1774. So Boucher believed at the time and in retrospect. The call to a congress and the economic boycott directed against Britain were decisions of "the highest moment," affecting "the very vitals of our Constitution," and putting America beyond hope of any accommodation with the mother country (*Rem.*, p. 128). As political events rapidly accelerated in the wake of the Boston Port Act, Boucher attempted to maintain a semblance of political neutrality, although his position already was essentially conservative. The colonial reaction to the British punitive measures worried him acutely and kept him "in a state of constant fever" (*Rem.*, p. 93). He questioned the legality and constitutionality of many of the measures to which the colonies resorted; in the stressful process his views crystallized on the side of conservatism.

The early part of 1774 was relatively quiet in Maryland and hardly prepared Boucher for the hectic months that followed. In the first five months of the year Marylanders were largely absorbed with internal interests and paid little attention to political affairs outside the colony. The clerical salary question continued to smolder, while Boucher quietly did his best to have the recent Vestry Act altered. The plight of the clerics seemed bleak enough, but in Boucher's opinion should the Vestry Act remain law it would soon produce even more adverse effects. In many Maryland parishes, he confided on 14 February 1774 to Rev. William Smith in Philadelphia, the new salaries would be inadequate for decent support, particularly because the cost of living was now rising rapidly. The Vestry Act, in his opinion, had done violence to the public faith. Worse yet, it would pave the way for additional "new modellings and reformation" by which, he thought, the church would soon cease to be an establishment (*MHM* 8:235-37).

Boucher's dim view of the state of clerical affairs was not shared by all Anglican clergymen. The Reverend John Montgomery, writing to Boucher with the hope of lifting his friend's spirits, expressed the belief that "some of the leading men in our Lower House" had promised to see to it that the act was modified in the approaching session. The letter failed to convince Boucher, who concluded that Montgomery was naive about the aims and schemes of politicians and had been taken in by either an empty promise or a mere rumor. Never one to neglect an opportunity, however, Boucher thought he saw an opening to exploit even the rumored possibility of an amendment to the objectionable act. Knowing that Paca was a key delegate in the lower house, Boucher immediately wrote to Smith, encouraging him to draft a letter to Paca urging a change in the law.[1] Such a move would be an expedient one, Boucher wrote, adding that Paca would have "no little regard to your judgment on such a question." He conceded that of late he had been forced "as a public man" to oppose Paca "with warmth," but Boucher assured Smith, with less than his usual candor, that "in the main, I take him to be good-natured and friendly" and likely to be "easily influenced" by such a letter (*MHM* 8:236). Smith obliged Boucher with the letter to Paca, but to no avail.[2]

Although Boucher seized every chance to improve matters in his battle for the clerical salaries, he had pinned his best hopes on a court test of the act. He and his colleagues of like opinion had retained legal counsel at a very considerable cost and had instituted a suit which their counsel had assured them would determine the validity of the Vestry Act. Unfortunately, the rising revolutionary crisis gave their lawyers cold feet. They refused to try the case, "alleging that it was *unpopular*, and that they would not incur the popular odium." The hopes of the clergy were suddenly "blasted" and Boucher was now in despair. He feared the worst; the House of Delegates might "*resolve* not to pay us anything at all" (*MHM* 8:237-40).

The Vestry Act affair, taken by and large, had been a disas-

[handwritten margin note: Commentary on effect of rev.]

trous one for the Maryland clergy, but Boucher consoled himself that his own losses were limited. He had suffered a nominal loss by the reduction of his parish salary from £500 to £250, but since in fact he had received no salary in nearly three years this blow was more theoretical than real.[3] Boucher's success as a planter and the prosperity and estate his new wife had brought him were ample compensation for a salary he had never collected.

Boucher's principal occupation that spring and summer, and he found it a pleasant one indeed, was the development of a newly acquired plantation. For some time he had been looking about for a good plantation to purchase, and an opportunity presented itself in June 1773, when Nelly's improvident brother John Addison, owner of the Lodge on the banks of the Potomac across from Alexandria, was obliged to part with his patrimony to satisfy his creditors. Addison's estate had for some time been in the hands of trustees, of whom Boucher was one. Their efforts to preserve the estate from dissolution were unsuccessful and in the summer of 1773 it was necessary to sell the estate at auction. In an ethically questionable transaction, Boucher, Samuel Hanson, and Thomas Addison purchased the property for £2,500. The three men thus found themselves in possession of about 1,000 acres of land, buildings, and some twenty-six slaves and their "future increase," as well as an additional 72½ acre tract in Locust Thickett.[4] Hanson and Addison, however, failed to hold up their end of the bargain, and the original contract of sale fell through. Nelly, who loved the estate and grieved to think of her brother's patrimony falling into the hands of strangers, then persuaded Boucher to purchase it on his own. Borrowing £1,500 and adding to it £500 of his own capital, Boucher acquired the deed on 29 December 1773 at the much reduced price of £2,000.[5] At last he could anticipate a home of his own.

Boucher had always believed in "making great attempts," and this venture was no exception (*MHM* 10:36). The plantation challenged him, and he was prepared to make a major investment in time, money, and planning. Time was less a problem than it had earlier been because his clerical duties had changed. He had found his role in his own parish in Prince George's County so onerous because of dissident parishioners that he retreated from his duties there, leaving the parish in charge of his curate, Rev. Edward Gantt.[6] He then assumed the responsibilities of curate to his friend Rev. Henry Addison, rector of Saint John's in Prince George's Parish. Capital also posed no particular problem, for his credit was firmly established. Although he was already in debt for the original purchase, he nevertheless invested sizable sums of money to carry out his varied and extensive plans, and he soon had more than doubled his plantation investment.[7]

With a fair amount of imagination and a strong sense of the need for soil conservation which he had found sadly lacking in the Tidewater area, Boucher set about the task of planning the operation of his new estate. Within a year after he acquired it, Boucher had reclaimed forty acres of meadowland and planted it in timothy. Several large swamps were grubbed and cleared and new fences installed around the grounds. On the sloping land along the river opposite Alexandria he built a delightful falling garden. He continued to plant tobacco, but he was determined to avoid relying solely on tobacco culture, and he put several hundred acres into grain. In anticipation of a good cereal crop, he built a millrace nearly a mile in length and contracted for the construction of a gristmill. Meanwhile, he also constructed a large tobacco barn, remodelled the house itself, and "fitted up a handsome library."[8] Most of his slaves were not sufficiently skilled for his ambitious projects and he augmented the labor of three good black craftsmen of his own with that of a hired carpenter, a blacksmith, and a gardener. He acquired in addition five or six white indentured servants, husbandmen and laborers, bringing his total family to above seventy (*Rem.*, p. 94).[9]

Boucher was anxious to move to the Lodge, for it had one further distinct advantage; it lay out of the area which was "much under the influence of those popular lawyers whom I was obliged to oppose." He settled into the newly remodelled mansion in autumn 1774. Much of the work he had planned was well under way, and living now on the premises, he could oversee the operations to advantage. He found such employment congenial to his taste and discovered in its pursuit "more rational pleasure . . . than [in] any others in which I had ever engaged." Boucher obviously enjoyed being a country squire in one of the best tobacco-growing sections of America. He could have been well content, he reflected later, "to have passed through life so employed" (*Rem.*, pp. 93-94). In effect he was a full-time planter and a part-time clergyman.

Boucher's economic position was now solid, but like many

another colonial he saw the opportunities in western land speculation. As an insider in Maryland government and a close friend
of Eden, he had an advantage which he was not likely to overlook.
Although the Proclamation Line of 1763 was still in effect, certain
wealthy speculators were applying for warrants for lands beyond
Fort Cumberland, west of the line beyond which the proclamation
prohibited settlement. In March 1774 Boucher, in partnership with
five other Maryland gentlemen, John Clapham, Robert Smith, James
Brooks, Francis Deakins, and Thomas French, applied for warrants
which they were granted as a "matter of favor."[10] Boucher acquired
additional land on a partnership basis with Francis Deakins. He
ultimately held more than 10,500 acres of good western land, part
of Lord Baltimore's preserve.[11]

Some irregularity must have occurred with respect to the
lands purchased by Boucher and his partners since the patents
were not issued at the usual time. The customary procedure after
securing a warrant for new land was to have it surveyed, after
which a certificate with a full description of the boundaries was
presented to the Land Office for recording. When this was accomplished, the patent was issued. However, Daniel of St. Thomas
Jenifer, Maryland's receiver general and a competent and conscientious man, had objected to the issuance of warrants in disregard
of the Proclamation Line. While George Stewart and Benedict
Calvert, the judges of the Land Office, acquiesced in the grants,
simply accepting the certificates presented for recording, the usual
patents were not issued. Indeed, Boucher still did not have his
patents by the time he left America in 1775. On the other hand,
as a practical matter the lack of patents was not particularly
important. To all intents and purposes those who had purchased
were in full possession of the various properties, and the patent
issuance was treated as a mere formality.[12]

Boucher's western land lay in what was then known as Frederick County. He acquired the first parcel of 4,000 acres on 25
March 1774, and obtained a warrant for a second parcel of approximately 2,000 acres on the following day.[13] He subsequently
purchased 413 acres from one Thomas French on 1 June 1774;
he bought four or five thousand more acres shortly after the first
certificates were filed.[14] Altogether, Boucher held a sizable stake
in western Maryland.

The investment was one on which Boucher realized profits

almost immediately. The value of land in the southern colonies usually rose as soon as it was surveyed, sometimes soaring to a price four times the initial cost. Boucher's land proved to be no exception. As early as July 1774 he found it convenient to sell three parcels of surveyed land in his western holdings in the Mount Airy, Good Hope, and Blooming Rose tracts, a total of 1,884 acres. In March of the following year he sold additional parcels in Crab Orchard and Non Pareil, reducing his holdings in those tracts by 2,185 and 2,482 acres respectively. The rest was still in his possession when he left America and it ultimately became subject to confiscation. As he lamented later in England, had he been able to keep his backlands the remaining 4,000 acres would have been "worth as many guineas" by 1783 (*Rem.*, p. 95).

Although Boucher was extremely busy with his plantation affairs in 1772-74, he found time for a number of personal kindnesses which on occasion caused him no little trouble. One such experience involved orphaned nephews on Nelly's side of the family. Lands belonging to them earlier had been leased to individuals whom Boucher now charged with having committed "sundry trespasses" with impunity. Boucher determined to put a stop to them. The matter was settled by arbitration and heavy damages were awarded to the children's estate. A branch of the Hanson family was involved, one of whose members, John, was to serve as the President of the Continental Congress in 1779. According to Boucher, the trespassers never forgave him and continued to harass him although his only offense was in not permitting them "to wrong my orphan nephews" (*Rem.*, pp. 95-96).[15] The ill will of the Hanson family was compounded by politics, for his antagonists were soon to become active leaders at the county and provincial levels, serving on various committees. From the point of view of political differences, Boucher could scarcely have been more vulnerable.

The whole incident gave Boucher many moments of uneasy reflection. He had antagonized prominent and active members of the community in the process of protecting the interest of the children. He might have anticipated the bad feeling that his action against Hanson was to engender, because it was essentially the same kind of situation he had encountered in Annapolis in pressing for an American resident bishop. He had in no way benefited from the settlement himself, but instead had been damaged per-

145

sonally. As events in Maryland evolved, Boucher came to believe strongly that these "private grudges" actually gave way to "public measures" which adversely affected him. Furthermore, he thought he saw the implications of such grudges to the writing of history. As he reflected later, "Such motives (in my mind by far the most prevalent in all public commotions) lie beyond the reach of ordinary historians; a circumstance that, among others, renders every history I have yet seen or expect soon to see, of the late war, exceedingly unsatisfactory" (*Rem.*, pp. 95-96).

Boucher refused to be intimidated physically, just as he declined to be pressured by the prominence of the Hansons into sacrificing the legal property rights of his wards for his own comfort. While living at Castle Magruder Boucher had demonstrated his ability to stand his ground physically, and in a most unclerical fashion. He had an encounter with a blacksmith into whose property a favorite horse had trespassed through a broken fence. The irate blacksmith shot the horse in Nelly's sight and then became abusive about her husband. Still angry, the smith came to Boucher, shaking a stick in one hand and carrying a gun in the other, while swearing and promising that "by G—d he would serve me as he had served my horse." Finding the fellow's fist in his face, Boucher feared he would be struck; being "utterly unused to boxing," he decided that he would have to count on a fast victory. Boucher "struck him but once when 'prostrate he fell and measured o'er a length of ground.' " Boucher earned an unexpected amount of credit from what he described as a lucky blow. He commented later with sardonic amusement upon a society in which it was more advantageous to have knocked a man down "than to have been set down as a Newton." But he had to admit that being known as a "d——d fellow" and able to defend himself later proved to be useful (*Rem.*, pp. 114-16).

Boucher's personality was in part responsible for some of his difficulties with his neighbors. He was forthright in expressing his opinion, and he had an opinion on most occasions. He was candid about his own shortcomings, conceding that when "thwarted and opposed" he became "obstinate and mulish." He was aware of the effect which he had on others, and described himself with disarming honesty. "There was nothing quite ordinary or indifferent about me; my faults and my good qualities were all striking. All my friends (and no man ever had more friends) really loved me;

and all my enemies as cordially hated me." At the same time, Boucher thought that there was little that he could not be coaxed into by those he loved. Nelly could at any time laugh him out of his sullen moods, but she always gave him credit for the ability to initiate the overture to a reconciliation when they quarreled (*Rem.*, pp. 80-81).

But Boucher's charm with Nelly and with women in general was little help in dealing with such men as Osborne Sprigg, who apparently found it easier to "cordially hate" him. Sprigg was a planter who was soon to become a warm Patriot, a member of several committees, and a leader of the militia. The enmity between the two men arose from a simple business transaction with an unnamed planter. Boucher had arranged for a purchase of corn, but had refused to accept delivery on the ground that it was in such poor condition that it was "not marketable." Sprigg, hearing of the incident, made a great outcry, although he was hardly the aggrieved party. Sprigg's developing political power did not deter Boucher from insisting on a fair bargain. It was not to be Boucher's last encounter with Sprigg; once more a private quarrel was to cost him dearly in the future.

Thus far in the spring of 1774 Boucher's difficulties with his neighbors had been for the most part personal. But like other Marylanders, while he was absorbed in his own concerns he was also becoming increasingly involved in Maryland politics. For some three years intercolonial and imperial developments had elicited little response in the colony. The Tea Act had caused no great consternation. The House of Delegates had passed no resolutions, nor had there been any flood of letters to the newspapers. But the shocking news of the Boston Port Act abruptly shattered the parochial insulation of the colony.

As dramatically as a release of adrenalin in a lethargic body, the arrival of the *Circular Letter* from Boston on 24 May 1774 and the printing of the full text of the Boston Port Act in the *Gazette* on 26 May energized Marylanders. Baltimore, which first received the news from Boston, within hours selected a local committee to correspond with other colonies and enacted a resolution supporting the cause of Boston as the cause of all. On 25 May eighty Annapolitans assembled and passed a series of resolutions adopting the cause of Boston and urging unity among the colonies in pressing for repeal of the Port Act. They committed themselves to the concept of a general nonimportation and nonexportation agreement; they approved of a provincial and a continental association "under oath"; they declared their readiness to break off all trade and dealings with "that colony, county, or town that should refuse to enter such an Association." To implement this last resolution, each county was advised to elect a committee of correspondence. The committee should be empowered to keep abreast of events and to elect representatives to a general meeting of all county committees to be held at Annapolis on 22 June 1774. On the following day the Annapolis committee of correspondence sent off a draft of its resolutions to the Baltimore committee. The Annapolitans also selected a committee of five to work with other local committees to expedite "such association as will best secure American liberty."[16] Following the directive of the Annapolis committee of correspondence, meetings were held at the county level in May and in early June, and delegates to a projected provincial convention were elected.[17]

Boucher took little comfort when he saw the names of those who had been elected to the forthcoming convention, for they included some who bore him considerable enmity. Prince George's County included Osborne Sprigg among its eight delegates, while Anne Arundel County and Annapolis numbered among their ten delegates both Samuel Chase and William Paca.[18] Even the Charles County committee chose an old enemy of Boucher, William Smallwood, who still bore Boucher some ill will in the aftermath of the broken romance with Judith Chase. Boucher singled out the delegation from his own county and Annapolis for particular criticism, bemoaning the fact that "Out of the whole county there were but thirteen electors, and in Annapolis there were but four" (Rem., p. 121). The small number of electors from Prince George's County should have given him no surprise. He had exhorted his flock to abstain from attending the extralegal meetings and recalled with pleasure later that not one of his parishioners had attended. Under the circumstances, Boucher waited for the results of the first Provincial Convention at Annapolis with little enthusiasm and much apprehension.

Ninety-two deputies assembled in convention at Annapolis and sat 22–25 June 1774. This body purported to be a representative one elected in the usual way by the freemen of the counties. But the convention's claims to legitimacy hardly reassured Boucher, who firmly believed that the group sitting in Annapolis was neither representative nor legitimate. The whole committee process, he insisted, was novel and not known to the laws of the land or the Constitution (*Rem.*, p. 128).

The Maryland Convention promptly endorsed the plan for a boycott of England's commerce and a union of the colonies to enforce it, initiated a subscription in the various counties for the poor of Boston, and appointed delegates to attend a general congress of deputies from the colonies, if and when such a congress were agreed upon. Boucher's unease was compounded when the names of the delegates who were to attend the congress at Philadelphia in September were announced: William Paca, Samuel Chase, Thomas Johnson, Robert Goldsborough and Matthew Tilghman. They were all Country party men. Boucher expected the worst when he found his most bitter opponents, Paca and Chase, now in positions of considerable prestige and potential power. The actions which Boucher decried had put Maryland into the mainstream of colonial events. But those same events were more than a protest against British policy and actions; they aimed a telling blow at the old feudal arrangements of Lord Baltimore's proprietorship. Long decades of House of Delegates' dissent now came to fruition in the revolutionary movement. The final process of usurpation of power in the colony had begun.

However, there were no spectacular developments immediately. A period of relative quiet descended on Maryland after the June convention, during which the various offices of the proprietary government resumed normal business. Marylanders looked forward to the congress at Philadelphia with various moods—some with hopeful expectation, others, like Boucher, with trepidation.

Boucher pondered the lack of constitutional legitimacy for a meeting of the colonies called merely upon their own initiative. He considered the Maryland committee to be without legitimate foundation, and so too the proposed congress at Philadelphia. However, he viewed the September meeting as vastly more dangerous, its potential for mischief being greatly increased by its intercolonial nature. He feared also that the radical composition of the Maryland delegation to the September meeting would be duplicated in other colonies. Although Boucher entertained serious misgivings about the impending congress and its possible actions, he was as yet by no means wholly unsympathetic to the American position.

149

He had been dubious about the wisdom of British policy at times
in the past, and he now doubted the prudence and practicality
of the British measures which had produced the present crisis. His
thinking was probably not unlike that of Daniel Dulany, and
indeed may have been influenced by the Maryland secretary general, whose opinion he respected.

Dulany believed that Parliament had gone beyond what was
sensible and practical in its relationship with the colonies.[19] He
had spoken frequently in the past against tampering with colonial
charters, and now Parliament had moved against Massachusetts,
destroying her colonial government. Basic constitutional issues were
involved, not the least of which was the exempting of certain persons from trial by jury in the colony where the offense was committed. Given Dulany's position, it was not surprising that he was
among the eighty residents of Annapolis who had spontaneously
gathered to protest the treatment of Massachusetts in a resolution
which declared that Boston was suffering in the common cause
of America. A second resolution calling for the cessation of trade
with Great Britain had posed a problem for him. He dreaded
the consequences, but had reluctantly advised in favor of the
resolution.

The real dilemma for Dulany lay in the matter of a continental
association. Like Boucher, Dulany objected to an organization of
this kind, believing that "extra legal authorities could lead only
to difficulties at home and would certainly offend the Ministry
and Parliament." This was the point at which Dulany drew a
sharp line, beyond it he could not subscribe to the Whig position,
confiding privately to Edward Lloyd, a recent Country party
member, that "a petition and remonstrance from Congress to the
King and Parliament was the properest mode of proceeding to
obtain redress."[20]

The actions in the various colonies looking toward a boycott
were no surprise to Boucher, for he considered them to be the
inevitable result of England's "strange inattention" to her colonies.
Boucher had warned his friend James on 16 November 1773 that
England, "without seeing, or at least without attending to it" was
"suffering a strange refractory spirit to grow up which ere long
will work her irremediable woe" (*MHM* 8:183-84). Now in 1774,
both the Continental Association and the network of extralegal
local committees appeared to Boucher to be a flowering of the

150

same spirit of growing colonial autonomy which England had allowed to go unchecked for so long. Such independence of spirit, he thought, left little room for mediation or accommodation. If it prevailed in Philadelphia in September he feared it might very well lead to reckless action which would jeopardize the outlook for a peaceful redress of grievances. In an attempt to avert such a development, he counseled caution from his pulpit and adopted the watchwords "sit still."

Recognizing the limitations of his pulpit appeals, Boucher at last resorted to his pen to gain a wider audience for his call to caution, reason, and accommodation. To conceal his identity and his Maryland residence, in order both to protect himself from his neighbors and to enhance the effectiveness of his message, Boucher assumed the stance of a Virginian and wrote a multipage pamphlet addressed to the members of the congress about to assemble at Philadelphia.[21] It is easy to understand why Boucher chose to write as a Virginian. He had lived in that colony from 1759 to 1770, and in 1774 was living just across the Potomac from Alexandria, Virginia. He was aware of the increasing difficulty of finding a press willing to print conservative articles. Jonas Green, the printer at Annapolis, seemed unlikely to publish the pamphlet considering his delicate position. Even had Green agreed to risk the displeasure of the various local committees, Boucher's anonymity would have been less secure with a printer so close at hand. No doubt he recalled his earlier experience when his attempt at anonymity in the *Virginia Gazette* during the Routledge murder case had failed and his identity had become known to Landon Carter. He finally sent it to Rivington in New York for printing.

The *Letter from a Virginian*, as Boucher titled his pamphlet, preserved a tone of careful neutrality and presented a reasoned argument against the adoption of nonimportation and nonexportation agreements. Reminding the members of the Continental Congress that they were not about to assemble by "any formal, constitutional authority nor invested with any legislative powers," he cautioned against precipitate decisions, for "your opinions will have the effect of laws on the minds of the people, and your resolves may decide the fate of America."[22] Boucher urged the delegates to give careful thought to the colonial charters, which he held to be of fundamental importance. Based on his own understanding of the charters and the conditions under which they had been granted, he argued the indivisible character of sovereignty in the empire and the obligation of subjects to give their obedience to the laws of the supreme power. Until lately, he asserted, the supreme power of Parliament over her colonies had been generally acknowledged. There had been no pretense of infallibility on Britain's part, and free British subjects had retained their legal right of petitioning, remonstrating, and of proposing plans of reformation and redress, but Britain's sovereign supremacy, Boucher was convinced, had been beyond challenge.

He then attempted to minimize the nature of the present crisis. The closing of Boston's port, he suggested, was but a temporary measure and its importance ought not be exaggerated. The tea tax itself was but "a trifling duty, on a luxury, unknown to nine-tenths of the globe." Protest by means of an economic boycott was fraught with danger. It was a delusion to believe that the colonies could exert enough pressure on Britain for repeal of the tea tax and the Intolerable Acts, although they had been successful with the Stamp Tax. The acts themselves were totally different in their principles, while the various colonial arguments and claims which had been used so effectively in 1765 were now inapplicable. Moreover, he warned, a great nation like Great Britain would not submit to bullying and thereby expose itself to the scorn of rival kingdoms in Europe.

The case for a boycott, he cautioned, was also weak. The basic assumption behind nonimportation was that the commerce of the colonies with Great Britain was sufficient to make its cessation an effective coercive device. Boucher thought this assumption unsound in any event. But even assuming its validity, the technique itself was unfair. Was it just to ruin or obstruct the trade of a fellow citizen "by the intrigues of a cabal, by innuendoes, insinuations," or threats? "Shall we levy a tax upon these innocent citizens, a tax unheard of, disproportionate, a tax never suggested by the most inhuman tyrant? A tax, to the amount of their daily bread?" Another pitfall was the highly developed colonial art of smuggling. "In all trading nations, where there are duties or prohibitions, there are smugglers, there ever were, and ever will be, until we find some nation where every individual is a patriot or a saint." Too often even a "trifling extraordinary profit" proved to be an "irresistible temptation" to some; with the substance of thousands at stake, what could the colonists expect from a "loose agreement?" A boycott, he thought, could be an unequal contest in which "while we are giving [Britain] a slight wound, we receive a mortal one."

But the major plea of the letter was for the formulation of some practical plan of accommodation. He reminded the delegates that taxation and government were inseparable. Boucher urged the delegates to devise some means of reconciling taxation, "the indispensable obligation of every subject," with colonists' ideas of the "peculiar and inestimable rights of an Englishman." His first practical plan of accommodation involved soliciting actual representation in Parliament, in place of the virtual representation to which the colonists objected so strenuously.[23] His second suggestion was a proposal by the colonies of "some adequate, permanent, and effectual supply" of money in place of the "uncertain, ineffectual requisitions"—a step which would obviate the necessity of taxation on the part of Britain.

Boucher's final suggestion was a negative one: avoid the "horrors of civil war." He reminded the delegates of the peculiar vulnerability of the South, of the Indians on the frontier, and of the enemy within (the slaves). He foresaw the ruin of trade, the surrender of ports and capitals, and the "misery of thousands." Why risk the "inestimable blessings" enjoyed by Americans who were happy in comparison to the "wretchedness of peoples over nine-tenths of the globe?" A man like Joseph Galloway would have understood what Boucher meant, but men of the stamp of Paca, Chase, Johnson, Goldsborough, and Tilghman were bound to give his comparison and his worries scant consideration.

Boucher and other conservatives who had earlier doubted the wisdom of convening such an assemblage were far from reassured by the deliberations of Congress at Philadelphia. Although news of that body's debates and actions was handled carefully and with great political acumen, particularly on the part of the popular leaders, one development that became known in mid-September was disquieting. Congress had approved the Suffolk Resolves and had ordered them published in newspapers and in handbills.[24] Conservatives both in and out of Congress soon realized that the Resolves in effect came dangerously close to an assertion of colonial independence and might well pave the way for war. This, then, was just the kind of mischief which Boucher had feared might develop in such a body. Although he could only speculate on the prospect for an economic boycott, he could hardly hope with much realism that his words of caution against one would now prevail. The spirit of accommodation had been dealt a blow. He feared that the damage was irreparable.

Meanwhile, Boucher turned his attention to Maryland affairs, where the radically controlled committees were not waiting for directions from Philadelphia and had seized the initiative. In August 1774, the brigantine *Mary and Jane* arrived in port with a cargo of tea, but the Frederick County committee compelled it to sail back to England with the cargo undischarged. So enthusiastic were the committees' operations that it was difficult even for sympathizers with the boycott to avoid trouble. Anthony Stewart, a merchant and owner of the brigantine *Peggy Stewart* and a member of the nonimportation association, learned this to his dismay. His ship arrived in port on 14 October 1774 with a consignment of tea as part of her cargo, although he himself was not the consignee. Inspection revealed water leaking into the hold, and in order to save the rest of the cargo from damage Stewart paid the tax on the tea in preparation for unloading. His mistake was in not first consulting the Annapolis committee.

A general meeting of the citizens censured the action taken by Stewart and a larger meeting of county delegates was called to consider the matter. Stewart prepared a "vindication" and had a promise that it would be inserted in the *Maryland Gazette*.[25] However Jonas Green, the printer, was threatened with destruction of his press if he dared print it. When questioned by the county committee, Stewart offered to burn the tea publicly, but the mood of the meeting was ugly and no one was inclined to listen to him, particularly the Baltimore men. Whether the vessel should be destroyed was debated by the committee and the overwhelming majority said no. However Stewart, who correctly gauged the public temper, boarded the *Peggy Stewart* on 19 October, drove her aground, and burned his ship to the water's edge. The *Maryland Gazette* hailed Stewart's patriotic gesture and desire to maintain public tranquillity, adding that he had in mind his personal safety also.[26]

The summer and fall were disquieting seasons for Boucher in which political opinions seriously affected his social life. At a large dinner party attended by relatives and friends of various

154

political attitudes, Boucher encountered Osborne Sprigg again. Dr. Richard Brooke, whom Boucher considered a "well-meaning, sensible, but blundering man," offered a toast: "May the Americans all hang together in accord and concord!" Boucher, without a moment's hesitation and "prompted no doubt by my evil genius," glibly supplied a bon mot: "in any cord, Doctor, so it be but a strong cord" (*Rem.*, pp. 116-17).

humour

Boucher somehow managed to talk himself out of this situation, but Sprigg, in no peacemaking mood as far as Boucher was concerned, was determined to precipitate a quarrel and offered a toast of his own: "Damnation to General Gage, the troops under his command, and all who wish well to them." Predictably Boucher refused to drink to such a toast, which further outraged Sprigg, prompting him to threaten several times to strike Boucher in spite of the rest of the company who were trying to restrain him. Boucher calmly and patronizingly suggested that they not worry. He had observed Sprigg swallowing "large draughts of wine" to render himself "pot-valiant." Boucher urged them to " 'sit still,' " assuring them that " 'the gentlemen will not think of coming near me.' " Sprigg, having had some second thoughts, now recollected that "bruising" was ungentlemanly and that Boucher "was said to have studied under Broughton" and therefore might possibly be "an over-match for him." Shifting his tactics, Sprigg told Boucher that he would hear from him the next morning *as a gentleman*, to which Boucher coolly replied that he would be at home all the next day, but since he had never yet heard of Sprigg having acted "in any instance *as a gentleman*," it would be exceedingly surprising if he heard from him in the morning (*Rem.*, pp. 117-18). No second arrived in the morning to arrange a duel, but the enmity between the two men persisted, and Boucher had taken on a formidable antagonist who would soon have tremendous power in Maryland.

The activities of Maryland's committees gave Boucher additional cause for concern. He still considered them illegitimate and a dangerous innovation, too quick to resort to coercion in situations such as the *Peggy Stewart* affair. Marylanders had had ample experience with extralegal committees during the crisis following the Townshend Acts. The targets then had been factors whose goods were appropriated and put in storage. The principal center of activity had been in the prime tobacco cultivation section of the Western Shore, Anne Arundel County and Boucher's own Prince George's County.

Perhaps his most disquieting thought concerned the similarities in composition between the old and new committees. The Sprigg family, for example, had furnished members in 1768 and now. In late 1774 the committees formed by Marylanders confined their activities to disputed incoming cargoes. But this situation altered rapidly with the adoption by the Continental Congress of an economic boycott.

The most crucial measure adopted by Congress, the Association, had been prepared by four members of Congress who were in favor of radical action, one of whom was Maryland's own delegate Thomas Johnson. The measure was debated from 15 October on and was passed and ready for signing on the twentieth. Effective 1 December 1774, the colonies would cease importation of all goods from Britain and Ireland, East India tea from any section of the world, certain products from the British West Indies and Dominica, foreign indigo, and wines from Madeira. The importation of slaves also was to stop, as would all commerce with those who continued in the slave trade.[27] Those who imported goods between 1 December 1774 and 1 February 1775 could reship the merchandise or let the local committee either store the goods during nonimportation or arrange for sale, with any profit beyond cost to owners being designated for the relief of Boston. After 1 February there were to be no alternatives; goods would be shipped back immediately.

Ancillary to nonimportation was nonconsumption, which was to become effective 1 March 1775. Nonexportation was not to be effective until 10 September 1775. The latter measure had been more hotly debated than nonimportation, and along sectional lines, primarily because southern planters were accustomed to harvesting crops both in the spring and in early summer and did not wish to suffer any disadvantage compared with their northern counterparts. The later effective date of nonexportation represented a compromise on this point.

Congress, having assumed a legislative function by adoption of the Association, then arrogated to itself enforcement powers by calling for the establishment of committees in "every county, city, and town" in America, each charged with the duty of enforcement of the Association. In response to the directive of the

Continental Congress, the Maryland Convention set up new committees. In each county, freemen qualified to vote for representatives to the old House of Delegates met at the courthouse and appointed a committee to "observe the conduct of all persons touching this Association" and to carry Association terms into effect. Each county, following Convention instructions, also selected a committee of correspondence, charged with the duty of "inspecting the entries of their custom-houses and informing each other, from time to time, of the true state thereof, and of every other material circumstance that may occur relative to the Association," following the recommendation of the Continental Congress.[28] Before adjourning each county meeting also selected delegates for the next Provincial Convention, which would convene on 21 November 1774.

Boucher's own county, Prince George's, selected eight of its citizens, including Osborne Sprigg and Edward Sprigg, to sit among the fifty-seven delegates, who attended the Maryland Convention when it opened in Annapolis.[29] A principal item of business was the passage of a resolution stating that "every person in the Province ought, strictly and inviolably to observe, and carry into execution, the Association agreed on by the said Continental Congress."[30] A second session, with eighty-five delegates in attendance, passed a resolution ordering Marylanders to obey strictly and carry out the Association's mandate. The Maryland Convention elaborated upon a variety of economic measures, designed to encourage self-sufficiency and to maintain an effective boycott, including encouragement for home manufacture of woolens, linens, and cottons, the production of flax and hemp, and the establishment of a percentage scale for price increases. This last was necessary since earlier suggestions to merchants that they refrain from raising prices had been disregarded. Other resolutions arranged for the raising of a provincial militia and authorized the various county committees to obtain in any manner they saw fit a sum of money based upon their proportion of Maryland's population. The convention set an overall goal of £10,000 for this purpose. Anticipating some objections to the enforcement of its resolutions, the convention also resolved that no lawyer "ought to prosecute a suit in favor of the offender, in those cases where the county committee declared a breach of Resolutions." It then appointed delegates for the next Continental Congress to be held in May 1775, and adjourned after calling for a new Maryland Convention for April 1775.

At the close of the Maryland Convention, freemen of the several counties met to organize the defense of the colony, and in a remarkably short time committees were operating effectively.[31] The immediate task was to raise a militia and funds to support it. Prince George's County was one of the first to assemble, on 21 December 1774, and fell to the task of raising ten companies and £833 by subscription for their support, the quotas assigned to it by the Maryland Convention. In accordance with the resolution taken at Annapolis by the Provincial Convention, five classes of subscriptions were to be offered, ranging from five pounds down to one shilling and six pence.[32] Such arrangements made it difficult for any freeman to refuse to contribute without revealing his political attitude and thereby becoming vulnerable to the county committee. The county committee was to be furnished with the names of all those who declined to subscribe.

The raising of a provincial militia proceeded rapidly. Apparently the county committees agreed with the Maryland Convention that "the natural strength and only stable security of a free government" is a provincial militia. Colonials understood also that to raise a militia would add political strength to the Americans' tax objections, since having an independent militia would "relieve the mother country from any expense in their protection, and obviate the pretense of taxing them on that account." Therefore all male citizens between sixteen and fifty years of age were to form themselves into companies, choose officers, provide themselves with arms and ammunition, master the military exercises, and be "in readiness to act in any emergency." According to the 22 December 1774 *Maryland Gazette*, two companies had already been formed in Annapolis.

By the end of the year the spirit of determined opposition and preparation for military defense was visible everywhere. Governor Eden concluded that the "spirit of resistance against the Tea Act or any mode of internal taxation is as strong and universal here as ever." He firmly believed that the Maryland colonials were prepared to "undergo any hardships sooner than acknowledge a right in the British Parliament," and that they would "persevere in their non-importation and non-exportation experiments" in spite of every inconvenience, even if it meant "the total ruin of their trade."[33]

Nonimportation became effective 1 December, and the *Maryland Gazette* reported on 15 December 1774 that attempted importations had already been detected by the committees. Following the terms of the option under Article X of the Continental Association, the goods seized were sold at public auction, the owner was reimbursed for his costs, and the profits were forwarded to the poor and needy sufferers of Boston. Some importers were called before committees and obliged to apologize to the public. Merchants who tried to sell goods at prices above those recommended by the Maryland Convention were censured.

Although Boucher was not personally jeopardized by the boycott against merchandising activities, still he continued to worry about the operations of the committees and their lack of legal sanction. He may well have felt, as did Dulany, that the raising of troops was one of the worst mistakes of the year other than the formation of the Continental Association itself. Civil disobedience was a grave matter but civil disobedience with arms was downright rebellion. "The raising of troops," Dulany warned, "is a measure I apprehend not proper; we have a constitutional militia composed of the freemen of the province." According to the Maryland constitution, officers were to be "appointed by the Governor." The raising of troops by the Maryland Convention "effectually supersedes the constitutional militia."[34] Worried by the threat posed to legitimate government by the existence and the great potential for power of the numerous committees, Boucher stubbornly faced the new year. He was determined to do whatever he could to halt the rush of events that he was certain could lead only to the horrors of civil war.

◡ Chapter 8 ◡

Dilemma and Decision: 1775

Boucher's incipient loyalism had been forged in the early Maryland years, particularly in the heat of his controversy with Paca and Chase. His confirmed position on the side of the Crown was to emerge in the course of 1775 during the furor over the burgeoning operations of the extralegal committees.[1] Boucher soon became aware of the gulf between his own firm belief in law and order, responsibility to authority, and freedom of thought and speech, and what he considered to be the irresponsible radicalism of the Whigs. Yet for some months he refused to describe himself as an outright Loyalist, preferring to think of himself as a good American dedicated to the best interests of the colonies.[2] But by August 1775 Boucher was to conclude that he was indeed a Loyalist, if only because he knew he could not be a Whig. Boucher, like men everywhere in the colonies, was being forced to choose.

Boucher already realized that in Maryland as in the other colonies the nucleus of the extralegal committee system lay in the committees of correspondence.[3] As the revolutionary movement gained momentum, extralegal committees became the nerve system of the entire operation. Their efficiency rested in considerable part on an effective exchange of information at all levels, both within the province and with other colonies; the substantial overlap in personnel between committees was an important factor. For example, members of the provincial committee of correspondence and the delegates to the Maryland Convention were all drawn from the various county committees of observation. At one time

160

in Prince George's County a total of nine of the fourteen men designated to serve on the county committee of correspondence, the principal subcommittee of the committee of observation, were also delegates to the Maryland Convention.[4] The consequence was excellent communication and a tightly knit operation.

Another dimension of cohesiveness developed out of family connections. In Charles County, for example, the Dent family was active in committee work, as were their relatives in Prince George's County. Members of the Sprigg, Hall, Carroll, and Harwood families were serving in both Anne Arundel and Prince George's counties. Committee members in one county found it easy to communicate with relatives in other counties who shared their revolutionary political sentiments.

Many of those who filled committee positions were already old hands in Maryland politics, staunch members of the Country party and often able lawyers who had earlier successfully challenged the proprietary government on the issues of tobacco inspection fees and Anglican clerical salaries. These men obtained key roles in the extralegal committee structure. William Paca and Samuel Chase were two such men, and Boucher noted their growing importance with unease. Paca and Chase now were serving not only as delegates to the Maryland Convention but also as members of the provincial committee of correspondence and as delegates to the Continental Congress. Boucher was no less dismayed to find that Osborne Sprigg had become first a member of the large initial Prince George's County committee and then a member of both the Maryland Convention and its committee of correspondence.

Meanwhile the local committees were arrogating to themselves the functions of local government, and in their enthusiasm often resorting to vigilantism or outright terrorism. They served as the eyes and ears of the Continental Association, ferreting out violators, publishing their names and misdeeds to the community, and persuading them by various means to mend their ways. By 1776 scarcely any aspect of daily life remained beyond committee scrutiny. As part of the effort to detect and silence political sentiment "inimical to the cause of America," the committees of observation, as the local committees became known, intercepted mail and censored it, monitored opinions expressed both privately and publicly, and scrutinized questionable associates.

161

Most of the committees were also engaged in what was suspiciously like an informal system of taxation. The money thus collected was used to purchase arms and ammunition. The Anne Arundel County committee, for example, resolved that "every inhabitant of this County, who, on personal application by any one of the aforesaid Committee of Observation, or by any person appointed by them, shall refuse to contribute before the 1st day of *February* next to the purchase of Arms and Ammunition ... is, and ought to be esteemed an enemy to *America;* and that the name of every person who shall refuse to contribute on such application be published in the *Maryland Gazette*."[5]

Boucher's own Prince George's County, no less enthusiastic in enforcement than its counterpart committees elsewhere, met on 16 January 1775 and "recommended to the gentlemen of the Committee of Inspection" that they "use their utmost diligence to procure subscriptions" and that they collect as soon as possible funds for the purchase of arms and ammunition. Prince George's County did not go as far as the Anne Arundel committee had in providing public censure for those failing to subscribe; however the instructions to those who were to solicit subscriptions obviously implied that heavy pressure could be brought to bear on the county's residents. In Charles County the committee took much the same action as in Anne Arundel County, agreeing that those who refused to subscribe for the purpose of arms and ammunition purchase would be reported to the committee "that their names and refusal may be recorded in perpetual memory of their principles."[6]

Not all citizens were happy with the prospect of this kind of enforcement. A merchant at Annapolis confided to a friend in Philadelphia on 28 January 1775 that there had been some "spirited opposition" to this "insolent plan of levying money upon his Majesty's faithful subjects, to raise a fund for the express purpose of purchasing arms and ammunition," and to join "*Adams* and the Eastern Republicans" in their "treasonable" purpose to carry on "a formal rebellion in the colonies." Indeed, the merchant told his Philadelphia friend, he hoped that they had now stopped the progress of one "busy demagogue," who was "A turbulent man, of no consideration except with the needy and desperate like himself."[7]

Two other objectors to the proceedings in Anne Arundel County aired their dissent in the pages of the *Maryland Gazette*. One did not approve of the manner in which resolves had been

decided upon late in the evening when many of the "country gentlemen had left town" and many other citizens had "in general retired." In short, the meeting of 200 or even 250 men could hardly be called a full meeting of the inhabitants of Anne Arundel County. A second letter writer questioned the equity of "proscribing many respectable characters, zealous in the general cause, yet dissenting from the plan of redress" recommended by the mass meeting. It hardly seemed "consistent with liberty—the distinguishing characteristic of *British* subjects—to condemn . . . those who dissent from any popular opinion," pointing them out as "victims of vengeance to the hazard of public peace, the distress of worthy families and the destruction of private property."[8] But these dissident voices scarcely interrupted the committee deliberations or the enforcement of the decisions taken.

How effectively the various committees of observation carried out their directives may be estimated by reports of their activities in the *Maryland Gazette.*[9] As goods arrived the committees called the importer to task and obliged him to apologize publicly for his daring. Merchants were censured if they raised their prices in violation of the percentage increases determined upon earlier by the Maryland Convention. Those who had the temerity to question or disparage the means used by the committees were soon brought before the committee of observation, severely censured, and forced either to disavow their position or to apologize for their ill-considered words.

Others, hoping to avoid notice at least until they were actually presented with the subscription for funds for arms and ammunition, discreetly said nothing publicly, but poured out their true opinions to friends in England. For example William Eddis, surveyor of the customs, could not believe that the "evils complained of" by the colonials justified the "mode adopted to obtain redress," nor could he justify it on "principles of reason or sound policy." When the moment of confrontation arrived, Eddis refused "to join in any of the proposed contributions" for military support, and "refused to appear in any of the associations, or to enroll in any military corps." He was certain that not all citizens who contributed as requested were entirely, if at all, approving. Some he thought responded out of a sense of duty, but many contributed out of fear and the desire to avoid public "shame and infamy." This so-called voluntary subscription was in truth simply "an arbitrary tax" and the whole procedure amounted to sheer coercion. If one's opinion differed from that of the multitude, then one could be deprived of "character and the confidence of . . . fellow citizens." Eddis decided that it was better "to suffer" all ills than to resign that "glorious inheritance of a free subject—the liberty of *thinking, speaking,* and *acting*" according to conscience.[10]

Although Boucher's clerical status excused him from military duty, he was not exempt from the subscription for support of the new militia. Understandably he refused to support it, or any of the "various Associations and Resolves," all of which were in his opinion "very unnecessary, unwise, and unjust" (*Rem.*, p. 105). He firmly believed that the committees were operating outside the law and that great injustices were being done to individuals. Boucher's personal life also was affected immediately by a decision taken by the Maryland Convention that all who had hitherto refused to sign the Articles of Association must do so before 10 April 1775. Persons who persisted in refusing to sign were given two options: departure from the province with all of their property, or permission to remain subject to disarming and the posting of a bond as a guarantee against treason.[11] It is likely that Boucher made one of his appearances before a committee at this time.[12] Although nowhere does he say that he was required to post a bond, it is quite probable that he did. He must at least have appeared to have fulfilled the disarmament decree as well, but if he did he withheld at least two pistols which he shortly found a use for in his pulpit. Like many another Loyalist, he probably turned in his oldest and most decrepit weapons, retaining the operative ones.

The crisis precipitated by Boucher's refusal to sign the Articles of Association was resolved well enough for the moment, so that Boucher for a time supposed that it was possible to live with the terms which the committees imposed on him. He endeavored to conduct himself with "all possible temper and even caution," particularly when it became evident that the committees were showing great interest in those who publicly disparaged the means taken to defend the "people's rights." Such remarks were considered treasonable, and those who uttered them were brought before the committees, severely censured, and forced to disavow or apologize for such sentiments. Boucher knew that he was extremely vulnerable. He had attempted "in my sermons, and in various pieces published in the gazettes of the country, to check the immense mischief that was impending," but with little success (*Rem.*, pp. 104-5). His misgivings about the Maryland Convention, the Congress in Philadelphia, and the proliferation of new committees were probably known or at least easily surmised.

In spite of Boucher's caution, in a short time he came to the attention of the provincial committee sitting in Annapolis.[13] His accusers were "a Papist and two Presbyterians"; the Catholic was "my own parishioner." This fellow had "eagerly stepped forward as a witness" and "with great virulence" preferred a charge to prove Boucher's "inimicality to America." The committee ordered that Boucher be taken into custody immediately, and about two hundred militiamen went to Governor Eden's, where Boucher was visiting, to seize him and carry him before the committee for interrogation (*Rem.*, p. 105).

Somehow Boucher had warning of what was going on, and had even heard the charges brought against him. Greatly alarmed for his safety, his friends pressed him so importunately to flee that he found it hard to resist them. His own reaction however was strongly against flight. He thought that his enemies would wish for it, and he was not about to oblige them. A second and more fundamental reason for his response was his own predictable reaction to a challenge or to danger. He had expressed it well himself during the encounter with Giberne in 1762. Injured innocence had a "kind of magic elasticity," he thought; "like some creeping plants, the more they are trampled upon the more vigorous do they rise and flourish." He firmly believed that such skirmishes added to his character and his image and gave him a kind of added luster, *"like silver tried in the fire"* (*MHM* 7:151). Accordingly, Boucher prepared to stand his ground in argument with the governor, the council, and "a large number of the most respectable persons in the province," who were strongly for his flying (*Rem.*, p. 106).

The arrival of the armed men brought the debate to an end. Resolutely, Boucher went out to meet the captain, whom he knew, and asked what his business was. The captain courteously answered his questions, and Boucher shortly discovered that Paca and Chase would be among the interrogators waiting for him in Annapolis. Having decided to meet the danger head-on, he then decided to make a virtue of necessity. Plucking up his courage, he peremptorily told the captain that he "would not be carried to this, or any other Committee unknown to the laws, *alive*." However he gave his word "as a gentleman" that he would "wait on the gentlemen who composed the Committee," and charged the captain with delivering his compliments and his message to the committee in Annapolis. The captain agreed and Boucher soon "followed him, single, and in high spirits" (*Rem.*, p. 107).

When he arrived in Annapolis and tried to enter the committee room through the immense crowd, a sergeant in the militia, a hatter by the name of Lindsay whom Boucher considered to be one of the most noted blackguards in Annapolis, whispered in his ear. The Irish sergeant encouraged him to go on with the same spirit with which he had begun the march into town, assuring Boucher that he had "more friends . . . than enemies" among the armed men present, "and *by Jasus if he lived he would die with me.*" This whispered support gave Boucher more courage than if it had been "a message in my favor from the Congress itself." Boucher's conduct at the hearing was both forthright and courageous; he refused to be intimidated by the presence of Paca and Chase among his examiners. When the chairman began to speak to him he insisted on being permitted to sit down first. Then he protested that the committee had no authority over him, although he conceded that since his intentions were good there were no questions which, as gentlemen, they could put to him to which he would not give fair and satisfactory answers. The charges were read and a copy given to him. A few members of the committee harangued loudly on the dangers of having such a man as Boucher publicly avowing principles which were inimical to the measures of the Americans (*Rem.*, pp. 107-8).

Boucher quickly concluded that his best defense was to make a good impression on the crowd. He thought it most effective to ignore his accusers and direct his remarks to the audience. Later he could hardly recall what he said, but he remembered reflecting on Lord Chesterfield's observation that the manner of a speech is of much more consequence than the matter. He was unaccustomed to this kind of public speechmaking, but "Necessity may perhaps be the parent of eloquence," he thought, for it was successful (*Rem.*, p. 108). Many bawled out from the audience that what he said was quite satisfactory, and Boucher was acquitted. He had come off well in this encounter, but had heightened the ill will of his particular enemies. It was impossible not to provide them with other opportunities to ruin him, as feeling against those who did not express all-out Patriot sentiment increased. It was no more than a temporary reprieve.

The whole incident hardened Boucher's opinion of the seriousness of affairs in Maryland. The militia, normally under the command of the governor, now was responding only to orders from the extralegal committees. Governor Eden had not been able to protect a guest in his own home, a stark demonstration that legitimate government was largely incapacitated and that orderly constitutional government had been subverted by Country party devotees. After his committee appearance Boucher found himself under far heavier surveillance and life became increasingly more difficult. With some dismay, he discerned the hand of the Hanson and Sprigg families behind some of his troubles. They seized every opportunity to lay charges against him. Unfortunately, they now had new "weight in the world" with the activist Patriots (*Rem.*, pp. 95-96). He was forced to conclude that his parish "swarmed" with Patriots who were forever "stirring up anybody they could find at all so disposed" to give him "trouble and vexation" (*Rem.*, p. 114).

Meanwhile, the new Maryland Convention was preparing to meet at Annapolis on 24 April 1775, and Boucher wondered what new measures would be considered. He had no intention of attending the debates, but if he had he would have found entry barred to him. No strangers were permitted to attend the sessions.[14]

Boucher's fears rose once more after the news of Lexington and Concord reached the convention, as that body prepared for armed resistance. The situation became even more tense when six men from the convention went to Governor Eden to request arms on the grounds that an uprising of slaves might occur or a ship of war might arrive in the harbor of Annapolis with instructions to seize the inhabitants. Eden could not know whether their request was based on genuine fear aggravated by knowledge of Lord Dunmore's efforts to incite the Indians to a frontier war, or whether the Marylanders were engaging in a clever maneuver. Eden, faced with a dilemma, consulted with his council and then agreed to furnish arms to certain men whom he himself had earlier appointed to the legitimate militia. The next day the militia colonels of four counties, proceeding under the Militia Act of the province, took into direct custody approximately one hundred stand of musket.

Thus in a manner thinly disguised as "constitutional custom," the governor in effect yielded the armament of the legitimate government to the extralegal committees. The Patriot party thus armed itself, in part with official consent. One cannot condemn Eden out of hand for his action; it is probable that he was genuinely convinced of the danger. Boucher soon expressed the same fear of a slave revolt, but he also found it useful as propaganda in his opposition to the Continental Congress.

The news of Lexington and Concord had its effect on the populace as well as on the Maryland Convention. Many who had been somewhat tepid sympathizers with American grievances became more forthright Patriots. Robert Eden, surveying the scene, wrote to his brother William: "We are in a state of thorough confusion."[15] As Boucher watched the developments, he became more disquieted than ever and turned to Rev. William Smith in Philadelphia to express his chagrin. He complained on 4 May 1775 that he had been "plagued, vexed, abused and injured in the extreme," and that all of his time and energy had been required just to keep his "head above water;" otherwise he would have written earlier (*MHM* 8:237).

The letter was an appeal to Smith to join with Boucher and the "true friends to our excellent constitution," to abandon his position as an "unconcerned looker-on," and to "take *a decisive part* in the present broils." Given the state of affairs in May, Boucher was uncertain that Smith could do any good, although he urged him to try. The present chaos was the result of the measures taken by the Continental Congress, which had ignored the instructions "you concurred in giving to your deputies." Congress was, in his opinion, "unequal to the great business they have undertaken," and the colonies were now rapidly "running into all the horrors of confusion, misrule and civil war." "For God's sake, command me," Boucher beseeched Smith, if he could be made useful. He apologized to his colleague for the ineffectiveness of his own position, being "a fellow of no mark nor likelihood" who had already acquired "so bad a name." He was certain that whatever he might do, he would be "sure to be found out, and of course . . . mauled by committees." He admitted to Smith that he was ashamed to acknowledge the fact, but he had been "deterred through fear."

Even were he willing to risk discovery and the consequences, he felt helpless to do anything constructive, for he knew "neither a press nor printer" who was even "tolerably impartial, save Rivington's—and he is proscribed." He had heard that the Reverend Thomas Bradbury Chandler of New Jersey and Myles Cooper also had been proscribed, but he hoped it was mere rumor (*MHM* 8:239-40).

Affairs in Virginia were no better than in Maryland, he advised Smith. He had conducted some business across the Potomac the day before, and had left with the impression that "they are even madder than in New England." Altogether the situation was frustrating. Boucher truly believed that "the Americans have most woefully mismanaged their cause; and as things are now carried on it is not easy to say to which side a real friend to liberty, order and good government would incline." Sadly he told Smith, "for my part I equally dread a victory on either side" (*MHM* 8:240).

Boucher now guarded his tongue and expressed his opinions judiciously, even in private, attempting to pursue what he perceived to be a neutral course. From his pulpit he continued to preach caution, hoping that advocacy of moderation would not be construed to be anti-American. Bolstered by his belief that "nine out of ten of the people of America . . . were adverse to the revolt," he determined to do what he could to slow the process of rebellion (*Rem.*, p. 121). At times he felt that he was working almost single-handedly, for he could expect little help from even pronounced Loyalists, whom he later characterized as having a "foolish good-nature and improvidence about them which leads them often to hurt their own interests by promoting those of their adversaries" (*Rem.*, p. 118). Still, he could not sit idly by and make no effort to halt the escalation of the civil upheaval. He had once admonished a friend: "Resignation is so far from being a virtue that it really is criminal, whilst there may be supposed to be a possibility of a cure" (*MHM* 7:162). With but few voices raised with his in Maryland, and with the hope of success slim, Boucher pursued his course undaunted. He even refused to alter the liturgy of the church by dropping prayers for the royal family, which the Patriots insisted be done.

Acting on his determination to wield a moderating influence on the populace, he presently produced a letter entitled "Quaeries Addressed to the People of Maryland." Boucher was handicapped

169

by having the Maryland press closed to him, but he said that he eventually turned to a printer in New York to get his words of caution into the hands of the public.[16] The letter raised the constitutional issue, pointing out that the extralegal committees, were "not known to the laws of the land or the Constitution," yet they had undertaken to "debate and determine on matters of the highest moment" which affected "the very vitals of our Constitution." These actions contrary to authority created a grievance greater than those complained of against Britain, particularly since the resolves being taken at these committee meetings were being "framed and supported so as to have nearly the force of law" (*Rem.*, pp. 128-29).

A second issue raised in the letter concerned the unrepresentative composition of the various committees. Although the "General Committee" (the Maryland Convention) published its resolves in the *Maryland Gazette*, they could not "with either truth or propriety" be said to express the sense of the people. Not "one man in a thousand" had voted for any of the members of the Maryland Convention, nor had one man in ten thousand approved the resolves, either directly or by his legal representative.

Enforcement of the resolutions was even more unjust, for a motion in the convention that the resolutions of the majority should bind the minority had been defeated. Thus common sense and commonly held ideas of liberty could not justify restraining individuals from debating or questioning public measures. Furthermore, the penalties imposed by the committees were controversial; they were such that no "regular legislature ever ventured to adopt," as, for example, "the denunciation of tar and feathers." It appeared to Boucher that neither "the laws of God or the laws of the land" restrained the committees. The whole situation amounted to tyranny: "What is tyranny but the assumption and exercise of power without any authority?" And where was liberty to be had, when there was no longer a free press, and even "the ministers of the Word of God are dictated to and controlled in their holy function?" Boucher hoped that his message would make his fellow Marylanders stop and think (*Rem.*, pp. 129-30).

Meanwhile the Second Continental Congress was about to reassemble at Philadelphia with no moderate voices among the Maryland delegation in attendance. In an attempt to put the case for the conservative side before the southern deputies, Boucher managed to address them "through the medium of a newspaper" with an anonymous letter purporting to be the work of a number of Virginians and Marylanders who had property and "were not in debt." According to Boucher, James Rivington in New York obliged him by printing it in his *New York Gazette*.[17]

The letter began with a plaintive comment that it was a "sad state of times" that the writers of the letter, though of some consequence in "our country" and well-known to the delegates, found it necessary to communicate in this fashion. The letter urged the southern delegates to observe the original purpose for which they had been sent, which was "to examine into and ascertain our alleged grievances, and to point out the best means of obtaining redress." The single question originally before the First Continental Congress had been "whether the Parliament of Great Britain can constitutionally lay internal taxes on her colonies, and if they cannot, whether the 3d per lb. duty on tea be a tax or not." That first Congress had resolved that Britain could not tax in this way, and had set up a boycott. Now the duty of the southern deputies in this second Congress was to avoid the "horrors of a Civil War," and to take action against the resolves of the first Congress. If they did not, severance from Great Britain would certainly follow. With independence, the subjugation of the southern colonies to those of the North was inevitable (*Rem.*, pp. 131-32).

The letter was intended to be an emotional appeal to "Virginia and Maryland Country" sentiment and to southern sectionalism in general. Bluntly, the letter pointed out that the South had more to fear from war than the North; "we have within our selves an enemy fully equal to all our strength [the slaves]." If that did not dissuade the deputies, Boucher urged that they consider the frontier hazards. "We have, too, an injured, a vindictive and a barbarian enemy on our frontiers, who, on the slightest encouragement, would soon glut their savage passion for revenge by desolating our out-lying settlements." Furthermore, if Britain were sufficiently provoked, she could easily exploit the dangerous situation by supplying these potential enemies with arms, ammunition, and officers by means of the Mississippi River (*Rem.*, pp. 134-35).

Boucher urged caution upon the southern deputies, appealing to them not to be "so fascinated by New England politics as to vote for destroying [the constitution of church and state] without

171

first well knowing what we are to have in its stead" (*Rem.*, p. 134). The letter pointed out how utterly defenseless the southern and middle colonies would be after years of "civil broils" and how subject to seizure by "our more enterprising and restless fellow-colonists of the North." This was no "chimerical conjecture," but a plausible development to expect given the history of mankind (*Rem.*, pp. 132-33). There would be as little likelihood of the southerners forming a "cordial union with the saints of New England" in a "monstrous and an unnatural coalition" as there would be of "the wolf and the lamb" quietly feeding together (*Rem.*, p. 134). At first the aggressive northerners "may be contented to be the Dutch of America, i.e. to be our carriers and fishmongers," but should the time come "when all North America should be independent," then Boucher supposed that "his Northern brethren would then become also the Goths and Vandals of America" (*Rem.*, pp. 132-33). Boucher's final arrow was aimed at the unrepresentative position of the delegates: "you have not the voice of the people with you" (*Rem.*, p. 136). Since they spoke for so few, he cautioned that the deputies watch their activities carefully.

Although Boucher continued to do his best to circumvent trouble, another crisis now loomed. The Maryland Convention in its session of 24 April 1775 had proclaimed 11 May a day of public fasting and humiliation. In his opinion the proclamation itself was an artful attempt to win the people to obedience to the committees' ordinances. He wrote to James on 31 October 1775 that he also had doubts about the wisdom of staged events of this kind which tended to work the common people into a frenzy (*MHM* 8:243). The atmosphere reminded him of the Puritan sermons of an earlier day which had had so great an effect on people during the Grand Rebellion in England (*Rem.*, p. 118). He mistrusted also the purpose of the collections taken on Fast Days; the real objective, he thought, was not to recommend the "suffering people of Boston to the charity of my parish," but to raise money "to purchase arms and ammunition" (*Rem.*, p. 105). He was determined not to serve the Patriots in this way.

Thus on 11 May he left the duty of the day to his curate, Walter Hanson Harrison, whom he described as "a weak brother, yet a strong Republican." Harrison preached a sermon which Boucher considered "very silly," indeed, "mischievous," and which blew "the coals of sedition" and rendered him popular. Boucher

Drama but fact?

had only contempt for that kind of popularity, for in order to obtain it one had only to be "very like the bulk of the people, that is, wrong-headed, ignorant, and prone to resist authority." If any really sensible man thus became the idol of the people, it was by virtue of "letting himself down to their level" (*Rem.*, p. 119).

The evasive ploy did not work. In spite of Boucher's effort to avoid trouble by keeping his "mouth . . . with a bridle" (*MHM* 8:243), some surmised that he had stayed out of the way on purpose, and correctly deduced that the rector disapproved of the Fast Day and its objectives. As a result Boucher received a number of threats, to which he made no answer except in his sermons. However, after that date he daily met with "insults, indignities, and injuries" (*Rem.*, p. 105). In spite of the unpleasant situation, Boucher thought it proper and necessary that he continue to go to church, but he sensibly decided to avoid Queen Anne's. Unfortunately he ran into difficulties even in Addison's quiet parish. One Sunday Boucher recommended peaceableness in his sermon, upon which one Mr. Lee and others abruptly rose and stalked out of church. They construed the sermon to be "a stroke at the times," and therefore unacceptable. That incident seemed to be a signal to his parishioners to consider every sermon "hostile to the views and interests of America," and Boucher soon found that every time that he went into a pulpit something very disagreeable happened. He received various messages and letters threatening him with fatal consequences if he did not preach what was acceptable to friends of America. Refusing to reply directly to any threats, Boucher "uniformly and resolutely" declared that he "never could suffer any merely human authority to intimidate" him and that he would perform his duty to God and his church as his conscience dictated. From then on Boucher preached, when he could preach at all, with a pair of loaded pistols lying on the cushion beside him. Quietly he told his congregation that if any man or body of men could possibly be so lost to all sense of decency and propriety as to attempt to carry out the threat to drag him out of his own pulpit, he would think himself "justified before God and man in repelling violence by violence" (*Rem.*, p. 113).

Meanwhile, during Boucher's absence from his own parish, his curate seized the opportunity to preach in his own way and to further the Patriot cause. From Boucher's point of view, Harrison had been "promoting factious associations and subscriptions"

173

ill becoming a minister and had materially assisted in shifting the temper of the parish even more to the Whig point of view (*Rem.*, p. 119). Thus when the Second Continental Congress designated Thursday, 20 July the first intercolonial Fast Day, Boucher knew that it might well mean more trouble. The furor had hardly subsided from Maryland's Fast Day in May.

Governor Eden, who attempted to keep a wary finger on the political pulse of his colony, sensed the rising emotional climate and sought to put a damper on it. He went to Boucher and suggested that he ought to make a point of appearing in his own pulpit on the forthcoming Fast Day. In order to please Eden, and to deprive Harrison of another opportunity to influence his parishioners, Boucher dubiously agreed. He hoped that in some way this gesture of seeming cooperation might preclude trouble for himself, as his deliberate absence in May had not. Boucher carefully prepared a sermon recommending "purity of life" as the best means of success for any cause, cautiously dwelling on general topics "with a modest and most humble vindication" of himself included (*MHM* 8:243). He then submitted the finished product to Addison, Eden, and his "most judicious friends," all of whom considered the sermon softened to the point that it "could not possibly give offense" and yet might be an effective brake to rising Patriot excesses (*Rem.*, p. 120).

Thus determined to use his own pulpit on the Fast Day, with the hope of restraining his parishioners from taking any active part in it, Boucher informed his curate, who was less than pleased. Harrison replied that he himself had prepared a sermon for the occasion, based on a theme against absolute monarchy. Tactfully Boucher commended the judiciousness of his choice of theme, surmising that Harrison had found a published sermon, transcribed it, showed it to the committee, and had had it approved. In his opinion, most topics were approved if they seemed to be "against power and for liberty," whereas in his own sermon "the jet of my arguments was that in taking a part they could not be sure they were right and doing good." Therefore it was "truest wisdom as well as duty" in so difficult a situation to "*sit still*" (*Rem.*, p. 120).

The Second Continental Congress convened on 10 May 1775. Everywhere a rising sense of unity was apparent. The religious and emotional appeal of the Fast Day, combined with the exciting news from Philadelphia, inflamed Patriot opinion. When the Fast

174

Day arrived, Walter Dulany, soon to be a major in the Maryland Loyalist regiment, accompanied a cheerful Boucher to Queen Anne's Church, where they arrived twelve to fifteen minutes early. Both were startled to find Harrison there, fully expecting to preach his own sermon in spite of Boucher's instructions to him. More disturbing was the sight of some two hundred armed men in the church, obviously under the leadership of Col. Osborne Sprigg, the confirmed Whig and declared personal enemy of Boucher.

Several of the men present interrogated Boucher, and to their questions he returned an equivocal answer that "though an advocate for the doctrine of resistance in general," he thought it "exceedingly unsuitable" to attempt to deal with so complex a theory with the compass of a sermon. His own sermon, he assured them, "spoke not of it." Not surprisingly, Sprigg forbade him to enter his pulpit. In reply, Boucher flatly told Sprigg that the pulpit was his own and he would use it; unless they took his life he would preach. He was surrounded by two hundred men, "under arms and in shirts," who threatened him with "horrid imprecations," promising that if he did enter the pulpit he would not "come out alive" (*MHM* 8:243).

In keeping with his long-established policy of facing danger head-on, the redoubtable cleric waited until the proper time for the sermon and then, with a loaded pistol in one hand and his sermon in the other, prepared to ascend the steps of his pulpit. David Crawford, a friend from Upper Marlborough, immediately stepped behind the beleaguered rector and pinioned his arms securely. He whispered to Boucher that "on his honor" he had both seen and heard explicit orders given to twenty handpicked men to fire on him the moment he stepped into the pulpit (*Rem.*, p. 122). Crawford was a member of three Prince George's County committees and conceivably was well informed. It was a tense moment.

Concession now seemed impossible to Boucher. He thought that his life depended on not "suffering these outrageous people to carry their point" (*Rem.*, p. 122). To flinch once was to invite danger forever, and unless he was out of their reach, out of the country, he had to try to intimidate them as he had in the past. Swiftly calculating the odds, he appealed to Crawford to go into the pulpit with him. Crawford was a friend but also a Patriot, and probably not foolhardy enough to risk his neck in the face

175

of twenty men, any one of whose aim might be faulty. Crawford refused.

Utter confusion and disorder prevailed. Those who wished to prevent bloodshed or death in the church forced Boucher away from the pulpit. Not all of the bystanders were opposed to him. As he remembered later, a considerable number insisted that he was right in demanding his own pulpit. More violent than the moderate men, Osborne Sprigg and his followers now attempted to shout down the proponents of compromise, and they managed to surround Boucher, jostling out the moderates and his friends. Cut off from effective help and realizing that the situation was rapidly getting out of his control, Boucher quickly took the initiative. With a suddenness that caught Sprigg off guard, Boucher seized the Whig leader by the collar, aimed his pistol at his hostage's head, and assured Sprigg that if any violence were done to him, he would "instantly blow his brains out." There is no doubt that Boucher intended to execute his threat (*Rem.*, pp. 122-23, 113).

With some of the aplomb he had displayed before the Council of Safety, Boucher now peremptorily told Sprigg that "if he pleased, he might conduct me to my horse, and I would leave them." With the militia company uncertain what to do, Sprigg agreed. The pair walked the hundred yards to Boucher's horse "guarded by his whole company" (*Rem.*, p. 123). Sprigg, intimidated, nonetheless had enough spirit left to order his men to play the "Rogues' March" on their drums. Boucher's boldness and courage had saved his own life, and somewhat diminished Sprigg's prestige.

On the following Sunday, the undaunted Boucher went back to Queen Anne's to preach the sermon he had prepared for the Fast Day. There were a few there to oppose him, but many fewer than before, probably, Boucher guessed, because they had not expected him to have the temerity to make another attempt at his pulpit. He calmly ascended his pulpit at the proper time and preached the sermon he had intended for them earlier, adding some comments on the fracas of the previous Thursday. During the service, the word went out of Boucher's presence and a crowd assembled after the sermon. Again surrounded, jostled, and hustled into a position with his back against a wall, he harangued the mob in the manner he had used to appeal to the crowd during his interrogation before the committee in Annapolis. Again he was successful; the affray ended "in a war of words" (*Rem.,* p. 124).

Threats and abuse by Boucher's enemies nonetheless now became more and more frequent and more furious, and it was clear to him that the time was fast approaching when his position would become absolutely untenable. People like Sprigg considered even an attempt to appeal to moderation as treasonable activity. Perhaps Sprigg and the other members of the Council of Safety were aware of Boucher's pamphleteering and had guessed at his authorship of the letters addressed to Marylanders and to the southern deputies sitting in Congress, in spite of his attempts at anonymity.

Meanwhile, the pace of military events in the colony accelerated. On 26 May the Continental Congress had recommended that each colony put itself in a state of defense immediately. Soon thereafter the Congress called on Maryland for two companies of riflemen to join the forces in Massachusetts. By mid-July, Frederick County had raised the two companies and they had departed. Public feeling ran high with the news of the Battle of Bunker Hill; enlistments increased as did support for the militia companies which Maryland had been raising for some months.

On 26 July, a new convention assembled at Annapolis with 140 deputies in attendance. Following the recommendation of the Continental Congress, the Maryland Convention resolved to put the colony into a state of defense. "The cruel prosecution of the war against the people of Massachusetts" and General Gage's proclamation declaring the inhabitants of the colonies "rebels and traitors" were declared to be "sufficient causes for a free people to arm in defense of their liberty." A formal association of the freemen of the province was entered into, and the committees of observation in every county were instructed to appoint persons in each parish or hundred to "offer or carry the said Association to all Freemen resident within their County." Anyone not subscribing upon application, or within ten days thereafter, was to be reported by the committee of observation to the next Maryland Convention.[18]

The Maryland Convention also created a sixteen-member Council of Safety, eight each from the East and West Shores, to act as an executive body between convention sessions. The Western Shore members included Paca, Chase, Johnson, and the two Carrolls, Charles Carroll, barrister of Annapolis, and Charles Carroll of Carrollton. The convention granted the new council broad powers, which included the right to grant commissions for courts martial, the right to hear and punish high and dangerous offenses (defined according to the resolutions of the Maryland Convention), and the right to print paper money.[19] The council also was granted the power to call out the whole militia if necessary. All members were required to take an oath of silence before a justice of the peace regarding all convention business.

It was clear to Boucher, as well as to others who had been subject to the tender ministrations of various committees, that more than ever personal animosities might find in committee action a convenient means of revenge. Even the Maryland Convention itself recognized the possibility of misdirected or vengeful "enthusiasm." In an attempt to forestall such situations, it took upon itself the responsibility for hearing petitions from citizens who had grievances against a committee action. Its purpose was commendable, but the action had tremendous implications for the balance of power in the colony. The governor's civil power had not been challenged previously, although for some time the various committees had been regulating the commerce and controlling the militia and the armament of the colony. Now, in July 1775, the Maryland Convention usurped this power too. It assumed practically unlimited authority by designating itself as a kind of supreme court of appeal, with the power to consider and dispose of petitions. It could choose to uphold the decision of the county committee of observation, ameliorate the sentence of the county committee, or set the sentence aside if it did not find the facts to be as the county committee presented them.

The creation of the Council of Safety represented a landmark in Maryland affairs. The civil authority of the governor had been challenged successfully, and from this moment on Eden's position deteriorated. For a time he retained control of his magistrates and sheriffs, but the new council's exercise of its powers as supreme arbiter and enforcer of the public peace soon rendered the legitimate civil officers incapable of performing their duties. Legitimate local enforcement officers were in close competition with committees of observation which grew in power as the authority of the Maryland Convention increased. For one thing, the convention made certain changes in its enforcement committees designed to improve their organization and to make them more efficient. Each county now had a designated number of persons serving on its committee of observation. For example, Prince George's County was allotted thirty-three members serving one-year terms, while Anne Arundel County had thirty-four. Any seven members were vested with full power and authority to execute the Association's directives and the resolves of the Maryland Convention and of the Continental Congress.

By now the committees were empowered to act well beyond the confines of mere boycott concerns. The committees of observation had full power and authority to apprehend any persons "on probable proof" that they were "guilty of any high and dangerous offense tending to disunite the inhabitants of this province in their present opposition or to destroy the liberties of America." Such persons were to be sent, together with the charges against them, to the Council of Safety "on that Shore where the offense shall be committed." If the charges were proved the persons were to be imprisoned until the next convention met. The convention might then take further action, or insist that they depart from the province within a specified time.[20]

By now a structure of government at each level of the political process had been erected. Contrary to Locke's theory of a new government replacing that of the old in the process of revolution, Maryland Whigs had imposed a supralegal government upon the province while the old government still existed. Well before any formal declaration of independence on the part of the Continental Congress at Philadelphia, a de facto revolution in government had been accomplished.[21]

If any doubted that a transfer of power had taken place, the case of James Christie, which came to the attention of the Maryland Convention in early August, carried the message.[22] The facts were simple. Christie had written a candid letter to one of his relatives, Lt. Col. Gabriel Christie, who was stationed with the Sixtieth Regiment at Antiqua, in which he described the "terrible confusion here with our politics" and hazarded the opinion that Maryland was "little behind the New Englanders." He thought that the trouble was traceable to some "violent fanatical spirits" among them who had pressed matters to the point that Marylanders were "threatened with expulsion and loss of life and for not acceding to what we deem treason and rebellion." A regiment here "would keep them quiet," he suggested, a line which he was

179

soon to regret writing. The letter was intercepted and fell into the hands of a county committee of observation.

Christie was promptly summoned before the committee to explain the "damning evidence" in the letter. Being ill, Christie sent a representative asking for a postponement, which the committee refused to grant. Instead the committee attended him, demanding to know "who he had united with." Christie denied any activity other than the writing of an indiscreet letter, but to no avail. The committee found him manifesting "a spirit and principle altogether inimical to the rights, privileges, and liberties of America," and published his name as an "enemy to his country," desiring all persons to break off all connections with him. His offense was considered "a dangerous crime and atrocious enough to lay before the Continental Congress." The beleaguered Christie, although confined to his bed, was considered sufficiently dangerous to require guards (whom he was obliged to pay) posted around the clock. Soon rumors began to circulate that Christie had ammunition in quantity in his home, resulting in a thorough search of the house. Two guns and a pair of pistols were found, but no ammunition.

The upshot of the Christie case was that Congress at Philadelphia declined to make a decision on it, and referred the matter instead to the Maryland Convention. Ultimately Christie was given permission by the latter body to leave the confines of his home, but only to "ride out with a guard for exercise." Later he was required to post a bond whereby he guaranteed his appearance before the Maryland Convention and agreed not to leave the province, upon which arrangement the guard was finally dismissed. The convention eventually banished him from the province and ordered him to pay £500 as his share of charges and expenses in defense of America.

A spirit of vigilantism flourished in all the counties, but Prince George's County displayed more aggressiveness than others. Boucher's uneasiness during the earlier months of the year grew steadily as the directives of the Maryland Convention proliferated. He was well aware that the phrase in the convention's directive for dealing with Loyalists which threatened to be his undoing was "guilty of any high and dangerous offense tending to disunite the inhabitants of this province." Boucher knew that many of the men on the Prince George's committee would construe his attempts to steer a middle course as tending to disunity. He could only wait and see what happened.

The case of Richard Henderson soon showed the temper of the committee of observation, and worse yet, the emotional attitudes of many in the county who were not members of the committee.[23] Henderson was a member of the Prince George's County general committee, a post which he had held since January 1775.[24] Clearly his sympathy for the American cause was not ambiguous, although this fact seemed of little help to him when he ran afoul of the committee of observation of his own county. The problem arose on the day that Henderson took charge of a company of militia, one of whose members was George Munro. The soldier had written some unacceptable lines in an intercepted letter, on the basis of which he was arrested. The militia company, shocked that one of their own company should be guilty of such an indiscretion, proposed that instead of arresting him, someone in the company should volunteer to be answerable for his appearance before the committee of observation on the next day. Henderson refused, and sentries were then duly posted to guard Munro. Meanwhile, the soldier fell ill, and Henderson belatedly agreed to guarantee his appearance. No trouble was expected from the sick Munro.

On the following morning, Henderson talked to Munro, who showed no apprehension about appearing before the committee. Thus reassured that there was no hazard in the guarantee he had made, Henderson withdrew the sentries and returned to his company, remaining with his soldiers until Tuesday evening. He did not see Munro again. That evening the committee of observation sent for Henderson and Munro, but to Henderson's great consternation he found that Munro had departed without leave.

Anticipating the displeasure of the committee, Henderson questioned his men and learned the facts which he then relayed to the outraged committee. Unknown to Henderson, a "great number of men with loaded arms came to town," declared their intention to tar and feather Munro, and brought along an old lean horse to set him on in order to drum him through the town. Apparently this motley, impromptu group had its plans ready, whether the committee found Munro guilty or not, and in spite of any penalties which that body might choose to impose. Munro had seen the mob and had ridden off afraid.

181

In no way had Henderson connived with Munro. In fact he had been a reluctant security agent for him, acceding only when his militia company pressed him. None of these explanations, however, placated the committee, which then decided to hold Henderson wholly responsible for the escape. He was given until the following Monday morning to produce Munro. Henderson, seeing no alternative, arranged to send out several search parties, bearing the expense of both men and horses out of his own pocket.

Although Henderson had acted in good faith, and continued to do so, he encountered more ill will than he could bear. He and his family became targets for the animosity of men who were either members of the Prince George's committee of observation or unauthorized men such as those who had wanted to tar and feather Munro without a hearing. Henderson was terrorized and threats were made to tear down his house. Finally, in desperation he sought relief from the Maryland Convention, asking that the Prince George's committee be restrained. Thomas Mangill, a member of the committee of observation, testified before the convention that Jasper Wirt, who had built Henderson's house some ten years earlier, was determined on vengeance against Henderson. Although Wirt had been persuaded at one time to disperse the "body of people" harassing Henderson, he had still threatened to appear again with the rabble-rousers. When questioned about his vengeful attitude, Wirt glowered that "he had not yet forgot the building of Mr. Henderson's house," apparently a reference to some ten-year-old grievance which he was still nursing. More moderate neighbors were unable to control the situation without the intervention of the Maryland Convention. It seems obvious that in this case at least, personal animosity had become entangled with committee business to the diminution of justice.

Boucher worried over such incidents and with good reason, for he saw a personal hazard. The whole Henderson incident had been triggered by interception of a letter written by a militiaman. Surely even greater scrutiny would be accorded the correspondence of people such as himself. Boucher fretted, for he had just dispatched a letter to James by Captain Rothery bound for Whitehaven.[25] His fears were intensified when a "very worthy friend" (perhaps Christie) fell under the eye of the committee of observation on the basis of a letter "villainously intercepted," which Boucher knew personally was "not a thousandth part so exceptionable" as his own. His friend was sentenced to perpetual banishment and fined £500. Boucher dared risk no letters after that, and he continued to worry about his correspondence with James even after he was in England, hoping "in God you have neither answered mine nor of late wrote to me at all on any political questions" (*MHM* 8:242). Although Boucher's personal security at that time was no longer at stake, he still hoped to protect his American property and wanted no exposure by a stray letter.

Daily life became more precarious. On one occasion he found it necessary to cross the Potomac into Alexandria, and at once found himself in a new encounter with his ancient enemy Landon Carter.[26] In Carter Boucher had an enemy of consequence. In the years since their original encounter over the Routledge murder, Carter had moved to the forefront of the Patriot cause with essays calculated to convince the public that the cause of Boston was the cause of all, and that to consent to the British repressive measures meant that all Americans must submit to arbitrary taxes and say farewell to liberty.[27] Sometime after the murder Carter had been irritated by a Tory-flavored epigram which Boucher had prepared for publication in the *Virginia Gazette*.[28] Unfortunately the printer of the *Virginia Gazette* was also anxious to secure the Assembly's printing business, and in an effort to "curry favor with some of the leading men" in the legislature he showed them Boucher's "poor epigram" (*Rem.*, p. 110). Colonel Carter had immediately recognized the handwriting as Boucher's, and had promptly declared the article "exceedingly obnoxious," and the author "inimical to America" (*Rem.*, p. 110).

The incident of the epigram set the stage for a much more serious situation which occurred in April or May 1775, when Boucher went to Alexandria on business. Boucher had been in town scarcely half an hour when Carter sought him out and attacked him about the epigram. A mob gathered, and although Boucher looked around for an ally, he could find no counterpart to the friendly Irishman Lindsay at his earlier hearing in Annapolis. Indeed, one of the loudest of the group was a "virulent" Presbyterian, a Mr. Ramsay.

Again a stratagem seemed necessary. After the initial violent onslaught, Boucher got permission to address the crowd and he made the most of it. He silenced Ramsay by describing him as an improper judge of what was wrong and what was right in a priest of the Church of England. Next he recounted the savory particulars of the Colonel Chiswell-Routledge murder and Carter's role in it. He begged his listeners not to allow themselves to be duped by a "cowardly man" seeking to revenge a private quarrel. Although Carter complained of Boucher's artifice, he dropped the matter of the epigram. The rabble-rousers were mollified and allowed Boucher to go free. Again he had had wit enough to extricate himself from a most unpleasant situation. But Nelly, who with Jane had watched all this from an adjoining house, was so disturbed that she extracted a promise from Boucher that he would never go back to Alexandria. The promise was easy to make.

Boucher's position was now rapidly becoming impossible. He later told James that for the last six months of his life in America he dared not venture out of his house unarmed (*MHM* 8:243). He lived only from day to day, endeavoring to keep out of difficulty, yet hoping to maintain his principles as well as he could. He believed that "nobody, no merely human authority," could intimidate him (*Rem.*, p. 113). He hoped against hope that his belief would not be shaken, but he felt more and more isolated. The failure of Rev. William Smith of Philadelphia to rally to his support only increased his sense of isolation.

Boucher had thought as late as May 1775 that the cause of law and order had an ally in Smith. Boucher was among the Anglican clergy who had met in Philadelphia in 1773 and drafted a plan for concerted action on church problems and against "republican" activities. Now Boucher too hopefully assumed that because of this earlier alliance he could rally Smith to support the Loyalist cause. Eagerly he wrote Smith and settled down to await an answer. But there was no answer to his letter, nor was there the least evidence that Smith was taking a stand against the measures of Congress and the provincial committees. Boucher soon learned how little the clergy of Philadelphia regarded this agreement, and how generally they—and Smith—now supported the views of Congress.

With a sense of shock and great disappointment at what seemed to him to be cold betrayal, Boucher learned of Smith's "defection" to the American cause. Boucher received the hard news from a published copy of one of Smith's sermons; Smith did not even do Boucher the courtesy of a more personal reply. The sermon "vindicated the Congress, conventions, insurrections, and military enrollments." Boucher never forgave Smith for this means of notifying him of his position, and continued to view his action "with aggravated poignancy" as a discourtesy and a "breach of friendship" (*A View*, p. 455).

Boucher was to recall later that he had told his parishioners that Smith had been "my particular friend, that it is not long since I conversed with him on these very subjects, respecting which he then professed to think as I thought, and as every true son of the Church of England must always think, because it is impossible any one of our communion should be disloyal without first renouncing his religion." Thus Boucher labeled Smith a traitor and an incendiary and from that date forward always wrote disparagingly of him. He was persuaded that Smith's selfish concern was to continue his good relationship with the Presbyterians of Philadelphia. Later, when Smith was appointed a bishop in the newly created Protestant Episcopal Church of the United States, Boucher was more than ever convinced that Smith had served self-interest, not principle (*A View*, pp. 453-55). Boucher may not have known that Smith wrote a series of eight letters under the pseudonym "Cato" and published them in Hugh Gaine's *Mercury* 18 March–6 May 1776, in which he argued that independence was unjustified.

The month of August was a misery of anticipation. Boucher knew that it was only a matter of days before he would be approached for his signature on the Articles of Association which the Maryland Convention had promulgated in late July. He could not as a matter of principle sign any paper that approved of opposition by arms without immediately being in violation of his double oath to the church and to the state. His moderate stance, his constant theme of "sit still" to his parishioners, could not be tolerated any longer by those who were demanding that patriotic Americans take up arms in defense of liberty. If a course of neutrality, of mere lip service to a cause to buy time and ride out the storm had ever been possible for a man with Boucher's convictions and principles, that time was now past.

It was inevitable that he would once more be in open confrontation with the committee of observation should he refuse to sign. He was aware that he could expect little consideration when that happened, for he had not endeared himself to Patriots in the past months. Even before his summons to Annapolis from Eden's dinner table, he had twice been called before extralegal committees. Although Eden nominally retained the office of governor, the Maryland Convention and the Council of Safety now held the substance of power. Proprietary government was a corpse, waiting only a decent burial. Eden's dismissal in the near future was inevitable. There was no hope of help for Boucher in that quarter, no more than there had been in the earlier confrontation with the militia.

Nor could Boucher expect any help from Washington, now commander of the Continental Armies, despite their "very particular intimacy and friendship" (*Rem.*, p. 48). The two men had not seen each other since a chance encounter while crossing the Potomac. Boucher, Jinny, and some friends were enroute to Alexandria, where Boucher found the Virginians "on fire, either with rum, or patriotism, or both." Boucher recalled the occasion later as a celebration in honor of Washington's departure for Cambridge to assume command, but he may have been mistaken, for there is no record that Washington returned to Alexandria after taking command of the army in June. Some Patriots in the boat gave three cheers to the general, but Boucher and the Reverend Henry Addison merely raised their hats. Although the encounter was brief, Boucher told Washington of his fears about the consequences of the military preparations. There would certainly be a civil war, he said, and very soon the Americans would declare for independence. Washington thought not, and replied earnestly that "if ever I heard of his joining in any such measures I had his leave to set him down for everything wicked" (*Rem.*, p. 109). Washington was quite sincere, Boucher thought.

In spite of their seven years of friendship in America, however, what Boucher recorded about Washington in his *Reminiscences* were the biased comments which reflect his own Revolutionary War experience. They accord Washington faint praise. "Mr. Washington was the second of five sons," Boucher was to recall, "of parents distinguished neither for their rank nor fortune." Lawrence was the eldest Washington son, a soldier who sold his commission as an aftermath of a scrape and who died later at Barbados. Boucher apparently took some pains to deprecate the family's prestige. George Washington, he wrote, had had no education at all except for the reading, writing, and accounting which had been taught him by a convict servant hired by his father for a schoolmaster. The young Washington was a surveyor of Orange

County, at a salary about half the value of Boucher's own Virginia rectory, or about one hundred pounds a year. His 1754 expedition against the French, Boucher thought, had earned some ridicule, and so had the journal which he had published on the subject. In subsequent military engagements, Boucher continued, Washington had conducted himself in "the same manner as in my judgment he had since done, i.e. decently, but never greatly" (*Rem.*, pp. 48-50).

Although he was not impressed with Washington's military ability, he never failed to concede his integrity, honesty, and morality; however, he took the opportunity for a jibe, adding parenthetically, "except that as a Virginian, he has lately found out that there is no moral turpitude in not paying what he confesses he owes to a British creditor." Washington's most distinguished characteristic in Boucher's opinion was that he was an "excellent farmer." Otherwise, Boucher found him to be "shy, silent, stern, slow and cautious," and not "affectionate in his nature." He was a religious man, "having heretofore been pretty constant, and even exemplary, in his attendance on public worship in the Church of England." Just before the close of the French and Indian War Washington had married the widow Custis and thus came into possession of her "large jointure." "He never had any children; and lived very much like a gentleman at Mount Vernon in Fairfax County," Boucher recalled from his visits there (*Rem.*, p. 50). In part his bitterness stemmed from the fact that Washington had offered him no assistance, although he must have known of Boucher's tribulations.

Boucher knew that he had no choice except to refuse to sign the articles. "I should have been most base, and of course most miserable, had I done otherwise," he wrote to William Eden on 27 June 1776. Boucher began to think of retreat to England. It was a step which he knew would be ruinous to all his American property and interest, which was then all that he had in the world. But he was aware that were he to insist on remaining he might endanger not only his property but his life (*Rem.*, p. 124). If he were to decide to go, he realized that the decision would have to be made very soon. The Continental Congress had set 10 September 1775 as the date for the cessation of all commerce and shipping with Great Britain.

Once he had made up his mind to leave, he enjoyed a certain

187

peace. He did not regret his stand, and always believed that "sadly as things went against loyalty and loyal men, I have the comfort to reflect that some good was done by my efforts in their favor." He believed that his "character and credit" with his clerical colleagues had restrained some of them "within the bounds of duty" (*Rem.*, p. 120).

On 6 August 1775, Boucher wrote his farewell letter to Washington, renouncing their friendship and denouncing the Patriot cause.[29] It was a bitter letter, although it began with regrets that he would no longer be able to enjoy the pleasures of being Washington's "old friend" and neighbor. He recognized that they were involved in a force greater than either of them; therefore he was unprepared to blame Washington wholly for their trouble, nor did he think Washington would think harshly of him. In any case, Boucher reflected, "If I am still in the wrong, I am about to suffer such punishment as might satisfy the malice of even the most vindictive enemy." He thought it useless to go over their political differences again; they had already debated the great issue of the Patriot course of action long and fruitlessly, and Boucher had never been persuaded by Washington's argument. But he could not help complaining that his own convictions would never have justified him in molesting his enemies as the Whigs had persecuted him. Furthermore, he resented Washington's lack of concern about his plight: "You have borne to look on, at least as an unconcerned spectator, if not an abettor," while he had "in a manner been petted to death," like "the poor frogs in the fable." He found Washnigton's conduct neither friendly, just, manly, nor generous.

He let his Tory sentiments spill into his farewell. He maintained that the majority of Americans were not in favor of the Patriot cause.[30] Furthermore, his own decision was one of "truth and justice"; he could not have done otherwise "without doing violence to every system of ethics yet received in any civilized country." On the other hand, Whig principles, "at least as I see them exemplified in practice," he told Washington, "lead ... directly to all that is mean and unmanly." What a contradiction their actions were to "all that liberty which Whigs are forever so forward to profess," he observed. Boucher was a Loyalist by default, because he could not be an unprincipled person. He was convinced that to be a Whig required that he be without principles.

Boucher was more resolute in his Tory convictions than Gov-

188

ernor Eden, who had been in England and had not returned until 1775. Eden was in fact somewhat sympathetic with the Patriots, and once suggested that the Whig leaders dine with him to thrash matters out over the table. In spite of their personal regard for Eden, the Patriots realized the awkwardness and compromising appearance of such a dinner. Instead, Charles Carroll of Carrollton invited both Eden and the Whig leadership to dinner at his home, and they exchanged some confidential information. The Patriots admitted overtures were being made to France; Eden conceded that the British government was hiring Hessians. Eden thereafter was not molested, but a letter to him from George Germain telling of a proposed expedition by the British to secure the southern colonies was intercepted. Gen. Charles Lee had picked up the letter and immediately requested the Maryland Council of Safety to arrest Eden. Eden's behavior had been so moderate that the council defied the order and permitted the governor to depart for a British ship—at his "early" convenience, of course, but without armed force or an arrest.[31] During the last months he had given his parole to the Maryland Convention, and in effect had been a governor in exile though still in residence.

Boucher's plight had become more precarious than Eden's, and at a much earlier date. In the summer of 1775 Eden advised Boucher to leave for England and hazard all, relying on Eden's letters to help him find friends once he was there. The governor knew that ultimately he himself must flee, and he wanted Boucher to be settled in England where they could continue their friendship (*MHM* 8:343). The decision was made, and only the physical details of the departure remained. Nelly had at first concurred with a plan to leave her in Maryland "to take the best care she could of our estate," in the hope that in six months or so the storm would blow over and Boucher could return. Addison, on his part, was completely against the idea of their leaving Maryland. Boucher concluded that Addison's reaction was based on his opinion that he himself could not leave. His wife had died the year before, and he dreaded being left behind and alone (*Rem.*, p. 124). But suddenly Addison capitulated. He made arrangements to leave with Boucher and to take his younger son with him. The departure of the men had to be accomplished speedily if they were to avoid being caught by the closing of the ports. In mid-August Boucher rode into Annapolis to make arrangements for their passage.

Nelly now contemplated spending six months without her husband and concluded that she could not face the prospect. It was a difficult choice. Leaving with Boucher meant deserting their property, leaving her family, and facing an unknown future in a country foreign to her. On the other hand, she may well have realized that there was little hope that the troubles in the colonies would be over in six months. In some agony of spirit she finally decided to accompany her husband.

All departure plans had to be completed in less than a week. Eden, as good as his word, wrote a letter of recommendation to the earl of Dartmouth for Boucher to hand carry, while a second letter to Dartmouth on Boucher's behalf was given to Lloyd Dulany for delivery. Eden also wrote to the bishop of Bangor, who had married Eden's sister, and to the bishop of London.[32] Jane Boucher, Jonathan's sister, had already decided to stay in America, but Nelly's change of plan necessitated new arrangements. Boucher's friends had counseled him to create the impression that they were leaving with the intention of returning soon, hoping thereby to preserve their property. To do so the Bouchers took none of their effects with them, not even clothing. Boucher wrote later that he took "one suit of clothes, and Bills of Exchange to the amount of a little better than four hundred pounds" (*Rem.*, p. 127). Boucher's letters to James in subsequent years reveal that Addison had lent him about two hundred pounds and that he had been able to ship a cargo of tobacco to England to help him meet expenses in England for the supposed six-month stay.

After the passage to England had been arranged for in Annapolis, Boucher rode back to the Lodge, arriving on a Saturday and expecting to leave again on Sunday morning. He had been alerted earlier that "on Monday morning Mr. Sprigg and his myrmidons," of the Council of Safety would "wait on us with the new oaths and proscribe us if we declined to take them" (*Rem.*, p. 126). Kind friends, come to take leave of the Bouchers, filled the house that Saturday. While their belongings were carried on board a small craft to be transferred to the transatlantic frigate, Boucher gave his power of attorney to young Overton Carr, his long-time pupil and a "worthy" man, who was now a member of the family by virtue of his marriage in February 1775 to Nelly's sister, Ann Addison. The two had been living with the Bouchers and thus the delegation of responsibility to Carr was a convenient and natural arrangement. Boucher took the time to write down full directions for all that he wished to be done during his absence, for it was "highly inconvenient" to leave his affairs at that time (*MHM* 8:343). August was a busy time on the plantation and the harvest season was approaching. However, Boucher knew he could trust Overton Carr. Finally the harried cleric made his last will and testament. Dawn broke, and the moment of departure arrived. Boucher had not had time to go to bed that night.

The hectic preparations and the sudden change of plans gave Boucher little time to think of long-range consequences, but they did serve to blot out for the time being his sadness at having to leave. He deliberately thought about his absence in terms of six months. He was leaving "a country where now almost all my attachments were, to go to another now become foreign to me, where I had no friends, and knew not how to live for even the six months I expected to be absent." "Even a little self-delusion on such occasions is not to be discouraged," he wrote later. "I wished to believe we should return, and therefore was not too nice in examining how far it was probable or improbable" (*Rem.*, p. 127).

Jane Boucher and young Jack Addison (who were remaining at least for the time being) accompanied the two Addisons, Nelly, and Boucher to the schooner *Nell Gwyn*, which in turn was to take them to the frigate *Choptank*, then lying in the Potomac off Quantico. On 14 August 1775, "amid the tears and cries of our slaves," the exiles left the Lodge.[33] Their voyage on the schooner was short but miserable. Exhausted, they slept on one of the bunkers with a piece of old sail for a cover and a small bag of hominy for a pillow. They reached the *Choptank* a day and a night later. Jack Addison and Jane Boucher took their leave. The frigate then dropped down the river to the mouth of the Potomac, where it lingered several days before setting sail for Dover. It had been sixteen years and two months since the day in July 1759 when Boucher had first glimpsed the American shore. Then he had been an Englishman, a stranger embarking on a new life. Now, thoroughly at home in America, he was being forced to flee his adopted land and return to England, again with the feelings of a foreigner. On 20 September 1775, straining his eyes for a last glimpse of the sunset on a "charmingly fine evening," Jonathan Boucher lost sight of the capes of Virginia, "never to see them more" (*Rem.*, p. 142).

Few Patriots mourned Boucher's departure. The degree of his unpopularity may be measured in several ways. The *Virginia Gazette* recorded a bon voyage item on 22 September 1775 which Boucher may not have heard about. It was a piece of news apparently relayed by a man aboard the *Choptank* who noted the departure of "parsons Addison and Boucher, with families." With these two parsons gone, and Lloyd Dulany and others embarked, Annapolis was thinned out, the writer thought. He closed with a partisan barb: "May we not rejoice that America is in so fair a way of being disgorged of all those filthy, grovelling vermin," fit only to be trampled upon by tyrants. Meanwhile, let them "herd with their kindred" and breath the contaminated air of "villainy and corruption." So ran the impassioned prose of a fellow American. Boucher fared no better on the streets than he did in the press in those wild disordered days. Within a few more months, in May 1776, a thousand or more Sons of Liberty paraded an effigy of Boucher through the streets, and then shot and hanged it (*MHM* 9:234). His American career was at an end.

The English Years

ᴖ Chapter 9 ᴖ

Boucher the Émigré

Jonathan Boucher's sad voyage to England as an exile from the America to which he had become so accustomed was short and tempestuous, requiring about a month on the Atlantic. Nelly survived it in good spirits; Boucher suffered a severe fever and was in a dangerous state at times. The *Choptank* made port at Dover on 20 October 1775, and the Bouchers proceeded to London with the two Addisons. Fortunately, they were able to turn to one Mrs. Brooks, whose son they had known in Annapolis. They boarded with her temporarily at Queen's Square, Westminster.

London was a surprise to Nelly. The crowds overwhelmed her, and the first time she was with Boucher in the streets she asked him to stop until the crowd passed, not realizing that this was the usual street traffic. Boucher, with time on his hands and no occupation, found it "exceedingly amusing and flattering" to be "so much at the fountainhead of . . . all literary matters." He candidly admitted that he contrived to "see and be acquainted with *living authors*"; he was pleased to have met Governor Hutchinson, a "spinner of newspaper paragraphs" (*MHM* 8:350). Boucher also busied himself in pursuing an acquaintance with those men to whom Eden had written about him. Both Lord Dartmouth, the colonial secretary from 1772 to 1775, and the bishop of London encouraged Boucher to think that something might be done for him.

In spite of this initial encouragement, Boucher was to know hard times and bitter disillusionment. But he was to be luckier than many Loyalists. He may well have been more persistent and ingratiating. Furthermore, his efforts on behalf of the Anglican church in America and his friendship with Myles Cooper gave him a little advantage in England in the long run. Boucher hoped primarily for a parish living, although he was aware that he could not command an income comparable to that of his Maryland parish and plantation operations. For a time he hoped strongly that William Eden, undersecretary of state and brother of the former governor, would be able to help him. Eden's brother-in-law was the bishop of Bangor and Boucher thought it possible that through him Eden might procure a living. But all this came to nothing, apparently because the bishop refused to depart from his policy of appointing only native sons to livings in his diocese. It is possible that Boucher expected some sort of governmental office in return for his services to the proprietor in America and those he was about to offer in London. He also aspired to a pension; it seemed to him that he had some basis for both hopes.

Shortly after arriving in London, Boucher met with Lord George Germain, the British war secretary, and volunteered a wide variety of information, political, geographic, and military, about the colonies. This meeting may have been arranged as a result of Robert Eden's letters to the earl of Dartmouth in the Colonial Office and the intercession of William Eden. Robert Eden had indicated that Boucher was an intimate friend, knew most of the important men both in Maryland and Virginia, and was knowledgeable about the affairs of both colonies.[1] Boucher and Germain talked freely about America, and Germain asked him to give, in writing and in detail, his sentiments and his advice (*MHM* 8:344). This Boucher did in a lengthy paper on 27 November 1775.[2]

Boucher dealt first with the causes of the revolution, stressing its inevitability. The colonies, Boucher explained, had been founded merely as fishing and trading settlements, and for a long time no one in Britain had paid any attention to them other than to improve trade arrangements. The consequence of this policy had been the neglect of political affairs. Britain had failed to realize that for over a century she had allowed the colonies to drift nearer and nearer to independence. In short, Boucher advanced what twentieth-century historians have called the "theory of salutary neglect," an idea which Edmund Burke also proposed in his celebrated speeches in the House of Commons.

Boucher then turned to the problem of military strategy. The heart of the rebellion was in New England; it was only just that the king's generals should make the New England colonies "feel the miseries of a country that is the seat of war." He urged that Washington be forced into a decisive action. One good victory could decide the quarrel; otherwise the Americans would be encouraged to pursue hostilities indefinitely. Boucher next volunteered some specific military advice. The defense of New York was imperative; an army of 10,000 men should be dispatched there and an occupation force of 5,000 men should be stationed in the city. Britain would have port facilities and accommodations for the soldiers. Armed vessels could then go up to Albany and easily cut off communication between the northern and southern colonies. Thus in his imagination Boucher foresaw the ill-starred Burgoyne campaign of 1777 that was to end in disaster for Britain.

Boucher also thought New York to be a desirable seat of operations because there were more friends of the British government there than in any other colony. He suggested that Britain capitalize on the disaffection toward the government which many New Yorkers harbored after its refusal to grant protection. Winning New York to the Crown would be a powerful example to the other colonies. Pennsylvania offered another strategic opportunity, according to Boucher's analysis of the situation. The Whig cause was weak there; not a single minuteman had yet been raised. No military operations were likely to be necessary there, but Philadelphia must be kept in constant fear of the navy. The province could become an excellent source of provisions, with good water transportation to move supplies to other colonies.

As for Virginia and Maryland, Boucher believed that they had comparatively little military strength. He recalled that fifteen years earlier, in 1760, the Maryland census had shown that there were only 15,000 able-bodied men in the colony. He could not estimate the potential number of men Virginia and the Carolinas could furnish, but he was positive that it would be poor policy to attack them. The two colonies if provoked would fight "in their own way, in woods and behind trees." Boucher's forecast was sound for frontier regions and rural wilderness areas, as the British learned to their sorrow at Lexington, Bennington, and King's Mountain.

Maryland and Virginia would be doing well, Boucher observed, if they were able to control "their own internal enemy." The situation in these colonies presented good psychological opportunities to keep the South constantly off balance by playing on the fear of slave uprisings with arms furnished by the British, and of Indian frontier attacks. He did not suggest the actual use of such measures, but only the threat. Humanity aside, he thought it would still not be good policy to exploit either slaves or Indians as weapons. "They resemble the elephants in the armies of old"; they might well turn on their allies. Boucher also held out the possibility that the British might use the white indentured servants in the southern colonies to advantage. These people had been decoyed to America and the tobacco colonies by romantic promises, only to find themselves "to all intents and purposes, slaves." It would be worthwhile to enlist them and harness their ill humor and their knowledge of the country, its manners, and its people. What was more, they were seasoned to the climate.

In Washington, Boucher commented, the Americans possessed a commander of decidedly limited abilities. "In the military line, it is not possible his merit can be considerable," but Boucher warned that Washington would "atone for many demerits by the extraordinary coolness and caution which distinguish his character." The only reasonable course of action would be to harry him with a thousand difficulties daily and to keep him "perplexed and confounded with stratagems." He would, Boucher thought, stand up well in a regular action, but would be defenseless against artful maneuvers. Furthermore, Washington was already distressed by internal problems which would further distract him. There was serious dissension within his staff, which, Boucher deduced from his own knowledge of the army and of the men commanding it, could only increase with time. The enlisted men were "wrangling about their pay" and their clothing and distrusting their leaders. Furthermore, the American enlistment system handicapped Washington seriously. The short enlistment periods, with reenlistment lagging due to the lack of military success, would shortly present the American commander with "insuperable difficulties." Many enlistments, he pointed out, would expire about Christmas, at which time many soldiers would go home.

Boucher then made a series of suggestions for winning the Americans back to loyalty. He recommended appeals to British freedoms. As soon as possible, Britain must arrange to publish "full and liberal manifestoes" promising good and loyal subjects "a free press, free inquiry, and free trade."

This letter to Germain was extraordinarily knowledgeable, dwelling shrewdly on the weaknesses of the colonial cause and suggesting ways to exploit them. The absolute commitment to England which Boucher must have felt in order to write such a letter marked a turning point in his life. Although it would be more than two years before he would admit, even to himself, that he could not return to America, this letter marked the psychological moment when Boucher's sense of country shifted. He had turned his back on America and was no longer the "good American"; he had channeled his talents toward suppressing the rebellion.

Boucher received "some little assistance" by order of Lord Germain for his information and advice, together with personal assurances of "a little farther supply of money" from Secretary Pownall of the Board of Trade. On the basis of these reassurances, Boucher requested a pension of £200, knowing that others who had done less than himself for the British cause in America were now in possession of "comfortable and established pensions." Furthermore, many high-ranking officials in the church had also assured Boucher that he "deserved to be made some amends." Boucher reminded Eden, however, how necessary it was to maintain strict secrecy about such a pension. He was concerned about the possible reaction in America. In 1776 Boucher still "cherished an idea" that William Eden was most likely to assist him in getting reestablished in America, where he thought it in his best interest to cast his lot, even if it was "not the most to my inclination" (*MHM* 9:61-63).

When weeks dragged by with no word of a pension forthcoming, Boucher's appeals to William Eden for assistance elicited a positive but restrained inquiry from Eden to Pownall on his behalf. Eden described Boucher as a "modest and worthy man" whose abilities were "good enough to be useful" and who used his talents with "zeal and discretion." He did not "urge the request" for a permanent provision, but expressed his intention to get something for Boucher from some of the bishops. His restraint on the pension request stemmed from his knowledge of "the poverty of the public purse." Yet he wanted some assistance for Boucher in the meantime, for "you see that the poor gentleman wants bread" (*MHM* 9:63-64). A pension would eventually be forth-coming, but it was months in the future.

Now that Boucher had joined the ranks against the Americans, he found himself full of criticism of colonial society. The letters he wrote during 1776 often expressed little charity toward his former American neighbors. On 28 April he wrote James that he admired the "compendious plan of your Mr. Graham" who, "I am told, proposes a total excision of the whole race of the present colonists and then to set about a new plantation from better stocks" (*MHM* 9:56-57). He informed William Eden on 7 January that undue emphasis on the popular element was a major problem in the colonies because of "early prejudices, fostered by education and confirmed by religion," which made Americans "cherish republicanism." Church and state in the colonies were both "presbyterian; ... literally and truly all power flows from the people." Boucher knew it was "better to have the meanest committee-man your friend, than the best and most powerful governor" (*MHM* 8:339-42). So he told William Eden out of the depths of his own unhappy experiences before committees.

In another letter to James on 10 July 1776, he directed his ire against Thomas Paine's *Common Sense*, which had recently come to his attention. Parts of the letter are damaged or missing, but its meaning is clear. Boucher was both outraged at the implications of the pamphlet and reluctantly envious of its author's pamphleteering skill. He considered it so inflammatory that he thought it must be the work of Dr. Benjamin Franklin. It seemed to him politically portentous, intended "to persuade the people of America at once to declare for independency." Inasmuch as it had been published under congressional auspices, he supposed that the pamphlet was a precursor to such a declaration. Boucher could not, however, withhold his praise for its "boldness" and "originality of thinking"; he assumed that its vein of imagination and a warmth of coloring" would command attention. As for the contents, he believed that it proved the truth of his own conjecture that the issue in America was not "about taxation only, or even supremacy" of England over America, but a "downright, premeditated [action?] against the Constitution" on the part of Patriot leaders on both sides of the Atlantic (*MHM* 9:67).

Boucher told Eden on 7 January that the Americans were not solely responsible for the turn of events. Some of the evils of the times he blamed on the English. It was not America's "transatlantic devotees alone, her Hancocks and her Adamses," he wrote, but "your Chathams, your Camdens, and their satellites, the Burkes and the Barres, even down to Priestly" and his "paltry pamphlets," who were responsible. And Boucher was still certain that nine-tenths of the people in America, "exclusive of the New England govt.," were against the measures that had since been adopted. "Their passions . . . are inflamed, . . . but still their reason remains unconvinced." While he hoped that the "*still small voice*" of reason would again prevail, he lamented that the dispute was apparently going to be left to the "sad arbitration of the sword" (*MHM* 8:342-43).

By April 1776 Boucher was becoming irritated by the delays and alterations in the plans of the British. The best season for action would be over before the troops could be deployed. What was worse, he was sorry to learn that the numbers to be committed were far fewer than originally planned. Disconsolately he concluded that there could be no defeat for the Americans in 1776. It was a sad prospect for Britain; she was committed to "prosecuting a disgraceful war, which is sure to cost far more than all the profits to be derived from America" for many years. Yet Britain must continue the war, and with vigor and success, or "'twill soon be over with England" (*MHM* 8:352).

Throughout the Revolutionary War years, Boucher followed military developments as closely as his circumstances permitted, reading the British newspapers and copies of the *Maryland Gazette* when he could get them. He was probably as well informed as any member of the public could have been, since he also attended sessions of Parliament regularly. When the British made a gain, Boucher reiterated his opinion that he never had a doubt of conquering the Americans, "if the men sent out for that purpose are but faithful to their trust, and in earnest (which, by the bye, has not I fear been the case hitherto" (*MHM* 9:65). However, news of British victories must have caused some mixed feelings on Boucher's part. Nelly had anguished thoughts about her only brother, who had become an officer in the Continental army (*MHM* 9:233). Late in the year she expressed the fear that he had been involved in the Long Island engagement of 27 August. The British had inflicted 1,500 casualties on the American force of about 5,000 under Gen. Israel Putnam and his subordinate generals, William

Alexander (Lord Stirling) and John Sullivan, at a cost of only 400 British. Boucher commented that the "cunning Yankees" had contrived "to have our Southern fools principally concerned" (*MHM* 9:232).

Boucher marveled at the few occasions when the Americans enjoyed a measure of success. But he managed to account for them by his conviction that English newspaper narratives were vastly different from what happened on the spot. However, if the accounts which he read were correct, then it was the result not so much of "their good management as our ill-management." He was also certain that "a deal of people" with whom he conversed were secretly "Patriots, not from any affection to the Americans but disaffection to the Ministry" (*MHM* 9:233). In Boucher's opinion, one explanation for the periodic American victories was the downright disloyalty of British commanders in the field, who were sometimes "anti-ministerialist" and wished "for ill-success." He had heard tales from America which he believed supported his negative conclusions about British commanders and British strategy. Not a single British ship, Boucher had been informed by friends in America, had been stationed in the Delaware River since he had left Maryland. Yet trading was brisk there, some persons had grown rich, and the Patriots had "laid in vast [quantities of?] warlike apparatus." In the same letter to James in which Boucher told of the shortsighted policy toward the Chesapeake section, he confided that he had a plan to prepare and publish a series of letters he had had from America that would prove his point (*MHM* 9:60).[3]

In November Boucher rejoiced in the prospect of a general engagement which the news from New York seemed to promise. But by the end of 1776 he was certain that the Continental army would not risk such a confrontation because he was positive it would be defeated. Good policy on the Patriot side dictated that they "disperse in small bodies" (*MHM* 9:235). He was correct in his estimate that a policy of delay and avoidance of major confrontations would serve the Americans best, given their knowledge of the terrain, their strength in guerilla engagements, and the open field training of European armies. Washington's effectiveness as a general, it is now clear, increased as he took cognizance of these circumstances.

The ill management of the Patriot army in New York and on Long Island Boucher attributed to "divided and distracted counsels." He thought some of the Patriot accounts which he had seen in their own papers confirmed his opinion. Very likely he had been reading the *Maryland Gazette,* for he seemed to have had information on how the Marylanders fared. "Our Maryland fools suffered the most; many of my parishioners and quondam persecutors being knocked in the head" (*MHM* 9:236). Boucher noted that one who had suffered that fate was the same man who had had cart loads of stones carried to church to stone Boucher for having said, "as it was alleged," that a rifleman "would be no match for a common musketeer in the field." With pardonable satisfaction, he observed that most of these riflemen had fallen or been taken prisoner, and he noted with relish that "Several of my neighbors, I find, have gotten their bellies full of liberty, in the shape of musket balls, and bayonets" (*MHM* 9:335). He still hoped that the Americans would have just and liberal terms given them, but not until their "rebel armament" had been effectually demolished and their leaders punished as examples. Until that was done, "it is absurd to expect any accommodation that can last much longer than it is a-making" (*MHM* 9:236). It was at this time, while Boucher still held a strong belief in the ultimate success of British arms, that he began his plan for the future government of the colonies.

The British ministry appeared to Boucher to be remiss in planning for the "settlement of things"; nothing was being done. His concern for the future government of the colonies, together with his desire for recognition from the British government, motivated him to write a plan for government himself. His project entailed a "very laborious and most difficult enquiry" and had already cost him much thinking and research (*MHM* 9:237). By January 1777 Boucher had finished the pamphlet on future government for the colonies. He placed it in the hands of Sir Grey Cooper, whose judgment in the matter was to be decisive. What he had proposed for the Americans is not clear. In spite of Boucher's interest in the plan, nothing further developed.[4]

The year 1777 provided Boucher with ample opportunity to criticize both Sir William and Admiral Lord Richard Howe. In January he learned that they had proclaimed a general pardon to "all who will come in within 60 days." The timing was poor, Boucher pointed out, for they had just gained advantages "far beyond their most sanguine hopes," and now had thrown them away with an "unaccountable" pardon offer. He railed at the "timid, dastardly, irresolute, shilly-shally way of going on which, more than anything else, encourages the leaders of the revolt" (*MHM* 9:240). In the fall Boucher again criticized the Howes. They had been "roused from their lethargy," he wrote James on 18 October 1777, after hearing the news that they had moved against Philadelphia, "but, to be sure, all this might just as well have been done many months ago." He continued with caustic criticism of General Howe's strategy: "I defy any man upon the earth to give any good reason for this monstrously tedious and expensive voyage from New York to our Bay; when, from all that yet appears, Washington might have been forced to have fought out of his entrenchments in the Jerseys." In his opinion, "Never, surely, was there so singular a history" (*MHM* 9:334-35). He did have an indirect word of praise for the Americans, however, embodied in criticism for the Howes. He thought the Howes no match for the Americans, and considered the rejection of all overtures by the colonials "most providential" for the British (*MHM* 9:236). Howe's extended delay in New York and the long voyage to Chesapeake Bay to move against Philadelphia were never comprehensible to Boucher. The only bright spot of news was that eight Maryland, three Pennsylvania, and two Virginia counties had submitted and petitioned for the king's protection. He sincerely hoped that there might be a good settlement in the end, one that would be of durable advantage "to the whole Empire" (*MHM* 9:335).

Boucher's next letter to James reflected the disillusionment and feeling of impending disaster that was shared by most of the Loyalists after the defeat of Burgoyne at Saratoga in 1777. It was a crushing blow to Boucher, as his words to James on 23 December indicate. "It knocked me up; for I seemed to myself just before to have been set up a little, only to have the heavier [blow] fall" (*MHM* 10:32). In spite of James's cautioning about the "mistaken confidence" of Boucher and of the other "wretched refugees," he refused to budge from his opinion that the British had the capacity to suppress the rebellion. In defense of his position he wrote James in the same letter: "The people were such as we described them; and, if things have hitherto gone on most perversely . . . it has not been owing to their good management, but to your ill-management." Boucher's faith in history was also being shaken at seeing "a greater event than it has ever yet recorded likely to be brought about by the most unlikely of all human means" (*MHM* 10:26-27).

In one of his most bitter diatribes against the Patriots to that date, Boucher maligned his former compatriots: "I say it again, and will say it as long as I have common sense and common honesty, that the people who now bid defiance to this great and glorious nation are in every point of view worthless in the extreme." He refused to concede that the "understanding" which the Americans had displayed was true knowledge, but asserted that it was instead a "subaltern bastard sort" which could more aptly be described as "cunning," and was on a par with their "integrity." With a few deprecating remarks about Washington, Hancock, and Adams, Boucher pursued the subject. The nation "seems not to have got a true idea of the contest." It was an American war only because the scene of action happened to lie there; in reality, it was "a war against the Constitution, and a Catalinarian combination of individual scoundrels." To support his argument, Boucher pointed out the origin of the best brains of the American opposition. "Some of the best heads, and certainly the best hands employed in it, are not of American growth," he wrote. "Two-thirds of Washington's army were born in this hemisphere, a fact I never could persuade them to believe till they found it so at Brandywine." Furthermore, he added, "a majority of their generals are also of Europe." As for the greatest of American plans, they were conceived, he believed, "within but a little way of the spot where I am now writing" (*MHM* 10:26-27).

Stern criticism was not reserved for the British command in America; Parliament came under his fire regularly. Boucher confessed to James that his hopes were at the lowest ebb, and not from the "little gleam of success which seems to have attended the efforts of the factions yonder, but from that of their compeers here." He told James bluntly that he had been attending Parliament regularly and he did not like what he saw there. "Your Government is rotten at the core," he declared. He had "heard speeches there which would have been thought licentious, seditious and treasonable in America," even when he had left it. Ministers seemed, "when baited by these dogs of faction, to be in but little better plight than I used to be, when had up by the committees for my inimicality to liberty. They are weak and timid in a manner

205

that shocks one; as suggesting so melancholy a proof of the weakness of Government" (*MHM* 10:27).

Boucher's remaining slight attachment to America comes through in his repeated use of the words "your government." He no longer identified with the Americans, but neither did he feel wholly like an Englishman. While he understood the weakness of Parliament, "where would you get a better?" He had learned that Parliament was "exceedingly dissatisfied (and surely they have reason) with their commanders; and yet are afraid to recall them, or at a loss where to find better." Sarcastically he commented on Burgoyne, who was "to come home a Patriot; and instead of beating rebels, to carry on a safer war with administration." Boucher deplored Britain's current preparations to carry on the war even more vigorously, while at the same time making overtures of reconciliation. He concluded that the government would soon be willing to end the war on "almost any terms." Thus, "after all this waste of blood and treasure, a peace will be patched up not so good for either side as might have been had three years ago" (*MHM* 10:27-28).

Boucher did not write to James again until two years later, on 10 November 1779. His great depression had silenced him. "Tired and sick of politics, myself, I think I have not lately plagued you with my conjectures and opinions. Indeed, everything has turned out so unlike what, I think, any reasonable man could have expected that I am afraid and ashamed even to offer a conjecture." It seemed to him that "If the history of the last four years were now faithfully written, fifty years hence, it would be set down as marvellous and romantic." "Folly and mismanagement are not peculiar to us," he wrote. If the rebels were successful, they owed it not to their "superior wisdom but superior villainy." But he could not exonerate the British command. He thought that from Howe to Keppel all the British misfortunes were owing to "incapacity" of commanders. He could not cease to be amazed at the great effects that had developed from "such apparently inadequate causes." He sadly reflected: "It is all a paradox and a dream; and I have never been able to see an inch before my nose, through the whole progress of it." It seemed incredible to him that thirteen colonies, "the majority of whose inhabitants wished not to be so lost," had indeed been lost, and "without a single decisive battle." Somehow every action "has been in favor of the losers" (*MHM* 10:35).

With a feeble attempt to see the brighter side, he volunteered to James that perhaps it was as well for the world. Maybe mankind was no longer warlike, and "wars must hereafter be determined by long purses, rather than guns or swords." He thought the French in the past had managed even worse than the British; certainly the Spaniards had. He closed the letter with disillusionment: "My private affairs in America are in perfect unison with the public. Everything there is turned topsy-turvy; mankind have lost all principles of religion and every thing else by which societies are held together." Americans, although "not so fierce . . . really are every whit as savage as the aborigines who now have ample revenge on their European invaders" (*MHM* 10:35).

As late as December 1780 Boucher was hopeful that Maryland could be recovered by the next summer, "if no very great disaster befalls us." It seemed possible because the leaders were quarrelling with one another, and because though the "miserably enslaved multitude are by no means alert and active enough in availing themselves of the opportunity to emancipate themselves," yet he thought that they "must do it in some degree in their own defense." This, he thought, "will force the British generals to cooperate with them, their distrust of whom is the true cause that any rebellion at all still exists." It is apparent that by this time Boucher wholly identified himself with the British, and his old neighbors and friends had become "those Americans." Even the Maryland clergy was optimistic, Boucher told James. They were so cocksure that they had sent over a commission "empowering four of us here in England to take care of the interests of the American Church" (*MHM* 10:114-15).

In January 1781 Boucher was not yet completely discouraged about the prospects of Britain holding her colonies, although he was using forlornly the term "us poor refugees." He hoped that they would not be "Cassandras" for long. "I do still think, as well as hope, that things will come round again; a bold hope . . . considering who and what they are that must conduct them."[5] Boucher was heartened by a military development, the "affair of Rodney," in which Eustatia Island, a depot for supplies from the Dutch, was captured. As he wrote to James on 15 March 1781, "It was a great deed, and will be sorely felt by our rebels." However he could not help expressing the wish, which he thought James might share, "that the French, rather than the Dutch, had gotten so heavy a blow?"[6]

Boucher had always had a conception of himself as both a literary man and "a public man," and it was natural that these two roles would provoke in him a desire to write about the country of his adoption during this period of political turmoil. He had continued to work on a history of America, and had had it ready for the press in 1779. On 11 September he told James that he had sent to press a large quarto "History of America," but still had on hand some letters "taking to pieces our infidels." Historians can only speculate on what this history was. So far as anyone knows, it has never been published. It is possible that Boucher suffered the disappointment of having his work suppressed, as was that of George Chalmers in 1782. It is also possible that portions of it may have been incorporated into his preface to A View.[7]

In common with most of the first exiles, Boucher was beset with financial fears. Of the funds which he had managed to bring with him from America, passage for himself and Nelly had cost forty guineas, and his living expenses in London since his arrival had consumed another forty by January 1776. He had no income and no immediate prospect of an appointment to a living, and he began to realize that he had even less expectation of receipts from his property in America. In America he had always been able to fall back on teaching for an income and there he had been better qualified than most who took up the profession. In England, however, he faced competition from more learned men. He had no other training and experience and few avenues to earning a living.

Like many of the refugees from America, Boucher found living in England a hardship.[8] The cost of living was higher than in America. Most Tory exiles had lived in affluent circumstances in the colonies, and only the thought that such trials were temporary in England made life bearable. Boucher told James that he and Nelly were learning to economize, to live frugally, but were learning very painfully and not very well. "I live expensively, I cannot help it," he wrote on one occasion (*MHM* 8:352). In Maryland Boucher had had social prestige; in England he had almost none. "Here, everybody I see eclipses me," he complained. He had been introduced to the bishop of London and the archbishop of Canterbury and thought them cold and formal and not very liberal. They seemed to think that they were doing "wonders when they give you a dinner" (*MHM* 8:344-45). The exiles were sensitive to the rebuffs they received when they attempted "to enter fully into English political or economic life," and in part this was responsible for their withdrawal into "small refugee societies" based on their concentration in certain London neighborhoods along provincial lines.[9] Boucher finally concluded that there were just too many refugees clamoring for places. Some Englishmen who might have liked to help him, he decided, were dissuaded by the thought that if they could not help the others they ought not set a precedent, or many more would leave America to seek aid in England.[10]

Meanwhile Boucher did manage to catch on as a writer, which added a little cash to his dwindling supply. In the fall of 1775, Boucher had written several articles for the best daily of the time, the *Public Advertiser*. Presumably he set forth the Loyalist point of view and possibly some of the same opinions he had earlier expressed to Germain.[11] Boucher stated later that he received two payments of £40 each directly from Thomas Pownall, secretary of the exchequer, for his newspaper work, part of £177 distributed by Germain to "particular Objects of the Attention of Government," according to the minutes of the treasury of 27 February and 30 May 1776.[12] When the situation looked absolutely desperate in midwinter 1776, Boucher encountered a piece of good fortune. Myles Cooper, former president of King's College and also an exile from America, had been lately serving as the curate to Dr. Richard Browne at Paddington in London. Now he was returning to Oxford, and he arranged for Boucher to have the vacant post. Cooper told him it would pay about £70 a year, but Boucher was grateful for any material help.

Boucher moved to lodgings in Bell Lane, Paddington, in February 1776 and stayed there until midsummer, when Addison and his son left, the former to take a tour of England and the latter to enter an academy in Soho Square. Nelly and he then took a house in Paddington to themselves at twenty pounds a year, furnished it, and in the process spent "every farthing of money I then had, which was seventy-five pounds" (*Rem.*, p. 145). But he now could expect the income from his curacy (he recalled it later as sixty pounds, which later was increased to one hundred pounds), and he now had the regular Loyalist's pension of another hundred (*Rem.*, p. 145). He garnered an additional forty pounds a year for reading prayers to the Honorable Mrs. Trevor in Curzon Street every Sunday between his own two services, bringing his annual income to a total of two hundred pounds.

By summer 1776, Boucher concluded that there was little likelihood of Nelly and he being able to return to America very soon. He had received no remittances from America nor did he expect any in the foreseeable future. He concluded that his most rational course was to alter his "plan of life" and "take a select number of young gentlemen into my house to educate." Boucher was "without money, connections or friends, and more especially without learning," but he was well endowed with "competitors all round me, all possessed of all these advantages and many more." He thought it was "little less than madness in me to hope for success" (*Rem.*, pp. 145-46). He disliked teaching, but he and Nelly needed additional income.

Once the decision was taken, Boucher took a larger house in Paddington called the Hermitage, for forty pounds a year, then promptly took in two lodgers for three months to help defray the cost until some students should arrive. Boucher was in his thirty-eighth year, and found himself beginning a career once more. It had been fourteen years since his early Virginia days as a minister and schoolmaster. Life then had been arduous, but his expectations had been great, and by comparison with the meager salary he could now command, his American salary and the opportunities of his plantation had gone far to offset the drudgery of colonial life.[13] By November 1776 Boucher's financial circumstances were such that he offered to provide "bed and board" for James's oldest son, Thomas. Boucher had learned that James planned to bring his son to London the next spring to find some opportunity in commerce for him. Boucher immediately suggested that Thomas become a member of his own household, so that "I might, for one winter at least be to him what for nearly twenty you have been to me—a father." He assured his friend that he could afford it, and even if no good business opportunity presented itself that winter, "we will at least . . . rub off some of the Cumberland rusticity." Although Boucher had seemed resigned to his own childless state in America, as the years went by in England he tended more and more to fill the void in his life with affection for James's two sons. Mindful of the "drudging beggarly way" that Cumberland lads all too often had to begin in the world, and remembering his own first limited ambition to be a clerk in a counting house or an assistant in a shop, Boucher wanted a better prospect for Thomas. He offered to make inquiries about apprenticing arrangements with assurances of being taken into partnership after three or four years. Although this approach would require an investment of money and thus James's concurrence, Boucher made it clear that he thought the partnership opportunity most attractive for Thomas (*MHM* 9:237-38). As it turned out, a merchant in Lombard Street later took Tom as an apprentice.

Meanwhile, Boucher's operation of a boys' school ushered in a period of intense activity unparalleled since his early years as an usher with James at Saint Bees. Boucher found it a difficult adjustment. He was often too tired to write letters at the end of a long day of "fagging" with boys. "Were there any room left for choice," he remarked to James, "I certainly should not have chosen" teaching as a means "of getting a livelihood." He had neither the health, spirits, nor temper for it, and Nelly was "hardly ever well two days together." He knew he would find it less difficult were he a "younger and less shattered and weather-beaten man."[14] Boucher nevertheless managed to cope with the boys, and slowly the school grew. Robert Eden was of some help by sending his own son to Boucher, which lent a kind of aristocratic sanction to the undertaking. Another London schoolmaster referred a prospective student to Boucher when he could not accommodate him in his own school. His success was assured when Lord Galloway investigated and found the school suitable for his eldest son, Lord Gairlies (*Rem.*, p. 151).

Such patronage was necessary to Boucher's long-term prospects, but the demands often exceeded his capabilities. He had always been weak in Latin grammar and probably knew but little Greek at this time. When the opportunity arose to take on the son of one Mr. Glassford, a merchant of Glasgow, Glassford wished to ascertain Boucher's competency in Greek and ordered the young man's tutor to go down to Paddington and interview Boucher for that purpose. Astonishingly, but with his usual resourcefulness, Boucher passed the screening by employing his wits, keeping the lead in the conversation, and utilizing his knowledge of the classics to the utmost (*Rem.*, pp. 149-50). From that day forward, Boucher worked desperately hard, laboring to teach himself sufficient Greek to instruct his students.

After a time the task of keeping ahead of his students became overwhelming and he turned to James for a solution. Although he could not afford an usher, it was imperative that he engage one and he begged James to find him a competent assistant as soon as possible. To go on as he had been would lead to disaster, he thought, but he would not give up. "No calamity can gall me so much as having the boys taken from me, through any suspicions of my incompetency," he admitted, for that would cover him with disgrace. James was to send him a young man "more learned than myself," with good sense and honesty, and a willingness and ingenuousness to conceal his superiority.[15] It was a difficult order, but James presumably was able to oblige him, for the school prospered and Boucher soon enrolled both Lord Shaftesbury and the son of Sir Thomas Broughton.

Fluctuating enrollment caused uncertainty for any schoolmaster, and Boucher was no exception. Boucher's goal was an enrollment of between twelve and fourteen boys. When it dropped to eight, as it occasionally did, Boucher fretted until replacements appeared. However, he usually had twelve to sixteen boys with him, and soon found it necessary to keep two ushers constantly in his employ, while he varied the number of masters to suit the enrollment. Boucher credited much of the success of the school to Nelly's efforts.

In 1779 another break came his way. With the assistance of William Stevens, a newly found friend whom he considered "one of the prime blessings of my life" (*Rem.*, p. 146), he applied successfully for the post of undersecretary of the SPG. His first attempt at the position in 1778 had failed because he refused to promise that he would not leave. The practical benefit was the annual salary of one hundred pounds, although it was later reduced to eighty. The post allowed him to cement his friendships with many of the men who would soon fill the American bishoprics created by the establishment of the American Episcopal church after the war.

Boucher doubtless hoped that his new position would be sufficiently influential to secure him either one of the bishoprics abroad or an important church office in England. John James, Jr., who knew of his aspirations but was dubious about the prospects for Boucher in America, wrote to Nelly on 13 November 1781 expressing his opinion: "It would be vastly agreeable to you to live to see America reduced and submissive, and Mr. Boucher a bishop or archbishop there; neither of which perhaps is likely to take place before our present scanty term of years is up and the scene closed." John was very nearly wrong, for if Thomas Bradbury Chandler had been free to choose the man whom he believed most fit to be the first bishop of Nova Scotia, Boucher, not Charles Inglis, would have had the appointment.[16]

A chance gain developed in 1779 when Boucher aided an eccentric and wealthy woman in solving a series of personal problems. A certain Miss Mary Barton, the daughter of a silk merchant, had a servant who appeared to be having delusions and was about to be institutionalized. Miss Barton sympathized with the woman and asked for Boucher's assistance in finding her a house in Paddington, in order that she might take the servant woman to live with her. Boucher also assisted Miss Barton with her financial affairs. It appeared that her lawyers had her assets entangled with their own, and he successfully intervened to protect her interests. By this time Miss Barton was "wonderfully taken" with her new friend and when her health presently failed she invited Boucher to accompany her to the baths at Bristol.[17] Before they left she insisted on making out her will in Boucher's favor. The baths were no help, and Miss Barton soon returned to die. At her death in 1782 Boucher inherited Cheshire "property worth not less than £500 per year" (Rem., p. 158). Unfortunately, he also inherited a year-long legal battle with her attorney. Boucher eventually settled the case at a cost of £700–£800. With the windfall of an annual income and with an increase in his income from the Paddington curacy to £100, Boucher was in a much better financial position.

Later, when the British government made its first compensation payments to Loyalist exiles, Boucher received £900, out of which he promptly loaned £250 to James Brooks, an exile from Maryland who was in straitened circumstances and wanted to establish himself in the wine business. Boucher also arranged an annuity for his sister Jinny, who had long served his household. He was sensitive to her need for some feeling of independence and grateful to her for her years of service and affection. Ironically, he had just made these arrangements when Robert Eden's debt

213

to Henry Harford, to which he was a cosigner, fell due, totaling £1,500 with interest. It was a most inconvenient time. None of the Edens offered any help, and Boucher was forced to borrow money to pay for Eden's debt (*Rem.*, p. 188).

As the American war progressed, Boucher often reflected upon its consequences for his return to Maryland. From time to time he convinced himself that America would be reduced by British power, but he now doubted that it ever would "be a country for me again." "The wretches who now rule there," he wrote to James on 23 October 1776, "have so exceedingly injured and insulted me, that it is not to be expected from human nature that they should ever forgive me" (*MHM* 9:234). He knew that he could expect no remittances from his parish, nor from his estate in America. He valued his American estate in land, slaves, and other assets at £5,000 sterling, plus another £1,000 in debts owed to him. He recognized that he could not recover the latter because of the "confusion of the times and the suspension of all law and justice." He owed a total of £2,500. However, he was convinced that the value of his property would decrease as a consequence of the war, and if the British lost he thought it possible that he would be reduced "to my original nothing." "Would to God I had been in circumstances never to have emigrated," he wrote despairingly (*MHM* 8:345-46). Sir Robert Eden's future plans were crucial to his own decisions about any return to America. "If Sir Robert Eden should go back, I think I too certainly will; as I may then, un-soliciting, have anything that is to be had in America." Eden, however, leaned to staying in England. "I trust, however, he will find some way or other of providing for me somewhere, as he certainly is desirous to do" (*MHM* 9:234).

Boucher endured other irritants in these years, one of which was an unhappy epilogue to his former affair with Judith Chase, the young Maryland woman whom he had once hoped to marry. The two children of this alliance, Betty and Kitty Strange, were still in England under James's watchful eye. For years Boucher had been making covert annual remittances of twenty pounds for their care.[18] He originally had arranged to leave the children with his sister Mary at Blencogo. The situation had given rise to some gossip in Blencogo which had distressed him considerably. In some annoyance he wrote James that there was a fellow "in Blencogo, a true Cumberland clown, very ignorant and very cunning,"

214

who "with almost as much folly as malice, first formed the conjecture that my two little orphans were [Jinny's] because their little fingers were like [those of] our family." Boucher charged James to watch over the girls, to "inquire how they go on, and see how they look." He worried about their welfare. Although he did not want James to suffer any loss on their account, neither did he wish to see them become mere servants. Yet he was in no position to take them off James's hands, "as would best become me, and I dare not think of removing them" to Paddington. Occasionally, he had the pathetic thought that he ought to write to the girls, and asked James's advice on that point. Apparently he did not know precisely where they were, having earlier required James to remove them from his sister Mary's care.[19]

Boucher's letters to James continued to include inquiries and instructions concerning the "two unfortunates." He hoped to have them trained in some way in order that they might earn a living for themselves other than as servants (*MHM* 9:239). He offered to get them places in London, but he did not really want them there. He told James that he "should dread to see them here, with the constitution of their warm latitudes" (*MHM* 8:347). Yet it is more than likely that they were in the Cumberland area at the time, in a climate which Boucher must certainly have remembered was colder than that of London. The real obstacle was Boucher's unwillingness to have them too much under his own eye.

James thought it necessary to send Kitty down to London, and Boucher reluctantly agreed to find her a domestic place near Windsor.[20] Here she continued to be a source of concern to him. "Poor Kitty!," he remarked in a backhanded reference to her mother, "I am afraid she, too, is to be an adventuress." "I have done all I can for the poor girl, and if she has any caution she may do well. But there seems to be a something about her that makes me afraid." Kitty was "giddy" and thought of little but "new caps, white petticoats," and such.[21] In fact, Boucher's pessimism about Kitty's potential career in the Windsor household was wellfounded and her domestic service there was to end in August 1780, when her mistress closed the house for an extended vacation and took only one servant with her.

Two months later, the Jameses suggested that Betty be sent down to Paddington to the Bouchers. Again this posed a dilemma. "Nelly seems not to like to have her, and I cannot find another place at all proper for her," Boucher told his friend sadly. He asked James not to send her until he had the opportunity to talk to Mrs. James. Like her sister, Betty was obviously a problem and neither Boucher nor Nelly wanted to have her in the house. In the end, Boucher reluctantly agreed to have the girl come down to Paddington, but she almost immediately took French leave. He was only moderately concerned. When she was found the straggler was temporarily put in Jinny's care. The presence of the girl continued to trouble both his conscience and his convenience. He wished that she would somehow disappear. Wistfully he hoped that Mrs. James would take her off his hands. He was willing to pay for an apprenticeship, whatever the cost, preferably within reach of the Jameses. He hoped fervently that in a year or two he might be released from his care of both girls.[22]

Meanwhile, when Kitty lost her place in Windsor the Bouchers in despair took her into their own home, turning out their unsatisfactory upstairs maid to do so. Although Kitty was "honest and good natured," Boucher confessed that he was "full of fears." The real difficulty lay in the relationship. "I hate ... to have her a servant to me." Happily Kitty got on "more than tolerably" in the Boucher household, and Boucher even admitted, in spite of his evident embarrassment, "we really love and esteem her."[23]

Thus Boucher, in spite of his reluctance, dutifully assumed the responsibility for the two girls for years. His failure to acknowledge the children may seem callous in the twentieth century. But Boucher indeed assumed more responsibility for his illegitimate children than most eighteenth-century gentlemen. It is clear that in his own eyes Boucher behaved as an honorable man. His later letters are strangely silent about the fate of these children. After the 1780s Boucher no longer wrote of them. Whether Kitty simply disappeared into the London streets, as Boucher feared, or whether she managed to become an acceptable domestic servant is unknown. Only one thing is certain: Mrs. Chase did not entirely forget the children. She remembered one Catherine Strange in her will.[24]

Boucher had other family matters that distressed him in these years. His sister Mary had made a bad marriage to Isaac Tordiff, a notoriously poor manager and provider. The Tordiffs were still living on the Boucher family land, although title had fallen to Boucher at the death of his parents. He had been determined to hold the land, although to do so had cost him considerable effort and had made it necessary for him to borrow money in order to pay the encumbrances on the land and his sisters' legacies of one hundred pounds each. It disturbed him to have his relatives living on the land while it returned him no profit, for he thought Mary a "strange-tempered woman" with a "disagreeable husband."[25] But his natural kindness caused him to conceal his dislike.

To manage all of the difficulties of the Blencogo land, Boucher had given James a plenary power of attorney and many instructions. Mary had to be dealt with, and James was to show her "all possible justice" and yet persuade her to become more self-reliant and to refrain from her propensity to bother him with her imaginary problems. Mary was to be given the first chance to lease the land rent free for six, seven, eight, or nine years, or long enough to return her legacy in rent. Mary and Isaac were to pay the taxes. Not surprisingly, when the rent-free period expired they showed a very natural reluctance to pick up the payments. They showered him with a "world of complaints" and boldly asked that the rent be remitted. Boucher's irritation with them was intense; he had no real affection for them and he could not understand why they could not pay so small a rent when they were both young, had met with no misfortunes, and Tordiff had a good trade. He feared that they were either "lazy, or manage ill" (*MHM* 9:55-56). But his good nature again rose to the surface. He decided not to forego the rent, but then enjoined James to temper his terms to the Tordiffs if that seemed too harsh a decision. He relied on James to settle the matter in fairness to both the Tordiffs and himself. In spite of the fact that Mary was a "poor, helpless, complaining creature," and he doubted not that her husband was little better, yet "she is my sister and I can not bear that she should want, whilst I, at least *seem* to live in plenty" (*MHM* 9:60).

Before long the pair were threatened by a lawsuit, and they again turned to Boucher and begged his assistance. The scattering of facts which Boucher picked up convinced him that the claim against the Tordiffs was all too valid. Reluctantly Boucher engaged an attorney who managed to settle the affair. Boucher was intensely irritated. It was bad enough that he was maintaining Mary and her children on the Blencogo estate, but it galled him to be "saddled also with the maintenance of a sorry fellow, of no use or significance that I know of, but for bringing more beggars into the world." But again he concluded, "she is my sister, and friendless and forlorn" as she is in the world, "I cannot, I must not, desert her" (*MHM* 9:327). Ironically his "poor, helpless" sister, whose health was presumably so precarious that Boucher expected news of her death at any time, managed to raise two daughters who later married, while she herself outlived Boucher by many years. Boucher left a substantial inheritance to each of his nieces; his bitterness was long forgotten.

In the fall of 1776, Boucher learned to his dismay that the Sons of Liberty had hanged him in effigy. Somewhat surprisingly, his main concern was the impression this would make on his slaves. "My poor slaves and servants have been true and trusty to me beyond example; and their conduct when they saw their hapless master hanged and shot (in effigy, I thank God only)... has and shall endear them to me whilst I live." But the event also caused him to doubt that he could return to America. He still believed that Britain would defeat the rebels, but he questioned whether he would ever live in Maryland again. "God knows whether even I shall see them again, or not," he said of his slaves (*MHM* 9:234).

Boucher continued to worry about his American property. He wondered whether Overton Carr, his agent in Maryland, had found it possible to carry out the detailed instructions Boucher had left for him. Finding out the status of his property was the more difficult because Boucher was reluctant to put any of his friends or relatives in jeopardy. Attempts by Maryland Loyalists to communicate with Loyalists in England were dangerous. The mere receipt of letters from England was very hazardous and might expose an individual to severe reprisals. A long-time friend of Boucher's, probably Overton Carr, was to be imprisoned for several months on the basis of letters from him.[26] Boucher was also reluctant to write to inquire about his affairs because he feared that interception of his correspondence might interfere with whatever chance he had to recover his property.

In an attempt to protect his interest, Boucher arranged for a "fictitious sale" of a portion of his American properties. But when he learned that this sale might be challenged, he made further arrangements with his attorney in Maryland to carry on a "complete" sale. He hoped against hope that this procedure would shelter his property from the colonists' "madness," although the second sale may have been equally suspect (*MHM* 9:233). Boucher was even more disturbed when he learned from a correspondent in America that Col. William Smallwood, the friend of Judith Chase, had moved in convention for the confiscation of Tory estates, and of Boucher's in particular.[27] The rumor may or may not have been true, but what is certain is that no such motion passed. In reality Maryland was very reluctant at this time to embark on a policy of general confiscation, and would not do so until the October session in 1780.[28]

Meanwhile, disagreeable bits of news of American affairs reached Boucher from time to time. In September 1777 he learned that his former curate Harrison had been appointed to Queen Anne's, and Boucher began to read in the *Maryland Gazette* of meetings being held in "Mr. Harrison's Chapel." He reflected bitterly that it had once been "Mr. Boucher's Chapel" (*MHM* 9:335-36). Boucher told James the news of Harrison's appointment on 8 September, referring to him as a "dirty puppy," whose brother was serving as secretary to Washington. In the same year Boucher mourned the disestablishment of the Church of England all over the continent of America, leaving every man free to support any religion he pleased. He thought it an invitation to popery or "worse systems," and an exact repetition of an old story one could read in Lord Clarendon.

Reports from America about his slaves may have shaken his earlier fondness for them. "Even some of my Negroes, they tell me, are gifted, and will hardly be restrained from holding forth," he observed to James. Boucher was saddened to read an advertisement in a newspaper valuing his library at the Lodge at £1,000 and offering it for sale. He had had no direct information about the sale, which occurred in October 1777. Such events were creating chaos in Maryland, he thought, "and my private affairs [are] going to wreck and ruin as fast as they well can" (*MHM* 9:333).

Two years later, Boucher was warned by a friend in America to expect confiscation, and Overton Carr arranged for two additional transactions in an attempt to protect Boucher's property. On 18 September 1779 Garland Carr "bound himself" to Boucher in the amount of 500,000 pounds of inspected tobacco, in exchange for "all the lands and premises, together with the Negroes, the stock of cattle, hogs, sheep and horses with their future increase."[29]

The transaction included the provision that if Garland Carr later returned the property to Boucher, having observed certain stipulations regarding the use of profits to improve the property, then the obligation of 500,000 pounds of tobacco was to be null and void.[30] Like the previous fictitious and valid sales, this was another attempt to protect Boucher's interest. But it was to be no more binding, since Maryland soon declared all conveyances of any kind made between 19 April and 1 December 1779 by British subjects null and void. Garland Carr had little hope of proving the legitimacy of his purchase.

In spite of constant rumors about confiscation legislation and numerous attempts on the part of the more radical Marylanders to bring about such a law, the new state government moved slowly toward seizure of property. In part, this cautious approach was a reflection of Maryland's historically conservative society, and in part of a less retaliatory spirit than existed in colonies which experienced occupation by British troops and their wanton destruction of property. The earliest legislation concerning Tory property was enacted in 1776 and 1777, and provided for the forfeiture of property as a penalty under statutes against treason and misprision of treason. Unless Boucher were singled out for treasonable activity, he had reason to hope that he might yet retain his holdings in America. But Boucher's optimism was blasted by Maryland's Confiscation Act, which passed in the October session, 1780. Under its terms all absentees who did not return to the state by 1 March 1782 and take an oath of fidelity to Maryland were to be considered British subjects whose property would then be confiscated. There is no evidence that Boucher gave any thought to returning upon this news, but if he did he was soon dissuaded.

The General Court, in its May 1781 session at Annapolis, declared Boucher treasonous. His name appeared in the indictment along with twenty other Maryland Tories, including Daniel, Walter, and Lloyd Dulany, Anthony Stewart, George Chalmers, Bennett Allen, Henry Addison, and half-a-dozen others.[31] In May 1782, however, the General Court quashed the treason indictment against Boucher, as well as charges against nineteen others whose names had appeared on the court docket. Nevertheless, Boucher was still subject to the Confiscation Act, and in spite of all his efforts in cooperation with Overton Carr, the whole of his estate was seized. Apparently there was some mishandling of his estate, for in 1781 the commissioners for forfeited estates reprimanded Thomas Williams, sheriff of Prince George's County, for having sold some of Boucher's Negroes after the General Assembly had already confiscated and appropriated them to the use of the state. He was warned that if he attempted to receive the money for the sale or to give any title for the Negroes, he would be in violation of the law.[32]

Although Boucher's attempts to protect his estate failed completely, they became known to the public and produced much ill will. An anonymous letter writer who signed himself "Bye-Stander" arranged to publish a diatribe against Boucher in the *Maryland Gazette* on 29 March 1781, charging him with perpetrating fraudulent transactions. The evidence on which he based his accusations consisted primarily of letters of January 1777 and July 1780 which the Council of Safety had found when it seized the correspondence of Garland Callis and Overton Carr.[33] Obviously Bye-Stander was fully conversant with the contents of the letters, and he also knew that the deed under suspicion had been drawn by William Cook, a nonjuror and a Tory, who was privy to the plan and who had probably advised it. Anthony Addison, another son of Henry Addison, had used the same device and had conveyed his father's property to his brother-in-law Garland Callis.

Because of their assistance to the refugee parsons, the letter writer labeled both Garland Callis, husband of Henry Addison's daughter Ann, and Overton Carr, Boucher's brother-in-law, Tories and agents for two of Maryland's bitter enemies. Furthermore, he charged the sheriffs of both Prince George's County and of Frederick County with acting officially in their aid, threatening them with hearing "more of it" unless they moved promptly to collect the treble tax from the property of both parsons.

Bye-Stander also accused Boucher of arranging to discharge debts to the Loan Office and to his creditors in depreciated Continental money, thereby substantiating the political character he had established before he fled the country, "in which he raised himself from a poor pedagogue to an affluent fortune." Boucher's correspondence, according to the letter writer, was "full of bitterness and resentment" and breathed "sedition." He strongly recommended that no compassion be shown by Maryland either to Addison or Boucher.

221

This last advice to the readers of the *Maryland Gazette* was prompted by a request from Henry Addison, who was now in New York, for permission to return to Maryland. Addison, like many colonial refugees, was most unhappy in England and nearly destitute in 1780 when he decided to sail to America.[34] From the relative security of British-occupied New York he pleaded with the new Maryland government to allow "an old man broken by age and infirmities" to "find a grave among his ancestors." But the letter writer was unmoved by such sentiment, preferring to believe that Addison's request was simply a means of saving his fortune. It was not love of his country that prompted his petition, but "the dirty acres in Prince George's and Frederick Counties" that "he loves, he adores."

The letter was a heavy blow to any lingering feeling for the colony which Boucher may have had, and the damage to his reputation rankled. He was determined to find out who had written it, although he already strongly suspected Samuel Chase. For the time being there was nothing he could do about it, but he waited for some opportunity to present itself. That moment came in October 1783, when Samuel Chase arrived in London.[35] Boucher confronted him personally and charged him with being the author of the defamatory *Maryland Gazette* letter. Chase declined to answer. Under these circumstances, Boucher decided that it was his duty to his friends and to the public to declare the remarks in the letter "uncandid, ungenerous, and many of them grossly untrue."[36]

Although Boucher had nothing left in America, he was still contentious and determined to salvage his reputation. He drew up a letter in which he denied any fraudulent actions "either in Maryland or anywhere else." The letter was not an apology; instead he described his private letters to his friends in Maryland as "natural" and not necessarily "unbecoming" in a man who was perhaps too apt to be "warm" and who had never dealt with his friends with the "cold correctness" necessary for "a political inquest in times of great heat." He expressed the hope that the public would form its own opinion of the anonymous, mean, and cowardly Bye-Stander who had aimed the blow at him when he could not defend himself. Boucher gave Samuel Chase his signed and witnessed letter to deliver to Maryland for publication. But he did not trust Chase in the matter, and subsequently appealed to Gen. John Cadwalader of Philadelphia to arrange for publication of another copy of the same letter. He explained to Cadwalader that Chase had promised to arrange for publication, but if he did not, then he wished Cadwalader to forward the letter to an editor. This was Boucher's final concern for Boucher the American. Everything he had owned in America, and the life there which he had valued so highly, were now beyond his reach.

As he stood at the end of his American career, Boucher had just turned forty and Nelly was thirty-nine. The fortunes of the two former Marylanders had improved dramatically, and they could afford to commission the artist Daniel Gardner to paint single portraits of each of them, as well as another canvas in which they are seated together on a bench with a garden backdrop. All three pictures are in pastel gouache, and show Nelly in a white dress with flowers in her hand and with a white cap on her head. Jonathan is in clerical garb, holding a book. Gardner has captured the strong personality of Boucher in a pose that reveals an imposing man, tall, with wide shoulders and a solid look. His round face, broad across the cheekbones and with an ample nose somewhat flattened over the bridge, had just a hint of a double chin. His prominent grey eyes were accentuated by dark, pyramid-shaped eyebrows and a hairline with a slight widow's peak. His hair style (possibly a wig) was long enough to turn under in a large sausage curl over each ear, then caught up and tied in the back. He had the look of a virile, intelligent man with a sense of command. His countenance was open and alert, with a smile about the lips and a generally cheerful aspect. Nelly, on the other hand, appeared fragile and ill. Her rather small, heart-shaped face, with a narrow, pointed chin, a rather long nose, and short upper lip, had a patient, kindly look. Her deeply set eyes and hollow cheeks bore testimony to her precarious health.

Jonathan Boucher and Nelly stood at the threshold of the postwar years. He was to have two productive decades in England, but Nelly's death was little more than a year away. Nevertheless, with courage and all the energy she could summon, Nelly joined with Boucher in establishing their lives in England. They concentrated on the Paddington school, in which John James, Jr. had joined them some months before.

John was a tremendous source of pride and satisfaction to Boucher, who loved this boy as if he had been the son he had longed for. "Sure I am, I love him most sincerely, and even your wishes for his doing well are hardly more earnest than mine," he told the boy's father.[37] John had been born at Saint Bees on 21 March 1760, about a year after Boucher's departure for America. He was educated by his father at Saint Bees and later at Arthuret until he was admitted to Queen's College on 6 October 1778. Although Boucher earlier had taken an interest in Thomas James, the boy was less talented academically than his brother John, for whom Boucher developed a deepening concern and affection with the passing years.

While John was at Queen's and Tom was apprenticed in London, Boucher's proximity to both places had made it natural to invite the two boys to Paddington and they spent several vacations with the Bouchers. He was always careful to have the approval of James for such Christmas, Easter, or summer periods, and John wrote dutiful, informative, and affectionate letters to his parents describing his pleasure with the arrangement. "A visit of this kind has as much power as a sudden gleam of sunshine on a dull day." John was comfortable in the Boucher household. "Mrs. Boucher," John wrote his mother, "is a sensible, agreeable woman," who is "open, frank, and well-bred." Although Nelly did not dress with "gaiety," she was very neat. The Bouchers "do not live in any very high style," John observed, noting also that Nelly seemed constantly busy with her needle.[38] He soon discovered that Nelly had much good humor and that the household was a lively one. On 22 February 1780, his father wrote to Boucher urging him to act as a parent to John in every way.

Boucher encouraged John constantly, either lending or giving him books from his own expanding library, and inspiring him to further academic achievement. In a sense, John represented the university-trained scholar that Boucher should have liked to have been. In 1781 Boucher had urged John to think about the prize poem competition sponsored by the chancellor of Oxford University; however, time elapsed and John found his time so engrossed that it was too late to engage in the effort. Again in 1782 Boucher made the attempt at persuasion, and this time he succeeded. The subject for that year's competition was Christopher Columbus, and John thought he might produce a respectable poem, particularly if he referred to Virgil for inspiration for beautiful language. Soon he sent his father the first 94 lines for his comments, and the first 159 to Boucher for serious criticism. "Bravo,"

Boucher wrote after reading the first portion. "It has no faults, or I no faults can spy:/It is all beauty, or all blindness, I." Boucher then followed his lines of encouragement with many specific, constructive criticisms and suggestions for improving the poem. No father could have been more pleased than Boucher when John's poem won first honors, public exhibition of the poem, and a prize of twenty pounds.[39]

Boucher tried to impart to John some of the wisdom which he had acquired in his own lifetime, and most of all his spirit of adventure. He dreamed of wonderful European vacations for John, but he also tried to make practical plans to bring them to fruition. He found John's conversation a delight, second only to that of his father. John was a great assistance to him and a source of companionship.

On 4 July 1782 John took his B.A. at Queen's College and then returned to Arthuret for six months. While there he assisted his father with his twenty pupils and pursued his studies independently. Boucher, however, had pressed John to come to Paddington to work with him, a plan he first broached to the James family in 1779. A move to Paddington was a difficult decision for John, for his father was barely lukewarm about the proposal. For one thing, he wished John to return to Oxford for an additional year; for another, he remembered his own hard years of teaching at Saint Bees with their drain upon his health, and did not want so demeaning a life for his own son. But John decided in favor of Boucher's school, and in January 1783 he took up residence in the Hermitage. Boucher then divided the students into two groups, giving John the responsibility for half of them. The arrangement was so satisfactory that Boucher was soon to propose that John become his partner, a plan that was consummated in April 1784.

Meanwhile, Boucher encouraged John to enter the clergy. John agreed, and was to be ordained on 13 June 1784 in Chelsea. On the basis of his expectations, he promptly proposed to Elizabeth Hodgson, the sister of Sir Richard Hodgson, the high sheriff of the Carlisle area, and made plans to bring her to the Hermitage after their marriage. It seemed to Boucher that a move into such a large household might well appear formidable to the young woman, and accordingly he wrote her a welcoming letter of great warmth and sensitivity. He assured her that she had "fair prospects" for happiness with James, for he possessed the "best understanding" and "the best temper" he had ever met with in a man. "You will have much to say to me, and I to you," he wrote, adding that she should come to them "with confidence," for "though as yet, we are in some measure still personally strangers to you, when you change your home you shall still find yourself among friends." Nelly, his "dear, suffering martyr to a long and severe sickness," added her assurances.[40] Boucher promised that if she were spared to him, Nelly would be a real friend to Elizabeth.

Nelly's health had been declining through 1782 and became worse in the winter of 1783 in spite of a stay at Windsor. It occurred to Boucher that when the weather improved Nelly might benefit from some leisurely travel, and he began to make plans for the summer. He engaged a phaeton and a pair of horses and arranged for a servant to accompany them. He proposed that they leave on 18 August 1783, journey first to Staffordshire, Cheshire, and Buxton, and then pause for a day or two before continuing. If Nelly kept "stout" or improved, then Boucher hoped to see James at Arthuret by 28 September. The brief reunion with his old friend in 1782, when James received his doctorate at Queen's, had whetted his appetite to see more of him, and he looked forward to showing Nelly the scenes of his childhood in Cumberland.

✑ Chapter 10 ✑

New Roots in England

Boucher's sentimental journey with Nelly to the familiar Cumberland hills intensified his concern for the tradition of the family and the remains of the estate, and inspired a renewed interest in the history of the district. His concern was to come to fruition in three ways: in acquisition of land to enhance Blencogo farm holdings; in biographical sketches and county material for William Hutchinson's *History of the County of Cumberland* (published 1793-97); and in 1792 in a sweeping proposal for economic, cultural, and conservation measures for the county. Although he enjoyed a "kind of melancholy satisfaction" by "retracing all the old haunts" of his boyhood days, such as the place where he had caught a large trout, found a bird's nest, or fought a successful battle, still the visit to Blencogo was disappointing. The barrenness of the village appalled him, the rusticity of the natives reminded him of his own coarse childhood manners and customs, and he had a less than warm welcome from the neighbors who barely remembered him and came to stare at him with curiosity and envy rather than "to rejoice" in his return (*Rem.*, p. 165). The cool reception the natives gave him was in fact quite understandable, for he had last been in the village some twenty-one years before.[1] He was further saddened by the plight of his sister Mary, whom he found "battered by age and disease" (*Rem.*, p. 164). Boucher and Nelly stayed at Blencogo for three or four days, and on Sunday Boucher preached the sermon at the Bromfield church, the last time Nelly was to hear him from the pulpit.

Boucher's search for his past was equally disappointing at Wigton and Carlisle. At Wigton he sought out Johnson's tavern, which he had remembered as a spacious and respectable house, and now he found that he could "scarce find room to swing a cat" (*Rem.*, p. 166). With some difficulty the proprietors convinced Boucher that the place had not been altered. At Carlisle he searched in vain for a landmark from his past, the King's Arms, but learned from an old-timer that the building was long since gone.

His spirits were lifted by the warm reception the Jameses accorded him and Nelly at Arthuret. Nelly now had the opportunity to know the family that had meant warmth and love to her husband for so many years. Boucher was delighted to see Nancy James for the first time since 1769, and he reveled in conversation with James. Arrangements were made for taking John as a partner in the school, with the understanding that gradually he would succeed Boucher in the business. Before he left Cumberland County Boucher visited Edmund Law, the bishop of Carlisle, at Rose Castle, and his son, the bishop of Killala, who was there to see his father.

The reunion at Arthuret was marred by Nelly's rapidly failing health, although she bore her infirmities stoically. Boucher knew that she was very weak, frequently sick, and often in pain. Both were aware that she stood on the "brink of the grave," yet she never failed to astonish her husband with her good spirits on the arduous journey (*Rem.*, p. 167). She attended to everything and exerted herself so that she never detained Boucher by five minutes, he recalled, although they frequently set out on their daily journeys by five in the morning. She knew Boucher's penchant for punctuality, and was not surprised at being back at Paddington within five minutes of the time Boucher had proposed to return, a schedule projected before their departure.

The months that followed Nelly's return from Cumberland were filled with a "sad succession of wearisome nights and days," although she continued to attend to all of her domestic concerns as well as she could. Her "poor frame was emaciated and worn down to a skeleton," and by late February "she could hardly be said to be alive" (*Rem.*, p. 168). Her malady, "ossifying of some of the vessels that lead to and from the heart" (*Rem.*, p. 161), defied the treatment of her London doctors, including Dr. I. Carmichael Smyth, who attended her throughout her last days. Finally, on the night of 1 March 1784 her condition worsened, her breathing became more labored, and she begged to be lifted out of bed and onto a sofa. Boucher hastened to take her in his arms and grant her wish. She put her lips to his, murmuring "My dear Boucher," and within moments died in his arms (*Rem.*, p. 170).

Boucher had expected her death, had known that she desired the release from pain, and had thought himself prepared for it. "I wept only for myself," he remembered. He had not realized the extent to which all of his "habits of thinking and acting" had revolved around Nelly. He felt her loss keenly, "as if I wanted some of the parts essential to life, a leg, an arm, or an eye" (*Rem.*, p. 170). He had long been accustomed to sharing every thought and to doing nothing without first discussing it with her. He was brought to sharp reality shortly after her death when he was asked to make some decision concerning her funeral and found himself about to leave the room in order to consult with Nelly about it. She was interred in a vault at Paddington, and Boucher took pains with an epitaph for her which recognized the devotion to him which had led her so far from her home and family in Maryland.

> On the cold pillow that supports the dead
> My Eleanora rests her weary Head;
> She was amid those flowers whose gentle form
> Shrunk from the pressure of that civil storm,
> Which ancient systems into Ruins hurled
> And shook the Basis of th' Atlantic world
> From these rude scenes, Though Int'rest urg'd her stay
> And friends entreated, Still She turned away;
> Turn'd from the comforts of a Native Home
> An Exile with the man she lov'd to roam.[2]

Nelly's death left Boucher devastated. Although John James brought his bride Elizabeth to the Boucher household soon after his marriage 15 April 1784, an arrangement agreed upon some time before, the Hermitage still seemed too bleak to be endured. He felt " 'In every varied posture, place, and hour,/How widowed every thought of every joy' " and his mind sought to "wander from its woe" (*Rem.*, p. 172). Nelly had anticipated his state of mind after her death and his need for comfort of sorts, and some time before had suggested a change of scene.

Boucher accordingly devised a plan that would also benefit young John, to whom he had transferred some "disorderly and unmanageable" students. He proposed to the Countess of Shaftesbury, the mother of one of his most obstreperous students, an excursion around England during the summer vacation. The jaunt was speedily approved by the earl of Shaftesbury and his wife, who sweetened the prospect with the suggestion that their son should bear all of the expenses of the tour except those of Boucher's servant. Early in August they left John in Paddington and set out on horseback, each with a servant, travelling in a leisurely fashion. Their first stop was Derbyshire, then Lichfield, Manchester, Liverpool, and Chester, after which they traversed both the north and south of Wales, punctuating their enjoyment of the Welsh countryside with visits at Cardigan, Carmarthen, Cardiff, and Cyfartha.[3] The change of scenery and the break in his routine was some solace, and Boucher was pleased to learn upon his return that a long-deferred wish was about to be fulfilled.

For the past ten years Boucher's efforts to secure a rectorship with the aid of his American friends and their British contacts had yielded nothing. Now in 1784 he was offered the Epsom parish. Almost certainly Boucher's good fortune was the result of a friendship begun in London in 1777 with William Stevens. Stevens was a hosier with a thriving business, self-educated in French, Hebrew, the classics, and theology.[4] Stevens, who was sensitive to Boucher's discomfort and loneliness as an exile, tried to ease the situation by introducing both Boucher and his friend Addison to the many clerics in his wide circle of friends. It was he who arranged for Boucher to meet the bishop of London and the dean of Canterbury. Two weeks later Boucher had occasion to ask Stevens for advice on some matter and Stevens invited him to his home. From then on the friendship flourished, and they dined, corresponded, and exchanged favors.

The two men had much in common. Like Boucher, Stevens was self-educated in several areas, politically conservative, interested in literary pursuits, and concerned with theology. Furthermore, Stevens's success in business did not escape Boucher's notice, and he soon sought his new friend's advice in financial matters. Stevens in turn encouraged Boucher's writing, about the American

Revolution as well as other political and theological subjects. On occasion he commended Boucher for his business ability, traveled with him to sundry meetings, stayed for days at a time in the Boucher home, and when it was convenient borrowed Boucher's horse. Later the men were to work together for union between the Anglican congregations in Scotland and the Scottish Episcopal church. The friendship continued throughout Boucher's life. Stevens, who was six years older than Boucher and described himself as a good friend, served as a kind of counselor and mediator for Boucher. On occasion, he gave Boucher sound criticism with dry, sharp wit and a great deal of humor.

It is clear that Stevens aided Boucher in obtaining the benefice at Epsom being vacated by the Reverend Samuel Glasse, who had served the parish since 1782. Stevens had learned that Glasse intended to resign, rode to Epsom to see John Parkhurst, author of a Hebrew-English lexicon and patron of the Epsom parish, and then rode on to see "his patron's patron" as well. Parkhurst was favorably impressed with Boucher's credentials and his friends' recommendation. He appointed him to the living "because Mr. Boucher had distinguished himself in America during the revolution by his loyalty and by teaching the unsophisticated doctrines of the Church of England to a set of rebellious schismatics at the hazard of his life."[5] Once more Stevens was Boucher's advocate, just as he had been in encouraging Boucher to apply for the post of undersecretary to the SPG.

Boucher was pleased with his new position; it offset the frustration he had felt in 1780 when his hopes to succeed Dr. Richard Browne as rector of Paddington had come to nothing. The income was an improvement over the Paddington curacy, and he had for some time longed to recapture the prestige as a rector which he had enjoyed in Maryland. But there were other enticements as well. The countryside of Epsom Downs was attractive, and Saint Martin's Church had a venerable history which Boucher could appreciate. The parish lay in the old Epsom Manor (originally known as Ebesham, Ebbisham, or Eppesham), and had belonged to Chertsey Abbey from a time before the Norman Conquest to the dissolution of the monasteries. The church itself had been dedicated by the bishop of Tours and in 1331 had been licensed and endowed with a mansion and fifteen acres. After an interval of almost nine years, Boucher was once again a beneficed clergyman.

His installation in the ancient church 20 January 1785 marked the beginning of nearly twenty years of faithful service at Epsom. However, his pleasure in the occasion was dimmed by the recent death of his substitute father, Dr. John James, on New Year's Day 1785.

For several reasons Boucher's move from Paddington to Epsom was not accomplished immediately. One difficulty was how to dispose of his school. Boucher had determined earlier that John would inherit it. On the death of his father, however, John had been offered the vacant post at Arthuret and he had accepted it, leaving Boucher with the task of closing the school.

Boucher had been gradually freeing himself from teaching duties at Paddington, after John had settled in at the Hermitage. In August 1784 Boucher had left John in charge while he had taken a summer excursion around England and Wales at the expense of the Honorable Ashley, Shaftesbury's son. While Boucher was gone the three oldest boys of Nelly's eldest brother arrived from America. Boucher had been the guardian of these children in Maryland, and when he fled to England Overton Carr assumed Boucher's duties. Now he had sent them across the Atlantic to Boucher's care once more. John and Elizabeth left Paddington on Lady Day, 25 March 1785, the school was closed, and Boucher could find no suitable substitute. He found it necessary to take the Addison boys with him to Epsom, boarding them with his sister Jane at the Vicarage. His hopes for complete freedom from teaching duties vanished. The arrangement also proved to be a financial liability, for remittances from America were few and Boucher later estimated that he had expended more than six hundred pounds on behalf of the boys. He sought no reimbursement, perhaps because the prospect of the Epsom salary and the inheritance from Miss Barton had made the burden less heavy.

The move to Epsom was delayed in order to allow his curate Joseph Golding until June or later to find other quarters and to relinquish the parsonage in which he had been living. Furthermore, Boucher's many books involved a heavy moving expense. His library of some 10,000 volumes was now too extensive to be shifted, he thought, in any but a summer month when rates were reduced (*Rem.*, p. 178). (By 1806, when the library was sold at auction by Leigh and Sotheby, there were some 10,000 volumes and a large collection of manuscripts.)

Thus stalemated, Boucher saw that the interval was convenient for a tour of Europe which suddenly became available on the most attractive terms. Through connections he had made in his Paddington school, Boucher had an opportunity to accompany Lady Suffield on a journey to escort her son to Germany and bring home Delves, the son of Sir Thomas Broughton. For his escort services Boucher was to live and board as a gentleman with all expenses paid. Parish duties posed no particular problem, for he left those to Golding. Although Boucher thought Golding odd, he was clever and could write and deliver a good sermon. The Addison boys were apparently left to their own devices and to Jinny's watchful eye.

The travelers proceeded by Calais and Saint Omer to Brussels, where they spent a week with the recently widowed Lady Eden, who then accompanied Boucher to Antwerp. Next they journeyed through Liège, Spa, and Aix-la-Chapelle, completing a circle of Dusseldorf, Westphalia, and Hanover to Brunswick.[6] Boucher enjoyed a month's stay at the court in Brunswick, where he was the recipient of some attention by the duchess, sister of George III. Boucher later remarked: "In no part of my life, and in no part of the world, did I ever spend my time more entirely to my own satisfaction than I did . . . at Brunswick" (Rem., p. 180).

From Brunswick Boucher traveled down to southern Germany, boated along the Rhine to Strasbourg, turned westward into France, halted at Rheims, and then continued to Paris and Caen, returning to London on 7 October 1785 (Rem., p. 180). In all he traveled about 1,800 miles. At long last he had had something of the Grand Tour which he had envisioned for himself and John Parke Custis. A journal which Boucher kept during this tour has not, unfortunately, been discovered; one which he kept in 1784 was lost when Elizabeth Hodgson, who was carrying it to Cumberland, was robbed of her portmanteau.

Upon his return to Epsom Boucher resumed his clerical duties with as much enthusiasm as he could muster. He was even more lonely now, with John James up north at Arthuret. While John had been in Paddington there had been opportunity to see him; now the much greater distance between Epsom and Carlisle precluded the pleasure of his company. Boucher's spirits were further dampened by his sudden dismissal from his position as undersecretary of the SPG. In spite of the assurances of Secretary Morrice that "he had no wish to be rid of Boucher and had acted only in the interests of the Society,"[7] he was not comforted. He later wrote that he had resigned "by the advice . . . of his Grace the Archbishop of Canterbury" (*Rem.*, p. 181).

Depressed with his personal affairs, and as yet not much engrossed in the life of the parish, Boucher turned his attention to affairs of the American church and initiated a complex exchange of letters with Bishop John Skinner in Aberdeen, a member of the Scottish Episcopal church, with Rev. Charles Inglis, resident at Halifax in Nova Scotia, with Thomas Bradbury Chandler of New Jersey, and with Samuel Seabury, who was to become the first resident bishop in America. His correspondence with these men was to last for some years.

Boucher had long argued in Maryland that fulfillment of the Anglican church constitution in America required only a primitive bishop, that is, one without civil authority and possessing only the right to ordain and discipline clerics. However, protests to that effect had never been accepted by most colonials. The great importance to history of the power of what people believe, whether it be true or not, is nowhere more vividly demonstrated than in this eighty-five-year-long emotion-charged controversy. Boucher thought the postwar situation in America supported his belief that the earlier opposition had been illogical at best and insincere at worst. "Hardly was their independence gained before an episcopate was applied for and obtained." The same men who had once been so violently opposed were now the chief promoters. How, he wondered later, could any one fail to see that "those persons who . . . were vilified and persecuted" in 1771 for wishing to introduce an episcopacy were "not the enemies to America." Wistfully, he asked if the time would not be distant when the same judgment might prevail concerning "the same men and their conduct respecting the revolution?"[8] Obviously Boucher's toryism was still showing. The new bishopric appointments were totally unlike those which would have been made through Parliament had the American colonies not become independent.

Disquieting news reached Boucher in 1785, which he promptly shared with Bishop Skinner in Aberdeen. The Anglican church in the southern states had developed alarming symptoms, largely because the few Episcopal clergy left there were men Boucher considered not "distinguished for abilities or worth." Enemies of the church were quick to take advantage, and were promoting a wild project—a coalition between the Episcopalians and Presbyterians. Boucher's reaction was immediate and negative. "I have by every means in my power put those over whom I have any influence in my old neighborhood of Virginia and Maryland on their guard against a measure I cannot but deem insidious and therefore likely to be fatal." Furthermore, Boucher reported to Skinner, he had already called for the assistance of those champions, Dr. Thomas Bradbury Chandler of Elizabethtown, New Jersey, and Rev. Samuel Seabury, earlier of New York and now bishop of Connecticut and Rhode Island. Boucher confessed that it worried him that all these things were being carried on "within the vortex of Dr. Smith's immediate influence," because he was a man who was "bent on being a bishop." Boucher had followed Smith's career with some interest, but thought no better of him in 1785 than he had when Smith had supported the Whigs in 1775. Boucher distrusted the man's motives. He was certain that if Smith "cannot otherwise compose his ends," he would surely "unite with the Presbyterians, and so Herod and Pilate shall again be made friends" (*MHM* 10:116-17).

The Seabury consecration opened up a relationship between the bishop in America and Boucher that was to last for some years. Although Samuel Seabury had hoped to be consecrated by bishops of the Church of England, they had declined and he had then turned to the Scottish church. Less well known is the fact that he applied to the nonjuring bishops in England, with Boucher serving as intermediary. (The nonjuring bishops believed their power derived from those who had refused to take the oaths of allegiance to William and Mary in 1689, believing that James II was still the rightful king.)

When Seabury requested Boucher's good offices in his appeal to the nonjurors, Boucher turned to Dr. Kenrick Price of Manchester, once a grocer and now a nonjuring bishop. At Boucher's request, Price forwarded his appeal to Bishop William Cartwright, who was also an apothecary and practicing surgeon.[9] Cartwright then replied to Boucher. William Stevens probably put Boucher in touch with Cartwright through Price, since Cartwright's activities as the last nonjuror of any consequence were well known to the hosier. Cartwright, who wished to be known as "Bishop of the Orthodox Remnant of the Ancient British Church," served a nonjuring congregation at Shrewsbury. He did not want to be considered a Dissenter, and allowed his family and his entire congregation to attend the Anglican church.

Boucher had made a point of familiarizing himself with the nonjurors' liturgy, and it seemed to him that it did not include anything to which Seabury could not "very safely assent." Boucher's purpose, however, was to have Cartwright furnish a statement to Seabury outlining the nonjurors' requirements for consecration, in order that Seabury himself might be assured that there were no "requisitions of a spiritual nature" to which a "conscientious member of the Church of England" could not subscribe.[10] Cartwright did furnish information, but in the end Seabury was consecrated by the Scottish Episcopal church 14 November 1784. Cartwright rejoiced with Boucher in the news, delighted that Seabury was now "vested with sufficient authority to consecrate a bishop for every state in America."[11]

Boucher correctly assessed the tenuous existence of the nonjuring body, and for that reason he thought it his duty to attempt to bring this splinter group back into the fold of the established church. Boucher offered the nonjurors his friendship and service, which Cartwright gratefully acknowledged. However, when Boucher initiated his persuasive attempt to welcome Cartwright to the orthodox church-state relationship, he was considerably less grateful and said so bluntly. Although Boucher persevered, he met with the same intransigence. Boucher never converted him, but he did exercise a measure of influence over Cartwright's religious writing, and did what he could to ease the stringent economic burden imposed upon him by a large family and an inadequate salary. The two men finally simply agreed to disagree on the fundamental religious issue which divided them, but continued to explore each other's arguments and exchanged opinions on a variety of subjects. Thus began a correspondence which lasted for eleven years, fostered in part by their common concern for the American and the Scottish churches.

Boucher was actively interested in the American church, and passed along information he received from Seabury to Bishop Skinner at Aberdeen, including the word that Dr. Smith was pleased with Dr. Seabury's return to America. The reason was obvious to Boucher; Smith had learned lately that "one bishop alone may in certain cases consecrate another." All of Smith's maneuvering to become a bishop would require "poor Seabury's utmost skill to manage" (*MHM* 10:117). Although he thought it possible that Seabury might find it necessary to consecrate Smith in order to curb the trend toward unification with the Presbyterians in Virginia and Maryland, where Smith still commanded a considerable following, Boucher felt such an expedient would be too high a price to pay.

By 1786 Seabury had ordained twelve persons, eight of whom were "from the middle and southern states," which Boucher hoped would prove that "the rage for reformation is not so very general as some forward men wish to have it believed." Seabury's welfare was a source of concern to Boucher, for he was shocked to learn from the Connecticut bishop that no salary provision had been made for him in America, contrary to the understanding of both that "a subscription of £50 a year would be made up for him among my friends." Somehow the plan had failed to materialize, for Seabury had written: "No provision is made for me; so that for time and for eternity I have no trust but in the goodness of my heavenly Father, and may his will be done." Boucher confided to Skinner: "I have, this day, written to him to draw on me for [fifty pounds]." He added a caution: "It is not fit, however, as will be obvious to you, that this should generally be known" (*MHM* 10:118).

Boucher followed with interest the developments of the first general convention of the Episcopal clergy of North America which opened on 27 September 1785 in Philadelphia. The clergymen, together with an equal number of laymen, endeavored to form a general plan for the whole Episcopal church. Seabury declined to attend, but Boucher expected that his steadying influence would be felt through the attendance of Dr. Thomas Bradbury Chandler. For that reason only, Boucher dared to hope for at least some good results. The meeting, which the Americans called an ecumenical council, provoked Boucher's sardonic amusement. Americans, he observed to Skinner, were so parochial as to think of "no other *world* or people but their own and themselves." The results of the convention he found less amusing than the title, attributing them to the fact that the lay members had prevailed, "having been more used to public haranguing and the management of popular assemblies." The church constitution which the conference produced was "crude, rash and weak." On the subject of discipline, the convention had seemed to follow King's *Constitution of the Primitive Church*, which had been "ill understood and worse applied." Thus both bishops and presbyters were to be deposable by a consistory of presbyters and laymen. As for the liturgy, the convention had "at a stroke, knocked off the Athanasian and Nicene Creeds," and one clause of the Apostles' Creed, the Descent into Hades. The Lord's Prayer and the Te Deum were "corrected." Boucher wondered if Skinner might not say "it were well for them if they could alter the Commandments" (*MHM* 10:119).

The prime mover in all of this mischief, in Boucher's opinion, was Dr. William Smith. The constitution reflected "very exactly about that pitch of learning to which I have thought his mediocrity of talent equal." Boucher was not alone in his opinion of Smith, for Charles Inglis, after reading the minutes, noted that some resolves were "very degrading to the Episcopal authority," resolutions which he attributed to Dr. Smith who still commanded a following and who was disappointed in his hopes for a bishopric.[12] Fortunately from Inglis's point of view, he was able to inform Boucher directly of some changes in the church constitution which he thought put bishops on a "more respectable footing." When a bishop attended a convention he was to preside ex officio. In cases where a bishop might be tried for any offense, two bishops at least must be present in the convention "besides the culprit," while all sentences of suspension, degradation, and so forth "were to be pronounced by a bishop." In spite of such changes, Inglis considered the constitution still "miserably defective—a linsey-woolsey piece of business in which the spirit of republicanism and Presbyterianism is predominant."[13]

Boucher was aware that the validity of Bishop Seabury's ordination had come into question, a situation which he attributed to "Dr. Franklin, a notorious infidel as well as a rebel," who had charged that "some breach was made in the Scottish Succession of bishops." Although the convention voted down the measure invalidating Seabury's consecration, it arranged for what Boucher considered to be a "very decent letter to our archbishops and bishops requesting them to consecrate bishops for America." Furthermore, Boucher observed, Congress desired its ambassador in England to inform the British ministry that such a measure "would give no umbrage to the American States, while it would greatly oblige the Episcopalians in general." The reply to the convention and Congress was, in Boucher's opinion, a judicious one; the ministry could give no answer until it had seen the plan of discipline and worship and could judge "how far they are still of our Communion and the Church of England" (*MHM* 10: 119-20). In 1786, Parliament responded favorably with an act granting authority to the archbishops of York and Canterbury to consecrate nonresident bishops. William White and Samuel Prevost were consecrated in Lambeth Palace Chapel within the next year, for the dioceses of Pennsylvania and New York respectively.

Throughout these developments, Cartwright freely volunteered his opinions to Boucher; he more often approved of the American church than did Boucher, particularly if decisions taken in America coincided with any of Cartwright's primitive church tenets. Obviously he approved of the American trend toward separation of church and state, and in 1787 he commented tartly on English bishops who thought themselves obliged to have an act of Parliament "to empower them to do what was their bounden duty to do," while at the same time restraints were being laid upon all clergy that were unparalleled "in all former ages" by acts of Parliament. Cartwright could see no sense in "kings being nursing fathers to the church!"[14]

Boucher often neglected his correspondence with Cartwright and others in 1785-87 when personal affairs engrossed his attention. In November 1785, John James suffered a riding accident while delivering medicine on a cold, rainy night. His horse slipped on the wet road, and he suffered internal injuries followed by violent hemorrhaging a few days later.[15] Severe illness plagued John for two months, after which he sought unsuccessfully to recover his health at a hot spring at Clifton.

By May 1786 John had fallen ill again, and was in serious condition at Bristol.[16] Still attempting to regain his health, John resorted to a dubious treatment consisting of sailing in rough weather, which was intended to bring on seasickness as a cure. He journeyed to Southampton, made several short voyages for the purpose with no benefit, and then crossed the Channel to Le Havre in July 1786. His companions suffered seasickness, but John felt fine. The intended cure failed, but John caught a cold at Le Havre which was aggravated by the becalming of the ship on the return voyage, during which the passengers were forced to remain on board without food or sleep for forty-eight hours. After a long period of invalidism, he managed a short visit with Boucher at Epsom, but died soon after at Brompton, 23 October 1786, aged twenty-seven. The immediate cause of his death was pneumonia. Boucher arranged for his interment in his family vault at Paddington where Nelly earlier had been laid to rest, after a service in the church where John had served for a brief time as curate.

The loss of John, who was almost as close as a son and whose promising career he had nurtured, was a heavy blow to Boucher. John's widow and their only child, Mary Ann, apparently returned to the Carlisle area. Thus Boucher was denied even their company in his grief. Three of his closest human ties had been broken in each of three successive years. Only his sister Jinny survived of those whom he had held most dear.

Soon afterwards, in 1786, Boucher determined to pay his respects to "an excellent and amiable" lady in Epson, Mary Elizabeth Foreman, who had a "handsome fortune." Probably Boucher was extremely lonely, although he was not a man to gainsay prudence and once again he made a fortunate marriage. The ceremony took place in Saint Michael's Church, Saint Albans, 15 February 1787. Boucher took a house in an expensive neighborhood in Woodcote Green, paid two hundred pounds for a coach, and lived in a handsome style with seven servants.[17] This way of life was unfamiliar to him. He soon tired of the seemingly endless round of social events which consumed so much of his time. He neglected his correspondence.

Cartwright had read of Boucher's marriage in the newspaper and promptly wrote to wish him happiness. With his usual candor he added that he did not approve of the marriage of priests after ordination. Boucher, busy with his new life, did not reply, leaving the Shrewsbury apothecary and bishop to wonder if he had offended his friend. He fretted for some months, then wrote Boucher to ask if he had indeed damaged their relationship with his remarks. Feeling somewhat remiss, Boucher replied promptly and reassured Cartwright that their correspondence was on the same footing as when it had begun. Cartwright was mollified and again dispatched a lengthy letter, entreating Boucher to reply soon. Again he was disappointed, for Boucher was again absorbed with his own affairs.

Mary Elizabeth was pregnant and Boucher was delighted.

For years, unwilling to add to Nelly's frustration and unhappiness, he had smothered his longing to be a father. Instead he had lavished his affection on Tommy and John James, and particularly on John. Now, after the death of his substitute son, the prospect of parenthood was appealing. Initially the pregnancy went well. For his wife's comfort they removed to Egglesden, the country estate of her brother John, and Mary Elizabeth seemingly progressed through the expected stages for several months.

Then Boucher's dream took on the quality of a nightmare. His wife was discovered to be not pregnant at all. Instead she was suffering from "an enlarged ovarium," according to Dr. I. Carmichael Smyth, who was regularly consulted. He told Boucher in confidence that he feared it was a bad case. Cartwright, learning of the difficulty, expressed his concern and recommended, "if it should be approved by your better physicians," a series of "the most gentle electrical shocks transmitted through the abdomen and drawing breast milk from a healthy woman."[18] But nothing reversed the illness. The next months were ghastly for Boucher as he watched his wife deteriorate into a mere skeleton plagued with bedsores. Unlike Nelly, Mary Elizabeth was not a silent sufferer, which made a bad situation even more difficult. Finally, on 14 September 1788, Boucher "again became a forlorn widower." Although this marriage had not been as "loving as my first," Mary Elizabeth's death left him desolate. With his "mind shaken and unhinged," he wrote Sir Frederick Eden, son of his old friend Robert Eden, about his loss and told him that his friends had advised him to shift the scene and go to his native northern hills for comfort.[19]

Boucher had a great love for the rugged Cumberland hills; the land of his forebears formed a stronghold of continuity and tradition for him, and it gave him pleasure to return. But it was not Blencogo that interested him. The small patronage which he had inherited from his father had cost him seventy pounds to discharge debts and another hundred to his two sisters to satisfy their inheritance. He had not received "a shilling" from it by 1786 (*Rem.*, p. 33). He felt no attachment to the homestead itself; indeed, he thought James already knew that he had "some reason to dislike the place." However, James "could not possibly know or imagine how thoroughly I detest it. Never do I mean to live there." Boucher consequently looked upon the acquisition of land adjacent

241

to the Blencogo house as an investment opportunity. In March 1781 he proposed to buy "the little estate" adjoining his when it came on the market for "upwards of £300." An income of fifty pounds "when a rainy day overtakes me" would be useful. He thought it prudent to think about the future, for "I have for so long been eager in the chase of the good things of the world," and even now "I am too apt to fool away my money, however hardly earned, in books."[20]

After the death of Mary Elizabeth he thought again of investing in additional land, adding two or three parcels in Caldbeck Parish, which he described in appreciative terms in Hutchinson's *History*. The Caldew River tumbled rapidly down from high ground and on to Hudscales, where "in a most commanding situation, just at the foot of the mountains," Boucher had a manor consisting of about twenty-four tenants.[21] He purchased in addition an estate in Sebergham Parish which he found equally pleasing.[22] The manor provided a fair view of two contiguous bridges, one at the foot of Sebergham Brow and one called the Bell Bridge. Here, too, the River Caldew, or Caudey, afforded a landscape that delighted Boucher. The "woody and beautiful" banks of the river were "particularly picturesque and interesting" against a background formed by the mountains of Scotland and Northumberland.

Although in 1781 Boucher had to ask the elder John James to stand surety for him when he bought his first parcel of land, funds were no problem now. Mary Elizabeth's entire estate of £14,000 now belonged to Boucher, and in 1789 he purchased Long-Holm-Row (now known as New-House), an estate of 112 acres (*Rem.*, pp. 195-96). The real estate purchases occupied Boucher's mind when little else interested him. Planning improvements on his estates, such as building a farmhouse, gave him pleasure as similar projects once had in Maryland. All of these Cumberland ventures did much to reestablish the prestige of the Boucher family, a fact which must have pleased him when he remembered his father's charge to him as a young man.[23]

Boucher had no great desire to return to Epsom, but he could not postpone it indefinitely. In November 1788 he was back in his melancholy parish house to pick up the threads of his clerical life once again.[24] After the luxury and spaciousness of Woodcote Green the Epsom house seemed even more cramped and inconvenient than before. His constantly expanding library could scarcely be housed in his quarters. He determined to purchase a better house on Clay Hill, west of Epsom, and an attorney of Lincoln's Inn sold him a sturdy house on five acres of land for £1,025.

In these years the security which Boucher had struggled for and won in America, only to lose as an exile, was again his to enjoy. In 1788 he saw the culmination of all his efforts to salvage something from his American property. He had filed a claim for £5,906 14s. sterling in 1784, submitting with it documentary corroberations of its value and testimony from character witnesses. For a time his claim was in jeopardy because of overly zealous friends in Maryland, who had tried to falsify some claims of debts in America. The Maryland authorities had discovered the deception and made a point of relaying the information to the British Claims Commission. But since the scheme had been perpetrated without Boucher's knowledge, he somehow managed to rectify the matter (*Rem.*, pp. 196-97).

When in 1788 William Pitt offered his plan for the compensation of Loyalists,[25] Boucher disliked it, declaring "Pitt is a fool." Part of Boucher's loss, of course, had stemmed from passage in Maryland of the Vestry Act of 1773. His parish salary was supposed to be almost £500, but his parishioners had taken advantage of the political quarrel over clerical salaries and most had stopped paying tithes at all. Boucher had not received any salary in the three years before he left America. Under the terms of the Pitt proposal Boucher could get no recognition of his real salary loss. As compensation for being deprived of the income from his Maryland parish he was to receive £120 a year for life. In 1787 Boucher had been paid £900, and his final allotment was fixed at £1,850 more (*Rem.*, pp. 196-97).

Boucher resumed his life at Epsom and became more sociable once he was released from the trials of his wife's long illness. He enjoyed having dinner with the Eden family, and Lady Eden offered Boucher the hospitality of their home whenever he had business in London. He had established a friendly relationship with her son Sir Frederick, and he soon became something of an adviser to the younger man on career and financial problems. Later, when Eden was writing his book *The State of the Poor*, Boucher offered him advice and indeed furnished him with material for it, both on Epsom Parish and on certain other parishes in Cumberland.[26]

Pleasant as these occasions with the Edens were, they were no substitute for the love and domestic serenity which Boucher had once known with Nelly. Nelly had often suggested that Boucher write his memoirs, and on the second anniversary of her death, Ash Wednesday 1786, Boucher had begun a journal which became his *Reminiscences.* Even two years after her death, the poignancy of his loneliness permeates the pages. Perhaps the memoirs were useful in assuaging his grief by fulfilling his wife's wishes that he record his experiences. Boucher continued to write in his journal after Mary Elizabeth's death, at least for a short period of time. Then abruptly, he discontinued the project, turned his back on the first half-century of his life, and contempated a new romance.

During Boucher's three-month retreat to Cumberland in autumn 1788, after the death of Mary Elizabeth, he had had the opportunity to visit with Elizabeth, young John's widow, and her daughter, Mary Ann, who was by now nearly three years old. Boucher had know Elizabeth well in Paddington; he had welcomed her warmly when she had arrived as a bride just twenty-two years old.[27] The two had much in common; like Boucher, Elizabeth had a Cumberland heritage. Both had loved young John dearly, and now both were lonely. Elizabeth had already adjusted to the life of a minister in her brief years with John. Elizabeth was a comely young woman, a fact which Boucher did not fail to notice. Furthermore, she was in radiant good health, a welcome contrast to the ravages of illness which had marked his years with both Nelly and Mary Elizabeth. Boucher, now fifty-one, began to think of marriage to Elizabeth and the pleasing prospect of domestic happiness and children. He began his courtship of John's widow, and confided his hopes to his friend Stevens.[28]

Elizabeth, aged twenty-eight, married him 29 October 1789. The ceremony took place in Saint Mary's, Carlisle. Within a year the family which Boucher had yearned for became a reality with the birth of a son, James.[29] The child was baptized on 7 September 1790. The pleasure Boucher took in his first child is explicit in an enthusiastic letter to Edward Jerningham, the poet and dramatist, whom Boucher asked to write what he described as a "Genethliacon," a didactic poem setting forth "those educative influences under which the infant, whose training is the object of the poem, shall grow up a young man loyal to the Constitution in Church and State." By now Boucher was a thorough conservative. He begged Jerningham to write "what would not only highly delight two fond parents," but would "render him a worthy and useful man, and thus do him more real service than all the little savings of money that I can hope to leave him." He wanted the poem to dwell on "the two most important objects of his attention, politics and religion," in order to inspire his son to be virtuous, "loyal and monarchical," and to eschew "all the low and levelling arts of republicanism." In short, Boucher wanted his son to be "pretty nearly altogether as I am," except that he did not want him to be "a poor vicar." Boucher hoped that he would become a "true son of the Church of England," and as such even "farther removed from Presbyterianism" than from "popery."[30] Boucher's letter to Jerningham revealed the extent to which he had become a high Tory.

Boucher's experiences as a teacher were reflected in his aspirations for his son. "I should ... stimulate him to exertion—to cultivate his powers, to be impatient of ignorance, and to abhor low-mindedness and illiberality." He had stood in loco parentis for so long to a series of boys in his schools that he had had ample opportunity to think about that which was important for the training of his own children.

A year later the first of five daughters was born in the Clay Hill house, Ann (1791-1812), was followed by Eleanor Mary Elizabeth (1793-1861), Jane (1794-1810), Elizabeth (1797-1866), and Mary (1799-1871). Two other sons were also born—Barton (1796-1865) and Jonathan (1800-1801), the only child who died in his father's lifetime.[31] The burgeoning household at Clay Hill also included Mary Ann James.

However, Boucher's sister Jinny had returned to Cumberland. In April 1794, aged fifty-two, Jinny died at Bromfield and was buried in the family plot there. She had made her home with Boucher for so many years that he experienced her death as the "snapping asunder of one of the nearest connections he had." He expected the loss of his "poor dear sister" to make "a cripple of me for the remainder of my life," he confided to Sir Frederick Morton Eden.[32]

Of all the girls, perhaps Eleanor most endeared herself to her father; at least she was said to be "her father's child." She was "very dear, very little, sweet-tempered, agreeable, full of good sense and consistently religious . . . gay without levity . . . serious without gloom."[33] She sounds much as Boucher had once described his first wife, for whom the child was named, and she may have been a special child to Boucher on that ground alone. However, in spite of her favorable position in the family, Eleanor remembered her early days at the Epsom parsonage as a "stagnant monotony of existence," broken only by the arrival of a number of French refugees from the revolution in France. Such refugees were not allowed to live near the coast and thus frequently found their way to Epsom. Several Catholic priests among them sought Boucher's advice and assistance, but others were secular persons of whom Eleanor retained vivid memories which she later shared with her children. Monsieur Chabot reminded her of bows and snuff boxes; Monsieur Jerduke, whom she had thought conceited, absurd, and "a dressed up horror," taught dancing. Boucher allowed Eleanor, and perhaps the other older girls, to have lessons in the minuet. She remembered well the slow tempo, the head turned gracefully, the practiced art of giving and withdrawing the hand. "It was all very elegant," she recalled.[34]

The 1790s found Boucher, twice thwarted in his dreams for a family, surrounded by offspring in a vital and satisfying marital relationship. Elizabeth was youthful and energetic; she provided the domestic order which he had known with Nelly and the love and affection which he needed to thrive. The kind of family life he had first glimpsed and envied in the household of John James and Nancy at Saint Bees was now his own.

◡ Chapter 11 ◡

In Search of a Mitre

Boucher's long search for a manner of life more congenial to his temper and his talents ended with his marriage to Elizabeth. She had both a stabilizing and a stimulating effect on him. His concept of himself as a public man, submerged in the years of the Revolution after the victory at Saratoga, reasserted itself, and his literary work took on more significant proportions. He prepared a plan for a British federated government intended to bring universal peace which he presented to the ministry for consideration, and he proposed a detailed series of social and economic developments intended to benefit his native Cumberland County and its inhabitants.

Boucher's several visits to Cumberland had sharpened his interest in the region, in its rugged landscape, in its undeveloped natural resources, in its primitive economy, and in its lack of civic amenities. Consequently, when a publisher in Carlisle, F. Jollie, solicited his "patronage, aid and advice" for a county history, Boucher acquiesced in the project. He suggested that if authentic accounts of distinguished Cumberland natives could be obtained, they would be a desirable addition. "To deserve well of mankind is to deserve being handed down to posterity with applause," he declared, making clear that "distinguished" should not mean of "great opulence or high station," but those whose contributions had never before been acknowledged in print.[1]

At the time he suggested the biographical sketches, Boucher had not foreseen that he would be asked to do them himself.

Neither had he realized when he consented to prepare the articles, perhaps too hastily he thought later, that he was taking on "an attempt of considerable difficulty for which I was but very indifferently qualified." He found that the materials were miserably scanty and widely dispersed, if they existed at all. Nevertheless, he completed some twenty-five sketches which were published anonymously in William Hutchinson's *History and Antiquities of Cumberland* (1793-97) and were afforded favorable attention in the *Monthly Review*.[2]

Some of Boucher's selections were decidedly eccentric, including Thomas Morpeth, the "remarkable free booter or land-pirate." The sketches gave Boucher some difficulties with the editor and publishers. He thought himself particularly ill treated in the disposition of his article on the Reverend D. Graham of Netherby, whom Boucher thought an eminent Quaker. John Mitchinson of Carlisle, another Quaker, objected to the article on the grounds that it was "not written in that mystic style so affected by Quakers." Without even the courtesy of informing Boucher, the printer laid aside the article and substituted one drawn up by Mitchinson himself. Boucher was also indignant when the printer rejected a poem written in Cumberland dialect, possibly by Boucher, which described the customs and manners of Cumberland rustics in the early eighteenth century with spirit and fidelity. Again the publisher accepted Mitchinson's opinion; he felt that the poem was not grave or decorous, and therefore not suitable for a history of this kind. Boucher felt the rebuff keenly; he insisted the poem had not "a single sentiment or expression unfavorable either to good manners or good morals." In any case, no known copy of it survives.

Boucher himself was quick to admit some weaknesses in his literary venture. He was aware that he was not a professional writer, and he discovered relatively early that writing biography was no "easy undertaking." Nonetheless, he was not altogether without some sense of confidence in his project. He knew he was possessed of "an independency of mind," and he had no intention of writing fulsome panegyrics. All too soon Boucher encountered a problem that has always plagued biographers—the relative or descendant who considers a reasonably honest piece of biography to be an insult to the memory of a revered ancestor. Boucher's sketch of Sir James Wallace, at one time attorney general for the

Crown, proved to be deeply offensive to Wallace's son. With what perhaps was excessive caution, the printer showed the younger Wallace the sketch of his father before it went into the finished history. Outraged, the son taxed Boucher with "imbecility and rancor" and insisted on writing the article himself. The result, as might have been expected, was a panegyric that had little or no relationship to reality. Boucher presently found a way of venting his own sense of outrage in his unpublished "Secret History" of Hutchinson's *History*. In this piece he told the true story of the Wallace contretemps, and attached his original sketch as he had intended it for the printer. The "Secret History" was destined never to come to publication, yet it is far more useful today as a guide to Wallace's life than anything else available. The incident left Boucher with a lingering sense of injustice and resentment at being "brow-beaten and traduced by a pert boy" who had no talents of his own and whose influence rested solely on the accomplishments of his father.

Boucher himself was not entirely free of paternal motives in his biographical undertaking. He believed that he was setting up a model of great lives which might serve Cumberland youths who wished to be successful. His life of Sir James Wallace had been intended to point out an avenue of opportunity through training in an attorney's office, which was not the usual route to a high government post. " 'One might as soon expect to arrive at a princely mansion through an *avenue of narrow lanes* or to sail by a navigation of ditches to the metropolis of a powerful country,' " Boucher had written, quoting another writer.[3]

The "Secret History" has been useful to posterity, for when he confided his secret thoughts on the subject he also noted that he was marking with vertical lines in the margin all of those sections of Hutchinson's *History* which he himself had written. Thus, in the opinon of R. S. Ferguson, president of the Cumberland and Westmorland Antiquarian and Archaeological Society in the late nineteenth century, Boucher deserves credit for "some of the best parts of Hutchinson's *History*," and for considerably more than just the biographical sketches in the first edition. In addition Boucher wrote a series of parish histories, including accounts of Bromfield, Sebergham, Penrith, Saint Bees, Wigton, and Caldbeck.[4] They are valuable as sources of Boucher's social thought in the 1790s.

Boucher's interest in county history had been stirred by what he considered defects in earlier local histories, which he thought contained too few suggestions for local improvement. Nor had such histories given so much as a line to the subject of discommoning the immense wastes that still disfigured the country (*MHM* 10:31). Boucher supposed that they once enclosed the lord's hunting grounds. The hedges ran in zigzag lines, and he wondered at the origin of those boundaries when mutual advantage to owners would seem to have dictated straight ones. In an effort to remedy the omissions of previous historians, Boucher wrote parish accounts which were replete with a variety of information. He first engaged in etymological discussions of the place names involved, gave attention to the topography, noted remains of antiquities, and then added the history of ownership of various manors. His descriptions of the natural beauties of the Cumberland area are vivid ones, clearly the work of a man who loved the region. But the histories are more than that; they furnish detailed material on population, housing, occupations, poor rates, wages, agricultural practices and production, and a wealth of comment on, and remedies for, whatever deficiencies met his eye. He paid particular attention to Caldbeck Parish. Much of the contemporary data he obtained through his own effort.

Local history, Boucher thought, should be made interesting to others than local people. Such histories provided a great opportunity for a more universal appeal, because they permitted authentic historical documentation of progress from barbarism to civilization. In Cumberland during the Border Wars, for example, the inhabitants were almost savages. This observation reminded him that on the western frontiers of Virginia he had seen the counterparts of the former occupants of the Cumberland marches. The border inhabitants in Virginia subsisted entirely by hunting, and "no laws have yet been devised sufficient to restrain them from their incursive, predatory wars on their hapless and (comparatively speaking) civilized neighbors, the Indians." These backwoodsmen formed "those companies of rifle men in the Rebel army," he had written James on 23 December 1777, scarcely complimenting them in this negative comparison with the more civilized American Indians (*MHM* 10:29). By 1792 some of his ideas had germinated and had become his anonymous pamphlet, *An Address to the Inhabitants of the County of Cumberland*.[5] Boucher's ideas stemmed from his critical perspective on his native area, which in turn led him to suggest some wide-ranging plans for improvements that were at once visionary, yet specific about financing.

Boucher also took time out in these years to write a bit of didactic verse. Back in Maryland he had written a few lines to an actress who performed in the theater in Annapolis; now, in these less romantic years, he penned some verses addressed to "a very old and remarkable Hawthorne Tree which formerly grew by the pond on the Cross-Green at Blencogo." The twelve stanzas represent a kind of pastoral moralizing sermon arising out of his contemplation of the hawthorn, using its greenness to symbolize the renewing spirit of virtue.

> Whence is it, Batter'd Bush, said she,
> That thus, worn down with Age, I see
> Thy Limbs, though broken, fresh & clean,
> And thee still full of Bloom, & green.
>
> A Dryad made her this Reply:
> True Virtue ne'er can wholly die:
> This Tree's still sound at Heart, I ween
> And thence it blossoms, & is green.
>
> Thus toiling on Life's dreary Road,
> Whilst no foul sins his Peace corrode,
> My Bard's still cheerful & serene,
> And, though now old, like me is green.[6]

It is also possible that Boucher wrote the lengthy pamphlet, *Remarks on the Travels of the Marquis de Chastellux in North America* (1787).[7]

Although Boucher recognized that he was not himself a poet, he was an ardent patron of Thomas Sanderson, a Cumberland poet, and persuaded him to write the "Ode to the Genius of the Cumberland" which was published in Hutchinson's *History*. He later arranged for an offer to Sanderson of a post at Barbados, although the poet refused it. Sanderson was grateful, and dedicated his edition of the poems of Josiah Relph of Sebergham (1797) to Boucher. Boucher also erected a grave slab to the memory of

Relph in the Sebergham church, for which he prepared a Latin inscription which was also published in Thompson's edition.

Boucher had intended to remain the anonymous writer of the biographical sketches in Hutchinson's *History*, but somehow his identity became known. The modicum of success which he enjoyed encouraged him to reconsider the possibility of publishing a book of sermons, an idea which he had thought about off and on since his early exile days in London. Then he had needed money, and he had hoped that the sermons would attract sufficient attention to warrant an appointment to a good benefice. When Boucher finally published his book of sermons in 1797, *A View of the Causes and Consequences of the American Revolution, in Thirteen Discourses, Preached in North America between the Years 1763 and 1775, with an Historical Preface*, his purpose had become essentially political and the book firmly established his reputation as a High Tory.

Once Boucher's book and the reviews appeared, the number of his correspondents increased. Joseph Jefferson, who had earlier appreciated the biographical sketches in the *History*, now learned Boucher's identity and wrote to congratulate the learned author whose work had so enriched the Hutchinson book. He had been impressed particularly with the treatment Boucher accorded dissenting ministers, and had concluded that the author was "a liberal gentleman—he thinks for himself on subjects of literature and religion and he indulges others with the same privileges."[8] Jefferson, who identified himself as a "methodistical" minister at Basingstoke, was born close to Blencogo, in Wigton, Cumberland County, and educated at the Wigton Grammar School. He served as the master of the Free School at Bothel for four years and then attended Homerton College in London, a seminary for dissenting ministers, from 1789 to 1791, after which he accepted the responsibility for an independent congregation at Basingstoke. Jefferson was something of a Hebrew scholar and often referred to John Parkhurst's *Hebrew Lexicon* in his current project, a reading of the Bible in Hebrew. Thus he was aware that the "late learned Revd. J. Parkhurst," patron of Epsom Parish, had inscribed the last edition of his lexicon to Boucher.

However, the two men found additional ties in their common heritage and love of Cumberland, and in their mutual interest in provincial dialects. In his first letter, Jefferson referred to various distinguished natives of Cumberland, such as William Wordsworth, and enclosed a pamphlet or two of his own writing. Boucher replied promptly, and encouraged the correspondence by sending Jefferson a copy of his book of sermons by coach. Boucher apparently queried him about his political sentiments, to which he replied: "If I am not an High Church Tory, I may perhaps claim some degree of merit in not being 'Whiggissimus.' " He added that there would be no strife between Boucher and himself, nor had he the time to dwell on politics at the moment. Jefferson was pleased to discover that they had a friend in common, Anthony Robinson, whose literary abilities he respected, saying that if Boucher had had any arguments with him on politics he already knew what his sentiments were. (Robinson had reviewed *A View* unfavorably in the *Analytic Review*.) Robinson was more restrained in his political discussions than Dr. Samuel Johnson, he added, who had been known to throw "a folio volume at the head of any one who disputes with him on a subject," particularly when he had "the worst side of an argument." Although Jefferson did not wish to discuss his politics, he was willing to make clear his present religious position. He was not now a member of the Church of England, yet he saw himself as a studious man, desirous of consecrating his learning "to the services of religion and to the advantage of my immortal fellow creatures."[9]

The correspondence between Boucher and Jefferson, which was to last until Boucher's death, was off to a good start, particularly when Jefferson was able to report that he had read the book of sermons and had been "highly gratified and instructed by it." Although he insisted that he had "little opinion on politics," and had spent little time informing himself on the subject, he admired the manner in which Boucher had treated the "difficult and complicated" subject of the American war, displaying both integrity and consistency. On the subject of Boucher's religious principles, however, Jefferson disagreed. "You are a Churchman by principle," he wrote, "and therefore you will not be surprised if I cannot subscribe to every sentence of your publication—and especially when the subjects of church government and episcopacy are discussed." This did not worry Jefferson, for "on these things, we have 'agreed to differ.' "[10]

Boucher, with his usual sense of mission, felt constrained to make an attempt to convert Jefferson to the true church, just as he had labored to that end with Cartwright. By May 1798 he had raised the subject in conjunction with a prospect of a new position for Jefferson at Banff. Although the dissenting minister vowed that he would always remember Boucher's kindness in the matter, he assured him that he had given the subject of "conformity and nonconformity" a great deal of thought and must take the liberty to inform him that "at present I cannot think of changing my situation." He expressed his trust that his "inability to comply" with Boucher's overtures would not result in the interruption of their friendship and correspondence. Boucher had expected that the emoluments at Banff would tempt Jefferson to return to the established church. However, Jefferson assured him that although "it would not become me to affect to despise worldly interest," he was pleased to report that "divine providence" had placed him in a situation more favorable than that of many of his brethren both among the dissenters as well as in the established clergy.[11]

Boucher's friendship with Jefferson developed rapidly, and he felt a sense of closeness which was absent in his relationship with Cartwright. Perhaps their shared native roots helped. Boucher trusted Jefferson with information which he did not want either his contemporaries or posterity to see. Jefferson respected that trust and in one instance assured him, "at your particular desire, I have just destroyed your letter. You need not fear anything dishonorable from me in the affair."[12] The subject of Boucher's confidence remains unknown.

Boucher took the young man's declaration of his independent religious stance with good grace, although he did not entirely desist in his proselytizing efforts. Jefferson in his turn, however, expressed his conviction that evangelical ministers had something to offer, a "happy method of preaching" which had been found to be effective. It is doubtful that Jefferson knew how much opposed Boucher was to such preaching, an attitude that he acquired in experiences with the backwoods Dissenters in Virginia and Maryland. However, this was Jefferson's effective counterweight to Boucher's pressure for conformity.

Boucher's interest in the welfare of the church at large, particularly his own scheme for the union of the Anglican congregations in Scotland and the Episcopal Church of Scotland, led him into other correspondences. Soon after publication of Boucher's book of sermons, Charles Daubeny, a minister at North Bradley and later at Bath, wrote to compliment Boucher on a "valuable and interesting publication," and so began a correspondence which lasted until 1803.[13] Daubeny had entered Winchester College and then received a fellowship at New College, Oxford. A considerable fortune from his father, a wealthy Bristol merchant, enabled him to prepare for holy orders. After ordination in 1773 he held a Winchester fellowship for two years, and then removed to a college living at North Bradley, Wiltshire. He later founded and endowed an almshouse for the poor at North Bradley, and built a school at his own expense.

Although Daubeny was quick-tempered and indifferent to the opinion of others, retiring and little interested in social life, his reputation as a scholarly theologian grew. Frugal, if not penurious, in his personal needs, he was generous with his money, time, and talents in the pursuit of those projects of which he approved: education, parish improvements, and the union of the differing parties of the Christian church. He attacked popery as stridently as he did Protestant nonconformists, on occasion departing from common courtesy to do so. The preface of Boucher's book had attracted him, for it evoked in his mind a disturbing contemporary parallel. England seemed to him to be enmeshed in the same principles which had led to the American Revolution. Daubeny had been at Versailles at the outbreak of the French Revolution, and he entertained firm ideas on the disastrousness of that event, an opinion which Boucher shared. Daubeny was also a strong supporter of the SPG, with which Boucher had once been affiliated. But above all, the pair shared the same concern for bringing Dissenters back into the Church of England.

After he had become the minister of Christ Church, Walcot, Daubeny published *A Guide to the Church* (1798), which advanced his scheme for the union of dissidents in the Anglican church. When he first wrote to Boucher in 1798, another manuscript was in preparation and soon he was sending Boucher packets of papers. He asked Boucher for his criticism of specific sections concerning Calvinism, and church unity and schism, as well as for his general opinion of the scope of the work. Later, when the revised manuscript was ultimately published under the title *An Appendix to the Guide to the Church* (1799), he incorporated

255

many of Boucher's suggestions. After publication of the *Appendix,* which was in effect a second volume intending to prove that the discipline of the Church of England was of apostolic origin and that any departure from it would be schismatic, he requested Boucher to review it, deeming him "the fittest person" for the task.[14] Boucher, for reasons unknown, declined to review the book, although Bishop Skinner and Dr. George Gleig had both given Daubeny strong approving letters and he expected them to write good reviews. Daubeny, however, did not take offense at Boucher's refusal, for less than a month later he assured him that he would use his influence at Winchester College on behalf of admission for Boucher's son.[15]

These two men recognized in each other dedication to similar principles with respect to church and politics. Indeed, Daubeny pointed out to Boucher that a review of his own book, *A Guide to the Church,* had called Boucher, Samuel Horsley (later bishop of Asaph), and himself "the Lauds of the present day."[16] He commended to Boucher the "sound constitutional principles" of the *Anti-Jacobin,* at whose service he put his own abilities, and considered "that schismatic courier," the *Gospel Magazine,* a danger to the constitution of the church. Both Boucher and Daubeny held popular preaching to be a great disaster. The latter firmly believed that "a doctrine that faith is necessarily productive of works is a most dangerous error, a true child of enthusiasm," an opinion to which Boucher could heartily subscribe.[17] In fact, Boucher seldom missed an opportunity to criticize popular preaching. The two men exchanged frank opinions on church issues and clerics, and seemed generally to agree. Daubeny, for example, praised Boucher's "handsome review of a work by the Bishop of Lincoln," but felt free to doubt "whether the bishop is as orthodox and apostolical as he is represented to be." He also volunteered to tell Boucher about the bishop of London, whom he thought neither sound nor honest.[18]

The religious subject of greatest interest to Boucher, however, and to Daubeny to a somewhat lesser degree, was that of the Scottish church. Boucher favored a union between the Anglican congregations in Scotland and the Episcopal Church of Scotland, and had discussed such a union with William Stevens as early as 1793.[19] Stevens, who approved of the union but thought it should take place gradually, advised Boucher to let the negotiations for the merger be handled by Sir William Forbes, a close associate of Bishop Skinner of Aberdeen and an advocate of the plan. Boucher had a close personal interest in the plans for such a merger; he hoped to be made bishop of Edinburgh. Skinner had invited Boucher to Aberdeen in October 1793, and had discussed his hopes that Boucher in that position would aid the project. The winter of 1793 had passed with no news of further developments. Then in spring 1794, Boucher received a letter from Sir William Forbes and the vestry of Saint Paul's Chapel in Edinburgh "respecting the important business now pending there." The Epsom minister was delighted: the letter was "exactly such an one as I could have wished, and must bring the matter to some crisis; I hope to an happy one," he confided to Sir Frederick Eden. A few days later, Boucher met with "His Grace of Canterbury," after which he planned to stay with the Edens for a few days and tell them of the outcome.[20] Unfortunately, the plan was temporarily shelved, primarily because of Presbyterian opposition.

Four years later, when Boucher was "on the verge of 60," as he put it, the Scottish union plan was revived. Cautiously, Boucher refrained from any comments to friends for the time being, but he was not able to conceal his hopes from Frederick Eden, who had guessed his "great secret." Boucher promptly charged his friend to secrecy, for he wanted no one at Lambeth Palace to know his plan until he had had more time to reflect upon it himself. Now that Eden had guessed, he decided to solicit his opinion before presenting it at Lambeth. The caution was necessary, Boucher thought, for he was not yet very confident that "it ever can be put on such a footing . . . that it would be prudent for me to go to Edinburgh; yet I have more than a notion that it is already on such a footing as to make it my duty." The outcome rested on the approval of the archbishop, but Boucher had many doubts about that official. If only he would see the thing as I do, Boucher reflected, he could not find a better opportunity "to promote the true interest of true religion," or to benefit me.[21] Although Boucher had hoped for approval of his plan from Eden, he was afraid that Eden might agree with William Stevens, who had already advised Boucher not to accept a mitre in the Scottish church. Boucher, feeling rebuffed, did not favor Stevens with his confidences for some time, causing Stevens to comment tartly that he had been "struck out of the Privy Council."[22] Stevens never failed to speak his mind bluntly, and on the subject of a Scottish bishopric he no doubt irritated Boucher with an attitude so contrary to his own.

The ,decision about the union of the Scottish churches remained in abeyance, while Boucher's chances for a mitre seemed to be improving. In the summer of 1798 Boucher was pleased to be invited to give two sermons—one at Guildford and one at Carlisle—both of which he expected to add to his already considerable reputation as a good Anglican sermonizer. There was a fair touch of pageantry when the assizes held a session in a county town. The robed judge walked to court in a procession which was headed by the sheriff in traditional costume and was accompanied by trumpeters. The pomp appealed to Boucher, particularly in that summer of suspense while he savored the prospect of a bishop's headdress.

Boucher prepared a sermon for the assizes at Guildford, Surrey, for 30 July 1798, before the Lord Chief Justice Kenyon. Kenyon complimented him, and the gentlemen of the grand jury unanimously requested that his excellent sermon be published.[23] The *Monthly Review* took note of the sermon, commenting that it contained some thoughts and observations which were not common, but which were no less estimable, on the subject of mercy. The reviewer agreed with Boucher that mercy, improperly directed, could produce great evil: "The weakness of good men serving on juries, while it has favored unfortunate individuals, has proved in its consequences . . . very detrimental to the public." Boucher turned to Stevens once again, wanting to share his sense of pleasure in his popularity. However, Stevens was still somewhat offended at the distance Boucher had earlier put between them, and his reply to his old friend was a little more sharp than usual. He expressed the hope that the "notice" Boucher had lately received would prove a real gain, but in his own experience, he wrote, "to gain popularity is often little better than a man's filling his belly with the east wind." If Sir Frederick thought Boucher had "blossomed," Stevens added, "the blossoming is the blossoming of a thorn."[24]

Later that same summer Boucher preached his second sermon at the assizes held in Carlisle on 12 August 1798, before the Hon. Sir Giles Rooke. Again the sermon was to be published. Boucher fretted that his pulpit presentations would do him less credit in print than they had when he read them. Stevens reassured him while still managing to prick his pride. "Don't be squeamish," he counseled, "I'll warrant you they will do; and they are in excellent hands for correction."[25] The *Monthly Review* later described the sermon at Carlisle as "political and patriotic," with good language and "laudable" in general.[26] The two sermons are the last formal political statements of Boucher's career; they reflect his increasing conservatism in the wake of the French Revolution. As he commented in a letter to James Maury, he expected his friend to find them "Toryish." Boucher was now one of the three "Lauds of the present day."

The decision about the Scottish church was still pending, and Boucher chafed. Always a restless man, he decided on a move of his own, one that clearly indicated his expectations. In August 1798 Joseph Jefferson acknowledged Boucher's startling decision to terminate his ministry. "At length, after having toiled for so many years, an earnest if not successful laborer in the vineyard," he had "come to the resolution to quit the service," and to move to Cumberland. Jefferson, much surprised, assumed that he was depressed with his parish duties and endeavored to cheer him up. He admitted that he, too, suffered an occasional sense of lack of accomplishment in the "vineyard." He hoped that Boucher's move to Cumberland would not dissolve their relationship, although he confessed that it would give him pleasure to think of Boucher living in a part of the kingdom that engaged so many of his own musing thoughts.[27]

Boucher implemented his plans with little delay. By late summer of 1798 he had taken a house at Holme Hill, near the Caldew River, convenient to Carlisle and to his new estates in Caldbeck and Sebergham parishes. With some insight into Boucher's reasons for the shift of residence, Jefferson commented that the new residence would be "peculiarly pleasant" because of its situation two miles from Rose Castle, the retreat of the bishop of Carlisle.[28] Boucher contemplated his new quarters with pleasure, and invited Jefferson to visit him as soon as the family was moved and settled. It is clear that Boucher also sought the approval of his long-time friend Stevens in this Cumberland venture, but Stevens was less inclined to be reassuring than he was to give Boucher some plain talk. In Stevens's opinion, the move meant being "buried alive at Carlisle," which he found "equivalent to being dead and buried elsewhere." On the other hand, his disapproval should be of no importance. "Whether I approve or not it does not signify three skips of a louse." To Boucher's suggestion that he might think of joining the Bouchers in the Cumberland neighborhood, he put a curt negative: "To think at my time of life of making Carlisle a half-way house to Aberdeen on a future date, you must take me to be as wild and romantic as somebody that shall be nameless." Boucher had confided to Stevens that he had hoped that the archbishop of Canterbury "might have prevented the necessity of the measure," but Stevens refused to speculate on what the archbishop might or ought to have done to obviate Boucher's need for a house near Carlisle.[29] It is clear that both men thought of the move as an intermediate stop on the way to Aberdeen.

All through the month of September, the Scottish church plan was still a possibility. Arrangements were made for Boucher to visit Edinburgh. Boucher was thoroughly at home on a horse, a result of his plantation days in America, and he set out for Scotland on the first of October with considerable enthusiasm. The welcome accorded him upon his arrival in Edinburgh was gratifying, and he enjoyed the warm hospitality of the city that he found both "curious and interesting." He admired the ruins of Roslin Castle. With his usual practical turn of mind, he envisioned the day when he and Frederick Eden might tour Scotland together. Eden could capture the curious scenes in drawings, while Boucher would capitalize on his writing ability. Together, they might "make a book to bear our expenses."[30]

Boucher remained in Scotland several days, and then rode the nearly one hundred miles to Carlisle on horseback, arriving on 15 October 1798. The journey amazed and interested him; he saw places so picturesque and remembered them so vividly that he was certain he could describe them to Eden well enough that he might draw them. As he jogged along the roads on a heavy Irish horse, he amused himself by composing some epigrams.

> In dress the fancies of mankind are such
> We generally do too little or too much
> Both these extremes in Scotland here we see

Women go naked ev'n above the knee
In men, a diff'rent, but not less fault is found;
A filthy plaid envelops them all round.
No longer let us these extremes deplore;
But men be cover'd less, & women more.

Although Boucher sent his verses to Eden, he would not tell him in a letter what his business in Scotland had been. "It was not mere amusement, still less any vain projects of authorship," was all that he would say for the time being. "I have a great, and I hope good purpose in view, but whether I shall ever be able to bring it to bear, God only knows." He did promise to tell Eden everything when they met.[31] Boucher lingered in Carlisle for two weeks, probably making further arrangements about the house which he had taken. Perhaps he found time for some fishing in the Caldew with its picturesque scenery and woody banks. Boucher considered himself a *"brother angler"* of Izaak Walton, and thought no river finer than the Caldew for sport fishing, even though, as he had observed in his essay on Sebergham Parish, its trout were less delicately flavored than those in neighboring smaller streams.

Boucher returned to Epsom with pleasant expectations of enjoying the society of William Stevens and his London friends. Jefferson encouraged him in his aspirations by speculating on the possibility that his "learned friend" might later "be called upon to fill the office of the arch-deaconry of Carlisle."[32] Throughout the winter, the Scottish plan of union remained in limbo, but he still contemplated a move to Carlisle. In a letter to Jimmy Maury on 17 February 1799, he discussed his plans to move with his large family in the coming summer, hoping to "sit down...quietly for the small portion of my life that may now remain." The lack of news from Scotland had begun to cause him some disquiet, however, and he confided to Maury that the move was a very serious and "important measure." "We have actually taken a house," he wrote, "and as it is entirely a sacrifice to prudence, I trust we shall never regret the taking it" (*MHM* 10:126). Unfortunately, the eighteenth century slipped away, and Boucher had had no further word from Edinburgh.

At last, sometime before 8 February 1800, Boucher was offered the position of principal minister of the English Episcopal Chapel in Holyrood Castle, Edinburgh (the equivalent title today would be dean). One Mr. Fitzsimmons, the previous incumbent, had been dismissed or forced to resign. The vestry of the chapel "have done me the honor to invite me to succeed him," Boucher wrote to Bishop John Douglas. The post itself was no financial plum; Boucher understood the annual salary to be only one hundred pounds. But like Saint Anne's Church at Annapolis, to which Boucher had waited to be appointed for years, it was the *Gradus ad Parnassum*. It was a difficult decision for him to make, but he had had to make such a decision twenty-five years before in Maryland. Then he had clung to his loyalty to the Church of England and obedience to the Crown, and put in jeopardy all his worldly goods. Boucher refused the position, although he understood that the incumbent of the post would be the heir apparent to the mitre of Abernethy Drummond, the bishop of Edinburgh. In spite of all the attempts to persuade them along the way, the Scottish Anglicans refused to "render obedience to the Scottish bishops." Boucher thought he would be acquiring a parish which was Episcopalian in name alone. Under these circumstances he refused it. As a man of principle, and one who had thoroughly studied the Scottish problem for years, he would not compromise in his belief that it was an unsatisfactory arrangement and detrimental to the true church.[33]

Filled with dismay at the turn of events, Boucher wrote Stevens on 21 April 1800 of the failure of his hopes of a Scottish mitre. Stevens tried to lift Boucher's spirits by twitting him, and by attempting to give him a commonsensical perspective. "I am sorry to see you moralizing in so gloomy a strain; your letter may be called, 'The Lamentations of Jonathan.'" Stevens reminded his disgruntled friend that it was not the first time that a position which he had sought had entailed provoking delays or had eluded him completely; nor was it the first time that he had failed to get the Scottish bishopric. "Through life it has been your lot to be tantalized with hopes and prospects of advantages which have never been realized. Oh sad." On the other hand, not all of Boucher's prospects had failed, and some advantages had been realized when he had had no hopes or prospects. He had had an ample fortune bequeathed to him by Miss Barton, Stevens recalled, and the thousands he had obtained from his second wife must somewhat balance the account. As a matter of fact, Boucher had received an additional legacy in 1791 from Charles Foreman, an uncle of his second wife. Furthermore, Boucher had once lamented that he did not have a family; "now you must allow that you have little reason to complain on that score." "I must wonder that you should sigh for what you might so easily obtain without a sigh," Stevens wrote. "If fortune has sported with you, she has likewise sported for you; and upon the whole I think you may be said to have had pretty good sport." Dr. Samuel Glasse and Rev. William Horne, rector of Otham, were both familiar with the circumstances of Boucher's disappointment. They had read his various complaining letters on the subject, and were moved to tell Stevens to recommend to Boucher that he give up his projects of one kind and another, and try living "quiet and happy."[34]

For some months Boucher had determined to leave his parish by the first of May 1800, at the latest, presumably to spend the early summer in Carlisle.[35] Now he had to consider the alternatives. Although Boucher had told Jefferson that he would "quit the service," it seems doubtful that he resigned from his pulpit. Saint Martin's Church at Epsom has no record that he left his post as rector. He was a practical man and perhaps he hedged to some extent, knowing that a financial risk was involved, and had not yet offered a formal resignation when his years of planning for Scotland collapsed. It is also possible that he did indeed resign, but rescinded his resignation so quickly that it was never formally recorded. On the other hand, it is entirely possible that Boucher never had any intention of resigning as rector at Epsom, but instead determined to leave the parish in the charge of his curate while he absented himself from all but occasional parish duties. Whatever Boucher's earlier plans had been, the family remained at Epsom in July and entertained the Edens. Boucher spent August through September at Brighton, Sussex, providing a seacoast holiday for his growing family. It is not clear what Boucher did about the house at Holme Hill that summer. Whatever his intentions about living in Cumberland, the fact is that Boucher was back in Epsom by February 1801, and Epsom remained his mailing address until April 1804.

The year 1800 was a year of disquiet and discontinuity for Boucher. The collapse of all his dreams of a bishopric, first dimly perceived and unexpressed in Maryland, then thwarted first in

Nova Scotia and now in Scotland, was more than a blow to his pride. The emoluments of a bishopric were permanently out of his reach. Although he was now a man of considerable property in Cumberland, when he rented the house at Holme Hill he had envisioned a higher standard of living than that of a parish minister. Furthermore, he had taxes to pay at Blencogo and elsewhere on the manors he owned, as well as the burden of an agent to oversee his affairs in the north. More importantly, his expenses at Epsom were spiraling and demanded ready cash. The house at Clay Hill was a large one, with a handsome library which he continued to stock, an expensive pleasure which he refused to deny himself.

The needs of his growing family were also a burden. The youngest of his seven children, Mary, was still under a year old when Elizabeth presented him in 1800 with a frail son, Jonathan, who was to die in infancy. Considerable domestic help was required for the brood, which included Mary Ann James, the child of Elizabeth's first marriage to young John James. The death of Boucher's sister Jinny six years before had deprived the family of a devoted and hard-working second mother, a loving spinster who had served her brother most of her life. Although Boucher had not wanted Jinny to seem a servant to him, and had provided her with a fifty-pound annuity for that reason, nevertheless her services to the family had been worth far more.

The cost of educating his sons was a grave concern to Boucher, for he wanted them to have the kind of preparation and university education that he himself lacked. Although Boucher had supervised the earlier training of his eldest son, James, the boy was now nearly ten years old. Boucher was thinking in terms of Winchester College soon, and a consequent expenditure of at least sixty pounds a year for tuition alone. His second son, Barton, was still only four years old, but he too would require education. Depressed with the developments in Edinburgh, Boucher felt the full gravity of his sixty-two years and contemplated his responsibility for the welfare of his wife and eight children. Elizabeth would have a heavy burden to assume at his death, even with adequate financial support.

Boucher announced a new decision: he would resume teaching. With as little relish as he had had when it had become necessary to teach to earn his bread at Paddington, Boucher once more established a school–his fourth. Boucher prided himself on his "happy pliancy" for accommodating himself "to any circumstances and any situation," and what he lacked in enthusiasm for the task he balanced with determination to succeed (*Rem.*, pp. 26-27). But the venture taxed his patience sorely. William Stevens, who was once again in Boucher's good graces, bore the brunt of his complaints: "I don't wonder you should growl and grumble at the idea of beginning life again, as it were," he sympathized with the Epsom cleric, although he was pleased to know that he was taking the "employment of pupilizing more kindly" than Boucher had originally expected. Stevens could empathize with Boucher's trials, for he conceded that he himself could not imagine anything that could reconcile him to teaching. "I should sooner creep into an augur hole."[36] In an effort to be helpful Stevens offered to find students for Boucher's school. He arranged for the grandson of Dr. Samuel Glasse to attend, which gave Boucher's venture some of the prestige necessary to success. Glasse, in turn, was to be vastly pleased with his grandson's progress. Again with Stevens's assistance, Boucher began to acquire those students whom Tom Hooker at Rottingdean could not accommodate. The continued operation of the school was now assured.

As in the past, Boucher encountered the perennial problem of obstreperous pupils and distasteful negotiations with parents, as well as the constant difficulty of finding suitable assistants for the school. As was his custom, he told William Stevens of his present distresses. One of Boucher's current assistants had "ill-used" him. Stevens attempted to find a better one for his friend. Unfortunately, it was no easy task. "Among all the men of great *larning* I am acquainted with, I know not one to suit your purpose. I have ne'er a ragged arsed parson in my eye at present, and indeed, now forsooth, they must all have silk breeches, or the situation is not good enough for them."[37] Boucher then hit upon the idea of inviting his friend Joseph Jefferson to consider teaching with him. Jefferson declined, having already agreed to work for Homerton College, the first Dissenting college to offer classical learning for the Dissenting clergy. Jefferson was to serve as a tutor "in the field," preparing young men for two years and then sending them on to a four-year residency at Homerton. The novel idea failed to come to fruition, and Jefferson instead established a school of his own.[38] Boucher managed to carry on, presumably with his less than satisfactory usher.

The cares and responsibilities of his school did not prevent Boucher from watching developments in the Scottish church. In spite of his own disappointment, he endeavored to maintain a careful exterior of impersonal concern in his letters to church officials. He did not always succeed, and one can detect an acrimonious edge to his remarks here and there. On one occasion Boucher expressed his firm opinion that the Scottish church should be put on the proper footing by the requirement that the clergy take an oath of loyalty. In a letter to the bishop of Salisbury, he urged him and the bishop of Rochester to write pastoral letters to that end. Boucher expressed particular irritation over Edinburgh's captivation with popular preaching, and decried the trend in the church toward selecting popular ministers. Boucher had had his fill of the evangelistic style in the backwoods of Virginia and Maryland. In spite of Jefferson's best efforts from Basingstoke, Boucher had never been persuaded of the value of enthusiastic preaching, preferring instead "ability, piety, orthodoxy, and learning," all qualities which he believed he himself possessed. Boucher deplored the stipulation of Bishop William Abernethy Drummond who was about to fill another vacancy in the English Chapel, that the "English assistant . . . must be a good preacher." With some perhaps forgivable malice, Boucher could not refrain from expressing his opinion to Bishop Douglas that "it must, however, surprise you I think to be told that even the grave and sound Bishop Abernethy Drummond begins to think popular talents in the pulpit of some moment." He now found Drummond "querulous and intemperate." Boucher concluded: "I was sanguine enough to hope that I might be the means of remedying some of these evils, but I found that it was beyond my strength," and thereafter he appears to have ceased writing to the bishops.[39] He turned to some pressing business of his own.

Boucher's agent for his affairs in Cumberland had been acting against his interests, and as usual he turned to Stevens for advice. Stevens was pleased to remind Boucher that he had had trouble with the same man before and had been in hopes that he had "long ago done his worst and that he had no more farewell plucks to take." Boucher, it seemed, had not learned from experience. "Was it not the practice in some places to strip geese

of their feathers while alive, and leave them to shift for themselves?," he asked Boucher. Stevens hoped that at last he had
taken the "necessary steps to prevent any more last plucks." If
he had not, then he deserved to be "cut for the simples." Acidly,
he reminded Boucher that he was always guarding against being
imposed upon, because it irked him so when it happened. Stevens
declared himself "too lazy" to take such measures, "but I sometimes think you are a greater fool than I am and that is saying
a great deal."[40] Boucher took with good grace Stevens's blunt comments and sharp jibes at his frustrations and follies, along with
his hard-headed advice. He knew that underneath the crusty exterior and the tart tongue lay a warm heart and a deep and
abiding friendship for Boucher, whose strengths and weaknesses
Stevens knew very well. Stevens had encouraged Boucher in every
venture he had undertaken for more than twenty-five years. It was
Stevens, not James, who encouraged Boucher in his "Historico-
Politico-Theological work" in the mid-1770s, which was to come
to fruition, in part, in a book of sermons in 1797.

◟ *Chapter* 12 ◞

Reflections of a High Tory

Boucher is best known for the political thought which he expressed in his book of sermons, *A View of the Causes and Consequences of the American Revolution in Thirteen Discourses Preached in North America Between the Years 1763 and 1775*. It was the major political work of his career and reflected many of the ideas which germinated in America and came to fruition in England.

Boucher had first thought about the possibility of publication of some of his sermons after his return to England when his circumstances had been "really bad." At that time he wrote six sermons over a period of six weeks "for this express purpose" (*MHM* 10:33). However, he did nothing with them at that time. Then, in 1779, he thought of them again and begged James to send him "half a dozen sermons, with leave to print them, or even a less number—along with my own."[1] His primary motive was to earn him "the credit of a little cleverness" which he hoped might aid him in his search for an appointment as a rector. Although Boucher was convinced that such a venture might be "the making of me," the project slipped into dormancy (*MHM* 10:33).

Two years later Boucher renewed the subject with James, urging him to give the plan serious thought and to take pains with criticizing and editing his sermons. He excused his demands on his friend on the ground that "by doing it, you may help me to bread." Realistically, he conceded to James that his sermons probably could not be published until the "American War terminates, and perhaps not at all if it does not terminate successfully."[2] James seems to have taken the request lightly and to have questioned Boucher's motives with some sarcasm, causing Boucher to complain that James had "almost knocked the whole matter on the head." Once again, the publication project faded from consideration until years after James's death, when Boucher brought the work to fruition in the 1790s.

Boucher was delighted when it appeared in print in 1797. Under the guise of a collection of sermons purportedly delivered in America between 1763 and 1775, the book consisted of two parts: an eighty-nine page preface, setting forth one of the first historiographies of the American Revolution, and thirteen sermons which constitute a political tract explaining Boucher's political theory. Although the preface would hardly do as modern history, it is a surprisingly knowledgeable, though British-oriented, treatise, assigning essentially economic and political factors as causes of the Revolution. Boucher pointed to the competition of Americans with their counterparts in England, the immense American debts held by English creditors, the great prosperity of the mainland colonies, Britain's neglect of the colonies over a long period of time, irresolution and mismanagement in colonial administration and in the military, "the loyal opposition" in England, and the prolific political pamphleteering" (A View, pp. xix, xxxviii-xlii, xliv).

Encouraged by Boucher's assurances that he was publishing his sermons "very nearly as they were delivered from the pulpit" between 1763 and 1775, most historians have accepted his political ideas as a consistent body of thought without distinction as to time. Since he also asserted that his "opinions and principles" had "undergone no change" (A View, p. lxxxv), it was natural to conclude that Boucher's political thought from 1763 to 1797 was consistent and that his sermons were veritable reflections of his ideas a generation earlier. It is hazardous, however, to consider the book as an accurate representation of Boucher's thought in America because of a problem in dating the sermons. In spite of Boucher's assurances that his opinions had undergone no change, his contemporary correspondence indicates otherwise. He also admitted in his introduction that he had expunged a number of "seeming contradictions" and had corrected certain "inaccuracies" in preparing the sermons for publication (A View, p. lxxxv). Furthermore, he added an impressive body of footnotes, at least one of which was essentially a complete political essay on the respective merits of Lockean and Filmerian ideas (*A View*, pp. 524n, 533n). Finally, internal evidence of suspiciously prescient writing and examples of misdating in the sermons themselves lends substantial weight to the case for caution.[3]

The book is valuable as one excellent source of Boucher's thinking in the late phases of his career, but it would be injudicious to ignore the evidence that the published sermons are not actually those which Boucher delivered in America; the text of those which Boucher had earlier delivered in Virginia and Maryland did not survive his flight into exile. In a letter to William Eden 7 January 1776, Boucher mourned that he had "lost most of what I had ever written concerning America" (*MHM*, 8:343), and on 9 September 1781 Boucher told James that of his sermons in America he had nothing but his "first loose hints on scraps of paper to work from—my fair copies were left behind."[4] He also stated to the Loyalist Claim commissioners that the loss of all his American papers and documents hampered the preparation of his claim.

It is clear that some of the published sermons purporting to have been delivered in America were reconstructions which Boucher developed from minimal notes. It also seems reasonable to assume that at least six of the sermons were written in England between Boucher's arrival in September 1775 and 1779. The sermons then would be less than reliable as a statement of Boucher's opinions and principles when he was actually participating in American events. Boucher may, of course, have delivered sermons in America on the same general themes as those in the book. But it is difficult to imagine that his reconstructions or his newly composed sermons could be unaffected by his difficult experiences in the American Revolution, by his bitterness at not finding preferment in England for so many years, and by his hatred of the French Revolution. Even the lapse of twenty-two years since his escape from America would have had its effect at the moment he set himself to the task of the final editing of the sermons. His motives in publishing at that time were even more important. Although he wished to set down for the benefit of his children the principles which had guided his actions in the American Revolution, Boucher's practical sense would have given him another powerful incentive. In the 1770s he hoped to gain a benefice;

in the late 1790s he was in search of a mitre, and it would be natural for him to represent himself as a high churchman and high Tory.

One of the most interesting ideas incorporated in the preface of *A View* was Boucher's plan for a British federated government. His proposal for the reunion of Great Britain and America was based on the concept of two "distant, distinct, and completely independent States," wholly unlike the old parent-child relationship to the colonies, unlike the relationship between Great Britain and Ireland or Scotland, and even less like that of France. Boucher's proposed constitution would be an alliance broad enough to encompass the community of commercial interests, with "some considerable degree of community in government." He envisioned "the subjects of the one" as subjects of the other, with each making laws for itself. Each would guarantee the defense of the other, "not merely as an ally and a friend, but as an integral part of itself, one and indivisible" (*A View*, pp. lxxiii-lxxvi).[5]

Boucher saw his plan of a federated government as a way of realizing the towering project of universal monarchy, something which France had once tried to arrange, thereby convulsing Europe for centuries. Britain would be a depot, supplying the European market with the overflowings of the three quarters of the world united in "a triple cord of irresistible strength." England's small size would be an advantage, since it was most easily defended and least likely to interfere with others in any staple produce. England would be the workshop; the others, however superior either in size or opulence, would be her children. There is much of the old mercantilist spirit here, but presumably with more autonomy for the parts of the system. The colonies, if children in respect to trade, would be comparable to the mature offspring of a parent. Boucher hoped that such a plan might be a means of universal peace, a barrier against ambitious, disorderly, and refractory men of all countries. It had to be strong enough to overawe aliens into peace and to keep its own turbulent members within bounds. In summary, Boucher envisioned a grand alliance to maintain world peace, a Pax Britannia of the nineteenth century.

The benefits to England of such a federation were obvious to Boucher, but he thought America had something to gain as well. When he set forth his federated plan of government in 1797 he had been following American politics closely and had observed

John Adams's difficulty in maintaining diplomatic neutrality in the face of party factionalism. America was not in "confirmed health," he believed, but in "an intermission of sickness," "kindly granted by Providence" (*A View*, p. lxxx). America, he thought, might be expected to recognize some virtue in his constitution. Boucher, however, was completely skeptical about recognition of the value of his plan of government on the part of British politicians. He wrote bitterly that England's statesmen were "wholly occupied" with "financial calculation and the balance of parties," and he expected nothing but ridicule for his suggestion. His plan for a federated government died as quietly as the earlier plan of government he had submitted to Sir Grey Cooper in the 1770s.

With a straightforwardness characteristic of Boucher, he dedicated the book to George Washington as a tender of renewed amity and sent him a copy. The dedicating lines are in no way an apology for his earlier letter to Washington on the eve of his departure from America. He praised Washington for having asserted in his farewell valedictory address that the only firm supports of political prosperity were religion and morality. Boucher also complimented him on the United States' form of government, which fortunately had been "framed after a British model" and therefore had "the unity of its executive and the division of its legislative powers," in spite of its many defects. Several months later Washington acknowledged receipt of Boucher's book. Since he had not yet read it, he made no comment on its content. He politely recognized the honor of the dedication, adding that he regarded Boucher as a man of principle for whom he entertained "no unfriendly sentiments."[6] Thus Boucher had a minimal reconciliation with Washington.

Boucher had also sent a copy of the book to Jimmy Maury, who obviously disapproved of some of its contents. He took Boucher to task for having had the temerity to dedicate such a "pointedly disgusting" book to Washington and then to send him a copy. In reply Boucher chided him and Americans generally. "You are such gluttons of praise that you wish to be praised even for rebelling." Boucher felt that Maury's opinion reflected the narrow point of view of a Virginia merchant, "a *beggar of tobacco*," and a man of Jacobin politics.[7] He dared to hope that Jimmy's son would be neither a revolutionist nor a Republican. Boucher found it impossible to resist a final barb at the weak position of

the new government which seemed so slow to "resent the indignities and the injuries of their new sister [France]." How long
will "your rising states" tolerate being "kicked and butted by the
Grand Nation," for "the sneaking purpose of some little commercial
gains?" Boucher asked, adding sourly, "You would not have put
up with an hundredth part of it from us" (*MHM* 10:120-21).

Boucher could do without Maury's approval while he basked
in compliments from others. He had just received a Virginia ham
from a merchant (one not in the tobacco trade) with an accolade
on Boucher's seasonable work which he thought would be very
generally read in America. Furthermore, he had just been offered
a D.D. by a Scottish university, which he had declined. Perhaps
the approval that pleased him most was that of Peter Porcupine,
to whom Boucher had sent the first copy of his book. In his reply
on 24 August 1798, William Cobbett expressed his thorough agreement with the remarks in the preface, particularly Boucher's statement that Britain had received vile treatment at the hands of
historians of the American Revolution. "The demon of falshood
[sic]" seemed to have guided "their prostituted pens," wrote Cobbett, though he hoped that "truth may, however, at last come out,"
and Loyalists would receive some overdue honor. He too decried
the "dreadful fraternity of France (one of the fruits of the Revolution)." Nonetheless, Cobbett discouraged Boucher's hope for
a second edition of his book of sermons. The book, he said, was
"too serious and too long" to sell in America, since "a very few
copies of any thing above a pamphlet will find sale in America."
Although he expressed the wish that he could publish it anyway,
Cobbett felt certain that the loss would be at least fifty pounds
and therefore prohibitive. Cobbett concluded his letter with reminiscences of England and his birthplace in Surrey, assuring Boucher that he expected to be there in a few years and would look
him up at Epsom.[8]

Until late January 1798, Boucher had no idea how his book
would be received by the literary critics. During the suspenseful
period he cheered himself with the thought that at least he had
written it. He wrote to Maury: "I think I could not have gone
to my grave quite so easy in my mind...had I not left to my
children somethig like a testimony" to principles that he had
adhered to "pertinaciously" at great cost to himself. He wanted

them to know that he had been "neither a fool or a knave" in doing so (*MHM* 10:126).

Meanwhile, Boucher was pleased when Lord Kenyon and the archbishop of York approved of his book and gave him some reason to hope for favorable reviews. Unhappily, the first intensive commentary on the book appeared in the *Analytic Review* and was unfavorable, while those that followed bestowed praise or censure depending upon the political views of the critic.[9] The writer in the *Analytic Review* complained that he had expected "a detail of interesting particulars" from a firsthand witness, but had not found them. Furthermore, he characterized the causes of the war which Boucher had identified as unexceptional, causes "of which no child in England could be ignorant." He lamented the absence of information on the "progress of the American union, the combination of the rebels, the march of treason and revolt," and the key figures involved. On the latter point, the reviewer found only "a little abuse of Franklin and Washington." He also took exception to Boucher's conclusion that the Revolution had resulted in a weak American government; on the contrary, the new government was strong and the suppression of the Whisky Rebellion proved it. Finally, the reviewer challenged Boucher's conclusion that the revolution in France was a consequence of the revolution in America; instead he thought the upheaval was the direct result of "the national debt and the feudal system of old France." Boucher had written with "all of the bitterness of party" and was obviously a Tory "of the very first water."

The treatment accorded the book in the *Monthly Review* was scarcely more favorable.[10] The critic attacked Boucher in a spirited fashion for first renouncing class bias and then treating the unsuspecting reader to a full dose of it in discourses resembling "senatorial speeches or popular harangues" more than instructive sermons. At length a comprehensive review appeared in the *Gentleman's Magazine* in November 1799, assigned the book considerable importance, and gave it "unqualified approbation."[11] This reviewer welcomed Boucher's "elegantly and correctly written" preface and pronounced his judgment that it had been much needed to fill the vacuum caused by the lack of an impartial history of the American revolt. The author, he declared, had displayed "considerable acuteness," and "discrimination," and had earned the right to enjoy "the society of the learned." Boucher must have savored that review.

Whatever contemporary critics thought of Boucher's book, it established its author in the public mind as a staunch high churchman. He had closed his book with a quotation from the sermon Archbishop William Laud delivered from the scaffold before his execution. In doing so, declared a reviewer, he had proclaimed himself a high churchman who hailed Laud as "one of the ornaments of human nature and greater than Lord Bacon." That image of Boucher persisted into the next century. It is not strange then that historians who have relied upon Boucher's book of sermons should have portrayed him as a high Tory.

The published sermons and Boucher's elaborate preface are an excellent summary of his thinking of the late 1790s, although they do not represent the whole body of his thought in the late phases of his career. More importantly, they do not represent his thought in America and in his early years as an exile in England. The fact is that Boucher's life consisted of three distinct careers, demarcated by radical alterations in his social position, economic interests, and friendships, with parallel and substantial differences occurring in his political thinking.[12] The element of chance played a considerable part. In Virginia Boucher was an American Whig patriot, a man whose ideas dovetailed with his economic interests. Only later in Maryland, and ultimately in England, did he become conservative and indeed reactionary in his political thought.

The Boucher whose thoughts the world has known best has been largely the Englishman who reintegrated himself into British society at Paddington, Epsom, and Cumberland. He bore little resemblance to the American Boucher. The years in exile deepened his already substantial conservatism. Like most of the Tory refugees, he suffered a severe cut in his economic and social position, and had to face up to the reality of dwindling funds, empty promises of a parish, and the need to earn a living. He had no sense of security until his hard work in the Paddington school began to pay off, but even then his income was a poor one compared with his handsome salary in Maryland. Few men experience such reverses without becoming both embittered and more reactionary; Boucher was no exception.

A major factor in Boucher's political shift in England was the outcome of the American Revolution. Never was he to admit that it was other than a catastrophe, an opinion which he defended to his death. The disservice done to mankind by the American rebellion was, in his opinion, equalled only by its "acknowledged and most distinguished offspring," the "dreadful" revolution in France and "the first-born, in direct lineal succession of numerous progeny of revolutions, of which that of America promises to be the prolific parent" (*A View*, pp. xxvi, lxxxiv, lxiv). Boucher followed closely the action across the channel of "yonder Devils," and in 1798 speculated that there would "assuredly be yet another revolution in France, and [that] these d——d Jacobins, who now carry all before them, [will] follow [the] fate of their predecessors the Brissotines and be made shorter by the head."[13] Meanwhile, Boucher seized every opportunity to remind his audiences that underlying the French tragedy was the loss of respect for religion, the attack by reckless men upon the French social and political order, and the loss of reverence for the French constitution.[14] For those willing to see, the French Revolution was "that yet more awful lesson which the world has since been taught by that more fatal exemplification of the effects of false principles" (*A View*, p. xxiii).

Beyond the revolutionary events, an additional but no less powerful force propelled Boucher in the direction of greater conservatism during his English years. This force was his great desire, bordering on anxiety, to find a place for himself within the English establishment similar to that which he had won in Maryland. He never succeeded in duplicating the intimacy in government circles of his colonial Maryland days, but his pursuit of that will-o'-the-wisp continually reinforced his conservatism. His deepening interest in affairs of the Church of England in America and in Scotland, as well as in her various dissenters, accentuated his commitment to his oath of office to church and state, while invitations to give assizes sermons both at Guildford and at Carlisle entrenched him even more solidly with the established church. Some of his most reactionary statements are contained in the assizes sermons of 1798; Boucher's political shift from his days as a Virginia planter was complete.

Boucher entertained some archaic and curiously reactionary ideas, yet a careful reader of his published and unpublished writing must also admit that he was above all an eighteenth-century conservative constitutionalist. Except for his flat rejection of the

Lockean explanation of the origin of government, his frame of reference is well within that body of thought shared by the English Whigs of the seventeenth century. And like most of the others who became Loyalists, he cited the same authorities as did his revolutionary opposition, although often with greater care in quoting accurately and fully from his Whig sources. Order meant legal order, the rule of law, to most Americans. In this respect, Boucher was no different from the founding fathers who "sought stability, just as they sought personal security."[15] Like John Adams, he had great admiration for the British constitution, which he always held to be the most magnificent instrument ever devised for the governance of man. However, he did not revere the constitution as an end in itself; instead, he perceived it as modern conservatives do, as a means to an end. It led to the reign of law and the protection and preservation of justice and liberty.

Like Burke, whose writing influenced him substantially, Boucher believed that constitutionalism makes possible great stability in a society.[16] Although he does not write of a contract as Burke does, as existing between generations past, present, and to be born, still he felt strongly the sense of that continuity, and his own forceful language conveys that belief clearly. The fabric of society, as he sometimes expressed it, must not be torn, for stability and continuity alone make possible the environment which is essential for law, order, justice, and liberty to exist and prosper. Only "just principles and righteous laws maintain...human society in a settled and established dependence" to produce order and security. For this reason Boucher firmly believed in the principle of obedience, which he regarded as "the great corner-stone of all good government." Obedience in turn must be based upon reverence for the state (A View, pp. 306, 310-11). Even modern writers, Boucher observed, agreed that "no government does or can possess force or power sufficient for its own support, were it not for the general opinion and persuasion, if not of its sacredness, yet of its inviolability" (A View, p. 306). Obedience and reverence were not mere ends in themselves; they were the means to protect government and organized society against disorder and anarchy, the twin weapons which threaten law, order, justice, and the general peace and happiness of mankind.

For Boucher, two premises were particularly abhorrent and subversive of social stability. One was the idea "that government

277

is a combination among a few to oppress the many," a "palpably absurd" conspiracy theory which he found completely incompatible with reverence for the state as the fountain of law, order, and justice; the second was the hypothesis that "all government is the mere creature of the people, and may therefore be tampered with, altered, new-modelled, set up or pulled down," merely as "tumultuous crowds of the most disorderly persons in the community" may determine "in some giddy moments of over-heated ardor" (*A View*, pp. 313-14). Like Alexander Hamilton, who did not consider government an evil, Boucher praised lawful government, which could be "the greatest blessing that mankind enjoy, and the very life and soul of society, without which men must live together rather like wolves and tigers, than like rational creatures" (*A View*, pp. 422-23). To believe that government was evil, Boucher thought, was just as illogical as to believe that a surgeon "who saves our lives by amputating a putrid limb" is an enemy (*A View*, p. 315). But like many another eighteenth-century constitutionalist, he was convinced that no state can be subjected to immediate popular control without disastrous instability.

Boucher held beliefs remarkably similar to those of another American constitutionalist, Fisher Ames. Just as Boucher had been affected by the operations of the extralegal committees of the American Revolution, so Fisher Ames had been deeply conditioned by Shays's Rebellion. He became one of the most ardent of Federalists, forcefully stating in his first political essay that the excesses of an uncontrolled democratic enthusiasm would jeopardize all government. Rioting, Ames thought, was high treason; "no sooner is the standard of rebellion displayed, than men of desperate principles and fortunes resort to it; the pillars of government are shaken; the edifice totters from its centre, the foot of a child may overthrow it; the hands of giants cannot rebuild it." Furthermore, lenience against insurgents would only encourage further challenges on the part of those who believed that a state could not enforce its authority. While many "would rebel, rather than be ruined," most would "rather not rebel than be hanged."[17] A majority of the members of the Constitutional Convention also would have agreed with Boucher and Ames.

The dilemma posed by the conflict between the principle of reverence for the state and the importance of resistance to unwise or corrupt governmental policy troubled Boucher as it did all constitutional conservatives. As was the case with most political thinkers of the late eighteenth century, Boucher could not accept the concept of a loyal opposition, because of the difficulty, if not impossibility, of distinguishing between opposition to a particular administration and its policies, and opposition to the state in a seditious sense. The idea that the activities of a "self-created body of men, who are generally known and described under the settled title of the Opposition," should be "absolutely necessary to the preservation of liberty," was foreign to his understanding. It mattered not "however generally entertained and acted on," such an idea might be; in his opinion it was "ill-founded" (*A View*, pp. 315-16). He would concede only that on occasion "some good" might come out of the activities of the opposition, but he retained his doubts that "the good that is thus done" could be sufficient to offset the disproportionate evil which results. Indiscriminate political opposition also carried with it an inherent danger as well, in its impact on "ill-informed or misdirected minds," who are then "naturally led, instead of reverencing government, to do all they can to dishonor it" (*A View*, pp. 318-19).

This rejection of the idea of loyal opposition was consistent with classic eighteenth-century conservatism, or even with Whig liberalism. Richard Hofstadter has pointed out that few men in America before the Jacksonian period were willing to accept the loyal opposition concept as compatible with, much less integral to, free constitutional government. Washington and Hamilton had condemned it as subversive.[18] Another good Federalist, John Adams, thought such opposition was deplorable, dividing the republic "into two great parties, each arranged under its leader and concerting measures in opposition to each other." Such a prospect, Adams considered, "is to be dreaded as the greatest political evil under our constitution."[19] Jefferson also shared the reservations about opposition, believing that the only sound government was one based upon Bolingbroke's idea of a union of all patriotic men.[20] Boucher's contempt for a "loyal opposition" was not an archaic remnant of seventeenth-century thought, but was instead a part of contemporary thinking.

Nor should Boucher's cynicism about the necessity for a loyal opposition be taken as naiveté or complacency about the existence of inefficiency and corruption in government. "Mal-administration, corruption, and tyranny, in those who govern," he wrote, "sap the

279

foundations of all good government" as much as they are "sapped by sedition and rebellion in those who are governed." Therefore, careful surveillance over the conduct of all administrations as well as over all policies adopted was the "common duty of every man in his sphere, and the especial duty of our constitutional guardians." Such overseeing of public business was not to be confused with "indiscriminate opposition" to government (*A View,* pp. 317-18). Many of these ideas sound like Burke, and they are not outside the frame of reference of eighteenth-century constitutionalism in general. One thing is certain: few or none of them can be traced to Filmerian thought.[21]

In two major respects Boucher disagreed emphatically with American political theory of the revolutionary period. The first was his flat rejection of Locke's compact theory of the origin of government. He based his objections on history, the Scriptures, and theory. It seemed patently implausible to him, judging from his observations of the wisdom and virtue displayed by the multitudes in real life, that "a large concourse of people, in a rude and imperfect state of society, or even a majority of them," ever gathered together and bound themselves "rationally and unanimously" within the framework of "various restrictions, many of them irksome and unpleasant." With some sense of the ludicrous, Boucher imagined a scene out of which Locke's compact might have arisen "in the decline perhaps of some fabulous age of gold." He conjured up a vision of "a multitude of human beings" who had been ranging the forests like their brother beasts, "*without guide, overseer, or ruler,*" at length having "in some lucid interval of reason and reflection" realized the "impossibility of living either alone with any degree of comfort or security, or together in society, with peace" now "met together in a spacious plain, for the express purpose of framing a government" (*A View,* pp. 519-20). The direct historical evidence in the hierarchical Hebrew culture bolstered Boucher's conviction. How much more logical to him was the proposition that the family was the nucleus of all government. The father served as the head of the house, and from that arrangement the patriarchal rule of the tribe evolved. Over a long period of time, the complex state structure of government emerged. Boucher never changed his position that Locke was historically inaccurate in his conception of a compact formed in a state of nature. His position here is more in tune with twentieth-century

political science than with that of his own day. The schism between eighteenth-century compact theory and Boucher's thought
is even more pronounced because he believed that the patriarchal
state, in addition to being a natural evolution, also reflected the
sanction of God and Scripture (A View, pp. 521, 525). Boucher
saw a special significance in the patriarchal government of the
Jews, for they were the chosen people and Jehovah had set them
under this system. Here Boucher most closely resembles Filmer.
Boucher's final objection to the compact theory of the origin of
the state was a theoretical one which arose both from his conception of the social order and from his philosophy of human nature.
His strong sense of tradition, born of his roots in Cumberland, had
never left him completely in America and had been revitalized
during the course of his repatriation in England. This sense of
the past was lacking in Americans, he thought; "Merely as Americans, they have no valorous ancestry to boast of, nor any history
but of yesterday" (A View, p. lv). They divested themselves of
habits and customs, which in turn made them less attached to
government from both principle and habit.

Boucher's return to English society, one much less open than
that which had permitted him to rise so rapidly in America, had
renewed his sense of stability. Change was not so rapid in England for an individual; Englishmen knew their places in society
and their obligations to the state. It was different in America,
where "Low people were . . . trained to be insolent and unman-
nerly; and were also taught that there was hardly any thing, however unreasonable, which they could not obtain, provided only they
were clamorous and audacious in demanding it" (A View, p. xli).
Boucher was reacting to the individualism of American political
theory and practice in the third quarter of the eighteenth century.
His own theories more closely resembled those of the medieval period, which advanced the idea of a highly integrated social order
in which all classes were part of one "great chain" (A View, p. 310).

Boucher's view of human nature accounted to some degree
for his rejection of Locke's compact theory. In general, he took
a Hobbesian view of the nature of man, a view which would
have made him at home in this one respect with the Puritans in New
England whom he almost despised. Boucher was not himself a
cynical man, but there is no question but that he had a realistic
attitude toward human behavior and toward human civilization

in general. His reading and his several experiences with irresponsible, cynical, and unethical men, both in America and in England, confirmed his less than optimistic view of men. He believed that as individuals men were a mixture of good and evil, and he looked to Hobbes's dedication to the earl ,of Devonshire for support: "man to man is a kind of God, and . . . man to man is an arrant wolf" (A View, p. 332n).[22] He saw man as a creature of prejudice, "in all respects a fallen and frail creature" (A View, p. 247), and he had no difficulty in believing that men had implanted in them a "degree of obstinacy" which made them "tenacious of what is opposed, for no better reason than because it is opposed" (A View, p. 84). Men were "more generally governed by their temper than their judgment," he thought.[23] He estimated that most men had a large share of the irrational in them, pointing out the "obsequiousness and pliability of human reason, and the facility with which men deceive themselves, when the interest of their passions requires that they should be deceived." Therefore, he said, one should not be surprised to discover the ease with which every man adopts "that creed which best suits his own inclinations, and seems most likely to justify his own practice."[24]

Boucher also had a good understanding of mob psychology. He was fully aware of the strategy often used by "movers of sedition," who reported that to have already happened which "they only wish may happen" (A View, p. 388). He also knew that the normal behavior of any individual caught up in a mass of people could be altered remarkably. "When once a multitude is tumultuously collected, there is no saying to what a pitch of mischief they may easily be led," he wrote. No matter how mild, beneficent, or humane any one of them might be acting independently, "I would not trust the milkiest man upon earth, when he is one in a disorderly and riotous crowd." It was Boucher's hard lot to have experienced mob action, so he knew that "collected together in a mob, we inevitably become irrational, violent, and tyrannical." To emphasize his point, he compared these quick changes of personality in a large body of men to certain chemical preparations, which "in their separate state, are perfectly innoxious; but, by being united, are rendered inflammable, and even poisonous" (A View, pp. 388-89). Nowhere did Boucher expect to find perfection among human beings, nor did he expect to find it among policy makers and administrators of any government. "No government on earth is infallible," he declared. "Perfection is not in human nature, and should no more be expected from aggregate bodies, than from individuals" (A View, p. 417). Fisher Ames expressed the same belief that only a dreamer expected perfection in government, someone who "had dipped his pencil in the rainbow."[25] Only disappointment awaited those who expected otherwise. "And what is the whole history of human life, public or private, but a series of disappointments," Boucher stated. In his experience, the history of mankind was little but a recital of quarrels, violence, strife, and wars. Such events "adorn the historic page," but "might better comport with the characters of wild beasts than of rational creatures" (A View, p. 332). Civilization itself was not an unmixed blessing, he had once confessed to his protégé, John James, when discussing the newly discovered South Sea Islands. He urged John to take "the proper position" in making the inhabitants the subject of a poem, by emphasizing "the misery of the savage life and the blessings of a well-regulated and improved state of society." But he added his doubts: "though I own to you I have often been tempted to think the other [position] was the stronger."[26]

Given Boucher's opinions on the condition of man, it is logical that he would reject the idea of human equality. In his youth he had been exposed to the summer visits to the Blencogo manor of the more affluent Boucher relatives, the Thomlinsons. Boucher was the poor country cousin who learned the English class structure through the back door of their country house. Their gracious manner of living was in sharp contrast with his own. Even the early days in Virginia had made him acutely aware of class lines in America, when he contrasted himself with the elegantly gowned and coifed ladies and the satin waistcoated gentlemen at the brilliant assemblies. Surrounded by plantation Negroes, he was certain to think about the inequality of men.

It is true that in Virginia Boucher had concerned himself with the idea of equal justice before the law and was much incensed over the Routledge murder and the lax manner in which bail was handled in order to accommodate a prominent Virginian. Boucher had been very conscious of the rights of Englishmen. His letters to James at that time were his historians, as Boucher put it, and they attest to his liberal spirit then. Nevertheless, Boucher denied that the whole human race was born equal and that no man was naturally inferior or in any respect subject to another. Thus he put himself outside the mainstream of American thought on this point. The proposition rested on false premises and conclusions, he thought. On the basis of his own observations, he firmly believed that men were not equal in talents and abilities. "Man differs from man in every thing that can be supposed to lead to supremacy and subjection, *as one star differs from another star in glory*" (*A View*, pp. 514-15).

As Boucher became more conservative, his old knowledge of the classes of men came to the foreground again and provided him with more evidence of inequality. The lower classes were "not industrious, frugal, and orderly," although once they had seemed so to him. They had characteristics, peculiar to their station in life, "of idleness, improvidence, and dissolution." He did concede that some of this resulted from "profligacy in the higher orders" of the community (*A View*, p. 310). Given these observations, talk of equality became something of a sham. Only "in times of popular commotions," he argued, "when revolutions are meditated," is the "doctrine of natural rights and the natural *equality* of mankind" countenanced. Then, he observed, "*all the congregation are holy, every one of them*" (*A View*, p. 419). Boucher had witnessed something of this in the rise of the republican spirit in America. At that time too he had not seen how men could be politically equal. Boucher held to his belief that some men were superior in endowment and position and ought to govern; those with different talents have a duty to accept governance. He could not conceive of a government "without some relative inferiority and superiority." To illustrate his point, he borrowed a metaphor from music: "A musical instrument composed of chords, keys, or pipes, all perfectly equal in size and power, might as well be expected to produce harmony, as a society composed of members all perfectly equal to be productive of order and peace" (*A View*, p. 515).

In addition to Boucher's disavowal of the equality of men, his quarrel with the compact theory rested upon yet other grounds. He detected a serious inconsistency in Locke's own theory. How could Locke insist upon the equality of all men under the compact, yet expect the submission of one man to another? "On what principles of equality is it possible to determine either who shall relinquish such a portion of his rights, or who shall be invested with such new accessory rights?," he asked. One could not have

284

it both ways, he reasoned; ~~submission immediately negates equali-~~ ~~ty.~~ "By asking another to exercise jurisdiction over me, I clearly confess that I do not think myself his equal; and by his consenting to exercise such authority, he also virtually declares that he thinks himself superior" (*A View*, p. 520). This hiatus in Locke's thought seemed to Boucher a serious defect, because he believed that most revolutions, including the American Revolution and its French offspring, were in fact the products of minority political move- ments. Unfortunately, in this process there was an additional hazard; one might "eventually subject himself to the possibility of being governed by ignorant and corrupt tyrants" (*A View*, p. 517).

Locke's system, based on consent, could only be "fantastic" and lead to chaos, Boucher reasoned (*A View*, p. 516). Consent itself was a "vague and loose" term, likely to mean little more than common feeling (*A View*, p. 513). But there was a further difficulty; even if one could maintain that acquiescence implied consent, agreement might have been "extorted from impotence or incapacity." And beyond the possibility of an invalid consent, there yet remained the question of the duration of the consent obtained: "Even an implicit consent can bind a man no longer than he chooses to be bound," Boucher could envision a constant process of consent followed by withdrawal, which could only result in a situation in which "governments, though always forming, would never be completely formed." In short, "the majority today might be the minority tomorrow," and "that which is now fixed might and would be soon unfixed." The same fallacious principle of equality of man "clearly entitles him to recall and resume that consent whenever he sees fit; and he alone has a right to judge when and for what reasons it may be resumed" (*A View*, pp. 515-16).

On the issue of the common good of mankind as a goal of government, Boucher again disagreed with Locke. He noted that what was commonly being affirmed as the end of government was the good of the inferiors, and ought to be understood as false. He thought that the confusion and misunderstanding of the com- mon good derived from the idea that "the end is above the means, and more noble"; therefore subjects were above their governors, and could call them to account. As a matter of fact, he observed, some governments existed for the benefit of the superior, as that of a lord or master over his servants: "Princes receive their power only from God, by him constituted and entrusted with the government of others, chiefly for his own glory and honor" (*A View*, p. 512n). The principal end of that kind of government was the advancement of God's honor. Only in a democracy was the safety of the people " 'the supreme law of the people' " (*A View*, p. 513n). In a monarchy the safety of the king is included with the safety of the subjects. Thus a king would be accountable only to God. He wished to make the point, a valid one for any day, that it would be very difficult even under a compact arrangement to establish what the common good actually ought to be. "What one people in one age have concurred in establishing as the 'common good,' another in another age have voted to be mischievous and big with ruin" (*A View*, p. 514).

Underlying much of Boucher's discussion of Locke's majority rule theory lay his deep and abiding distrust of the wisdom of the masses. He believed that the ignorant were more numerous than the wise and that mistakes in judgment and great errors in conduct were to be expected from the majority. Therefore the resolves of even large majorities of the poeple required the utmost caution, and the safety of the state should never depend on such determinations. All self-constituted assemblies aimed, it seemed to him, to "carry back social man to his supposed original independence, and to throw him once more into what has been called a state of Nature." The result, "if it be not anarchy, must at best be a democracy," and democracies "even when established without either tumult or tyranny, and by the very general though perhaps not unanimous consent of the community," were never satisfied with "an equality of rights." They naturally "aim at an equality of possessions," he believed. Thus one can attract the votes of a majority, and with great ease, when what is dangled before the masses is a proposition "not only to equalize property, but to destroy all those artificial distinctions in society which are created by property" (*A View*, pp. 363-64). Such thoughts as Boucher's did not disappear from American history. Even in the first glow of the new republic, Federalists such as Josiah Quincy, Fisher Ames, and others expressed the same sentiments. Hamilton is said to have remarked, in an unguarded moment of impatience with a dinner guest's long panegyric on the purity, intelligence, and "enlightened love of liberty" of the people, "Your people, sir—your people is a great beast!"[27] Hamilton was also certain that the masses were all too easily led by demagogues, particularly in a democracy, where uncontrolled by law and impressed with their sense of power, they were "liable to be duped by flattery, and to be seduced by artful and designing men."[28]

As a corollary to the problem of majorities, Boucher considered the subject of minorities, and developed a line of thought remarkably anticipatory of the thinking of John Calhoun in his pre-Civil War defense of the minority position of the South. "Abstractedly considered, or merely on the footing of natural rights," Boucher could see "no good reason why a minority should be bound by a majority." The principle had been adopted merely out of prudence and convenience and could reasonably be practiced only "in regulated societies, that is to say, in communities governed by laws" and even then minorities should be bound by majorities only in "specified" cases determined by law (A *View*, p. 362).[29]

At the same time, it is important to recognize that Boucher's seeming defense of minority rights is somewhat offset by his even greater concern for the serious consequences of minority group action. His indirect defense of minority rights is abstract and theoretical, while his sense of apprehension over the dubious accomplishments of minorities was conditioned by some hard realities in his own life which he would never forget. Fundamental to an understanding of his position here is the recognition that Boucher was firmly convinced until his death that both the American and the French revolutions had been conducted by political minorities. Boucher's overriding sense of the need for limitation of minority rights, a problem which he never resolved, pervades his writing.

Boucher disagreed entirely with his American Whig contemporaries on two additional points, the meaning of the word *liberty*, and the right of revolution.[30] On the first subject Boucher was clear and consistent. Liberty had been a constant topic of orators in America and he had had ample opportunity to learn what the Whigs meant by it, but he did not agree with their definitions. The kind of liberty which the Patriots had been talking about appeared to him to be something which bordered on mere pretense. The true meaning of liberty they had perverted to include that kind of liberty "of which every man now talks, though few understand it." Acidly, he commented that he had found the

287

word "in the mouths chiefly of those persons who are as little distinguished for the accuracy, as they are for the paucity, of their words" (*A View*, p. 504).

For Boucher, liberty had another meaning, one borrowed in part from John Locke, who believed in "absolute liberty, just and equal liberty, *equal and impartial liberty*" (*A View*, p. 268). Boucher recalled Hutchinson observing that liberty existed when the people could not " 'be subjected to any law or power among themselves without their consent.' " " 'Whatsoever is more than this,' " Hutchinson went on, " 'is neither lawful nor durable, and instead of liberty may prove bondage or licentiousness' " (*A View*, p. 533n). In order to bolster his argument, Boucher borrowed from Cicero, who had declared in his *Orations* that liberty consisted in a subservience to law. Liberty ought not to be the setting aside of law and the making of "our own wills the rule of our own actions, or the actions of others ... but it is the being governed by law, and by law only" (*A View*, p. 509). The one important prerequisite of liberty, Boucher thought, was that there be power sufficient to control the arbitrary and capricious wills of mankind, which if not so controlled, were dangerous and destructive to the best interest of society. Thus the primary aim of all well-framed constitutions was to place man out of the reach of his own power, and also out of the power of others as weak as himself, by placing him under the power of law.

Approaching the subject from another point of view, Boucher declared that he would write no flowery panegyrics on liberty, since they "are the productions of ancient heathens and modern patriots: nothing of the kind is to be met with in the Bible nor in the Statute Book" (*A View*, pp. 504-5). Asserting that true liberty "is a liberty to do everything that is right, and the being restrained from doing anything that is wrong," he quoted from Bishop Butler's sermon before the House of Lords 30 January 1740: "Civil Liberty is a severe and a restrained thing, [implying] ...authority, settled subordinations, subjection, and obedience" (*A View*, pp. 510-11). It was the "hard fate of unthinking multitudes," he thought, to be persuaded to "shake off a yoke, the weight of which they feel not, nor have ever felt, oppressive, and to change their old masters, without well considering who are to be their new ones" (*A View*, p. 393). The new liberty "may prove bondage, or licentiousness" (*A View*, p. 533n).

It was natural that Boucher should ultimately turn to the Bible for additional support, just as he had done to refute the compact theory, further describing liberty as freedom from the servitude of sin, and freedom to respect the laws. The clear duty of a Christian was to honor and obey the king, *"and all that are put in authority under him,"* a duty "essential to the peace and happiness of the world" (*A View*, p. 498). The love of liberty, which "carries us to withstand tyranny, will as much carry us to reverence authority, and to support it." Therefore a love of liberty which does not produce this effect was, Boucher believed, "hypocritical as a religion which does not produce a good life" (*A View*, pp. 510-11). Boucher was most at odds with American Whigs in his adamant rejection, on both theoretical and scriptural grounds, of any right of revolution. Like Thomas Hobbes, Boucher was convinced that states did not originate in a compact between the sovereign and the people, and thus the sovereign could not be held to any such agreement. Equally important, Boucher also accepted Hobbes's view that sovereignty carries absolute power (*A View*, p. 545). Any alleged right of resistance therefore was for Boucher a contradiction in terms. With his customarily practical turn of mind, Boucher carried the idea of the right of resistance to its logical conclusion: subjects would then have the power to determine when and to what extent they would obey. Such a state of affairs must result in magistrates being stripped of their "dignity, authority, and life itself," and could only create a "general confusion in the world" (*A View*, p. 484n).[31] Finally, because of Boucher's wide streak of pragmatism, he pressed the heavy argument that government cannot function effectively, if at all, unless it is "irresistible" (*A View*, p. 483). Lest some be lulled into a sense of security, he reminded his audience that "States, as states, have no prescribed period of existence," but they do have a *"time to die."* To expect them to arrive at perpetuity without principles of law and order and without irresistibility, he thought, was as vain a hope as that of a man who hopes for longevity "without any regimen or without temperance" (*A View*, p. 308).

In addition to his theoretical arguments against the right of revolution, Boucher argued from religious and scriptural authority. "Lucifer was the first author and founder of rebellion," Boucher declared, and the Scriptures charge rebellion with being "the first, the greatest, and the root of all other sins" (*A View*, p. 485).

289

Appealing to the New Testament for support against rebellion, he cited both the teaching of Jesus and his crucifixion. Christ commanded his followers to "render unto Caesar those things that are Caesar's," and then practiced his own precepts by his spectacular submission to execution, which set an example for Christendom for all ages since (*A View*, p. 538). The commandment to all Christians to love their enemies and to pray for their persecutors also embodied the basic rule for Christ's followers vis à vis the authority of the state—obedience for conscience's sake (*A View*, pp. 481-83, 508). By these canons, violence against sovereignty, no matter how tyrannical that sovereignty, could never be justified.

Boucher slightly modified his stand on the right of resistance on one occasion. In the preface to his book of sermons he admitted that sometimes revolutions were, "if not necessary, yet useful in states, by bringing forward some improvements in government." However, he compared improvements by such means to whatever good may result after a volcano's tremendous eruption. No man, he thought, would by choice live "in the neighborhood of a burning mountain" any more than "under a government liable to revolutions" (*A View*, p. lxvi). It is also worth noting that Boucher meant "lawfully established" government when he denied the right of resistance against government to "any self-commissioned persons." In Boucher's view, the most intolerable grievance in government existed when men disturbed the peace of the world in vain attempts to make government perfect, when the laws of nature ordain imperfection.

The foregoing argument against resistance to sovereignty and for obedience to government presented Boucher with the difficulty of reconciling it with the good Christian's absolute duty of obedience to the law of God. His solution was the concept of passive resistance much like that which civil disobedience theorists of the 1960s professed. A sovereign's command to a Christian to engage in polygamy, for example, would be contrary to the law of God and should be disobeyed (*A View*, p. 539). But his refusal must be peaceable; violence would only involve him in yet another violation of the law of God. The Christian must then submit to whatever penalty an unjust sovereign may impose for ignoring the fiat of the state (*A View*, pp. 495-560).[32]

Although Boucher's debt to Filmer on the subject of patriarchy is obvious, and has been well documented for decades, it is less well known that he was also critical of Filmer. It is true that Boucher did defend Filmer's theories against Locke, whom he thought had engaged in ungentlemanly conduct in his manner of criticizing the old royalist (*A View*, p. 529n). Boucher had thoroughly understood Filmer's thesis and did not find Filmer's writing and ideas on the beginning of political society deserving of the "extreme contempt which it seemed fashionable to give it." Filmer's work was largely known through Locke's treatise rejecting it, and Boucher suggested that "readers ought to read both Locke and Filmer and judge for themselves." Boucher's criticism of Filmer on the ground of his "very extravagant notions on monarchy, and the sacredness of kings" deserves to be known, along with his charge of Filmer's "less pardonable" and more serious "disparaging and unjust opinions respecting the supremacy of law" (*A View*, p. 530n). On these two issues Boucher joined forces with Locke, conceding that Locke's attack here was justified and well carried out. Filmer was a divine right monarchist without reservation, while Boucher's concern was with constitutional monarchy. He would not "argue for exclusive irresistibility of kings, merely in their personal capacity," for there was "no gallantry in taking a fortress that is no longer defended" (*A View*, p. 547).

Boucher was essentially a constitutionalist, a believer in the rule of law. It is true that Boucher leaned heavily on the divine character of the state and is liable to the charge of some inconsistency. But that did not make him an uncomplicated Filmerian. Instead, it becomes apparent that Boucher's long indoctrination in the Anglican church had had its effect, and that no biographer, however sympathetic, can reasonably proclaim him to be a profound or creative political philosopher. He was, like the Romans whom he admired, a good adopter and adapter.[33]

The last formal political statements of Boucher's career were his sermons at the Guildford and Carlisle assizes in July and August 1798, and they reflect his deep involvement with the Anglican church and his respect for the British constitution. At Guildford, for example, his theme was mercy and truth, virtues which he thought were no longer synonymous with justice in contemporary life. The mistaking of mercy for justice was especially damaging to the legal system. Witnesses who allowed themselves to be swayed by kindliness and affection damaged the objective quality of their testimony, while jurors who imagined that an error on the side of mercy was excusable were wrong. "In sparing the guilty," Boucher said, "they punish the innocent." The danger from misplaced mercy affected the body politic insidiously by lulling it into a sense of false security, just as "our bodily frames are subject to diseases which bring the certainty of death" before there is any warning of ill health. "A large portion of the public mind" had already been possessed by the "spirit of universal toleration and unrestrained indulgence of novel and untried theories," he believed, and it had been rendered forgetful of, and ungrateful for, "the long course of prosperity and happiness which we have enjoyed under the shelter of those fences and mounds with which our ancestors saw fit to guard our constitution." He cautioned his listeners to avoid undervaluing the constitution, which their forefathers "thought well worth the purchase, even when they paid for it with their fortunes and their lives."

Religion was not immune to the same dangers: "Modern infidels under the more specious name of philosophers sap the foundations of Christianity by the treacherous arts of false interpretation." Boucher alluded to the disastrous effects in France, where "a numerous train of self-sufficient philosophers" had deluged their country with pestilent writings on the subject of religion. Boucher reminded those at the session that the "wise master builders" of the church-state constitution had intended to create and preserve uniformity in "religious creed and professions." The world was imperfect, he concluded, but if ever "these virtues of justice and mercy" shall be united, they will be found . . . in that admired system of equal laws by which these realms are governed, and under that constitution which, blessed by God, is still the possession and the pride of Britons."

The sermon delivered at Carlisle was similar in its deeply conservative tone. He stressed the primary importance of "obedience to the laws and a reverent regard to religion," praising the infinite blessings of living in a country "distinguished equally by the purity and perfectness of its religion, and its wise and wholesome civil regulations." But the national religion was in an "awful crisis," and beset with dangers; *our worst enemies may be those of our own household.* He counseled his audience to withstand seduction into licentiousness in the name of liberty and to avoid being persuaded into atheism in the name of philosophy by reformers who discounted "the wisdom of experience" as mere "accumulation of error." Know when you are well off, he urged, and do not "quit the extended branches and protecting shade of that constitution" which has been of slow growth like the oak, but strong and stable, in exchange for a "stunted, leafless sapling of exotic origin and forced cultivation," a new "poisonous and pestiferous" plant.

The rise of Jeffersonian republicanism confirmed Boucher's poor opinion of government in America. When he wrote to Maury on 17 February 1799 he made clear that he had little respect for the Jeffersonians. He was appalled at their rise to power and was dismayed that "poor old Virginia" had played so prominent a role in it. Boucher recognized the conservatism in the position of Washington and Adams, and he took pleasure in pointing out a parallel between himself and those American gentlemen: "I daresay both the late and the present president of your States would think themselves affronted were they but suspected of being Tories," he wrote. Yet he thought it a happy thing for America that they were in practice as Tory "as I avow myself to be in principle" (*MHM* 10:125). Boucher thought his own political principles might be justified in American history itself: "A time will come, and may not be very distant, that the principles of my book, however they may now be scouted, will be cherished by all the true friends both of your country and mine."[34]

The modernity and liberality of Boucher's social ideas were in striking contrast with his political conservatism. He outstripped the great majority of his eighteenth-century "liberal" contemporaries in that respect. In general his opinions on the subject of race, his philosophy of education, and his "commonweal" social theories put him far more in tune with twentieth-century thought. On the question of race, Boucher thought all nations were of "one blood and kindred," and thus "in the eye of reason" every man ought to be allied to every other man "as his neighbor and his brother" (*Rem.*, p. 99). Yet he thought that every observant man who had ever lived in America knew that men were less attached to each other in bonds of social or political union in America than in any other country. He attributed the fact to the extraordinary variety of races in the colonies, particularly to that "very remarkable race of people" the Indians, whose very presence created a situation without any parallel in any other ancient or modern government,

293

and whose existence greatly influenced the manners and thinking of the Americans (*Rem.*, p. 98). Boucher had observed the individualism which de Tocqueville was to identify later.

Boucher championed racial equality for the Indians of North America and a positive program which embodied far more justice for them than did the contemporary British policy tacitly adopted by the Americans. Although it was Church of England policy to Christianize the natives, little had been done to carry it out. Boucher, however, had taken the policy seriously during his residence in Virginia and believed it his duty to assess the Indian situation. His reading and his own observations appalled him. Their culture was already in a badly decayed state. British and colonial officialdom had fostered policies so inimical to the Indians that a rapid decline in their numbers and independence was the result. The greatly reduced number of the Tidewater Indians bore silent testimony to the "benefits" of British occupation and Christianization, and the final history of many tribes had already been written by the time Boucher wrote his comments.

Boucher's attitude toward the American Indians was in sharp contrast to that of most of his neighbors, who considered that only dead Indians were good Indians. Too many men were murdering and scalping the Indians with a kind of religious fervor, as Boucher put it (*A View*, p. 29). Some settlers wantonly killed Indians to improve their shotgun skill (*A View*, p. 30n). Boucher thought the British and American policy of extermination was a violation of Christianity, and not worthy of the "genius of British government." He believed the American Indian to be intrinsically the equal of the white man and endowed with the same potential for civilization. He cited the Indians of Paraguay and Canada as examples (*A View*, p. 33n). He found historical evidence of Indian nobility of character, and thought it remarkable that English and colonial writers since John Smith had given the fact so little recognition (*A View*, p. 31n). Although the North American Indians lived in a state of barbarism, he thought them capable of becoming good citizens, farmers, and educated men. Furthermore, they were more entitled to the land than any others to whom it was being given (*A View*, p. 32). "I am morally certain," he wrote James 9 December 1765, that it would be "a much easier task to civilize every savage in America than Peter the Great had when he undertook to humanize the Bears of Russia" (*MHM* 7:296).

Furthermore, he wrote Tickell that he thought he could prove that the savages could be civilized in a few years "at hardly so great an expense as Virginia alone has been at in supporting the war against them but for one year" (*MHM* 7:163).

The first step was to put an end to hunting, stop selling gunpowder and implements of war (or sell only at exorbitant prices), and give little or nothing for furs. In addition large bounties should be given for whatever Indians produced as farmers, shepherds, or manufacturers. Under this regime, Boucher was certain they would learn the distinction of property, "like all the rest of the human race" (*A View*, p. 36). After all, the early history of even the most polished nations was once but the history of Indians who were no more savage "than our progenitors appeared to Julius Caesar or to Agricola" (*A View*, p. 33). And when he compared the frontier settlers of the Blue Ridge country with the early inhabitants of the English-Scottish frontier during the Border Wars, he concluded that the American Indians were the more civilized. A second step would be necessary; the land hunger of the colonials must be curbed. The white colonists were partly responsible for the difficulties of the Indian, Boucher wrote, putting his finger on a characteristic that distinguished the American national character. Settlers had a "very general passion" to be "forever running back in quest of fresh lands," which was "a practice detrimental to agricultural improvements and provocative of Indian wars" (*A View*, p. 32).

Boucher's views upon slavery and the Negro are both more complex and more ambivalent than those he entertained on the subject of the Indians. In his published sermons he espoused gradual abolition. A major reason for his belief was his firm conclusion that the institution of slavery had had a disastrous effect both upon the white master and upon plantation production in general. Virginia was the oldest British colony and it was blessed with "a genial climate, and a fertile soil." Yet it was Virginia's "great shame, and greater misfortune ... to be the most backward" colony on the continent. A visit to Pennsylvania, where Boucher had witnessed abundant production under free labor, had greatly reinforced his opinion of the economic lag in the Old Dominion. "If ever these colonies ... be improved to their utmost capacity," he wrote, "an essential part of the improvement must be the abolition of slavery" (*A View*, pp. 18, 40). "It would be to every man's interest that there were no slaves," he wrote, "because the free labor of a free man, who is regularly hired and paid for the work which he does, and only for what he does, is, in the end, cheaper than the extorted eye-service of a slave" (*A View*, p. 39). Boucher knew that abolition of slavery in the tobacco colonies would cause "some loss and inconvenience." Yet he believed that if it were done gradually, with "judgment and with good temper" the effects would be neither "great nor lasting." "North American or West Indian planters might possibly for a few years make less tobacco, or less rice, or less sugar," and the cost of production could be higher initially. But the disadvantages would soon be outweighed by higher prices or the reduced expense of cultivation (*A View*, p. 39).

Montesquieu's opinion of the effect of slavery upon the master impressed Boucher and he quoted from his *Spirit of Laws* in his sermons: "'By having an *unlimited* authority over his slaves, he insensibly accustoms himself to the want of all moral virtues, and from thence grows fierce, hasty, severe, voluptuous, and cruel'" (*A View*, p. 41). On the other hand, Boucher objected to Montesquieu's statement that the state of slavery was bad for the slave because he could do nothing through "a motive of virtue." Instead, Boucher thought that there were "some virtues growing out of slavery and peculiar to it, as there are in every other condition of life." Those virtues were fidelity, meekness, and humility, the "chief Christian virtues." Boucher's argument against slavery rested less on its "tendency to debase and injure slaves" (although he was "sensible it does this in a considerable degree"), than on the ground that slavery was "injurious to society at large." Boucher also chided Locke for having given "'every freeman of Carolina absolute power and property over his slaves'" (*A View*, p. 41n).

A decade before Boucher published his sermons he softened his attack on slavery in his *Reminiscences*. He conceded that it was an absolute moral wrong for one man to hold another in bondage, but at the same time he minimized the problem of slavery as one of little practical importance. It was lawful, and "if it is sometimes cruel it is so only from being abused" (*A View*, p. 39). Boucher may have been more optimistic about the treatment of slaves than was realistic. He himself seems to have been more humane in his treatment of his slaves than most planters, and he gave his slaves options about their disposition when he moved from Virginia to Maryland. One of his slaves paid him a compliment which "went near my heart" when he replied to the usual question posed to slaves on the road, "To whom do you belong?," by responding, "To Parson Boucher, thank God!" (*Rem.*, p. 96). His slaves were much upset by his abrupt departure from Maryland in 1775.

Boucher also anticipated John Calhoun and other southern apologists in his favorable comparison of the position of the southern slave with that of the "laboring poor in Great Britain" and in the rest of Europe. "The condition of the lower classes of mankind everywhere often seemed hard, when compared with that of those above them," but those in "a low sphere" were not necessarily less happy than others. It seemed to Boucher that those who were the "most clamorous advocates for liberty were uniformly the harshest and worst masters of slaves" (*Rem.*, pp. 97-98). Despotic nations treated their slaves better than those under republics; the Spanish were the best masters while the Dutch were the worst.

Boucher chose to sidestep the "abstract question of the right of one part of mankind" to make slaves of another, explaining in his *Reminiscences* that it was a lengthy subject unsuitable for his private memoirs. But he commented that slavery was "not one of the most intolerable evils incident to humanity, even to slaves," for he had known "thousands of slaves as well-informed, as well-clad, as well-fed, and in every respect as well-off as nine out of ten of the poor in every kingdom of Europe." "If a wrong be done" slaves by the possession of them, "as I question not there is," then their owners were sufficiently punished by the "unpleasant nature of their services." Boucher recalled a gentleman of his acquaintance in Virginia, the owner of many slaves, who insisted that the scriptural passage on the difficulty of a rich man's entering into the kingdom of heaven "must certainly have alluded to those who were rich in slaves" (*Rem.*, p. 98).

Boucher was aware of the dilemma which would develop with the freeing of the Negroes, for he believed, as did nearly everyone else of his time, that the black man's race and culture would make total assimilation impossible. He thought the color barrier which nature had placed in the way was insuperable (*A View*, p. 40, 40n). Meanwhile he believed firmly that it was the duty of every master to Christianize his slaves, to teach them to read and write, and to give them as much additional education as possible so that they might be granted at least spiritual freedom from bondage. Although he knew that most Negroes were lamentably ignorant, "compared with any other class of people in a Christian country," still he "saw no reason to think they were more so than many of the first converts to Christianity" (*Rem.*, p. 58). It is apparent that Boucher's extraordinary respect for law, combined with the indisputable fact that slavery was a legal practice, inhibited to some extent his moral condemnation of the institution. Moreover, Boucher never faced up squarely to the question of black racial equality, although he wrote of his abhorrence of slavery (*A View*, p. 39).

Boucher's earliest philosophy of education was essentially classical, the product of his own limited formal education, of his association with James, and of his own observations. The customary tutoring arrangements and the practice in American private schools emphasized Latin and Greek. Any differences from school to school were merely reflections of the different religious organizations that supported them. In general, British precedent was followed; although the Americans were great innovators when it came to adapting to their environment, they were singularly slow to change educational practices. James Maury, however, shared his unorthodox educational ideas with Boucher, thereby forcing him to reexamine his convictions on the subject. The older man, conditioned by his years of teaching in colonial America, was already acutely aware of the great gap between colonial needs and educational preparation. A significant gulf existed, Maury insisted, because Americans differed in so many respects from Europeans in "the genius of our people, their way of life, their circumstances in point of fortune, the customs and manners and humors of the country."[35] Consequently a European plan of education, however judiciously adapted, could no more fit the Americans than an almanac calculated for the latitude of London would fit that of Williamsburg.

The emphasis in American society was on the practical, Maury had observed. "A quack or empyric [could] get bread and fame, where Aesculapius himself would starve."[36] Few sons of the colonial families went into the professions; instead "masters of competent fortunes" in the colonies were more likely to engage in the production of tobacco or to become merchants. How could it be worth their time, trouble, and expense to get a classical education designed for those entering the learned professions? It seemed to Maury that the circumstances, the natural inclinations, and the talents of the learners ought to have primary consideration in determining the nature of the educational process. In order to correct the situation, Maury advocated deemphasizing languages, particularly the classical ones. Moreover, English grammar ought to be studied before Latin and Greek. History, geography, and some elementary business administration, he thought, would benefit the Virginia student.

Boucher's own theory of education put more stress on the classical than that of Maury, although his own experience in his American school had made him dubious about the value of a classical education for all students. The differences led to some lively discussions between the two men. Maury called Boucher's plan absurd; Boucher found it hard to defend. He sat down to the task "again and again," determined "to overset" Maury's novel plan, but he believed that he had not yet succeeded. He could not decide whether to attribute his failure to the merit of Maury's position, or to the "superioriy of his genius, or to both." Baffled, Boucher turned to James for assistance, since he knew that James and he shared the opinion that a method of education might be contrived to serve the needs of practicality while yet remaining "more extensive and enlarged."[37] Under Maury's arguments, Boucher found himself giving ground. He had read Maury's essay on the subject of a nonclassical education, and had urged him on 19 July 1765 to publish it, believing that the ideas contained in it could be "of infinite service in a country like this" (*MHM* 7:293-94). Maury agreed to do so, with the condition that Boucher "revise" and "retouch" it. Boucher complied, utilizing some comments from James.

The issue was not a mere speculative one for Boucher. In America, the success of his school depended on the progress of the boys under his tutelage. In the early years of his school he had thought that languages were the only "avenues to knowledge," and he conducted his classes accordingly. In 1765, when he had fifteen boys enrolled, his head class was reading Terence and Virgil. Gradually he shifted his views and began to think of languages as but a partial and imperfect approach to knowledge, although he continued to teach the classical languages in his school. As Boucher became critical of subject matter in his teaching, he observed the shortcomings of method. He confided to Washington that he had long held "in abhorrence that servile system of teaching boys words rather than things." "Getting a parcel of lumber by rote," he thought, might be useful and even necessary for a schoolmaster, but he doubted that it could be so to "a man of the world."[38]

Most of what is known of Boucher's opinions on education, other than those expressed in contemporary correspondence with John James and James Maury during his American years, are the product of his more mature thought in England. Although he published a sermon on the theme of American education in *A View*, it bears the imprint of his American teaching experience, of his years as a schoolmaster at Paddington, and of his editorial prerogative in 1797. The discussions with Maury and James had influenced Boucher's opinions and piqued his curiosity about the more general issues of education. His disquietude led him to extensive reading on the subject, and his reflections on the significance of education for society reveal a man of some intellectual stature. Boucher consulted both Milton's *Of Education* and Locke's *Some Thoughts Concerning Education,* but he was dissatisfied with their discourses; both were "wanting in results." People commend them," he wrote, "but how little has either one contributed to improve the national system of education." He objected to the great regard everyone had for speculative writing, "so rarely of a kind capable of being carried into practice," because such writing discouraged attempts on the part of others to write truly practical treatises. By his criticism, Boucher revealed to what extent he, too, had internalized the American penchant for the practical.

Rousseau, on the other hand, merited Boucher's high praise for his great service to France and neighboring kingdoms by "exposing in *Émile* the many ill-effects of confining limbs and bodies of infants in swaddling clothes, and by reducing the number of rickety and deformed children" (*A View*, p. 155n). History and the Bible also furnished some answers to Boucher's questioning of what education ought to be. He found a good example in the Persians, who sent their boys to school to learn justice. He appreciated the philosophy of education which stressed training for citizenship and quoted Ecclesiasticus: "He that teacheth his son grieveth the enemy" (*A View*, p. 159).

A national system of education intended to produce a good

citizen caught Boucher's interest. Perhaps this goal of education had had its genesis in Boucher's years of association with Jack Custis, who had serious limitations as a scholar, necessitating Boucher's stress on forming Jack as a "good man." For this concept of training for citizenship Boucher found support in Cicero, who wrote: "What better gift can we present to the State than an educated citizenry?" Juvenal expressed much the same philosophy, while Xenophon believed that learning was an apprenticeship to the business of life.

With these yardsticks for education in mind, Boucher then compared American education with that of other nations and found it too narrow. "We seem to restrain it only to the book; whereas indeed any artisan whatever" might be called a learned man if he comprehended the "secret and mystery of his trade." Boucher had adopted a new definition of education: "Whatever qualifies any person to fill with propriety the rank and station in life that may fall to his lot is education." Thus, any artisan or planter who perfectly understands the art he professes" could be said to be well educated (*A View*, p. 156n). He had expressed this idea first to Washington, writing that education is "preparation for the school of life" and is "of more importance than almost all the rest." "Considering the thousand unavoidable troubles that human nature is heir to," it was worthwhile to teach children "to bear misfortunes . . . with becoming fortitude." Thus, "one half of the evils of life" would not "afflict them," while others enduring the same mishaps would be "dejected."[39]

Once Boucher accepted a view of education as a training ground for the citizen, he then found the best means of education outlined in the Bible within the framework of Jewish polity. The means was obedience to God, the end was permanent security, and the prescribed study was the Bible. The history of creation, the people's own history, the history of other people, the system of civil law, the code of ethics, practical and humane, and the form of worship would all be included. With some thought of the American Revolution, Boucher expressed the opinion that more constitutions had been overturned by internal divisions than by foreign wars, a circumstance which the Jews had provided against by means of prudence and policy which had rarely been equaled. The excellent Jewish constitution had produced a more enlightened and happy people than most, a favorable circumstance which rested "in no small degree" on the superiority of their education, "which was not . . . restricted only to their earlier years" (*A View*, p. 174).

It is clear that Boucher's understanding of the role of education had been touched heavily by his experiences in the American Revolution. The Anglican church in America had been prevented from exercising her supportive role with respect to the state. Furthermore, the role of Dissenters, and the political activism of the Dissenters' colleges such as the College of New Jersey, had fomented disaffection. Boucher's ideal plan for education aligned with society would have none of that. As he looked back upon his sixteen years of tutoring boys in America, he concluded that in general America's system was a poor one. Too little regard was paid to parents' role in education, and no substitutes for their efforts were provided. He had been repelled by the common practice of permitting slaves to care for babies and young white children, saying, "I cannot be reconciled to having my bairns nursed by a Negro wench." He thought it "a monstrous fault" and a source of "many disadvantages to their children," and confided to James on 7 August 1759 that he thought he might remain single in America for that reason (*MHM* 7:6). Boucher had only to recall his own childhood and the attention his father gave him, teaching him a great deal before he was six years old, to be struck by the implications. Negro nurses, because of their own ignorance, could teach but little to their small charges.

Although he thought parents were the natural tutors of their own children, it was a privilege on which parents set little value. They seemed "perfectly indifferent who educates their children," as long as they themselves need not attend to it. "They persuade themselves [that] their duty is done, and done well, whilst they pay for having it done; no matter how, or by whom." Unfortunately, two-thirds of the education in America depended upon instructors who were either indentured servants or transported felons. Boucher wrote candidly of the appallingly low state of the teaching profession, observing that not a ship arrived with either redemptioners or convicts in which "schoolmasters are not regularly advertised for sale, as weavers, tailors, or any other trade." The similarity ended with the advertisement, for schoolmasters did not usually "fetch so good a price" as the others (*A View*, p. 184). Schools themselves were inadequate in number, Boucher believed, in spite of the fact that a "thriving if not opulent people" had ample ability to provide them. He found it a woeful fact of Maryland life that in a country of nearly one-half million souls, under British government and British laws, a people farther advanced in "refinements of polished life" than many large districts even in England, had not a single college and "only one school with an endowment adequate to the maintenance of even a common mechanic" (A View, p. 183).

The early neglect of children and the limited number of good schools may account for Boucher's observation that "we have amongst us very few who shine as accomplished scholars." On the other hand, he did concede to James on 9 December 1765 that "very great dunces are almost as great a rarity here as very great geniuses are with you." Apologizing for another of his "many romantic notions," he confessed that it would "really make me unhappy should I be so unfortunate as to have a son turn out a dunce," but he thought there was little danger of it "should he be born in Virginia." Somewhat sheepishly, he commented that he knew he ought be no more uneasy about having a son with "a mean capacity than I should for his having irregular features or an obliquity in his person" (MHM 7:299).

Since Virginia and Maryland left the education of children to the resources of each family, considerable illiteracy resulted. Prosperous families hired tutors; free schools were associated with charity. A large group in the middle created an illiterate class and many ignorant adults. Drawing on his own English rural background, he made an unhappy comparison between the laboring classes of his native country and those of America. The Americans were more ignorant and less religious. They were not depraved, but they had had little or no acquired information. If not particularly immoral, they were not moral, nor did they wish to know much of religion. The only excuse he could find for them was that "the great heats of our summers" indisposed one to habits of exertion and study. Boucher's early difficulties in getting his schooling and his acute awareness of his lack of a university background caused him to put great stress on the value of education. Without it, he thought, man is "a Caffre, a Peter the wild boy, a New Zealander; a little (and perhaps but a little) superior to an Oran-Outang" (A View, p. 158). Boucher had a healthy respect for a disciplined mind and a store of knowledge. His own education, meager in a formal sense but carefully nurtured, had been the means by which he had removed himself from a life he despised in Blencogo to one of considerable comfort.

Boucher never resolved to his satisfaction the problem of a practical education versus a classical one. He was still pondering over it in the early 1790s when he observed that "hardly half a dozen boys now pursue classical learning at Bromfield, Westward, Wigton and Sebergham," whereas forty or fifty years ago at least a hundred would have been so engaged (*A View*, p. 255).[40] It was easy enough to ask what use country lads would find for Latin and Greek while they toiled for their bread. The answer seemed less obvious to Boucher now, for he took a longer range view of the issue and wondered what effect this relatively sudden shift in public education might have on the country in general.

Boucher's open-mindedness about the need for some modification of educational practices was matched by similarly liberal thoughts on the subject of religion. In a spirit of ecumenism, Boucher reflected on the almost endless diversity of opinion on the subject of religion in the Christian world and concluded that such diversity was one of the greatest calamities with which mankind had ever been visited (*A View*, pp. 245-93). Furthermore, the division among Protestants made answering Catholic objections to the Reformation extremely difficult. In men so divided, religion had a tendency to exhaust itself in profession. "The more of it that they have in their mouths," he observed, "the less charity there is in their hearts." His criticism included those preachers of the "new light" persuasion who engendered "epidemic frenzy" and who used their oratory among "meager, dejected, squalid people crowding to hear field preachers" (*A View*, pp. 80-82). The multitude of splinter denominations had obscured the reality that they were "one body in Christ and members one of another; every separate communion may, and should, consider itself as a small part of a great whole; as still a member of the *Catholic Church* and the *Communion of Saints*." The differences of opinion in things not essential to salvation, he thought, should not be an argument for separation but a motive for "unity of the spirit in the bond of peace" (*A View*, pp. 68-69).

Religious toleration among Christians was an objective which Boucher believed in and practiced to a surprising degree in his personal relationships with Dissenters and nonjuring bishops. But

304

he had observed in Maryland that tolerance was chiefly "in our books and in our conversation," but nowhere in general practice (*A View,* p. 253). If any did not believe that, Boucher recommended that they ask any Roman Catholic members of Baltimore's province, many of whom had felt the lash of the "violent resolves of County Committees." The Quebec Act had triggered much anti-Catholic sentiment, some of which Boucher believed had been latent hostility and intolerance vented under pretense of objections to the Quebec Act (*A View,* p. 255).[41]

Roman Catholics had lived under civil disabilities in Mary- ✗ land since the Puritan Revolution in that colony. Boucher accepted that situation and did not suggest that "Papists" be allowed to hold political offices. He did believe that they should be free from "pains and penalties" (*A View,* p. 259). After all, Catholics justly deserved some gratitude. They had obtained the Magna Carta, and they had "laid all the broad and firm foundation of this unparalleled structure of liberty, the British Constitution" (*A View,* p. 289). Furthermore, they had "enacted most of our best laws, noble edifices, built and endowed almost all the national churches, founded eminent public *schools,* and two universities (*A View,* p. 287). These were great and substantial services, not the "puny efforts and wordy services of later times for which places, pensions, and titles have been lavishly bestowed" (*A View,* p. 289). Boucher believed that the Roman church had greatly reformed herself already, and was "daily reforming," with a general increase of "light and liberality" (*A View,* p. 281), but for all her reforms she was still "far gone in error" when it came to doctrine (*A View,* p. 255). At the same time, Papists in Maryland and elsewhere held tenets no more dangerous to the state than many of the ideas held by other separatists who were being treated with more lenience and forbearance. Catholics ought to have equal tolerance, he argued. Intolerance of Catholics had its own cost to America, for "ill policy and injustice" drove "them to foreign countries for education" where they had easy access to prejudicial ideas (*A View,* p. 292). With his usual hard practical sense, Boucher added that America "let our country be drained of educational sums of money while making possible the misdirection of many fine talents," thus perpetuating religious differences which were often begun in the education of Catholics.

The best hope of Christianity at large would be fostered by

an ecumenical movement which might put an "end to schisms and sects in a reconciliation and coalition between Catholics and Protestants of the Church of England (*A View*, p. 287). "Papists might not become Protestants," he cautioned, "for the name is commonly the last thing that is changed" (*A View*, p. 287n). But he expected that individuals would become more enlightened and informed, and thus by degrees they might incorporate into their creed many of the tenets of Protestantism, along with some of its spirit and moderation. What was needed, he thought, was "an authorized and legal conference of some leading persons among each of the three churches [the Church of England, the Church of Scotland, and the Church of Rome] for the purpose of developing some "general consolidating plan" (*A View*, p. 288). Boucher's plan for a consolidated church is consistent with his secular plan for a reunion of Britain with the liberated mainland colonies. He had adopted a kind of universalist philosophy both in politics and religion, which was not surprising nor unbecoming for a man who held himself responsible for the welfare of his church, his country, and for the improvement of mankind. Nor was his discourse on toleration antithetical to his desire for a bishopric, intended as it was to reflect his intention to save the Marylanders for the empire.

Boucher entertained even more liberal ideas on the subject of social welfare, many of which evolved out of his love of his native Cumberland. He was an ardent supporter of the Lake District, and gave considerable thought to its economic and social problems. A man might belong to the world at large, Boucher believed, but the paramount claims upon him were those of the neighborhood where his property lay and where "duty calls" were strong. Few men were called on to be ministers of state, or members of Parliament, but every man had abilities and opportunities to serve his country by improvements in agriculture, commerce, and in all of the peaceful arts of life.

Boucher's ideas for the improvement of Cumberland had germinated by 1792, and he incorporated them in the anonymous pamphlet entitled *An Address to the Inhabitants of the County of Cumberland*. He summarized the natural resources of the district, criticized Cumberland's deficiencies, and outlined some far-reaching proposals to bring his native land to a better state of prosperity. Cumberland County, he observed, contained ample supplies of slate of excellent quality, as well as good quarries almost at its doorstep; yet houses in the village were still thatched and built of mud or clay. With the best materials available for road building, Cumberland had the worst roads. And, Boucher believed, with the exception of a few remote counties in Wales, his own county was at least a century behind every other county in the British kingdom.[42]

Although county rates were collected, from Boucher's point of view there was a singular lack of evidence that any portion had been set aside for public works. The county had provided no poorhouses, workhouses, infirmaries, hospitals, libraries, or other institutions to promote the arts and sciences. Thus Cumberland's man-made assets could be summed up all too briefly: there were "a few mean bridges and a still meaner County Jail." No public works of any kind had been "set on foot by voluntary contribution." Furthermore, other Cumberland natural resources had been neglected. The coast swarmed with fish, yet no great trading companies to promote fishing had been organized. Scotland, on the other hand, had produced catches which outnumbered those of Cumberland ten to one. The value of products below the surface had been overlooked; even the old art of salt making had been lost. Although the county had plenty of fuel to carry on manufacturing, there were no longer any glassworks or ironworks.

From the time of his arrival in America until his death, Boucher entertained a variety of schemes and plans for public projects, both private and governmental, for the improvement of mankind. Now, appalled with the backwardness of his native county, he propounded an elaborate proposal for a public corporation to be financed by general stock subscriptions in order to develop the natural and human resources of the region. He envisioned the formation of a county association or society similar to those with which he was familiar in Bath, Manchester, and North America. He stressed systematic conservation and the development of natural resources. To accomplish these objectives, he outlined an incentive system based on either honorary or pecuniary rewards for those who performed valuable services to the community, even so humble a service as raising the best crop at the least expense or on the smallest amount of acreage. Meritorious servants or journeyman mechanics who had been steady and inventive were to be recognized. Anyone who discovered new mines or new

307

techniques to better the life of the community would be rewarded, as would a persuasive native who might prevail upon an ingenious foreigner to settle in Cumberland.

The proposed society would actively encourage agriculture by means of three experimental stations, each located in different parts of the county in order to take account of every possible variety of soil and climate. The society would initiate subsidies for promising enterprises, with attention to fishing, mining, saltworks, glassworks, and ironworks. Boucher thought that the development of an ironworks was particularly important.

In addition, Boucher's scheme called for the promotion of the arts and sciences by subsidies for a variety of groups. Authors and publishers of worth could be assisted in the circulation of useful publications at low prices. In this project Boucher was drawing on his knowledge of the widespread publication of Paine's pamphlet, *Common Sense,* and the efficacy of such organized circulation. Further subsidies for physicians and surgeons, meritorious magistrates, and impecunious but deserving members of Parliament were included in Boucher's plan. In order to encourage education, Boucher proposed a plan similar to the scholarships of today for "singularly promising" youths whose parents could not afford suitable educations for them. No doubt Boucher's own family background prompted this thought.

Of especial interest from a modern point of view were Boucher's suggestions for a comprehensive system of what would be called social security in today's terms. He proposed allowances for children of parents who had never had ten pounds a year other than as a result of their own labor, but had yet managed to put five children "out to honest trades and employments." Even this requirement might be dropped in the case of honest parents whose numerous children could not be properly supported. Boucher was mindful that many of his religious brethren of fair character with large families had salaries as curates or ministers which were woefully inadequate. He may well have been prompted by his knowledge of Rev. John James's struggle on an annual salary that never exceeded one hundred pounds, and of his own salary as a curate in Paddington. With some generosity of spirit, Boucher included dissenting teachers, who were Dissenters merely from "motive of conscience," unlike many of the Dissenters he had known in America whose motivation had been primarily political.

Boucher had in mind a system of pensions for retirees who had contributed to society, supplemented by a comprehensive system of poor relief for those who "through misfortune alone, are reduced . . . to straits and difficulties." Such relief, however, ought to be granted to those who had led a life of labor and who had not received "any parochial aids" and had not been beggars.

The means to fulfillment of this broadly based plan for the welfare of Cumberland society was precisely explained. The basis was to be voluntary subscription at the outset, until the Loan Office would carry it forward as a self-financing plan. Boucher pointed out the Loan Office in Pennsylvania and the Bank of England as models. Each operation had enriched itself and its constituents. The basis of the Loan Office operation would be a large proportion of all of the landed property in the county. No one could have a share in the Loan Office as either a lender or a borrower who did not have a "competent quantity of landed property in the county." For those who staffed the administrative positions, there would be handsome salaries to insure fidelity, and accounts would be audited quarterly. Surplus earnings would be used to carry on the other functions of the society. The rate of interest, he suggested, could be 3 or 3½ percent, and he particularly wished to exclude from the administration of the project both lawyers and "unfeeling usurers."

To bring the society to fruition, each subscribing member ought to deposit a specific sum immediately after its organization —for example, 1 percent of the rent roll of the subscriber's landed estate in the county, observing perhaps a minimum holding of not less than one hundred pounds a year. Boucher anticipated yielding on this point if too many persons had to be excluded. Each subscriber in the new association would pay not less than two guineas for every hundred a year he was worth in the county, which could entitle him to one vote in the election of each member of the committees designated to handle the business. The question of absentee landlords was a delicate one. Boucher estimated that a surprising quantity of the land in Cumberland, perhaps 50 percent, was held by such landlords. At the same time, he knew that his plan for Cumberland would stimulate the greatest interest among those who lived on their estates. Although this situation might well put his project in jeopardy, Boucher opposed the passage of absentee landlord laws as a cure far worse than the symptoms. The explanation for his reluctance may well be a simple one. He had himself been an absentee landlord for decades.

Boucher suggested a meeting at Whitehaven, Cockermouth, or Carlisle to consider his plan. He recommended that a chairman be appointed immediately, and that the first item of business be a discussion of the propriety of such an association. His project, he hoped, might serve as a "kind of platform, whereon to form and erect some better considered and better digested system." The time and specific place for "our Convention" Boucher proposed to leave in the hands of four gentlemen of distinction in the county, including Sir James Graham. Boucher would take no overt role. However, his pamphlet offered to answer any question directed to X. Y. Ware's Office, Whitehaven, or to Jollie's, Carlisle—to be "left there, unopened, till called for." Boucher took some pains to preserve his anonymity in the interest of his project. The voluntary nature of the proposal, the committee organization he envisioned, and the nature of the financing were all in large measure products of Boucher's American experience. Ironically, much of the administrative structure was framed in terminology more than a little reminiscent of the operation of the extralegal bodies of the prerevolutionary days he had known in Maryland. Boucher dared to hope that an idea so beneficial in its intent and so well thought out in arrangements could not fail to excite the Cumbrians. He thought it would provide a way to discard party interests and deal directly with those most concerned. To Boucher's disappointment, the plan died quietly, apparently for want of interest, in the Whitehaven or Carlisle anonymous mail box. The proposal was a far-reaching, liberal, and well-planned welfare concept far advanced for 1792 in Cumberland or any place in the world. Only in the twentieth century have societies begun to meet such needs in ways which Boucher suggested.

Boucher's disappointment with the Cumberland plan did not dissuade him from other attempts to improve the lot of those under his eye. Nothing was too minute to escape his attention, and he thought he saw a way to increase the nutrition of the poor of his parish at Epsom. He had observed that the indigent ate expensive white bread and seldom ate cheaper but more nourishing soup. "To be consistent, they should also be clad well in the finest broadcloth," he said. Impoverished people took what meat they could afford to buy and immediately went to the public oven with it for roasting or baking. Instead, Boucher believed, they ought to convert the meat to some kind of liquid nourishment similar to the economical dishes of Irish stew or to the Scottish hodge-podge. He hoped gradually to lead the people to a different, more frugal, and better system of cookery, and to this end he published in 1799 his plan for a soup establishment.[43] It is possible that Boucher may have read Benjamin Thompson, Count Rumford's published accounts of his experiments with army personnel and with the workhouses in Bavaria in providing nutritious diets based on soups.

Finally, Boucher's thoughts on the subject of women are worthy of comment. Although we know little or nothing about his opinion of the intellect of his last two wives, we do know that he admired the mind of Judith Chase, who thought like a man, an opinion which Boucher intended as a compliment. And he appreciated Nelly's good common sense, shared his thoughts with her, and consulted her opinion. Although she worked hard at his side, she was not treated like a subordinate dependent and they appear to have had a companionable marriage. Unlike many eighteenth-century men, Boucher was sensitive to the feelings of the women in his household, and he arranged to give his sister Jinny a feeling of independence by setting up an annuity for her at some financial inconvenience to himself.

Perhaps some of this same sensitivity accounted for one of Boucher's most strikingly modern social comments involving working women and wages. In the process of preparing his history of the parish of Bromfield, he painstakingly surveyed every aspect of life in that parish, including labor arrangements. He learned that day laborers earned from one to two shillings a day according to their merit and the kind of work involved. Men were hired "from half year to half year" at a wage of ten to twelve guineas a year, often without character references from previous employers. Women, on the other hand, "with difficulty get half as much," with dairy women getting no more than twice the hire of a boy ten or twelve years old. Male harvesters received one shilling, six pence, compared with women's ten pence. He also seems to imply that women may have had more difficulty than men in obtaining the six-month contractual arrangement, and that they more often than men were required to furnish references. In that part of the country a large portion of the farm work was done by women.

The problem was particularly acute, because so many then were poorly paid. "It is not easy to account for so striking an inequality; and still less easy to justify it," Boucher wrote in 1794.[44] The men who read Boucher's statement in the parish history may have been startled. If they had given the subject of wage disparity any previous thought, they probably did not agree with him. The disadvantaged farm women had an anonymous champion in whose words they might have taken comfort if they had had access to his Bromfield history, if they had been sufficiently literate to read it, and if their long, fatiguing hours of work had left them time to do so.

↶ Chapter↷ 13 ↶

The Lexical Study and the Race with Time

The last five years of Boucher's life were as busy as his years at Saint Mary's Parish in Virginia and at Paddington. His household seethed with the noise and bustle of his large family, the eldest of whom was only ten years old. In addition the house on Clay Hill reverberated with the recitations of Boucher's students, the number of which varied from nine to sixteen at any given time. But with the discipline and sense of scheduling which had long been a hallmark of Boucher's life, he regularly withdrew to his library to pursue his studies and his writing. What had begun in America as an amusing hobby had now become a consuming interest, if not a passion. His work on the provincial dialects of northern England engrossed more and more of his time. The drawling soft tones of Boucher's new Virginia neighbors in 1759 had kindled an interest in language in him which lasted his lifetime. His move to Annapolis in 1770, where the local idiom of the Maryland planters caught his fancy, provided an even greater stimulus to his curiosity about the development of language. He then had such leisure as he had never known before, and his social life increased, providing him with numerous opportunities to listen for and record local expressions and their meanings.

As a refugee in England in 1777, Boucher had turned to the

313

study of language both as an escape and a solace, as he wrote James on 23 December (*MHM* 10:30). Like most Loyalists, he experienced a crushing sense of depression at the defeat of Burgoyne at the battle of Saratoga, and for a time he deliberately turned his back on military developments and politics. As he began his strenuous study of Greek, undertaken in order to keep abreast of his teaching the Paddington school, Boucher's fascination with speech and language increased. He indulged his admittedly expensive tastes as a bibliophile, and he began to rebuild the collection of etymological books which he had lost in America. However, for some years Boucher's interest in language was more in the nature of a hobby than of a scholarly avocation. As a Cumbrian man, it was natural that the peculiarities of his own northern dialect would interest him. However, his serious concern with lexical work began with a request from a bookseller in Carlisle who asked for some contributions for a history of Cumberland which he proposed to publish. In reply, Boucher suggested that he ought to add to his history an account of the northern dialect, which he thought would be especially fitting for such a volume. Boucher was then asked to prepare such an account, which he agreed to do out of a sense of obligation to his native land. He believed that every man owed a large debt "to the country that gave him birth, though, as in my case, it gave him nothing more."[1]

Boucher soon learned that material for such an account was sparse. Most historians of the northern region had been "churlishly stingy" in dealing with the subject of dialect, and had dismissed it as merely the result of the "fluctuating nature of a living language." Part of the problem was the general lack of appreciation of the Cumbrian dialect, an attitude which he had felt keenly when the verses which he had submitted in his native idiom had been abruptly dismissed as not suitable for publication in Hutchinson's *History*. It seemed odd to Boucher that local northern historians neglected their own dialect, while beautiful specimens of Scottish poetry had been preserved. For example, the pastorals in the Cumberland dialect written by Josiah Relph of Sebergham impressed Boucher as "a very fair specimen of our language," which in his judgment "exceed everything that has anywhere been written in this way, since Theocritus" (*MHM* 10:31). The result of such inattention had been, Boucher thought, the impoverishment of the natural graces of the English language.

Boucher hypothesized that the language of Cumbria did not

merely reflect the customary changes that occur in a living language, as was the case with the languages of ancient Greece, France, and of England in general. On the contrary, Boucher theorized, the language of Cumbria had been relatively static, while that of other parts of England had been slowly changing. Perhaps the "true, unadulterated native Cumbrians" were now speaking as their ancestors had spoken two or three centuries ago. Boucher told James that the Cumbrian dialect was generally more stable than that of other areas of England, and thus, he suggested, the "dialect of your [daughter] Mary was once that of Queen Mary." He dismissed the hypothesis that the English language had been "corrupted" in Cumberland. Any corruption that had occurred had taken place elsewhere in England. This did not mean that Cumbrian speech had not changed at all, for changes in manners, modes of living, and the "disuse of things" had caused some words to fall out of use while "new wants" had resulted in the adoption of new words. The basic difference between his native area and others was the relatively slow pace of language alteration, which meant that many old words with strong emphasis were still in use, giving "pith and energy" to speech. He also believed that more of the beauty of the language had been retained in the writing of the north than elsewhere. Thus northern writers most resembled in language the authors of the seventeenth century, in whose works Boucher admired "sundry beauties which are seldom even aspired to" in the language of the eighteenth century (*MHM* 10:30-31).

In his initial research, Boucher discovered that in all the essential elements of dialect, the north of England was so completely Scottish that he must consider undertaking a Scottish glossary. Fortunately, Boucher's appointment to the parish at Epsom had put him in touch with Rev. John Parkhurst, the lexicographer of the Hebrew language, to whom he then turned for advice. Parkhurst discussed with him the enlargement of his project to include the Scottish dialect, and then advised him to abandon his first plan and "to explore the whole compass of the dialects of the North."[2] Thus with Parkhurst's encouragement, Boucher ventured to begin to compile a complete glossary of all the northern dialects. The foundation for Boucher's major literary work in philology was then effectively begun.

Boucher decided upon first-hand investigation, which required numerous journeys to Cumberland and elsewhere to hear, compare, and contrast the accents and idioms of his countrymen with those of other regions. He sought out "persons of almost all characters and description and, in particular, the lowest of the peasantry in different parts of the country" in order to converse with them, and, if necessary, to "coax and allure them to speak in their natural broad manner." It soon became obvious, however, that he had embarked on a vast undertaking for which he had little technical knowledge and which required a great deal of time. By 1797 he had recruited Jefferson, who diligently collected Hampshire provincialisms to add to Boucher's collection for what Boucher had begun calling his *magnum opus*. Boucher was soon importuning his friends in various districts to send him examples of poetry and prose for his project.

As his collection of language samples increased, he continued to ponder over the origin of dialects and sought the opinion of his friend Jefferson on the subject. Although Jefferson disclaimed any expertise on the topic, he hazarded the guess that dialects came about from "the different circumstances of temper and disposition—of ignorance in the rules of grammatical construction." Since children learned to speak by the imitation of sound, but often lacked "a taste or ear for accurate distinction," differences developed. This process was abetted in the case of children whose parents spoke to them "in a kind of lullaby" or half-language, Jefferson suggested. As for whether "dialect be an approach toward a sort of standard of language, or a falling off from such a standard," he hesitated to come to a conclusion, not knowing where to find such a standard. Of one thing he was certain; he disagreed with Dr. Samuel Johnson's definition of dialect as "the subdivisions of language." Johnson more properly should have been referring to the different "parts of speech."[3]

Although Jefferson thus criticized Johnson, Boucher was willing to follow the system of the great lexicographer in his own glossary. He intended to define each particular word as accurately as he could, and then confirm and illustrate each definition by a quotation or two from some modern writer or writers using the word. But Boucher also intended to carry his work beyond that of Johnson. Although he regarded Johnson's dictionary as "a stupendous monument of individual talent and exertion," he found it wanting in certain important respects. It incorporated only "the language as spoken and written by the best speakers and best modern writers," whereas Boucher envisioned a dictionary of words "as fairly entitled to the appellation of English" although "but one in a hundred" had found a place either in Johnson's or in any other dictionary. Thus many "good and significant words" were left unexplained, only because they happened to have fallen generally into disuse, although many people in provincial districts used them. Furthermore, many such words were still to be found in authors on whose works the nation had long "rested no ordinary portion of its high literary fame."[4]

Because Johnson's work was incomplete, Boucher believed that one could not obtain a fair and full historical view of the English language; one could not understand and appreciate English if the elements of the language in its infancy were missing. These early elements still existed in the various dialects of the kingdom and in the archaisms of speech which, "in most instances, may be regarded as counterparts of dialects." Boucher thought it a great loss that no scientific investigation of English dialects had ever been attempted and that there was no complete archaeological glossary. Furthermore, while the language of the provinces "is fastidiously rejected as vulgar, and that of ancient writers rejected as obsolete, we need not wonder that at length both are becoming unintelligible."

The waste was considerable. Besides the loss of many words of "sterling merit now buried in the rust of antiquity, there are still more that are disfigured in the rusticity of provincial dialects." Few literary men cared to spend any talent on these "outcasts of our language," save to "render their clowns more clownish by putting into their mouths, along with the tone of Scotland or the brogue of Ireland, some miserable jargon which is to pass for dialect." In this fashion the language had been impoverished, because exquisite and picturesque expressions diappeared. Boucher did not want his project to be merely an index, or even an explanation of words, in the fashion of dictionaries in general. He proposed to "enliven it" with items related to diet, dress, building, employments, sports and amusements, municipal regulations, legal terms, religious ceremonies, names of persons and places, and popular customs. Furthermore, comprehensive as this outline already was, he proposed to trace the various words through "all their doublings and disguises in other languages, whether of a Celtic or Gothic origin." In some instances he planned to trace words from the Saxon, through the Dutch, German, Danish, Swedish, and Icelandic. Boucher was aware of the many problems lying before him, embarked as he was "on a shoreless ocean with no rudder to steer with, and hardly a star to guide me." But he entertained the hope that his labors in comparative etymology might engage the attention of foreigners and thus repay the "many obligations which British philologists owed to German and Northern scholars."

Thus by degrees Boucher expanded his work; he now expected to produce a complete glossary of all of the dialects of the kingdom, including "all the antiquated and obsolete words in our old writers, from Robert of Gloucester down to Shakespeare and his contemporaries." And, "should there be room for them, and my life, health, and leisure be spared," Boucher wished to add collateral items which other lexicographers had neglected: anomalies in grammar which, "like the gypsy jargon," had crept into the language, peculiar idioms, oaths and common forms of swearing, "Scotticisms," and finally, "an inquiry [into] how far the common speech of Ireland and the United States of North America which . . . differs materially from any spoken in this Island, is, or is not, to be regarded as dialect." He then decided upon an introduction to the first volume of his work, designed to cover the origin, nature, and history of dialects, together with brief considerations on the importance and uses of etymology.

Boucher's fascination with dialects made the speech of North America an inviting linguistic contrast to that of England. Although he believed that "all the various languages spoken in all the world were once dialects," there were two notable exceptions: the language of the old Romans and that of the United States.[5] The peoples of Italy, who originally spoke many languages and dialects, later spoke only one language. However, in British America, settlers from England, Ireland, Scotland, Germany, Holland, and Sweden, who differed in dialect and in language, never mixed and incorporated with the aborigines of the country, unlike the Romans. Boucher could remember only two families in Virginia, the Bollings and the Brents, descendants of the celebrated Pocahontas, who had "any Indian blood to boast of," and he had never heard of any others in other parts of America. Yet in one particular of great moment, he saw a perfect parallel between Rome and British America; in neither were there diversities of speech which could correctly be termed dialects. Dialect in America was hardly known, unless one were to hear it in the "scanty remains of the croaking, guttural idioms of the Dutch, still observable near New York; the Scotch-Irish, as it used to be called, in some of the back settlers of the Middle States; and the whining, canting drawl brought by some republican, Oliverian and Puritan emigrants from the West of England, and still kept up by their undegenerated descendants

318

of New England." Boucher could not account for these exceptions
to dialect among the Romans, North Americans, and to some
extent, the Irish, other than by the history of their "first population." The first settlers of England had consisted of various tribes
from the continent which slowly coalesced into one nation. In
contrast, the colonies in Ireland and in America could trace their
origins to a few active English cities, mainly London, Chester,
and Bristol, whose "phrases and accents are yet discoverable in
the speech of the colonists." In Virginia Boucher had heard *holp*
for *help, mought* for *might,* and other expressions that had been
in full currency in England when Virginia was planted, but which
had long since become obsolete in the mother country.

Boucher wrestled with the difficulty of determining some cri-
terion by which to differentiate a language from mere dialect.
The speech of one people not being understood by another was
not a good measure, inasmuch as in all languages archaisms and
provincial idioms could make the speakers of one region unintelligible to those of another, even though both spoke the same
basic tongue. For example, a native of Wexford, Yorkshire, or
Somersetshire, each speaking in his own genuine dialect, "would
stand almost as little chance of being understood in London as a
native of Stockholm or Copenhagen." Londoners, of course, were
"peculiarly ill-qualified to judge of dialect, being hardly sensible
of their own." In spite of Boswell's encomium of Johnson for his
ability to distinguish dialects, Boucher thought the lexicographer
often mistaken in his dialectal opinions. Nor was Johnson's own
speech without dialect, even though he was from Lichfield, where,
Boucher thought, the purest English was spoken. One thing seemed
clear to Boucher: those who speak in dialect can generally understand the language as spoken by others, while they themselves are
often not understood.

In Boucher's opinion, therefore, there was no true dialect in
America; there were no words peculiar to some areas but dropped
from the speech of the country in general, and no striking local
peculiarities of enunciation or tone. This did not mean that there
were no "singularities of speech," both on the American continent
and in the West Indies. One was the "slow, drawling, unemphat-
ical and unimpassioned manner" which he first noted among the
Virginians and assumed was the result of the heat of the climate
which paralyzed all exertion, even in speaking. He traced the few
peculiar words he had noted to adoptions from naval or mercantile men with whom the first settlers had had contact, or to the
aborigines. With a crisp touch of bias, Boucher analyzed Ameri-

cans and their language, remarking that they were "too proud, it would seem, to acknowledge themselves indebted to this country for their existence, their power, or their language." They had revolted against the first two and were now "making all the haste they conveniently can, to rid themselves of the last." He foresaw that "in no very distant period, their language will become as independent of England, as they themselves are."

Boucher's years in America had also sharpened his interest in the various dialects of the North American Indians. "In no country in the world does dialect prevail more than it does among the savages of North America." He thought no two nations spoke exactly alike, and some tribes which had lived within ten leagues of each other would need an interpreter to converse. The basic American Indian language, he naively supposed, was that spoken by the Lenni-Lennape, or Delaware Indians. Furthermore, he believed that the continents of Asia and America had once been united, "possibly at more points than one." And without any justification in linguistics or philology, he believed that "unequivocal traces of the dialects of the confederated Indian nations in America are still to be discovered in some of the nations of Asia." There was more than slight resemblance between the languages both of South and North America, and of the Malays, between the language of "one of the blackest of the nations of Africa" and that of some of the American tribes, and between the Eskimos and the Greenlanders. He thought it a striking coincidence that neither the Cherokees nor the Chinese, nor some of the other peoples of the South Seas, could pronounce the letter *r*.

When Jefferson learned of the scope of Boucher's intended work he confessed that he was "almost overwhelmed with astonishment." "It is truly an Opus magnum — majus — maximum," he declared.[6] By 1798 Boucher had been working on the glossary seriously for some seven years. Although he could not anticipate precisely to what size his work would "swell," he thought it would not exceed two quarto volumes, closely printed, and anticipated delivering it in a period of three or four years, an estimate based on the considerable progress which he had already made in the work. He began to think of going to press. "With so large a family," he could not think "of adventuring on so costly a publication without some sure grounds on which to found any hopes of success."[7] He turned to preparation of a prospectus in order to solicit subscriptions, and for expert assistance he turned first to Frederick Eden and then to the duke of Somerset and several others. With good reason, Eden was to become his primary consultant.

Boucher's connection with the Eden family was of long standing. In America he had been a client of the family, but after the death of his close friend Robert, Boucher assumed a somewhat protective role with Eden's widow and the children. As Robert's son, Frederick Morton Eden, grew older, the relationship between Boucher and Frederick ripened into a close friendship. Boucher was consulted as a man of some consequence and good judgment, a trusted adviser on a variety of subjects. Eden confided his financial problems to him in 1794, for example, attributing his difficulties primarily to an expensive house which he had bought. Boucher's fondness for Eden was clearly demonstrated when he brushed aside the memory of the heavy loss he had sustained when he stood as security for Eden's father (for which he had not yet been recompensed), and suggested that Frederick apply to his father-in-law, James Paul Smith, for a loan for which Boucher would stand security. Within three months, Eden advised Boucher that his financial difficulties had been eased, but Boucher nevertheless urged him to practice economy. He pointed out candidly that Eden's annual income would be only eight hundred pounds, while his expenses were to be at least a thousand. Although he had earlier suggested that Eden had it in his power to render him an essential justice, no doubt a tactful request for compensation for Boucher's earlier loss, it is obvious that Boucher expected nothing from Eden while he was operating on a deficit budget.

Boucher encouraged and assisted Eden with his book concerning the poor of England, and had been gathering reports from Cumberland about tillage and absentee holdings. He had personally estimated the poor rate for his own native Blencogo at sixpence in the pound and forwarded other pertinent information to Eden for his use. As Eden completed sections of his manuscript he sent them on to Boucher for comment. Boucher gave him his straightforward opinions, at one point alerting him that the views on education which he had expressed might well expose the whole work to censure. Although he felt diffident about doing so, he nevertheless rewrote the section himself, and sent it on to Eden with instructions to determine for himself which version he preferred to use. At another time he thought it necessary to soften Eden's critique of William Pitt. Although Boucher had no formal legal training, Eden also consulted him on matters involving the law and on finding a publisher for a play which Eden had written.

Under these circumstances, Boucher turned naturally to Eden for his criticism and aid on the work in general, but particularly for assistance on his prospectus. The piece might make or break the success of the publication plan. He sent a draft of it to Eden, "my excellent and most dear and valuable friend." When Eden returned it, Boucher sent it to the duke of Somerset and to a third unknown correspondent, begging the last to erase or insert wherever he thought it could be done with advantage. Thus Boucher's prospectus was eventually completed, and when his sermon at Carlisle was published, the back pages contained not only an advertisement for Boucher's book of sermons, but also a notice that his "Provincial Glossary" was in preparation.[8]

As Boucher's work progressed, he made a number of decisions to alter it in one way or another. For a time he entertained the idea of a double glossary, the second to consist of words, terms, and idioms now lost even in the provinces and found only in the old writers. He knew that years would be required to complete such a project, particularly for a lone writer. He thought of collaborating with a reliable worker, but dismissed the idea. Meanwhile, he continued with his work. When he reached *T*, he came to a practical decision. Possibly on the advice of his critics, combined with his own more mature judgment, Boucher abandoned the idea of a double glossary. He recast the format, and blended provincial and obsolete words together under one alphabet. The new arrangement bypassed the difficuty of deciding whether or not a word was obsolete but not necessarily provincial, formerly provincial but now obsolete. However, the change in plan required considerable time to effect.

Boucher kept at his work diligently, hampered occasionally by bouts of illness. Early in 1801 he suffered a distressing malady which made writing both difficult and painful, although fortunately he was well by February.[9] By July 1801 he put his manuscript into the hands of a friendly critic. "I sat down ill-prepared to write such a treatise, which indeed I understood but imperfectly," he explained. He had had no "favorite hypothesis;" therefore the process had been a slow one. Now, in addition to comments on the material, he wanted an opinion on the advisability of printing a portion of the work in order to "feel the pulse of the public" and "to solicit material." He was by now considering publishing either the introduction alone (it eventually ran to sixty-four printed pages), or the letter *A*, although he thought this latter section was the least interesting. On advice he set about enlarging the subject of dialects, "my proper topic."[10]

Boucher's correspondence suffered under the pressure of his

linguistic work. Jefferson no longer waited for letters from Boucher, but wrote out of turn. He suggested that Boucher ought to investigate the Suffolk dialect, and was pleased to comment on the prospectus of Boucher's work which he had seen stitched into the *Gentleman's Magazine*.[11] Although Boucher was slow at answering letters, he still obliged his friends with literary assistance on various projects.[12] In addition, he worked from time to time on some new sermons which he was preparing for publication. These sermons, he told Jefferson, were not *"political."*[13]

The publication of the *Prospectus* had attracted the attention of literary men in both England and Scotland, many of whom furnished material for his lexicon, while others offered to read his manuscript. The Reverend Francis Leighton of Shrewsbury rendered considerable assistance to Boucher, particularly concerning the Welsh language. "There is hardly a page in the ensuing work in which I am not much indebted for his critical revision, for some necessary correction, or for some kind and useful suggestion," Boucher acknowledged. The Reverend Mr. Blakeway, also of Shrewsbury, had aided Boucher in much the same way, while the duke of Somerset, in addition to assisting with the *Prospectus*, had provided him with a list of provincial terms peculiar to the west, and had read a considerable portion of the manuscript. He had also been helpful with remarks on language.[14]

Illness struck Boucher again in early 1803, and this time he recovered slowly, until finally, in June 1803, he could write, "I thank God . . . that I have been gradually getting stronger, and I hope, better; yet still I keep my purpose of going to the north in hopes of great benefit from the air and exercise." Although it is not clear what this latest illness was, he had suffered from headaches constantly, an inheritance from his severe bout with malaria in Virginia and one which he expected one day would demolish him. He had also suffered from time to time with "the gravelly complaint" (kidney stones), hemorrhoids, and rheumatism. He worried about completion of his work when he contemplated the breadth of the project and what remained undone. He feared that he had but too few years in which to finish, and he made arrangements for some help. As he told a correspondent on 20 June 1803, he now had an assistant, "a Scotsman, along with me, and I hope by day we shall get on apace."[15]

Boucher still envisioned completion of the whole work in four parts, making two thick quarto volumes, the first of which would consist of six letters of the alphabet. He expected to finish the first part in 1804, encouraged in his ambitious undertaking by a list of nearly eight hundred subscribers.[16] The work progressed at a better pace with the services of an assistant, and Boucher prepared the final draft of the first portion of his work for the press. Now he began to worry. He had tried to make the work as "faultless as could reasonably be expected." Yet with all his industry and care in "unintermitted study" for the last ten years, he feared it still had many defects and errors. But his sense of the shortness of time induced him to forego further improvement and correction of the work, "approaching fast as I now am to the limits which David mentions as the natural period of *the days of our years.*" Still, since he had not been a young man when he had ventured on the task, he felt that he had done his best.[17]

Boucher's friends had confidence in his ability and it was not misplaced. Unfortunately, even though Boucher continued to work industriously on the manuscript, he did not finish it. His work won him recognition, however. He was made an honorary member of the Edinburgh Society of Antiquarians and of the Stirling Literary Society. He could now add F.S.A. to the M.A. after his name, as a fellow of the Society of Arts. He was also a member of the well-known Nobody's Club, an elite group founded in 1800 in honor of William Stevens, whose membership was chiefly composed of clerics of high church principles. Charles Dickens was to describe him in 1869 as a great scholar.[18]

Leaving the ruins of his life in America, Boucher had succeeded when many of his fellow émigrés had failed. He had more than fulfilled his father's impassioned charge never to lose the family estate at Blencogo; indeed, he had bought back all of the family estate and was now in possession of considerable property in Caldbeck, Bromfield, and Sebergham parishes. Some of the old lustre had been returned to the Cumberland Boucher name. Through his progeny Boucher was to furnish England with some able professional men, career officers, and a member of Parliament. His eldest son, James, became provost marshal of Grenada. His second son, Barton, who later changed his name to Bouchier, became the vicar of Fonthill, Wiltshire, and the author of many religious and other works. Boucher's first daughter, Eleanor Mary Elizabeth, married Edward Hawke Locker, commissioner of the Greenwich Hospital, and their direct descendant, Frederick Locker-Lampson, became a writer of some reputation. Oliver Locker-Lampson, Frederick's son, became a member of Parliament. Boucher's daughter Elizabeth married Edward James, a distant relative of Dr. John James and a captain in the army of the East India Company, while their son Edward Boucher James became a fellow of Queen's College, Oxford, and vicar of Carisbrooke, Isle of Wight. Other descendants were scattered around the globe, in Canada, Australia, China, and India, where Richard Boucher was governor of Bombay and Charles was governor of Madras. Still others emigrated in the late nineteenth century to the United States. Boucher's lifelong desire to maintain the family name was abundantly fulfilled.

His illness in early 1803, his persistent work on the lexicon, and his accumulated years all took their toll. When he visited Cumberland in the summer of 1803, he was in such a state of health that his friends thought he was near death. During the autumn, Boucher's sermons began to bear frequent allusions to the declining state of his health. One of his listeners, a visitor to the parish at various times who had always found Boucher's preaching impressive, noted his much altered appearance. When Boucher preached a sermon based on a text from Isaiah, "We all do fade as a leaf," the visitor was so moved that he sat down and wrote six stanzas, three of which are revealing:

> Our verdant spring, our summer gone,
>> Now autumn's pensive call
> Tells us the period is arriv'd
>> When thus we fade and fall.

> See the impressive preacher stand
>> This lesson to enforce,
> The trembling voice, the drooping head
>> Say life has run its course.

> The pallid cheek, the form reduc'd
>> An awful change disclose:
> Nature's exhausted pow'rs approach
>> Their long and last repose.[19]

Any benefit Boucher gained by his summer weeks in the north did not have a lasting effect. By 22 December 1803 he was in ill health once again, disabled by rheumatism, one of his recurrent headaches, and a slight fever. He continued working throughout the winter against the handicap of his deteriorating health. He was sympathetic with Jefferson, who was appalled to find serious errors in his published book, including "the most terrible affair of all — a whole line being omitted" by a "blundering printer," whose errors had defeated his best efforts. Jefferson closed his last letter to Boucher by wishing him "good eyes and patience, in preparing and printing your *Opus Magnum*."[20]

Aged in appearance and broken in health, Boucher died on 27 April 1804 "of paralysis," aged sixty-seven, with his work still incomplete.[21] He was buried in the Epsom churchyard on 4 May by his grieving wife and children, near his second wife, Mary Elizabeth Foreman. A tabletop monument with weathered but still discernible inscriptions marks his grave. The old Bromfield Church in Cumberland, the church of his youth, honored him with a plaque on the north wall of the chancel, commending his "unshakable loyalty, integrity and zeal" during the American troubles, his vain effort to stem them, and his return to his native country, "poor in all things but the riches of a blameless conscience." He died "regretted by the poor the learned and the good."[22]

Boucher wanted his glossary to be the lasting memorial of his life. Although his theory of language is now known to be untenable, and he clearly lacked technical knowledge of the subject when he began the undertaking, nevertheless it is the product of an intelligent amateur, an interesting combination of naiveté and shrewdness. In spite of the best efforts of his family and friends, the work slipped into relative oblivion, although the manuscript through *I* was used by the compilers of Noah Webster's *English Dictionary*.[23]

The most lasting tribute to him, or so it seemed for decades, was that given him by the parishioners at Epsom whom he had served faithfully for nearly twenty years. They installed a marble bust of him in a prominent place on the wall near the altar, flanked by a memorial tablet:

His loyalty to his King remained unshaken, even when the
madness of the people raged furiously against him; and,
for conscience sake, he resigned ease and affluence in
America to endure hardships and poverty in his native land;
but the Lord gave him twice as much as he had before, and
blessed his latter end more than his beginning.[24]

Appendix A

Judith Chase

A major romance of Boucher's life was not consummated in marriage. Instead the courtship shattered in the spring of 1767 when the charming widow, Judith Dent Chase, abruptly refused to marry him amidst a flurry of veiled charges about her past. Boucher was devastated, but his friend Henry Addison was pleased that he had had a hand in the broken engagement.

Within two months, on 22 June 1767, Boucher's sister Jinny made a hurried departure to England (*MHM* 7: 347-50), commissioned by Boucher to conduct some business for him and to seek the advice and counsel of John James in doing so. Thereafter, Boucher sought and received letters from James on separate sheets of paper from those which he customarily shared with Henry Addison and others; these letters make clear that he had settled two small girls with his sister Mary Tordiff at Blencogo, and had arranged to contribute twenty pounds annually toward their support "from the time of my sister's leaving England" (*MHM* 7: 45-46). Judith Chase was also expected to contribute, a commitment which she failed to meet for long periods of time, causing Boucher embarrassment and John James financial inconvenience. While Boucher remained in America he referred to the children as "my poor castaways" (*MHM* 8: 170-71), the "poor children" (*MHM* 8: 173-75), and "the poor orphans" (*MHM* 8: 178). Boucher wrote James in 1773 that he had "not seen their parent" for three years, "nor received from her a penny towards their support" (*MHM* 8: 183). This was his last comment to James about the girls until he arrived in England.

The closing of the ports in America further disrupted Judith's bills of exchange. Boucher wrote: "I advised, I entreated, I commanded her, if possible to make you a remittance of, at least, £100 before the ports were shut up" (*MHM* 8: 347), but he feared that she had not. Maryland soon prohibited the sending of remittances for the support of wards and children in England, allowing only sufficient funds for the return voyage. Boucher was living on limited funds and was cut off indefinitely from his property and income in America. In January 1776, Boucher was moved to assure James of his limited responsibility in the financial situation, to request an account of what he owed, and to fix a ceiling of £200 "for the support of these unfortunate girls" (*MHM* 8: 347).

Evidently James suggested that Boucher's presence in England might solve the problem of where the girls could live, a suggestion to which Boucher reacted by asking James to attempt to put them "into some decent way of getting a livelihood for themselves." He offered to be "useful to them" in the great city of London, but he did not want them there. He then furnished James with a mortgage to cover his debts to him, smarting from the "cutting" letter he received from him in March 1776 (*MHM* 8: 348). He did not want the children deserted, and he beseeched James to continue his attention to them, for "at this distance I cannot well take them off your hands as would best become me, and I dare not think of removing them hitherwards." Be frugal, he begged James; Boucher was afraid that his resources would be drained and that he could no longer support the children (*MHM* 9: 54-55). He inquired about their apprenticing, and offered to write to them if James thought it wise.

In spite of the provocations and irritations with Judith Chase, Boucher still cared for her, even though he knew much more about her than he had when he had courted her in America. Then he had understood only that she had married Richard Chase in December 1757, when she was sixteen, and that her husband had been poisoned by a slave a month after their marriage (*MHM* 7: 343; *Maryland Gazette*, 25 December 1757). Judith told him there were no children and she had been left with a sizable estate, but it had been diminished by poor management and litigation. Judith may have misrepresented some facts to Boucher. Her husband's will did not mention her or any wife (Charles County, Liber A.K. 11, fol. 3, Annapolis Hall of Records). It is possible that they were not married. Furthermore, Richard Chase bequeathed the bulk of his estate to a daughter, Frances, and a son, Jeremiah Townley Chase. In any event, Boucher did not know of their existence in 1766-67. Presumably Addison ferreted out the discrepancies in her stories and thought it wise to protect his romantic young friend from marriage.

In spite of the trials he experienced as a result of his alliance with Judith, Boucher thought about her in 1776 with more than a little admiration and affection; he remembered her "quickness of apprehension" and thought her "natural powers" too great "for any woman, circumstanced as women are with us, where they neither have, nor ought to have an elaborate education." He recalled "a vigor and a pith in her wit, which one is almost afraid to love in a woman." Yet she was "all woman," "overloaded with natural endowments" with gentle, delicate manners, and "truly *feminine*". She loved virtue, but had not always been virtuous; yet her foolishness, or viciousness on occasion was never for lack of "a good heart" ("A Character in Real Life in the Manner of Swift, on Stella," Boucher Manuscripts). Boucher excused her on the ground that she had been "ever the dupe of wretches whom she ought to have despised," one of whom was William Smallwood, "her first *ruiner*," who was "a fool as well as a knave," and through whose persuasion Boucher believed Judith had been "urged to use me ill" (*MHM* 9: 59).

Boucher concerned himself with the welfare of the two girls, who were called Betty and Kitty Strange in England, throughout the 1770s. After a series of trials in various households, including that of the Bouchers, Betty was apprenticed to a cloak-maker close to the supervising eye of Mrs. James in Cumberland, and soon dropped out of Boucher's sight. Kitty seems to have had more common sense, and made herself a place in Paddington, although Boucher disliked intensely having her "a servant to me." No further correspondence passed between Boucher and James about Kitty after March 1781. She may have remained as a satisfactory upstairs maid until Boucher moved to Epsom. It is probable that she determined to go to America in the early 1780s. What is certain is that she went to live with Judith Chase in Charles County and endeared herself to Judith. Whether she was a devoted servant or was conceded the status of a friend or relative is unknown. However, when Judith drew up her will on 3 November 1790, at age sixty, she bequeathed her entire estate to Catharine Charlotte Strange, described as "now a resident of this state and living with me, but formerly a resident of Great Britain" (Charles County, Liber A.K. 11, fol. 3, Annapolis Hall of Records). Judith died shortly before 30 December 1790; Catharine, as sole executrix, administered the estate with the assistance of Judith's brother, Warren Dent, whose inheritance appeared to be a list of Judith's debts.

ᴄ_ℐ𝒜ppendix_ B ᴄ_

𝒲ritings 𝒜ttributed to 𝒝oucher_

Letter to the *Virginia Gazette*, 25 July 1766

A search of the *Virginia Gazette* from 3 June 1766, the date of the Routledge murder, until the report of Colonel Chiswell's death published in October 1766, revealed letters by three anonymous authors—"A Man of Principle," "Dikephilos," and "Philanthropos"—and a fourth letter with no signature which was printed on 25 July 1766.

The letter signed "A Man of Principle" is probably not by Boucher. For one thing, Boucher expressed concern over "the very extraordinary manner" of the bailment, but no concern over freedom of the press (*Rem.*, p. 111). Insofar as this letter concerns the issue of freedom of the press to a greater extent than the bail issue, it is less likely to be Boucher's work. Second, the letter was written on 20 June 1766, before any "whitewash" letters excusing the behavior of the three judges had yet appeared. Since Boucher specifically said in the *Reminiscences* that he wrote only after vindication letters had been published, this letter would have appeared too early to have been Boucher's. Third, Leo Lemay presents convincing evidence that this letter of 20 June 1766 was written by Robert Bolling (J. A. Leo Lemay, "Robert Bolling and

331

the Bailment of Colonel Chiswell," *Early American Literature* 6 [1971]: 99-142).

"Dikephilos" had letters printed in the *Gazette* on 18 July and 29 August 1766, neither of which I believe are Boucher's work. Dikephilos acknowledged in his letters that he knew the men involved in the affair "with happiness and respected their honor." Of Routledge he wrote: "Mr. Routledge I was acquainted with and I esteemed him." This is primary internal evidence that Boucher is not the writer, since he stated specifically that Routledge was a stranger to him. Lemay believes that this letter was written by James Milner, a lawyer of Cumberland County.

The "Philanthropos" letter dated 22 August 1766 is heavily larded with biblical references and injunctions against murder, and might well at first glance seem to be the work of a minister, possibly Boucher. But Boucher's major concern centered upon the irregular bailment; this letter hinges upon freedom of the press. Lemay has concluded that if any of these anonymous letters were written by Boucher it is this letter of 22 August, a conclusion with which I do not agree. Byrd, by 22 August, had sued Bolling for libel, a cause which Byrd lost, and after which he challenged Bolling to a duel. The men were dissuaded by a magistrate who learned of the plans. It seems much more likely, then, that Bolling would have had a good motive for writing this letter denouncing tyranny and arbitrary power which had threatened "patriot spirits" with prosecution for using the press "to instruct and inform mankind" (Lemay, "Robert Bolling," pp. 99-142). Furthermore, Boucher wished to be anonymous. If one concedes that he was no simple-minded man, he would have avoided writing a letter with so heavy a religious flavor that his purpose would have been defeated.

By a process of elimination, the remaining letter, directed specifically to "J. B., Esquire" (James Blair, one of the judges in the bailment issue), seems to be the one most likely to have been Boucher's work. It is closest in date to the "vindication" letters which irritated him sufficiently to write. This letter deals at length with the question of bail, which he considered an affront to the court system involved. It is couched in terms of the constitutional issues, a subject of particular interest to Boucher; and the legal approach would not lead his readers to think of the writer as a cleric, thus preserving his identity. The writer's explanation for the lack of a signature sounds typical of Boucher: "I write on a public matter, and attacking nobody's reputation (but a wrong measure, as I conceive it)." Boucher considered himself a "public man" throughout his life. He went on: "The thing written should doubtless be regarded, not the writer. It is no matter whether he live in Northampton or Buckingham; it is enough that he values and tries to serve his country." The sense of service to one's country, and indeed, many of the very words used in this letter, pervade his writing both in America and in England. Lemay, on the other hand, believes that this letter was written by Robert Bolling, citing Bolling's commonplace book for the years 1760-67 ("Robert Bolling," p. 99). However, my search in the microfilm of the commonplace book did not turn up any direct evidence. It is possible that Lemay has seen evidence with which I am not familiar. However, I am now persuaded by internal evidence and the process of deduction that this letter of 25 July 1766 was written by Boucher.

Letter from a Virginian to the Members of the Congress to be Held at Philadelphia on the First of September, 1774

A careful examination of the internal evidence of style, diction, and thought, as well as a comparison with other pieces of Boucher's writing of the same period, has led me to agree with the authorities who have credited Boucher with the anonymous pamphlet, *Letter from a Virginian*. The Library of Congress has credited the letter to Boucher on the basis of a note in Allan McLane Hamilton, *The Intimate Life of Alexander Hamilton Based Chiefly on Original Family Letters and Other Documents Many of Which Have Never Been Published* (New York: Scribner's Sons, 1912), p. 442, which attributes it to Boucher. The *Letter* is also listed under Boucher's name in Charles Evans, *American Bibliography: A Chronological Dictionary . . .: 1774-1778* (Chicago, 1909), number 13168. More recently, Bernard Bailyn has included it in a collection of pamphlets as the work of Boucher (Bernard Bailyn, ed., with the assistance of Jane N. Garrett, *Pamphlets of the American Revolution: 1750-1776* [Cambridge, Mass.: Harvard University Press, 1965], vol. 1, 41n, 130n).

The *Letter* was first printed without imprint and then reprinted twice in Boston and once in London in the same year, 1774. On the basis of the type ornament, the printing has been ascribed to Hugh Gaine by Thomas R. Adams, in *American Inde-*

pendence: The Growth of an Idea. A Bibliographical Study of American Political Pamphlets Printed Between 1764-1776 Dealing with the Dispute Between Great Britain and Her Colonies (Providence, R. I.: Brown University Press, 1965), item 127.

Boucher's decision to write the *Letter* as a Virginian was not illogical. He wished to preserve his anonymity, and by now he was a well-known Maryland minister. He had lived in Virginia from 1759 until 1770, and in 1774 he lived not twenty miles from Mount Vernon, directly across the Potomac from Alexandria. A study of the thoughts expressed in the pamphlet prove that there are no statements made, nor arguments advanced, that are in conflict with Boucher's expressed political philosophy, his estimate of human nature, and his appraisal of the situation at hand in 1774. Furthermore, many of the arguments advanced in the *Letter* were essentially repeated in the two other political pieces reprinted in his *Reminiscences:* "Quaeries Addressed to the People of Maryland" and "To the Hon[ora]ble the Deputies in Congress from the Southern Provinces." The appeals in the *Letter* to accommodation, to knowledge in the process of decision-making at Philadelphia, to history, and to the charters and history of the American colonies particularly, square with Boucher's own process of determining his position in the crisis. The concern with constitutionality and fundamental principles is similar to that expressed in his personal correspondence and in earlier political writing in Maryland in 1772-73.

The *Letter* appeals to the preservation of what is good in the colonies, including freedom from poverty, lack of titles, individuals' ability to forge ahead, disregard of privileges of birth, and the American way of speaking freely as an equal of anybody. These are all characteristics that Boucher had written about in his correspondence with English friends since 1759. The author's use of the word "native" to refer to himself is easily explained. Boucher felt like an American, but he also wished to protect his identity and would hardly have advertised his English heritage at this time. He had already acquired a reputation as a conservative, as a supporter of a resident American bishop for the Anglican church and a member of the Court party. He knew he could not get such a political piece published in Annapolis, nor did he wish to have the impact of his persuasive attempt diminished by the knowledge of its authorship. Writing as a native abetted his desire to conceal his identity and added weight to his arguments.

The central themes of the *Letter* are similar to those Boucher deals with in other works. For example, the disparaging remarks about the New Englanders, their fractiousness, and their "common town meetings," appear elsewhere in his writing, particularly in connection with the episcopate issue. He consistently thought of them as "banditti of furious Dissenters in yonder mischief-making Northern Governments" (*MHM* 8: 177). The opinion of human nature expressed in the *Letter* parallels many of Boucher's statements. Men were corrupt; therefore the bodies composed of men were subject to corruption. Perfection in government was utopian. Smugglers, for example, would always be with us, wherever trade opportunities existed. Citizens were not saints, and too often submitted to the appeals of passion and emotion, to oratory and inflammatory pamphlets. Boucher laid great stress on the disruptive element of "party spirit;" it is almost a constant theme in his writing and is a prominent argument in the *Letter*.

Boucher had a good command of the thought of Locke, and his remarks on the use and abuse of his ideas by those wishing to serve their own purposes are familiar in all of Boucher's public and personal writing. Like Locke, he was concerned with the problem of majorities, particularly in 1774 when he believed that the great majority of his fellow colonials were trapped in a dilemma where neutrality was impossible and expedience dictated one's political decision. Boucher also believed that the grievances Americans might have were insufficient to justify the risk of a break with England and the horrors of civil war, an opinion expressed in the *Letter*, and one which Boucher retained until the day he died. The *Letter* is the product of a logical, coherent mind. The basic appeal is to reason, to the odds for success, and to law and order. There is an argument for a positive approach, for a plan of accommodation, as a substitute for the nonimportation agreements which he thought would be a mistake, grievous and irremediable.

In addition to the similarities in thought between the *Letter* and Boucher's other works, there are interesting stylistic similarities. Boucher uses a number of words not very common in other eighteenth-century writers. One such word is *teize*. Although spellings differed, Cotton Mather used it in 1693 (*teaze*), but the word in the sense of meaning "uneasy from trifling irritation" was becoming obsolete and the spelling had been shifting to *tease*, as Samuel Johnson spelled it in 1775. Nonetheless, he used it constantly in his writing for more than thirty years. Another favorite word in Boucher's writing vocabulary was *lenity* or *lenience*, along with *opprobrium, opprobrious,* and the phrase *generous mind.* The following words and phrases recur frequently in the *Letter* and in Boucher's writing, although they are not uncommon to eighteenth-century writers: *excess of zeal, parent country or state, mother country, reproach, horrors of civil war, party spirit, inflaming their passions, fabric of society, visionary ideas, demagogues, republican spirit,* and *deluded multitudes.*

Although this evidence cannot be conclusive by its very nature, and although Boucher nowhere stated that he had written this document, the internal evidence is persuasive.

The American Times, a Satire in Three Parts, in which are Delineated the Characters of the Leaders of the American Rebellion.
By Camillo Querno, Poet-laureate to the Congress

The Sterling Memorial Library, Yale University, credits *The American Times* to Jonathan Boucher and to one Reverend Smith of York, Pennsylvania. The Henry Huntington Library holds a copy of the play which contains a note: "The following poem is supposed to have been written by Jonathan Boucher, A.M., F.R.S., Vicar of Epsom, etc. Copies from the original manuscript at Baltimore by Howard Payne and presented to Doctor Jno. Osborn by his young friend T. Payne, New York, June, 1816." However, the New York Public Library ascribes the play to Jonathan Odell of New Jersey, with George Cockings listed as coauthor.

The play is filled with classical and biblical allusions and diatribes against Dissenters, but the thrust of the play is primarily against Franklin, Washington, Samuel Chase, John Adams, John Hancock, and others. Boucher would certainly have subscribed to the play's sentiments, particularly in lines concerning William Paca, Rev. William Smith, and George Washington. The recurrent attacks on "democracy" and "republicanism," as well as the play's concern for "reason" and "legal government," bear remarkable resemblance to Boucher's own thoughts on those subjects, especially the lines which express the hard lot of those who attempted to be "moderate" (pt. 3, p. 58). One of Boucher's extremely frequent expressions, "the still small voice" of reason, does appear (p. 62). However, it seems very unlikely that Boucher would have written this, alone or as a coauthor, given his activities in England in 1780.

Remarks on the Travels of the Marquis De Chastellux in North America

A number of authorities have credited Boucher with *Remarks on the Travels of the Marquis de Chastellux*. There is some supporting evidence in the preface of Boucher's book, *A View*, which criticizes the work of the marquis in much the same manner as the author of the *Remarks*. Boucher had strong feelings about the inaccuracies in the work of the marquis, but he expressed the thought that poor translation into English was responsible for some of the errors. Although I have not analyzed the style of this pamphlet, until there is better evidence, I am inclined to agree with Joseph Sabin that John Graves Simcoe is more likely to have written it (Joseph Sabin, ed., *Bibliotheca Americana: A Dictionary of Books Relating to America from its Discovery to the Present Time*, 29 vols.[New York: Printed for the Bibliographical Society of America, 1868-92], 16:582). Boucher's personal affairs in 1786-87 were complex and time-consuming; he was settling into a new parish, courting the woman who was to be his second wife, and entering the most social period of his life in England. At the same time, his interest in affairs of the church engrossed much of his time. His personal correspondence and his journal give no indication that he had resumed his earlier interest in pamphlet writing.

Appendix C

"A View" as the Product of Boucher's English Years

Although *A View* and its extensive preface are of great value in assessing Boucher's political and social thought, a number of instances of misdating and prescient writing are scattered throughout the book, lending substantial weight to the argument that one must be cautious about supposing the sermons to be representative of his thought in the American years. The evidence is clear that the sermons are essentially reconstructions necessitated by the loss of his papers and documents. None of this means that the sermons bear no relationship at all to Boucher's developing ideas between 1763 and 1775. The text he published in 1797 may very well expound in a general way the content of at least certain sermons which he delivered earlier in America, particularly in the last stages of his Maryland career. But they cannot be accepted simply as literal reproductions of his American sermons, and therefore as precise statements in all respects of his earlier political thought.

In his sermon "On the Peace of 1763," for example, Boucher referred to the "enormous load of debt" with which the recent war had "encumbered the mother country, (a share of which it is highly reasonable we should bear)," an obvious reference to George Grenville's celebrated analysis of the British budget problem (*A View*, p. 15). This is the only published sermon that can be identified reasonably certainly from Boucher's contemporary correspondence with a sermon actually delivered under that title in America (*MHM* 7: 156-57). But in fact Grenville did not present his report in Commons until 10 March 1764, and it is doubtful that Boucher could have had any great awareness or understanding of the problem nearly a year earlier (Great Britain: Parliament, *House of Commons Journal*, 1761-64, 29: 934). A little later in the same sermon, Boucher alluded to the "happy situation" in which British policy had placed the colonies. The ironic result, he added, had been to arouse "dissatisfaction among those who have long looked upon us with suspicion and jealousy," so that our friends in Britain "are told that the day may not be distant when even they shall sorely rue that so much has been done for the continental colonists" (*A View*, p. 43). Thus by his own account, Boucher anticipated in 1763 the bitter revolutionary controversy of several years later and in effect cautioned his parishioners against ingratitude and disloyalty to Britain.

Boucher's sermon "On Schisms and Sects," which he later dated 1769, expressed a point of view with respect to the current colonial controversy which was radically at odds with those set forth in various letters which he is known to have written at that time. In the sermon Boucher condemned those " 'half thinkers and bigots' " who " 'cannot distinguish between liberty and licentiousness' " and who by pretending " 'to freedom of thought and unbiased enquiry' " had brought about "so general a dissatisfaction with the existing government both in church and state" which lately had "been excited among you" (*A View*, pp. 59-60). It was loose thinking, Boucher assured his audience, that had led both to dreadful skepticism and to republican tyranny. Thus Boucher would have his readers of 1797 believe that as of 1769 he had already placed himself in opposition to the American patriot position. But, in fact, he then was still lending enthusiastic support in his letters to the Virginia radical cause (see chapter three). If this sermon was not entirely the work of the 1790s, it was at the very least "doctored" later to fit the stance toward the revolutionary controversy which Boucher adopted after 1772.

Another major example of the apparent prescience which permeates the sermons is Boucher's treatment of the subject of a resident American bishop. In his sermon "On the American Episcopate," purportedly preached in 1771, Boucher handled the matter as though he already was aware that the question would become a substantial cause of the break between Britain and the colonies. "In England," he represented himself as warning his audience, "prelatical power has never been objected to, except by those who meant to destroy it; and even such persons wished it destroyed, only because it was thought to stand in the way of their ultimate purpose to destroy the State" (*A View*, p. 142). The opposition to episcopacy, Boucher added, was fundamentally political; he purported to detect in it a change in the public mind which "cannot fail to have a mighty influence on the whole of our colonial system" (A View, p. 99). In short, he represented himself as detecting in 1771 a colonial spirit which would lead to the break with Britain four years later.

Numerous additional examples of prescience, misdating, and the like may be cited. For example, two sermons under the same title, "On Reducing the Revenue of the Clergy," which he later dated as 1771, contain substantial evidence both of too much prescience and of misdating as well. Here he leveled a blast at the "meddling, half-learned, popular lawyers of Maryland," whose attack on the church "may end, as it did in Cromwell's time, with the downfall of the State" (*A View*, p. 22). This was a reference to Boucher's later controversy with William Paca and Samuel Chase over Maryland's Act of Establishment of 1701-2, upon which the colony's church revenue depended. But Paca and Chase did not become involved in this controversy until Chase published a legal opinion about the church establishment in the *Maryland Gazette*, on 6 August 1772. The sermon "On Fundamental Principles," provides another example of dubious dating. Although Boucher dated it 1773, it refers directly to the "committees and sub-committees" and "conventions and congresses" which did not appear in Maryland until 1774, in the wake of receipt in Annapolis of the Boston *Circular Letter*. The same sermon predicted a "total destruction of foundations" through the operation of these committees, if indeed the damage was not already done. By Boucher's account, he already could see "An empire . . . within an empire," and "a new system of government of great power erected, even before the old one is formally abolished" (*A View*, p. 321). Boucher dated his sermon "Abram and Lot" as 1774 in Queen Anne's Parish, expounding on the theme that thousands of unfortunate persons who were shocked at the guilt of violating their oaths of allegiance and therefore refused to subscribe "to the wild notions which are so industriously circulated" were being subjected to having their "estates confiscated and their persons proscribed" (*A View*, p. 365). However, there was no confiscation of estates in Maryland until 1783.

Finally, Boucher dated his "Farewell Sermon" 1775, and it is filled with phrases indicating that it was his last, concluding with his wish that his parishioners have "patience under your sufferings, and a happy issue out of all your afflictions" (*A View*, p. 596). Boucher had not preached in his own parish since May 1775, and had preached for the last six months in Addison's church to avoid problems. But even then he kept two pistols on his pulpit cushions. More importantly, the circumstances under which Boucher left Maryland were not conducive to delivering a farewell sermon. The decision to leave and the plans to implement it were hastily taken and quietly managed. No man of even ordinary prudence would have delivered a farewell sermon, and Boucher had uncommon good sense. All of the evidence suggests it is wise to treat Boucher's book of sermons as a part of his English experience.

◡ _Appendix_ 𝔇 ◡

Boucher's Financial Worth

Boucher's Loyalist Claim

Boucher had estimated his worth in 1773 at £3,000 sterling, but he had improved his position considerably in the next year. The best estimate of the value lies in his Loyalist claim (American Loyalist Transcripts, 36: 137):

	Sterling
Lodge Plantation: 1,000 acres	£ 2,000
36 slaves estimated at	1,200*
8 white servants	120**
13 horses	130
44 head of cattle of different sorts	80
50 sheep	25
78 hogs	20
Plantation utensils	50
Corn, hay, and tobacco on hand	120
Plate, linen, and furniture	200
Library	500
Total	£ 4,445

*This figure was later corrected to 35 slaves at £ 1,285.
**This figure was reduced later at £ 60, to reflect the fact that 3 white servants had run away.

To this claim Boucher added loss of income from his "preferment." His claim stated that for the seven years prior to his appointment to the Prince George's County parish, the living had averaged "upwards of £500 sterling per annum," but that in "its reduced state, fees included, it could not be rated at more than £250 sterling per annum (ibid., p. 135). Actually, Boucher had estimated the living at £300-£400 sterling in 1772 (Boucher to James, 10 July 1772, *MHM* 8: 181). Finally, Boucher added a claim for his 4,000 acres of "back lands" at six shillings per acre, or £1,200, bringing the total claim, minus preferment losses, to £5,645 sterling.

Boucher at first estimated his losses without benefit of any proof from America, "owing to the loss of all his paper" (ibid., p. 131). Under these circumstances, he could only estimate his expense for his western lands at £500 or £600, but added that if "such lands have not been valued so high," he would "cheerfully acquiesce." In 1786, however, Boucher was able to produce a statement for the Claims Commission which indicated a sale price for all of his property (including the western land) of £6,394 14s. At the rate of exchange of 66 2/3, Boucher then revalued his property at £3,836 14s. sterling. Adding the increase in valuation to his prior claim at the lower estimated figure, he recalculated his whole loss at £5,906 14s. sterling (ibid., p. 134).

The sale price information rested upon information from one Mr. Cooke of the Maryland government, dated 15 September 1786 (ibid., p. 141). With this in hand, Boucher knew that the plantation land itself had been appraised at £3 sterling per acre, or £2,139 sterling. When the land was sold in May 1782, it brought £3,763 4s. in currency, which Boucher stated was the equivalent of £2,257 18s. 4d. sterling at the prevailing exchange rate. Given the rate per acre and the sale price, Boucher concluded that the Lodge no longer consisted of the original tract of land as he had held it, and assumed that it had been reduced in acreage by sales to cover the trebled taxes. By the same document from Mr. Cooke, Boucher learned that his personal estate in Maryland had been sold for £1,325 sterling.

Boucher owed £500 of the original £1,500 plantation debt when he fled. According to Boucher's claim, he had arranged with his attorney, his mother-in-law Mrs. Addison, to have any money collected applied to that debt. He owed a total of £1,200 when he left America, which was offset by debts owed to him of £1,500. Boucher's memory may have been faulty on the subject of his attorney. Nelly's mother had died May 1773, according to Bowie (*Across the Years in Prince George's County*, p. 33). Documents in the Annapolis Hall of Records indicate that Boucher had drawn up a power of attorney naming Overton Carr on 3 September 1775, although Carr did not file it with the court until 20 May 1776 (Prince George's County Deeds, Liber 21, fol. 270).

Boucher's Western Land Tracts and Record of Sales

Boucher had long had an interest in America's western land, which was stimulated by his contacts in Annapolis and his conversations with George Washington on the subject of making those backlands accessible by canals. As soon as Boucher was able to accumulate capital for investment, he took the opportunities available to those who were insiders in the proprietary government to acquire tracts of land beyond Fort Cumberland. According to the Records of the Commissioner of the Land Office, Annapolis Hall of Records, Boucher bought and sold several thousand acres beginning in 1774, as indicated below. (Maryland Historical Society tax lists are less useful since they do not begin until 1783.)

Tract	County	Patent Reference	
		Liber	Folio
Mount Airy	Frederick	IC A	633
Good Hope	Frederick	IC A	590
Non Pareil	Frederick	IC C	1-2
Blooming Rose	Frederick	IC H	392-3
Crab Orchard	Frederick	IC A	740

Tract	Date Sold	Acreage	Purchaser
Mount Airy: then Frederick, now Washington County	9 July 1774	395	Francis Deakins
Crab Orchard: then Frederick, now Washington County	10 March 1775	2,185	William Hayward
Good Hope: then Frederick, now Washington County	17 July 1774	389	Francis Deakins
Non Pareil: then Frederick, now Washington County	10 March 1775	2,482	William Hayward
Blooming Rose: then Frederick, now Alleghany County	9 July 1774	1,100	John Clapham
Total		6,551	

Boucher's Property in England

Although the value of his American property is easily ascertained because of his Loyalist claim, Boucher's assets in England are more difficult to estimate. The tax records for the pertinent years in Cumberland are now lost. The available information, including his salary at various times, the purchase prices of tracts of property which he was acquiring at Blencogo and in other sections of Cumberland County, the inheritance from Miss Barton and from his second wife, the purchase of the house at Clay Hill in Epsom and of the Coledale Hall residence just outside Carlisle, have been detailed in the text. Although Boucher considered his book and manuscript purchases a drain on his income, his extensive collection was in fact a valuable asset.

In summary, at Boucher's death he was in extremely good financial circumstances. His assets were between five and ten thousand pounds, according to the grant of probate of Elizabeth Hodgson Boucher dated 6 June 1804 (Probate 8/197, London, Public Record Office). The Prerogative Court, an ecclesiastical court, had no jurisdiction over land; therefore this sum did not include the value of any real estate. The house at Clay Hill was still valued at fifty or fifty-five pounds per year until 1803. From 1804 to 1830, Mrs. Boucher remained the owner, occupying it until 1807 or 1808, when Lord Byron rented it (duplicate land tax returns for Epsom, 1780-1831, Surrey Quarter Sessions and Clerk of the Peace Records, Surrey Record Office, Kingston-upon-Thames). Boucher was entitled to the vicarage of Saint Martin's at Epsom, which was listed separately but represented an asset to him even if he did not live in it after the Clay Hill purchase.

Some years before his death, Boucher estimated his Blencogo estate at £2,200 sterling, but since the tax records for the pertinent years are lost, it is impossible to know what the value of his other Cumberland holdings was, and what the rent from his many tenants might have been at the turn of the century.

The nine-page will drawn by Boucher in 1797 is on file in the Principal Probate Registry, Somerset House, London (fols. 378-1804 P. C. C. Heseltine), and reflects a substantial estate which Elizabeth inherited in full and as principal executrix, but for the bequests listed below (Prerogative Court of Canterbury, Abstract of Probates of Wills, June 1804, IR 26/88, pp. 10-11).

1. £100 each to Anne Tordiff Jackson and Jane Tordiff Harrison, daughters of Boucher's sister Mary
2. £20 to the Reverend Thomas Martin, curate of Bromfield
3. The "house they now live in at Sebergham for their lives and their survivors" to John Simpson and his wife and sister

In spite of his large family of young children, Boucher knew that he could afford to be a little generous at his death.

1. Vital statistics of Boucher and his family were established through manuscripts in the Jackson Collection, Cumbria County Library, Carlisle, England, and by a genealogical table in C. M. Lowther Bouch, "Jonathan Boucher," *Transactions of the Cumberland and Westmorland Archaeological and Antiquarian Society*, n.s., 27 (1927): 117-21 (hereafter *CWAA Transactions*). Boucher did not mention his uncle John (born 1699) in his autobiography (Jonathan Boucher, *Reminiscences of an American Loyalist 1738-1789; Being the Autobiography of the Reverend Jonathan Boucher, Rector of Annapolis in Maryland and afterwards Vicar of Epsom, Surrey, England*, ed. Jonathan Boucher [Boston: Houghton, Mifflin Co., 1925; reprint ed. Kennikat Press, 1967]; hereafter *Rem.*).

2. There are various spellings of the family name. Boucher had seen old documents respecting the family estate in which the name was spelled *Bourchier*. the *o* was not used before 1354; after that date the name was commonly spelled *Bourgchier, Burghcher*, and *Bourchier* in official records (Great Britain, Public Records Office, *Calendar of Close Rolls, Edward III, 1349-54*, ser. 4, 14 vols. [London: H.M. Stationery Office, 1906], 9: 24, 64, 129, 165; hereafter the Public Records Office is cited as PRO). Boucher's great-grandfather dropped the medial *r* from the family name; his own grandfather dropped the *i*, and his father further shortened the name to *Bouch*[r] or simply *Bouch*. After being orphaned when very young, Boucher's father was taken to Ireland, and later returned to England. Jonathan Boucher surmised that these circumstances caused his family to become confused with another still more numerous Cumberland family named Bouch. The argument that Jonathan Boucher belonged to the Bouch family and not to the Bourchiers is advanced by C. M. Lowther Bouch, who was apparently claiming him as his own ancestor. Boucher's son Barton reverted to the French spelling *Bouchier*, which was retained by some later descendants of Jonathan Boucher. Another descendant, born in 1855, restored the medial *r*, marking a return to the spelling of the early illustrious days when the family was part of official English history. The correct pronunciation of the Boucher family name is clear in an invitation to which various members of the Homony Club of Annapolis subscribed: "The Invitation's unanimous; I am a Voucher/

And am Yrs. &c Jonathan Boucher" (Gilmor Papers, Maryland Diocesan Archives on deposit in the Maryland Historical Society, Maryland Historical Society MS Collection 387, Baltimore, vol. 3, p. 14.). The pronunciation is substantiated in a poem about the club members which includes a few lines about Boucher:

> But to make the Club pious—and to carry the Farce on,
> Their superlative Wisdom's admitted a Parson;
> Tho a Parson of grace, savours much of a Layman,
> And thinks it no Crime to be sometimes a *Gay* man;
> As the Church I respect, tho you call not a Voucher,
> The man here described is Jonathan Boucher (ibid., p. 35).

3. John (1734-65), the eldest son, was later ordained in the Anglican church, married one Alice Dawson, and settled as a curate at Wickham near Newcastle-on-Tyne. He died less than a year after his marriage and before the birth of their child. In 1765 Alice wrote to Jonathan about his brother's death and of her pregnancy and indifferent health, appealing to him to see that the child was cared for if it lived and she died. She indicated that there would be funds available for support. Boucher responded to her appeal, enlisting the aid of his friend James to act for him in his absence. The child died soon after its birth and the widow within a year.

4. John James, M.A. Queen's College 1755, D.D. 1782. Headmaster of Saint Bees School 1755-71, he later became rector of Arthuret and Kirk Andrews 1782-85. He was married in 1757 to Ann Grayson of Lamonby Hall (*Maryland Historical Magazine* 7 [1912]: 2; hereafter *MHM*).

CHAPTER TWO

1. Boucher was recommended for orders by Rev. Musgrave Dawson and Gov. Francis Fauquier. After ordination on 26 March 1762, he received forty pounds and was authorized to receive His Majesty's Bounty of twenty pounds to defray the expenses of his passage to London. If he did not arrange to return to Virginia within three months, twenty pounds was to be voided (Fulham Papers, American Colonial Section, Lambeth Palace Library, London). Boucher's baptismal date is given as 8 March 1737 by the vicar of Bromfield, according to the ordination papers.

2. Boucher prepared a Latin epitaph and sent it to James for editing and adding to the monument at Bromfield Church. He saw it as his "last duty to parents I really loved and whose memories will be ever dear to me" (Boucher to James, 25 July 1769, Boucher Manuscripts, East Sussex Record Office, Lewes, England).

3. In addition to these "fevers unknown to Europe" (*MHM* 7 [1912]: 258), Boucher suffered from the "painful and excruciating disorder" which he called "piles" in 1769 (*MHM* 8 [1913]: 44). To make matters worse, the water at Smith's Mount was impure, and year after year he suffered illnesses, "often severe and tedious," as long as he remained in the colony (*Rem.*, pp. 40-41).

4. The aftermath of this romance is discussed more fully in chapter nine; see also Appendix A. Boucher revealed a second, differing account of it in his *Reminiscences,* in which he credited Rev. Henry Addison with

concerning himself in the romance and making some investigations. Addison discovered facts about Mrs. Chase that dispelled some of the mystery surrounding her. Although Boucher did not reveal exactly what this information was, he recalled: "I was enabled to unravel so very mysterious a story" about the woman whose "innocency" Addison had always suspected. Boucher also revealed that Addison's informant was one Mr. Smallwood, who was "much interested" in keeping the facts "secret," but who "little suspected" that he himself led to their discovery. Addison was apparently successful in his purpose of "the disengaging me from my attachment to Mrs. Chase" (*Rem.*, p. 53).

5. "A Character in Real Life in the Manner of Swift on Stella," 6 September 1776, Boucher Manuscripts.

CHAPTER THREE

1. Ralph Emmett Fall, "Jonathan Boucher, Turbulent Tory," *Historical Magazine of the Protestant Episcopal Church* 26 (1967): 330.
2. *Virginia Gazette*, 30 April 1767; 17 March, 5 May, 12 May 1768; 16 March, 4 May 1769; 22 March 1770. These are announcements of meetings and include Boucher's name, although he nowhere mentions that he held this post.
3. Boucher to John Waring of the SPG, 31 December 1762, Item 335, Bray MSS, SPG Papers, Library of Congress.
4. Fall, "Jonathan Boucher," p. 133.
5. Of Virginia's total Revolutionary War population of 500,000, 20,000 to 30,000 were Dissenters. In addition, great numbers were Anglicans, Deists, or indifferent (William Seiler, "The Anglican Parish in Tidewater Virginia, 1607-1775" [Ph.D. diss., University of Iowa, 1948], p. 115).
6. Fall, "Jonathan Boucher," p. 333.
7. Ibid.
8. Quoted in William Meade, *Old Churches, Ministers, and Families of Virginia*, 2 vols. (Philadelphia: J.B. Lippincott Co., 1906), 1: 409.
9. Jonathan Boucher, *A View of the Causes and Consequences of the American Revolution, in Thirteen Discourses, Preached in North America between the Years 1763 and 1775, with an Historical Preface* (New York: Russell & Russell, 1967), p. 42 (hereafter *A View*).
10. There was no system of public education in England. Until 1779 an English law prohibited any person from conducting a school or acting as a tutor unless he was a member in good standing of the Anglican church. Robert Raikes pioneered as a layman when the prohibition was lifted. The clergy in England opposed the schools, which were conducted on Sunday when people had more free time, because the curriculum was of necessity more secular than religious, concentrating on reading and writing (Erwin Lueker, ed., *Lutheran Cyclopedia* [Saint Louis: Concordia Publishing House, 1954], p. 1019). I am indebted to Dr. Edward H. Buchheimer of Detroit, Michigan, for assistance on this question.
11. Another son, James Maury, Jr., was aided in a commercial venture in England by Boucher's letters to persons able to assist him and by the extension of credit. Boucher also asked James to assist him. James

Maury later became the United States' consul to Liverpool. Boucher was to be introduced to Abbé Maury, later Cardinal Maury, through the Maury family, and the two were to carry on a literary correspondence for some years. Much of what is known of the James Maury-Jonathan Boucher friendship was provided by a letter written by a Miss Maury, niece of Abbé Maury, who was also the granddaughter of the Virginia James Maury and the daughter of young James Maury ("Thrax," "Reverend Jonathan Boucher," *Notes and Queries*, ser. 3, 9 [7 April 1866]: 282-83). See also Francis L. Hawks, *Contributions to the Ecclesiastical History of the United States of America*, 2 vols.⸀ (New York: Harper Brothers, 1836, 1839), 2: 269.

12. Richard Morton, *Colonial Virginia: Westward Expansion and Prelude to Revolution, 1710-1763*, 2 vols. (Chapel Hill: University of North Carolina Press, 1960), 2: 810-12.

13. Commissary William Robinson to Richard Terrick, bishop of London, 12 August 1765, in William Stevens Perry, ed., *Historical Collections Relating to the American Colonial Church*, 5 vols. (Hartford Conn.: Church Press Co., 1870-78), 1: 514-15.

14. Letter to *Virginia Gazette*, 25 July 1766; see Appendix B for evidence attributing this letter to Boucher. J. A. Leo Lemay provides new details on the Routledge-Chiswell case ("Robert Bolling and the Bailment of Colonel Chiswell," *Early American Literature* 6 [1971]: 99-142).

15. The law on this point of bail was printed in the *Virginia Gazette* on 13 August 1766.

16. Worthington C. Ford, ed., *Letters of Jonathan Boucher to George Washington* (Brooklyn, New York: Historical Printing Club, 1899), p. 13.

17. The revolutionary spirit was strong among Virginians, including clergymen. When Lord Dunmore dissolved the Houses of Burgesses in 1774, twenty-five clergymen became Loyalists, but thirty-six more declared themselves Whigs. Some served on the committees of safety and some in Virginia regiments as chaplains; five were in the army in a secular capacity (Seiler, "Anglican Parish," p. 115).

CHAPTER FOUR

1. Addison was to hold this post until his death in 1789 at seventy-two, except for the interval between 1775, when he escaped to England with Boucher, and his return to America after the war. Although Addison returned to New York in 1780 and petitioned the Maryland legislature for permission to return to his old home, his wish was not granted until after the peace. Boucher believed that Addison was of the same Cumberland family as the celebrated Joseph Addison, but he was probably wrong (*Rem.*, p. 51). See Effie G. Bowie, *Across the Years in Prince George's Country: A Genealogical and Biographical History of Some Prince George's County, Maryland and Allied Families* (Richmond, Virginia: Garrett & Massie, 1947), p. 32.

2. Saint John's Parish marriage records in *Genealogical Quarterly*, ser. 3, 10 (1900): 249. For an excellent account of the Dulany family, see Aubrey C. Land, *The Dulanys of Maryland: A Biographical Study of Daniel Dulany, the Elder (1685-1753) and Daniel Dulany the Younger*

(*1722-1797*) (Baltimore: Maryland Historical Society, 1955).

3. Boucher had already imported many books of sermons, including Masselion's thirteen volumes of French sermons. "I am almost overstocked with books of this kind," he commented to James on 9 December 1765 (*MHM* 7 [1912]: 299). In this letter he confided his fondness for Montaigne.

4. Boucher had broken off his arrangements with one Mr. Fell because the books he received were "worse-bound than common chapman books usually are," yet he was charged regular prices. He made a new arrangement with a bookseller in Glasgow (*MHM* 7 [1912]: 302).

5. William Eddis, *Letters from America, Historical and Descriptive: 1769-1777* (London: privately printed, 1792). Eddis was also secretary to Governor Eden 1769-76, and remained in the colony until 1777 to close the accounts of the Loan Office before returning to England as a Loyalist. Boucher later ordered three copies of this book (Records of William Eddis, Macalester College Library, Saint Paul, Minn.).

6. Boucher might have cited the example of the Charleston lawyer, Thomas Phepoe, whose income was between one and two thousand pounds in 1773, 1774, and 1775 (American Loyalist Transcripts, 60 vols., Manuscripts and Archives Division, The New York Public Library, Astor, Lenox, and Tilden Foundations, preface, li; hereafter Transcripts).

7. This summary of the Allen affair is drawn from Boucher's account in the *Reminiscences* and from Charles Albro Barker, *Background of the Revolution in Maryland* (New Haven: Yale University Press, 1940), pp. 281-89.

8. MS 1265, Dulany Papers, Maryland Historical Society, Baltimore; see also *Maryland Gazette*, 2 June 1768, and Barker, *Background*, p. 284.

9. Barker, *Background*, p. 285. Boucher's pseudonym may have been "Crambo," "Rusticus," or "Omicron" (*Maryland Gazette*, 10 March, 24 March, 31 March 1768). One earlier piece, according to Boucher, was "an allegorical portrait . . . somewhat in Swift's manner" (*MHM* 7 [1912]: 335). Other verses were written in 1769 (*MHM* 8 [1913]: 38-39).

10. Boucher told James on 9 March 1767 that he had heard the two had been surprised in each other's arms (*MHM* 7 [1912]: 341). Sharpe's opinion of Allen is quite clear in his discussions of the matter in a letter to Secretary Hamersley on 30 October 1768 (*Archives of Maryland*, 72 vols. [Baltimore: Maryland Historical Society, 1883-1972], 14: 538-44). Allen sank into poverty and degradation and died in London after 1782.

11. Nelson Rightmyer, "The Character of the Anglican Clergy of Colonial Maryland," *MHM* 44 [1949]: 101-2.

12. Fall, "Jonathan Boucher," p. 338.

13. Ford, *Letters*, p. 7.

14. Ibid.

15. Ibid., p. 11.

16. Ibid., pp. 10-11.

17. Ibid., p. 11.

18. Ibid., pp. 11, 10, 13.

19. Ibid., pp. 16, 21.

20. Ibid., p. 20.

21. Eden to Dulany, 10 May 1770, Sir Robert Eden Private Papers, Maryland Historical Society.

CHAPTER FIVE

1. William Eddis, *Letters from America*, ed. Aubrey Land, (Cambridge, Mass.: Harvard University Press, 1969), pp. 11, xiii, 32, 48. All subsequent Eddis quotations are from this edition.

2. William Oliver Stevens, *Annapolis, Anne Arundel's Town* (New York: Dodd, Mead and Co., 1937). Except where otherwise stated, physical descriptions of Annapolis are drawn from this local history. Annapolis was also Maryland's largest naval office; all ships leaving the upper Chesapeake were required to pay their export fees and register at Annapolis or Patapsco (Ronald Hoffman, *A Spirit of Dissension: Economics, Politics, and the Revolution in Maryland* [Baltimore: Johns Hopkins University Press, 1973], p. 14).

3. Eddis, *Letters from America*, pp. 12, 18.

4. Stevens, *Annapolis*, p. 21.

5. The following account of the social and intellectual background of Marylanders is based on Barker, *Background*, pp. 27-68.

6. Eddis, *Letters from America*, p. 14.

7. Eddis noted that the "quick importation of fashions from the mother country is really astonishing," and also observed that there were "throughout these colonies, very many lovely women who . . . might appear to great advantage in the most brilliant circles of gaiety and fashion" (*Letters from America*, pp. 20, 57-58).

8. A check of the Acts and Proceedings of the Assembly for 1770 and 1771 revealed no record of the letter, nor of any adjustment in salary. Boucher's vestry at Saint Anne's at this time included George Plater, Thomas Bordley, John Beale, Edmund Jenings, Daniel Dulany, Walter Dulany, Charles Calvert, Benjamin Tasker, Robert Gordon, William Fitzhugh, and Lawrence Washington (Frances Sims McGrath, *Pillars of Maryland* [Richmond: Dietz Press, 1950], p. 363).

9. For detailed accounts of the American episcopate question, see James Sims M. Anderson, *History of the Church of England in the Colonies and Foreign Dependencies of the British Empire*, 3 vols. (London: Rivington's, 1856), 3: 203-5, Carl Bridenbaugh, *Mitre and Sceptre: Transatlantic Faiths, Personalities, and Politics* (New York: Oxford University Press, 1962). For local church history, see Rightmyer, *Maryland's Established Church*, and Barker, *Background*, pp. 49, 216, 275-77, 359.

10. The Reverend Henry Caner of Boston, writing to Archbishop Secker, expressed the problem of the Anglican clergy clearly, an opinion with which Boucher agreed: "We are a rope of sand. There is no union, no authority among us; we cannot even summon a Convention for united counsel and advice, while the Dissenting Ministers have their Monthly, Quarterly, and Annual Associations, Conventions, etc. to advise, assist, and support each other in many measures which they shall think proper to enter into" (Caner to Secker, 7 January 1763, in Perry, ed., *Historical Collections* 3: 489-91.

11. Bridenbaugh, *Mitre and Sceptre*, p. 315.

12. Apparently the silence lasted two months, for by August Boucher dined with him and reported to James on 25 August that Eden was fond of him (*MHM* 8 [1913]: 172).

13. Boucher wrote James on 4 April 1771 that Myles Cooper expected one

Rotherham, a friend of James's, to "first wear lawn sleeves on this side the Atlantic" (*MHM* 8 [1913]: 177-78).

14. Boucher (*Rem.*, p. 66) wrote that he had written a prologue and some lines to an actress which had been printed in the *Gazette*. A thorough check of the *Gazette* from June 1770 through 1771 revealed two poems to an actress, and both were addressed to Nancy Hallam. Either could be Boucher's. "To Miss Hallam," printed 6 September 1770, is twelve stanzas long and unsigned. Charles Sellers attributes it to William Eddis (*Charles Willson Peale* [New York: Charles Scribner's sons, 1969], pp. 92-95). "To Miss Hallam, on seeing her last Monday night in the character of Imogen," printed 10 October 1771, is nine stanzas long and signed "Paladour."

15. Eddis, *Letters from America,* p. 8.

16. Allen Walker Read, "Boucher's Linguistic Pastoral of Colonial Maryland," *Dialect Notes* 6 (1933): 353-60. A complete copy of the poem is preserved in the preface to Boucher's lengthy glossary, a part of which was published after his death as *A Supplement to Dr. Johnson's Dictionary of the English Language* (1807).

17. H. L. Mencken, *The American Language,* 4th ed. (New York: Knopf, 1937), pp. 34, 35n, 120, 169, 313, 324n, 354.

18. For a full discussion of the clubs and their place in the life and thought of Annapolis and Maryland, see Barker, *Background,* pp. 56-60.

19. An advertisement appeared in the *Maryland Gazette* on 25 November 1773, offering a reward of one hundred guineas cash with "no questions asked" for the return of a missing folio bound in green vellum (Eddis, *Letters from America,* p. xxv). Only one folio is extant, held by the Historical Society of Pennsylvania (hereafter cited as Folio).

20. Folio, p. 4.

21. Ibid., pp. 55-56.

22. Boucher to Dulany and Jenings, n.d., MS 387.1, Gilmor Papers.

23. This is contrary to most reports in secondary sources, which credit Boucher with being the first president, if not the founder, and which do not indicate that his length of service was one month because of a monthly rotation rule (See, for example, Barker *Background,* p. 60; Rightmyer, *Maryland's Established Church,* pp. 163-64). Boucher's remark that he was the first president is probably responsible for the error (*Rem.*, p. 67).

24. Folio, p. 66.

25. The "Remonstrance" is so like the explanation of the name which appeared in the *Maryland Gazette* on 12 December 1771 that it may well have been written by Boucher. It was signed "Philomonous." Boucher's explanation conflicts with Seller's, who calls the club *Hominy,* and suggests an Indian origin and a "derisive play upon that of the politically oriented clubs . . . professing allegiance to Saint Tammany, aboriginal friend of the white man" (*Charles Willson Peale,* p. 97). Stevens, writing in 1937, says perhaps "the simple fare indicated by the name in its early spelling was a sign of the greater democracy of the group, for it contained not only men of great wealth, like Paca and Dulany, and a King's official, Eddis, the Surveyor of Customs, but also Charles Willson Peale, and Jonathan Boucher" (*Annapolis,* p. 53). One might question, however, whether the group was democratic. It was a prestige group, and what Peale may have lacked in wealth at that time was offset by his growing reputation as an artist; what Boucher

lacked in wealth was offset by his position in the Anglican church and his growing friendships in officialdom.

26. Folio, p. 69.
27. Folio, pp. 144-45.
28. MS 1265, Dulany Papers.
29. Folio, p. 146. Peale was engaged about this time in painting portraits of Washington and Jacky Custis, and was making frequent trips to Mount Vernon for this purpose.
30. This picture was given to Edmund Jenings as a gift, according to a letter of 20 April 1771 from him to Peale (Sellers, *Charles Willson Peale*, p. 85). About fifty years later, Peale remembered a picture of his wife and child "which was much admired and handsome verses wrote on it," although he mistakenly recalled that it had been painted about 1772. According to Sellers, the painting is lost (ibid., pp. 105-6). The *Maryland Gazette* printed some anonymous verses on 18 April 1771, entitled "On a Picture of Mrs. Peale," which may have been Boucher's. Judging by the verses, the subject of the picture was a mother and child.
31. Ford, *Letters*, p. 20.
32. Ray Allen Billington, *Western Expansion* (New York: Macmillan Co., 1949), pp. 150-51.
33. Ford *Letters*, p. 35.
34. Corra Bacon-Foster, "Early Chapters in the Development of the Potomac Route to the West," *Records* of *the Columbia Historical Society* 15 (1912): 110-12. Others interested and named as managers included George Mason, Rev. Thomas Bacon, Dr. David Ross, Thomas Cresap, and Jonathan Hagar; Col. George Mercer and Col. Thomas Prother were elected treasurers (ibid., p. 114). The letter reprinted in Bacon-Foster's article provides the only source for our knowledge of the Johnsons' effort to form a company. The location of the letter is now unknown.
35. The first English canal was opened in 1761 by an engineering genius, James Brindley, and was known as the Bridgewater Canal. It was designed to carry coal to Manchester from the Worsley mines (Charles Hadfield, *British Canals: An Illustrated History* [London: Phoenix House, 1950], p. 28.
36. Ford, *Letters*, p. 15.
37. Ibid.
38. Ibid. In a letter of 4 May 1772, Washington reported to Boucher that he had just returned from the session at Williamsburg, and that a bill had been passed to empower trustees (to be chosen by the subscribers) to raise money by subscription and lottery to open and extend navigation of the Potomac from Tidewater to Fort Cumberland. Execution was to be suspended until a similar law could be passed by Maryland's legislative body (John Fitzpatrick, ed., *Writings of Washington*, 39 vols. [Washington, D.C.: George Washington Centennial Commission, 1931-44], 3: 81). In 1785 Virginia and Maryland joined in forming the Potomac Canal Company.
39. William Eden became the first lord of the Board of Trade and Plantations (1776) and one of the peace commissioners to America (1778) (Robert Allan Eden, *Some Historical Notes on the Eden Family* [London: Blades, East, and Blades, 1907], pp. 37-39); see also Bernard Steiner, *Life and Administration of Sir Robert Eden*, Johns Hopkins University Studies, no. 16 (Baltimore: Johns Hopkins University Press, 1898) (hereafter *Robert Eden*); Rosamund Beirne, "Portrait of a Colonial Governor: Robert Eden," *MHM* 45 (1950): 153-75.

40. In 1784 Eden returned to America to salvage what he could of his property, contracted yellow fever, and died. Harford promptly called on Boucher for payment of the principal and interest. The request was very embarrassing for Boucher because of his own precarious financial condition. Boucher borrowed £1,000 in order to pay the note, Harford having agreed to accept the reduced sum in lieu of the full amount.

41. Frederick Morton Eden respected Boucher's counsel and consulted him on various matters, while Boucher in turn was always welcome in Eden's family circle. While Eden was in America, the deadline for filing a claim for losses in America approached, and Boucher and Rev. William Edmiston went to a great deal of trouble to assemble the necessary testimonials and prepare Eden's claim.

42. Robert Eden to the earl of Dartmouth, 27 August 1775 (*MHM* 8 [1913]: 240-41; see also Eden to Dartmouth, 9 September 1775 (ibid., pp. 241-42); *Rem.*, p. 104. Steiner's standard biography of Eden is surprisingly silent about Boucher. Much that Boucher did for Eden was behind the scene, but there is good evidence from Eden's hand that he was indeed a kind of confidential secretary.

43. Ford, *Letters*, p. 37.

44. Ibid., p. 15.

45. Ibid., p. 16.

46. Ibid., p. 18.

47. Ibid., pp. 16, 19.

48. Ibid., p. 19.

49. Ibid., p. 19.

50. Ibid., pp. 21, 24.

51. Ibid., pp. 25-26.

52. Ibid., p. 22.

53. Ibid., pp. 30-32.

54. Ibid., pp. 32-34. By 1771 Boucher had two students with him in addition to Jacky Custis: Benedict Calvert and Overton Carr. Calvert, the eldest son of Benedict Calvert, went on to Eton, where he died. Carr was to be sent to England (along with another Maury boy) for additional schooling with James in preparation for the gown (*MHM* 8 [1913]: 181; Ford, *Letters*, p. 34). On 9 December 1765 Boucher had written James: "I am but illy qualified for a schoolmaster." He added: "A few years more, and I hope to have done with it forever" (*MHM* 7 [1912]: 99).

55. Ford, *Letters*, p. 27.

56. Ibid., p. 28.

57. Ibid., p. 29. For Washington's replies to Boucher, see Fitzpatrick, *Writings of George Washington*, 3: 50.

58. Rightmyer, *Maryland's Established Church*, p. 158.

59. In 1960 Mount Lubentia was on what is now known as Route 202, between Largo and what was known as Oak Grove; it was the home of W. Beall Bowie.

60. Ford, *Letters*, p. 34.

61. Boucher contended that his wife's mother was soon reconciled to the marriage, and "happy to leave her daughters [Nelly and her sister Ann] under my care." Nevertheless, Mrs. Addison did change her will in 1773, instead leaving all of her property to Ann (*Rem.*, pp. 73, 76).

62. Ford, *Letters*, p. 46.

CHAPTER SIX

1. Boucher wrote *Gault* in the *Reminiscences,* but the Maryland Diocesan Library records indicate that Edward Gantt, Sr. is the man to whom he referred. Gantt is listed as Boucher's curate in 1771, and he may well have been the curate before Boucher's arrival.

2. For a full account of Maryland politics, see Barker, *Background,* pp. 290-377, to whom I am indebted for many of the specific facts below. For a more recent account of the importance of Maryland's economic problems in relation to politics and the Revolution in Maryland, see Hoffman, *Spirit of Dissension.*

3. William Paca (1740-99) was educated at Philadelphia College and admitted to the Middle Temple, London, on 14 January 1762. He and Samuel Chase were the outstandingly radical patriots of Maryland, having served together in the House of Delegates of the Maryland Assembly from 1762 to the Revolution. Paca had studied law in the office of Stephen Bordley before being admitted to the bar, and then established a law practice at Annapolis. He and Chase were elected to the Continental Congress; both ultimately served as governors in the new State of Maryland. Chase later became a justice of the Supreme court.

4. Arthur E. Karinen, "Numerical and Distributional Aspects of Maryland Population, 1631-1840" (Ph.D. diss., University of Maryland, 1958).

5. George Whitefield, the Methodist revivalist, made similar observations (Stevens, *Annapolis,* p. 59), and Rev. Thomas Cradock of Saint Thomas Parish castigated "the vile wretches and their preposterous conduct in the Church of England in Maryland" from Saint Anne's pulpit in Annapolis in 1753 (quoted in David Curtis Skaggs, "Thomas Cradock's Sermon on the Governance of Maryland's Established Church," *William and Mary Quarterly* 27 [1970]: 641). The complete sermon occupies pp. 637-53.

6. William Pinkney's account, recorded by his son, of the controversy over inspection fees and clerical salaries described the funeral given to the proclamation by the Country party during the general rejoicing after the declared overthrow of the Court party's arguments (Edward Pinkney's Notes on the Early Life of his Father, William Pinkney, Kennedy Papers, MS 1336, Maryland Historical Society).

7. *A Reply to the Church of England Planter's First Letter Respecting the Clergy* (Annapolis, 1770), Maryland Historical Society. The original handbill is summarized in this twenty-two page pamphlet, which is signed "A Constitutionalist."

8. Boucher may have checked the public records when he prepared *A View* in 1797. He said that the act was originally framed in Maryland, but was not wholly approved in England and had been returned for amending. The amendments were adopted in the next Assembly, and enacted into law. Meanwhile King William had died. The act, when sent to England for the second time, "modelled and passed according to the form directed by the late King," was approved and confirmed by his successor, Queen Anne (*A View,* pp. 223-24).

9. Charles Barker agrees with Boucher's conclusion (*Background,* p. 361). Boucher considered it his duty to defend the church, and wrote later that he drew up "sundry memorials, remonstrances, petitions, and papers" (*Rem.,* p. 70).

10. A test case was tried in Charles County when Joseph Harrison, a delegate, appeared as plaintiff against Sheriff Richard Lee, who had jailed him for refusal to pay the forty pounds per poll. Harrison claimed the jailing had been illegal. Paca, Chase, and Thomas Johnson were his legal counsel. The Charles County jury decided in Harrison's favor, awarding him sixty pounds sterling on the premise that the sheriff's demand for taxes was a violation of the rights of Englishmen (Barker, *Background*, p. 363).

11. Possibly Eden had promised Paca a post in the future because of his usefulness as a channel of intelligence between the Carroll forces and Eden. However, Boucher's disclosure placed Eden in an embarrassing position, forcing him to issue a disclaimer. Paca was, after all, an opponent of Eden's government. It is also possible that Boucher wished to divide Paca and Eden (Hoffman, *Spirit of Dissension*, pp. 119-20).

12. Anne Y. Zimmer, "The 'Paper War' in Maryland, 1770-73: The Paca-Chase Politial Philosophy Tested," *MHM* 71 (1976): 177-93.

13. Cooper to Boucher, 14 June 1773, Boucher Manuscripts.

14. Boucher to Rev. William Smith of Philadelphia, 4 May 1775 (*MHM* 8 [1913]: 238.

15. Washington visited Mount Lubentia 6-7 September, 4 and 10 October 1772, and 12 April 1773, according to a plaque on the entrance to Mount Lubentia. The September dates and dates of other visits are indicated in Fitzpatrick, *Writings of Washington*, 3: 37, 105, 148; 37: 496.

16. Ibid., 3: 45.

17. Ibid., 37: 497-98.

18. Ford, *Letters*, pp. 39-40.

19. Ibid., pp. 40-41.

20. Ibid.

21. Fitzpatrick, *Writings of Washington*, 3: p. 129.

22. Ford, *Letters*, p. 44.

23. Ibid., p. 45.

24. Cooper to Boucher, 14 June 1773, Boucher Manuscripts.

25. Fitzpatrick, *Writings of Washington*, 3: pp. 167-68.

26. "Thrax," "Jonathan Boucher," pp. 287-89. This description was supplied by a descendant of James Maury who knew Boucher well.

CHAPTER SEVEN

1. The manuscript is illegible at this point, with only the last two letters (*ca*) of the name of the man to whom Boucher wished Smith to write. However, the context makes it clear that the reference is to Paca.

2. On 4 May 1775 Boucher wrote to Smith and referred to the fact that he had "hesitated not to ask your friendly interposition" when he had thought Smith capable of helping, and added, "which you, with all the earnestness of enlarged humanity immediately indulged me in" (*MHM* 8 [1913]: 237).

3. Boucher's Loyalist claim indicated a salary of £500, although George Chalmers attested that Boucher's annual salary had been between £250 and £300. It is likely that Chalmers's reference was to the salary after the passage of the Vestry Act.

4. The indenture was recorded on 21 June 1773 (Prince George's County Deeds, Liber 20, fol. 265, Annapolis Hall of Records).

5. Although in other respects the conveyance of 29 December 1773 read much like that of June 1773, and specified that it included "all the lands devised to John Addison by his father," it did not mention any slaves. Boucher's individual purchase was recorded on 14 January 1774 (ibid., fol. 354).

6. In fact, the last recorded date on which Boucher attended a vestry meeting in his own parish was 24 September 1773. No parish record is available after that date. Rev. Walter Hanson became his curate in 1775 (Fall, "Jonathan Boucher," pp. 344-45).

7. See Appendix C.

8. Boucher's library at the Lodge was later to sell for more than £2,000 Continental currency after the estate was confiscated (Loyalist Transcripts, 36: 134).

9. However, Boucher's Loyalist claim indicates first thirty-six and then thirty-five slaves (Transcripts, 36: 141-42). It is possible that there was a larger number of slaves on the plantation during Boucher's residence there, and that the numbers were reduced by runaways or forced sales by the time he filed his claim.

10. This is the testimony of one of the partners, Robert Smith (Transcripts, 36: 148).

11. This is deduced from the fact that Boucher sold a total of 6,551 acres in 1774 and 1775, and still had 4,000 acres left on which he later filed a Loyalist claim. See Appendix C.

12. Lack of patents did not hinder the Maryland government from confiscating such property later, considering the certificate holders as the rightful owners. Nor did the lack prohibit the purchasers of 1773 from filing claims with the Loyalist Claims Commission for the subsequent loss of property by confiscation. Many witnesses attested to the fact that patent issuance was merely ceremonial, and the commission honored such claims, disallowing only those for uncultivated lands if the conditions of the grant had not been met. However, the allowance included only the purchase cost of such lands at the time of expropriation, and excluded any costs for surveying and patenting.

13. There is some discrepancy in the Land Office records. Some documents refer to a grant on 26 March of 2,000 acres (Non Pareil Patent), while the Mount Airy and Good Hope patents refer to 1,950 acres. They are either separate grants or one of the documents is in error.

14. Robert Smith attested to this in connection with Boucher's Loyalist claim (Transcripts, 36: 146-49).

15. A search of the extant court records under *Addison* did not reveal any case such as Boucher described; it may have been a private arbitration, which was a common arrangement then. On the other hand, it may have been a court matter, but filed under some other name. It is not clear whether this matter was related to Boucher's duties as one of the trustees of the John Addison estate. Since one of the other trustees was a Samuel Hanson and one of the trespassers was a relative of one Mr. Hanson, the matter could have been a sensitive one. This particular trusteeship had its origin in a debt and not in a death. Furthermore, John Addison (Nelly's brother) was still alive and did not marry until 1787; thus Boucher's term "orphan nephews" may have referred to another branch of the family.

16. *Maryland Gazette*, 26 May 1774. The committee consisted of Matthias

Hammond, Samuel Chase, Charles Carroll of Carrollton, John Hall, and William Paca.

17. See the resolutions of the county committees and the Maryland Provincial Convention published in the *Maryland Gazette* on 2, 9, 16, and 30 June 1774.

18. Prince George's County delegates included Robert Tyler, Joseph Sim, Joshua Beall, John Rogers, Addison Murdock, William Bowie, B. Ball, and Osborne Sprigg. The Anne Arundel County and City of Annapolis delegates were B. T. B. Worthington, Thomas Johnson, Jr., Samuel Chase, John Hall, William Paca, Matthias Hammond, Samuel Chew, John Weems, Thomas Dorsey, and Rezin Hammond (*American Archives: A Documentary History of the English Colonies in America from the King's Message to Parliament of March 7, 1774 to the Declaration of Independence by the United States*, 4th ser., 9 vols. [Washington, D. C.: St. Clair Clarke and Peter Force, 1833-37], 1: pp. 438-39).

19. See Land, *Dulanys*, pp. 308-19, for background and Dulany's position on this question.

20. Ibid., pp. 312-13.

21. *Letter from a Virginian to the Members of the Congress to be Held at Philadelphia on the First of September, 1774* (Boston: Hugh Gaine, 1774). See Appendix B; see also Anne Y. Zimmer, "Hugh Gaine, Loyalist Printer," *Societas* 7 (January 1978).

22. *Letter from a Virginian*, p. 7. All quotations until otherwise noted are from this pamphlet.

23. This discussion of virtual and actual representation in Boucher's pamphlet (pp. 27-28, 30) is similar to that of Daniel Dulany's *Considerations on the Propriety of Imposing Taxes in the British Colonies, For the Purpose of Raising a Revenue, by Act of Parliament* (Annapolis: Jonas Green, 1765).

24. Merrill Jensen, *The Founding of a Nation* (New York: Oxford University Press, 1968), p. 495.

25. For an account of this misadventure, in which William Stewart, a merchant and Anthony's brother, was also involved, see Land, *Dulanys*, pp. 313-14; Scharf, *History of Maryland*, 2: 159, 296-301; Eddis, *Letters, from America*, pp. 91-97.

26. Land, *Dulanys*, p. 314. The Dulanys heard Stewart's side of the story, that he had "destroyed property of great value to prevent worse consequences." A younger member of the family said that Stewart had agreed under pressure not to publish a vindication of his conduct. However, a letter of 27 October 1774 from Baltimore, Maryland, is probably closer to the truth. Stewart did not agree; he simply could not get it published. The printer had been threatened with destruction of his press if he printed Stewart's statement. An older source says that Stewart published an apology (John Archer Silver, *The Provisional Government of Maryland (1774-1777)* [Baltimore: Johns Hopkins Press, 1895] p. 10). However, later evidence in Land, *Dulanys*, pp. 313-14, is convincing; see also Eddis, *Letters from America*, pp. 91-97.

27. Jensen, *Founding of a Nation*, p. 506.

28. Journal of the Continental Congress, 20 October 1774.

29. The other members selected were William Bowie, Robert Tyler, Walter Bowie, John Rogers, David Crawford, and Joshua Beall (*American Archives*, 1: 1141).

30. The Assembly adjourned until 8 December since several counties were not fully represented because of late notice of the meeting.

31. County level meetings were held on 29 December 1775, 5, 19, and 26 January, and 2 and 9 February 1775, according to the *Maryland Gazette*. However, Prince George's County held its meeting on 21 December and Anne Arundel County, meeting jointly with the City of Annapolis, met on 23 December 1774.

32. *American Archives*, 1: 1056. Only clerics of all denominations, physicians, members of the governor's household, and those who objected on religious grounds were exempt.

33. Robert Eden to the earl of Dartmouth, 30 December 1774 (*American Archives*, 1: 1076).

34. Daniel Dulany to the Committee of Anne Arundel County, 16 January 1775, Maryland Historical Society; see also Land, *Dulanys*, p. 315.

CHAPTER EIGHT

1. Although the importance of the extralegal committees was neglected by research scholars for decades, a number of books and articles have been published in the past few years. See Pauline Maier, *From Resistance to Revolution: Colonial Radicals and the Development of American Opposition to Britain, 1765-1776* (New York: Alfred Knopf, 1972); David Ammerman, *In the Common Cause: American Response to the Coercive Acts of 1774* (Charlottesville: University Press of Virginia, 1974); Richard Francis Upton, *Revolutionary New Hampshire* (New York, Octagon Books, 1971), a reprint of the 1930 edition with the addition of a critical essay; Larry Bowman, "The Virginia County Committees of Safety, 1774-1776," *Virginia Magazine of History and Biography* 19 (1971): 322-37.

2. Boucher's concept of himself as a good American supports Wallace Brown's thesis that many Loyalists saw themselves as good patriots (*The Good Americans: The Loyalists in the American Revolution* [New York: William Morrow and Company, Inc., 1969]).

3. See Richard D. Brown, *Revolutionary Politics in Massachusetts: The Boston Committee of Correspondence and the Towns, 1772-1774* (Cambridge, Mass.: Harvard University Press, 1970).

4. The nine were Dr. Richard Brooke, John Rogers, Esq., Capt. William Bowie, David Crawford, Addison Murdock, Robert Tyler, Capt. Joshua Beall, Josias Beall, and Osborne Sprigg (*American Archives*, 1: 1011-12).

5. Minutes, Anne Arundel County (ibid., p. 1140).

6. Minutes, Prince George's County, (ibid., pp. 1011-12); Minutes, Charles County (ibid., 985-86); *Maryland Gazette*, 19 January 1775.

7. Ibid., p. 1194.

8. "To the Printers of the Maryland Gazette," unsigned letters, ibid., p. 1141).

9. *Maryland Gazette*, 15 December 1774; 5, 26 January, 23 February, 2 March 1775.

10. Eddis, *Letters from America*, p. 100; further quotations are from p. 103.

11. Scharf, *History of Maryland*, 2: 185.

12. Although a search of official provincial records has been fruitless, there is a certificate verifying Boucher's appearance attached to his memorial to the commissioners examining Loyalist claims (Transcripts, 36: 194).

Although the date given in each instance is November 1774, the sequence of events in Maryland makes a date early in 1775 more likely.

13. There are no records extant of committee activities in Prince George's County other than those which came to the attention of the Council of Safety, established in 1775, records of which begin with August 1775. Eden had written copious reports on events in the province from 1773 to 1775, but they seem to have disappeared. Some Maryland records, particularly those of Annapolis, were destroyed by fire.

14. Eddis, *Letters from America,* p. 107.

15. Gov. Robert Eden to William Eden, 28 April 1775, Bancroft Collection, American Revolution, vol. 1775, no. 1, Manuscripts and Archives Division, New York Public Library.

16. The letter is printed in *Reminiscences,* pp. 128-30; another letter, "To the Hon[ora]ble the Deputies in Congress from the Southern Provinces," appears pp. 130-36. Boucher wrote that these were among the very few pieces remaining of the many he had written as an "observing man on the spot," and that they conveyed the basis for his opposition. One statement in item 13 of the "Quaeries," referring to the confiscation of arms, indicates some confusion in dating, and may mean that Boucher later tampered with at least this section. The Continental Congress recommended in December 1775 the confiscation of arms from those who would not sign the Articles of Association. Those refusing to sign before 11 April 1776 were to give up their arms or be forcibly disarmed, and in addition a bond for good behavior was to be required. Maryland implemented the suggestions of Congress on 7 December 1775. Those wishing to leave the country were free to do so, and to take their goods with them (Silver, *Provisional Government of Maryland,* pp. 32-33). Boucher had left Maryland some months before this happened. No printer's name is indicated below the "Quaeries" in the *Reminiscences,* and a search of all Rivington material in the New York Public Library and issues of Rivington's *Gazette* for December 1774 through September 1775 failed to verify the publication of the letter.

17. Boucher, "To the Deputies" (*Rem.,* pp. 130-36).

18. *Archives of Maryland,* 11: 15.

19. Ibid., p. 23. The Maryland Convention authorized the printing of £266,666 worth of paper money valued at 4s. 6d. per dollar.

20. Ibid., p. 28.

21. This process of a new revolutionary government growing up beside old withering institutions is described by Crane Brinton in *Anatomy of a Revolution* (New York: W. W. Norton, 1938).

22. 7 August 1775 (*Archives of Maryland,* 11: 45-47).

23. Ibid., pp. 48-50.

24. *American Archives,* 1: 1141-42.

25. The letter was mailed in August 1775, but the specific date is unknown, and James apparently did not receive it. It is not with the extant Boucher-James correspondence.

26. The incident with Landon Carter must have occurred on 3 May 1775, inasmuch as Boucher stated in a letter to Smith dated 4 May 1775 that he had been in Virginia the day before.

27. Carter insisted that he, rather than Patrick Henry, was the first Virginian to oppose Great Britain in the struggle leading to the American Revolution (Jack P. Greene, ed., *The Diary of Colonel Landon Carter of*

Sabine Hall, 1752-1778, 2 vols. [Charlottesville: University of Virginia Press, 1965]).

28. This epigram, supposedly published in April 1775, has not been identified. Boucher says only that it was prepared for publication; since the printer showed the manuscript to various people and Carter promptly identified it and vilified Boucher, it may have been suppressed.

29. Ford, *Letters*, p. 47. All quotations until otherwise noted are from this letter of 6 August 1775.

30. Boucher believed at the time and later that the Loyalists were in the majority everywhere but in New England. It is difficult to judge the accuracy of his estimate at the time he wrote the letter to Washington, but there was some support for it in certain Maryland counties. As late as November 1775, Worcester County wrote to the Eastern Shore Council of Safety that "friends of liberty are in a bad situation. We have no ammunition and the Tories exceed our number" (*American Archives*, 3: 1572-73).

31. Stevens, *Annapolis*, pp. 148-49; Alan Brown, "William Eden and the American Revolution" (Ph.D. diss., University of Michigan, 1953).

32. William Eden introduced Boucher by letter to the earl of Dartmouth, and interceded with the bishop of Bangor on his behalf, but he could not get him a benefice. Even Lady Eden observed in London in 1776 that Boucher got only promises (*MHM* 8 [1913]: 344).

33. Boucher gives the date as 10 September 1775 (*Rem.*, p. 141). According to the records of the Grand Inquest in the archives of the county court of Prince George's County, 25 August 1778, however, Boucher and Addison were officially recorded as having left the colony on 14 August, "to avoid taking an active part in defense" (Brown Book, Liber 9, fol. 23). The August date is also supported by the fact that the colonial ports were to be closed on 1 September, the date fixed by the Continental Congress as the effective date of the nonimportation and nonexportation agreements.

CHAPTER NINE

1. Robert Eden to Lord Dartmouth, 27 August 1775; Eden to Dartmouth, 9 September 1775 (*MHM* 8 [1913]: 240-42). Boucher furnished Lambeth Palace with a list of clergy and livings in Maryland as of 1775 (Fulham Papers, American Colonial Section, III F, 217).

2. Boucher to Germain, 27 November 1775 (*MHM* 8 [1913]: 246-47). Until otherwise noted, the following quotations are from this letter. It was published by the *MHM* under a caption indicating that the letter was "possibly" to William Knox, undersecretary of state. However, the letter appears to be the result of Germain's request to Boucher to provide him in writing with "a pretty copious detail of all my sentiments and advice" on the subject of America, following Boucher's introduction by William Eden to "Lord George Germain, the new American Secretary, who talked pretty fully to me concerning that country" (Boucher to James, 8 January 1776 [ibid., p. 344]).

3. There is no further reference to these projected letters in Boucher's writings, although material from them may have been included in a

"History of America," which he sent to the press in September 1779. There is no record of publication, and the book may have been suppressed, as was George Chalmer's *History*, which was published long after the war, in 1845.

4. A complete search of all available Boucher materials and all of those of Sir Grey Cooper in various repositories in England have failed to reveal either a copy or any further information about the plan. Perhaps the difficulty lies in the fact that Boucher had concealed his identity. For obvious reasons, Boucher wanted his plan for the future government of the colonies to be a "profound secret" (*MHM* 9 [1914]: 240).

5. Boucher to James, 18 January 1781, Boucher Manuscripts.

6. Boucher to James, 15 March 1781, Boucher Manuscripts.

7. There is no record of publication in the British Library catalog, and no further mention of it in any of Boucher's writings.

8. For an excellent account of the problems encountered by other exiles in England, see Mary Beth Norton, *The British-Americans: The Loyalist Exiles in England, 1774-1789* (Boston: Little, Brown and Company, 1972). According to Norton, only a · handful of the exiles "achieved the distinction of having private conversations with members of the administration" (pp. 45-46), one of whom was Boucher. He also had conversations with the bishop of London, the bishop of Bangor, and several with the earl of Dartmouth.

9. Norton, *British-Americans*, pp. 68-72. Boucher did not follow this general pattern. When he arrived he settled briefly in Westminster, a section in which the New England refugees of 1775 congregated. Thereafter he moved to Paddington, then a suburb, following his appointment as curate in Myles Cooper's place. However, within a short space of time he moved three times in the Paddington section. He seems not to have limited his friendships to those from the southern colonies, perhaps because of his wider acquaintance among the clergy and his Eden connections.

10. In the latter part of 1775 seven Anglican priests went to England: John Ross, Philip Walker, Henry Fendall, Jonathan Boucher, Henry Addison, Bennett Allen, and William Edmiston. David Love, rector of All Hallows', Anne Arundel County, was also a Tory, but thought these departures a mistake and seemingly cowardly; he stayed until 1780 (Rightmyer, *Maryland's Established Church*, p. 113). Boucher wrote to James on 8 January 1776 that he himself had seen fifteen or sixteen of the American clergy in London (*MHM* 8 [1913]: 344).

11. Apparently Boucher signed the articles with a pseudonym, since a check of the *Public Advertiser* for the last three months of 1775 does not reveal any articles or letters with his name. Several written anonymously could conceivably be his; for example, one signed "A Detester of Rebellion" (25 October 1775), and another without a signature, captioned "An Address to the People of Great Britain from the Oppressed Loyalists of America" (7 November 1775).

12. Quoted in Norton, *British-Americans*, p. 283, n. 31.

13. His total annual income by 22 June 1776 was between seventy and eighty pounds. He still had no pension. In a letter to Eden, Boucher stressed the difficulty of living on seventy pounds a year, and asked Eden's aid in requesting Lord George Germain for a further supply of money (*MHM* 9 [1914]: 61).

14. Boucher to James, ? December 1780; 11 September 1779; 20 July 1780, Boucher Manuscripts.

15. Boucher to James, 18 January 1781, Boucher Manuscripts.
16. Margaret Evans, ed., *Letters of Richard Radcliffe and John James of Queen's College, Oxford, 1755-1783*, Oxford Historical Society Collection Publication No. 9 (Oxford: Oxford University Press, 1888), p. 167. Samuel Seabury wrote Boucher in 1792 of affairs in the church in America, of the possible appointee to the position of bishop of Canada, and of the forthcoming election of a bishop for Maryland, lamenting, "I would to God you was there, or at least that they may get some good man to fill that office" (2 January 1792, Archives of the Church Historical Society, Austin, Texas). The major contender in the struggle for the post at Nova Scotia was Thomas Bradbury Chandler, whose poor health and return to New Jersey in 1785 put him out of the race. Boucher was next for consideration, but imposed provisions which the church refused to accommodate (Boucher to Seabury, 12 June 1786, Seabury Papers, General Theological Seminary, New York; Chandler to Seabury, 28 July 1785, ibid.; Chandler to Thomas Hutchinson, Jr., 30 March 1785, Hutchinson-Oliver Papers, Massachusetts Historical Society). James S. M. Anderson, writing in his *History of the Church of England in the Colonies and Foreign Dependencies of the British Empire* (London: Rivington's, 1856), wrote of Boucher's near appointment on the basis of unpublished letters from Chandler and others to Boucher which had been lent to him, but which are unidentified. For an account of the struggle for appointment see Judith Fingard, "The Establishment of the First Colonial English Episcopate," *Dalhousie Review* 47 (1967-68): 475-89.
17. John James, Jr. to Mrs. John James, 22 January 1782 (Evans, *Letters*, p. 187). John told his mother that if Mrs. Boucher were to "give up her place," Boucher would be "in danger perhaps" from her "gratitude."
18. See Appendix A and my account of the early aspects of this affair in chapter two. There is no explanation of why the children were known by the surname "Strange."
19. Boucher to James, 25 July 1769, Boucher Manuscripts. This and other personal business was contained in four pages of a lengthy letter which were not printed with the other pages of the letter when it was published (*MHM* 8 [1913]: 43-45).
20. Boucher to James, 11 September, 12 February 1780, Boucher Manuscripts. Kitty told John James some wild tale of adventure which presumably had occurred on her way to Windsor, but which Boucher found hard to believe.
21. Boucher to James, 27 April 1780, Boucher Manuscripts.
22. Boucher to James, ? December 1780, Boucher Manuscripts.
23. Boucher to James, 15 March 1781, Boucher Manuscripts.
24. The bequest was to "my dear and well-beloved Catherine Strange" (see Appendix A).
25. Boucher to James, 25 July 1769, Boucher Manuscripts.
26. MS 1265, Dulany Papers.
27. William Smallwood had been mentioned a number of times in Boucher's letters because of his connection with Judith Chase. He received a command when the first independent troops were raised in Maryland.
28. A. C. Hanson, *Laws of Maryland Made since 1762. Consisting of Acts of Assembly under the Proprietary Government, Resolves of Convention, the Constitution and Form of Government, the Articles of Confederation, and Acts of Assembly since the Revolution* (Annapolis: Frederick Green, 1787), chap. 20; Philip Crowl, *Maryland during and after the Revolu-*

tion (Baltimore: Johns Hopkins University Press, 1943); Rolfe Allen, "Legislation for the Confiscation of British and Loyalist Property during the Revolutionary War" (Ph.D. diss., University of Maryland, 1937).

29. Archives of Maryland, Brown Book, Liber 9, fol. 48, Annapolis Hall of Records. Other transactions are recorded in Land Office Records, Annapolis: CC No. 2, pp. 269-70, 662-63; Blue Book 5, item 58 (1778); Red Book 23, item 156 (1786) and item 157 (1787).

30. Archives of Maryland, Brown Book, Liber 9, fol. 48.

31. Ibid.

32. *Archives of Maryland*, 45: 677.

33. Records at the Maryland Historical Society and the Annapolis Hall of Records were searched for these letters, but none was found.

34. Boucher and Addison had been very close in Maryland, and the Addisons had lived with the Bouchers for some time after their arrival in London. The relationship deteriorated under Addison's constant demands for money, which Boucher could not always meet. Before Addison left England, the two had disagreed on arrangements to indemnify Boucher for Addison's debts to him, and had consulted an arbitrator who said Addison should give Boucher a bond. Addison was angered, but complied. Boucher was relieved when he left (Boucher to James, 14 August 1780, Boucher Manuscripts). Presumably Addison waited out the years of the war in Delaware, whose government had agreed to his presence in the state. He returned to his parish after the war and remained there until his death in 1789.

35. Samuel Chase was sent to England in 1783 as an agent of Maryland to recover stock in the Bank of England that had been purchased when Maryland was a British colony (*MHM* 12 [1917]: 208-9).

36. Boucher to the printer of the *Maryland Gazette*, 2 October 1783. This letter, together with a copy sent to Gen. John Cadwalader of Philadelphia, is in the Cadwalader Collection, Historical Society of Pennsylvania, Philadelphia. Until otherwise noted, the following quotations are from this letter. Boucher may have selected Cadwalader, a stranger to him, because he was a well-known general in the Continental army, and because he knew of him through his marriage to Elizabeth Lloyd of Maryland. Whether the letter was ever printed is still in doubt. A thorough search of the *Maryland Gazette* from October 1783 through June 1784 failed to find it; it may possibly have been printed elsewhere.

37. Boucher to James, 12 February 1780, Boucher Manuscripts.

38. Evans, *Letters*, pp. 65, 59-60.

39. Ibid., p. 207, says £20,000, but this is an obvious error. According to the Oxford Historical Society, the correct amount is £20.

40. Boucher to Elizabeth Hodgson, 28 February 1784, Boucher Manuscripts.

CHAPTER TEN

1. In spite of the lapse of time, Blencogo in 1972 still resembled Boucher's description. The hamlet consisted primarily of an intersection at which the parish church stood, the New Inn, and a few weatherbeaten stone cottages.

2. The epitaph appears as published in *CWAA Transactions*, n.s., 27

(1927): 142. Edward Jerningham was commissioned to complete the epitaph from lines and thoughts furnished by Boucher. The original was in Boucher's Paddington church, but is now lost.

3. Boucher's itinerary can be deduced from William Stevens's letters to Boucher, 27 August and 15 September 1784, Boucher Manuscripts; see also *Rem.*, pp. 172-73.

4. Boucher wrote of Stevens's friendship as "one of the prime blessings of my life" (*Rem.*, p. 146).

5. Stevens to Boucher, 30 November 1784, Boucher Manuscripts; the quotation from Parkhurst is from a "Life of Parkhurst" prefixed to his *A Hebrew and English Lexicon* (London: W. Faden, 1762); see also *Rem.*, p. x.

6. Bouch, "Jonathan Boucher," p. 133.

7. Stevens to Boucher, 12 September 1785, Boucher Manuscripts.

8. *A View*, p. 151.

9. William Cartwright to Boucher, n.d., Cartwright Letters, Montagu Manuscripts, Non-Juror Papers, Bodleian Library, Oxford. This letter is the first of a series from Cartwright to Boucher dating from 23 April 1785 to 20 September 1796. The approximately eighty pages of correspondence are valuable for information on the life and thought of Boucher during this period, particularly since the correspondence with James ceased with the death of James on 1 January 1785 and the *Reminiscences* cease with 1789.

10. The contents of Boucher's letter are known since Cartwright summarized them in his letter of 30 August 1784, intended for Seabury but directed to Rev. Thomas Bradbury Chandler (William Phillips, ed., "William Cartwright, Nonjuror, and his Chronological History of Shrewsbury," *Transactions of the Shropshire Archaeological Society*, ser. 4, 4: 1-30).

11. Cartwright to Boucher, 23 April 1785, Cartwright Letters.

12. Bishop Skinner to Boucher, n.d., Protestant Episcopal Church Archives.

13. Charles Inglis to Boucher, n.d., Protestant Episcopal Church Archives.

14. Cartwright to Boucher, 26 March 1787, Cartwright Letters.

15. Evans, *Letters*, pp. xi-xiii.

16. Stevens urged Boucher to accompany him on a business trip to Wales, with a stop at Bristol to see "the poor invalid" (Stevens to Boucher, 27 June 1786, Boucher Manuscripts).

17. Boucher and Mary Elizabeth Foreman drew up a prenuptial agreement; she was to have £20,000 of Boucher's assets if she survived him, to be at her disposal by will (*Rem.*, p. 183).

18. Cartwright to Boucher, 2 August 1788, Cartwright Letters.

19. Boucher to Sir Frederick Morton Eden, 16 September 1788, Boucher Manuscripts.

20. Boucher to James, 15 March 1781, Boucher Manuscripts.

21. Jonathan Boucher, "Parish of Caldbeck," in William Hutchinson, *History of the County of Cumberland . . .*, 2 vols. (Carlisle: F. Jollie, 1793-97), vol. 2. Boucher's tenant paid £71 17s. 4d., "customary fines, and on alienation an arbitrary fine. However, on the change of tenant by death, only a "*god's penny* [was to be paid]; and upon the death of the lord, nothing" (ibid., p. 379). Boucher's own copy of the *History* is heavily annotated, containing manuscript notes, interleaves, maps, and prints, and is so bulky that it now consists of seven sections. Boucher's copy was sold at Bath in 1871 with the effects of his deceased daughter Mary (Mrs. George Dixon), and soon afterward it was purchased from

Messrs. Thurman and Sons of Carlisle by Richard S. Ferguson, chancellor of Carlisle, and president and editor of the Cumberland and Westmorland Antiquarian and Archaeological Society. Ferguson was the grandson of Sir Richardson Hodgson, brother of Boucher's third wife, Elizabeth. The book is now catalogued in the Cumbria County Library under the caption: Ferguson's Copy of Hutchinson's *History*.

22. Jonathan Boucher, "Parish of Sebergham," in Hutchinson, *History*, 2: 413.

23. A nine-page will drawn up by Boucher in 1797 indicates that he had accumulated a substantial estate (Principal Probate Registry, Somerset House, London, fols. 378-1804). Elizabeth was named executrix and inherited the full estate other than small bequests to his two nieces and to friends (Prerogative Court of Canterbury, Abstract of Probates of Wills, June 1804, IR 26/88, pp. 10-11).

24. Boucher informed Stevens that he intended to spend the winter at Epsom (Stevens to Boucher, 4 November 1788, Boucher Manuscripts).

25. Pitt's plan as discussed in the House of Commons on 6 June 1788 appeared in the *Annual Register* for 1788, pp. 136-39. Boucher attested to the good character and losses of several other exiles.

26. Sir Frederick Morton Eden, *The State of the Poor,* 3 vols. (London: J. Davis for B. & J. White, 1797).

27. Elizabeth was born 20 October 1761 and baptized at Saint Mary's in Carlisle. Her father, Richard, was a mercer; her brother became the mayor of Carlisle in 1797 and was knighted.

28. Stevens was eager to hear of progress, and wrote Boucher to inquire about "what passed between you and the widow" (Stevens to Boucher, 30 July 1789, Boucher Manuscripts).

29. James first married Mary Anne Blenkerne, a widow and daughter of Christopher Colclough, in 1815; he married Jane Houston, daughter of the Hon. Andrew Houston of Grenada, in 1820. One of his sons was Jonathan Boucher, later Bouchier, editor of the *Reminiscences*. James became provost marshal of Grenada. He was buried on the Isle of Man 21 January 1852.

30. Boucher to Jerningham, 15 November 1790, Huntington Library, San Marino, California. This was Boucher's second commission to Jerningham. Jerningham dabbled in poetry throughout his long life, but did not please the public until he wrote a poem in recommendation of the Foundling Hospital. In general, his poems were severely satirized. He may best be remembered for his arrangement of the royal library at the Brighton Pavilion, and for his friendship with Lords Chesterfield, Harcourt, and Carlisle, and with Horace Walpole.

31. Ann was baptized on 22 November 1791, married Lt. Joseph Taylor on 30 August 1811, and died without issue the following year. Eleanor Mary Elizabeth married Edward Locker in 1815 and six children were born to them. One of her children, Frederick Locker-Lampson, lent several of Washington's letters to his grandfather Jonathan to Thackeray when that author was writing *Henry Esmond* (Frederick Locker-Lampson, *My Confidences: An Autobiographical Sketch Addressed to My Descendants* [London: Smith, Elder & Co., 1896], pp. 4, n. 1, 10, 36-37, 344). Jane was baptized 17 November 1794 and died in London in 1810, aged sixteen, of "inflammation of the lungs." Elizabeth was baptized 7 June 1797, and married Edward James, a distant relative of Dr. John James, on 30 December 1817. They had eleven children. Mary was baptized 5 June 1799, and married George Dixon of Blencogo on 5 April 1836. They had twin sons, both of whom died within hours of

their birth on 27 April 1838. Mary died in 1871 and was buried at Bromfield. Barton was baptized on 4 April 1796. He became the vicar of Fonthill, Wiltshire, and married Mary, the daughter of the Reverend N. Thornbury, and died without issue on 20 December 1865.

32. Boucher to Eden, 23 April 1794, Boucher Manuscripts.
33. Frederick Locker-Lampson, *My Confidences*, p. 38. The descriptions of his mother, Eleanor Mary Elizabeth, are those which he heard from his aunts in Carlisle and elsewhere.
34. Eleanor recalled her childhood at "the Epsom Parsonage," which undoubtedly referred to the home at Clay Hill.

CHAPTER ELEVEN

1. [Jonathan Boucher], "A Chapter on the Secret History of Hutchinson's Cumberland," n.d., Cumbria County Library; hereafter "Secret History." It was probably written in 1793. All quotations until otherwise noted are from this manuscript.
2. *Monthly Review* 21 (September 1796): 30; 22 (March 1797): 328; 26 (May 1798): 366. The *History* was published in four parts, and reviewed at various times. Twenty-five sketches appear anonymously, including those of Isaac Ritson, Thomas Bacon, Archbishop Grindall, Thomas Wren, Thomas Tickell, John Leake, Rev. Thomas Robinson, Josiah Relph, and Dr. John Brown. It is also probable that Boucher wrote the sketch on Myles Cooper, according to marginal indications in Boucher's own copy. He was pleased that the *History* published accounts of low and poor persons, including schoolmasters. "If the notice here taken of this highly meritorious class of citizens may have the effect of procuring them somewhat more of respect and reward, we shall be happy" ("Secret History").
3. "The Suppressed Life [of Sir Wallace]," attached to the "Secret History."
4. R. S. Ferguson, "Explicatio," interleaved in Hutchinson, *History*, vol. 1. From the editorial statement in the *History*, we can substantiate as the work of Boucher only the histories of Bromfield, Sebergham, and Caldbeck. However, it is probable that he did many more, including those marked in the margin of his own copy, and supported by internal evidence.
5. A Cumberland Man [pseud.], *Address to the Inhabitants of the County of Cumberland* (Whitehaven: December 1792). The social ideas expressed in the pamphlet are dealt with in chapter twelve. A complete copy is included as Appendix 19 in Eden's *State of the Poor*, to which Boucher contributed much information.
6. Stanzas 2-4; the poem is interleaved in Boucher's copy of Hutchinson's *History*. Boucher was apparently imitating "A Merry Ballad of the Hawthorne Tree," in Ritson's *Ancient Songs*.
7. See Appendix B.
8. Jefferson to Boucher, 31 October 1797, Joseph Jefferson Letters, Southampton University, England. This series of eighteen letters from Jefferson to Boucher began on 31 October 1797 and continued to 18 April 1804. The information on Jefferson is based on internal evidence in the letters; he does not appear in the *Dictionary of National Biography*.

9. Jefferson to Boucher, 16 December 1797, Jefferson Letters.
10. Ibid.
11. Jefferson to Boucher, 2 May 1798, Jefferson Letters.
12. Ibid.
13. Daubeny to Boucher, 7 May 1798, Boucher Manuscripts.
14. Daubeny to Boucher, 10 April 1799, Boucher Manuscripts. In July 1799 Daubeny had his publisher, John Hatchard, send six copies to Boucher for distribution to his friends at Shrewsbury, to Bishop Skinner of Aberdeen and his father, and to Rev. Dr. George Gleig, later bishop of Brechin.
15. Daubeny to Boucher, 23 October 1799, Boucher Manuscripts. Daubeny kept his word and advised Boucher in January 1800 that the annual fees had nearly doubled at Winchester since his own time, and were now sixty pounds, which he feared would lead to "less learning in the Church" (Daubeny to Boucher, 7 January, 28 January 1800). The request was probably on behalf of James, then nine years old, but the records of Winchester College fail to reveal an application or an admission for James Boucher for 1799-1800. Daubeny had urged Boucher to enroll the boy immediately.
16. Daubeny to Boucher, 7 May 1798, Boucher Manuscripts.
17. Daubeny to Boucher, 10 April, 24 September 1799, Boucher Manuscripts.
18. Daubeny to Boucher, 7 November, 27 February 1800, Boucher Manuscripts.
19. Stevens to Boucher, 21 November 1793, Boucher Manuscripts.
20. Boucher wished to return to the Edens' house because there was smallpox in his usual lodging in London, Gray's Inn, and he feared exposing one of his children who had not yet had the disease. He also thanked Eden for "seasonable and substantial kindness" which "will make me . . . a free man for at least a year to come" (Boucher to Eden, 20 March 1794, Boucher Manuscripts). Eden may have repaid his father's debt.
21. Boucher to Eden, n.d., Boucher Manuscripts. The letter was written prior to 12 March 1798, Boucher's sixtieth birthday.
22. Stevens to Boucher, 5 September 1798, Boucher Manuscripts.
23. Jonathan Boucher, A Sermon Preached at the Assizes Held at Guildford, July 30, 1798 (London: J. Plymsell, 1798), British Library. See the review in Monthly Review 29 (May 1799): 117, which gives the date of delivery as 8 July 1798. 30 July is probably correct.
24. Stevens to Boucher, 5 September 1798, Boucher Manuscripts.
25. Ibid.
26. Jonathan Boucher, A Sermon Preached at the Assizes Held at Carlisle, August 12, 1798 (Carlisle: privately printed, 1798), Sterling Memorial Library, Yale University. The assizes sermons were reviewed together in Monthly Review 29 (May 1799): 117.
27. Jefferson to Boucher, 9 August 1798, Boucher Manuscripts.
28. Jefferson to Boucher, 23 April 1800, Jefferson Letters. My attempt to verify Boucher's tenancy or ownership at Holme Hill (Hawkes-dale District) and Coledale Hall (Caldewgate District) failed because no tax records exist for 1799-1804, according to the Cumbria County Record Office, Carlisle Castle. A search at the Public Record Office, London, was also futile.
29. Stevens to Boucher, 5 September 1798, Boucher Manuscripts.
30. Boucher to Eden, 16 October 1798, Boucher Manuscripts. The year is faded in the letter, but it is undoubtedly 1798.

31. Ibid. Boucher thought the verses were all original, but liked best one which he thought contained his "real handmark," and was good-natured. It does express his concern over the undeveloped lake region which seemed to him to lack inhabitants with the talent and application he saw in Scotland. He also had a little more fun at the expense of the Scotsmen:

> Bare and bleak are Scotland's hills
> And almost bare her plains
> Bare-legged more than half her nymphs
> And bare-a——'d all her swains.

32. Jefferson to Boucher, 15 November 1798, Jefferson Letters.
33. Boucher to Douglas, 9 February 1800, Egerton Manuscripts, British Library.
34. Stevens to Boucher, 21 April 1800, Boucher Manuscripts.
35. The *Carlisle Journal* for 2 February 1923 indicated that Boucher moved to Carlisle in 1799. He may have been spending part of his time there, but it is clear that his correspondents were addressing him at Epsom throughout 1799 and until his death in April 1804. It is also clear that Boucher was still preaching in his pulpit at Epsom in 1802 and in the autumn of 1803, although he may have been preaching only occasionally ("W. B.," letter to the editor, *Gentleman's Magazine* 95 [1804]: 740). Boucher's service to the Epsom church began 20 January 1785, and records indicate that he died 26 April 1804 (should be 27 April), presumably while he was still in the rectorship. His successor, Fleetwood Parkhurst, a relative of the patron of Epsom, John Parkhurst, began his incumbency 16 July 1804.
36. Stevens to Boucher, 7 September 1801, Boucher Manuscripts.
37. Ibid.
38. Jefferson to Boucher, 9 April 1804, Jefferson Letters. Jefferson took in eight boarding students and six others by the day.
39. Boucher to Douglas, 9, 26 February 1800, Egerton Manuscripts.
40. Stevens to Boucher, 1 September 1801, Boucher Manuscripts.

CHAPTER TWELVE

1. On the basis of Boucher's comments to James, one cannot ignore the possibility that some of the sermons may have been written by James. It is more probable that all of the sermons are Boucher's work. James may have thought the original request either unethical or too time-consuming, and therefore avoided answering at all in order to spare Boucher some embarrassment. Possibly James replied negatively through his son John, and Boucher tactfully dropped the matter until 1781. The gaps in correspondence may be accounted for by the fact that young John James was a frequent guest of the Bouchers at the Hermitage, and carried the manuscript and messages between the Bouchers and his parents. There are no credit lines to James in the book as it was finally published; in the absence of any evidence to the contrary, the sermons must be presumed to be Boucher's.
2. Boucher to James, 9 September 1781, Boucher Manuscripts.
3. The following interpretation of the dating of the sermons was advanced

in Anne Y. Zimmer and Alfred H. Kelly, "Jonathan Boucher: Constitutional Conservative," *Journal of American History* 58 (1972): 899-902. See Appendix B for more detailed evidence of the misdating of sermons.

4. Boucher to James, 9 September 1781, Boucher Manuscripts.

5. Boucher's plan was based on one advanced by Sir John Dalrymple in 1788, which Boucher thought had political wisdom, but which had been generally neglected by both politicians and the public. See Sir John Dalrymple, *Memoirs of Great Britain and Ireland*, 2 vols. (London: W. Straham and T. Cadell, 177-88), 2: Appendix, p. 42.

6. Ford, *Letters*, p. 53.

7. "Beggar of tobacco" was a derogatory term for a merchant who purchased tobacco in quantity.

8. Cobbett to Boucher, 24 August 1798, Locker-Lampson Papers. Boucher ordered the works of Peter Porcupine from his bookseller (Boucher to unknown correspondent, 19 February 1798, Montagu Manuscripts, Bodleian Library).

9. Stevens to Boucher, 5 September 1798, Boucher Manuscripts. The first review, signed "A. R.," was probably by Anthony Robinson (*Analytical Review* 27 [January 1798]: 36-41).

10. Unsigned review, *Monthly Review* 29 (August 1799): 369-72.

11. *Gentleman's Magazine* 69 (November 1799): 953-56.

12. Michael D. Clark agrees with this recognition of the stages of development in Boucher's thought, noting: "His political views had by no means fitted the stereotype of blind reaction into which some historians have tried to place them;" he describes Boucher as "less the picture of sour reaction than of stout eighteenth-century vigor" ("Jonathan Boucher: The Mirror of Reaction," *Huntington Library Quarterly* 33 [1969-70]: 19-20). A full examination of the reasons for the abrupt shift in Boucher's attitudes in Maryland first appeared in Anne Y. Zimmer, "Jonathan Boucher, Moderate Loyalist and Public Man" (Ph.D. diss., Wayne State University, 1966). Clark has also recognized the element of chance, "which more than anything placed him in a position which required him to define his political philosophy and to define it in a certain way" (p. 20). He further states (p. 22) that "from the time of his departure from America in 1775 until his death in 1804 he did not substantially modify" his political philosophy, which had crystallized in the revolutionary crisis, a conclusion with which I do not agree.

Clark, along with some other writers in the last decade, has recognized that Boucher, as well as other Loyalists, approved of American objections and measures against the Stamp Act and also voiced his disapproval of the Townshend Acts (Clark, "Jonathan Boucher," p. 21; see also Philip Evanson, "Jonathan Boucher: The Mind of an American Loyalist," *MHM* 58 [1963]: 123-36). Evanson's article contains some factual errors about Boucher's life, and an interpretation of his personality with which I disagree. Boucher's parish at Annapolis was Saint Anne's, not Queen Anne's, and his preface to *A View* does acknowledge that revolutions sometimes bring improvements in government (Evanson, "Jonathan Boucher," pp. 126, 131). It is difficult to think of Boucher's mind as "uncomplicated" (p. 130), and to give full credit to the assertion, "Unlike Franklin, who assiduously sought self-improvement, Boucher aimed for the time when neither cares nor wants nor striving for self-improvement would disturb his peace of mind" (p. 123). Although Boucher admitted that "both young and old I was naturally lazy and

371

hated work" (*Rem.*, p. 10), it would be incautious to take his words without balancing them against his actions.

13. Boucher to Sir Frederick Morton Eden, 8 January 1794, Boucher Manuscripts.

14. Boucher, *Sermon Preached at . . . Guildford.*

15. Benjamin Wright, *Consensus and Continuity: 1776-1787* (New York: W. W. Norton & Co., 1967), p. 53. My opinion of Boucher's essentially Whig frame of reference is shared by Mary Beth Norton, "The Loyalist Critique of the Revolution," in *The Development of a Revolutionary Mentality* (Washington, D.C.: Library of Congress, 1972).

16. Boucher quoted Burke at length in his footnotes to the sermons. He also relied on Hobbes, David Hume, William Blackstone, classical authors, and a host of religious writers.

17. Winfred Bernhard, *Fisher Ames, Federalist and Statesman: 1758-1808* (Chapel Hill: University of North Carolina Press, 1965), pp. 48, 49. Ames held views much like Boucher's on several other subjects. For example, he believed that people en masse were often blind and credulous, given to "sudden passions and ignorant prejudices," and that laws must be "irresistibly supreme" (ibid., pp. 50, 51). Ames refused to defend either extreme in government, and criticized those who had given up on republican principles and were extolling the virtues of monarchy "as if we were willing to take from the plough-tail or dramshop some vociferous committee-man, and to array him in royal purple, with all the splendor of a king of the gypsies." The presumption was, he thought, "that our king, whenever Providence in its wrath shall send us one, will be a blockhead or a rascal" (ibid., p. 51).

18. Richard Hofstadter, *The Idea of a Party System: The Rise of Legitimate Opposition in the United States, 1780-1840* (Berkeley: University of California Press, 1969), pp. 34-39, 31-110.

19. Quoted in Page Smith, *John Adams: 1735-1784* (Garden City: Doubleday & Co., Inc., 1962), p. 463.

20. Hofstadter, *Idea of a Party System*, pp. 122-69.

21. Peter Laslett, ed., *Patriarcha and Other Political Works of Sir Robert Filmer* (Oxford: Clarendon Press, 1949).

22. Clark states that Boucher did not agree with Hobbes's picture of human nature and society: "But although Hobbes's support of constituted authority was acceptable to Boucher, his picture of society was not. In one of his few allusions to Hobbes, Boucher recoiled from the notion that man in a state of nature was fiercer than wolves or bears were to each other. If Hobbes's assessment of human nature was correct, Boucher remarked, one might well exclaim, with the Prophet, 'Woe is me, my mother, that thou hast borne me a man of strife, and a man of contention to the whole earth!' " (Clark, "Jonathan Boucher," p. 29, quoting *A View*, p. 332). Other statements that Boucher held an opinion of human nature similar to that of Hobbes lead me to think that Clark may have misread Boucher's comment. He is not disagreeing with Hobbes's view, but agreeing with dismay. See also *A View*, pp. 62, 84, 172-73, 247, 523, for example; his opinion of human nature is consistently Hobbesian.

23. Boucher, *Letter from a Virginian*, p. 8.

24. Boucher, *Sermon Preached at . . . Guildford*, p. 17.

25. Bernhard, *Fisher Ames*, p. 51.

26. Evans, *Letters*, p. 127.

27. Quoted in Jacob E. Cooke, ed., *Alexander Hamilton: A Profile* (New York: Hill and Wang, 1968), p. 20, n. 31.

28. Ibid., p. 160. Later, with the rise of Jeffersonian republicanism in America, Boucher himself recognized the conservatism in the position of Washington and Adams, and took pleasure in it (*MHM* 10 [1915]: 125-26).
29. For an extended treatment of Boucher's concern for minority rights, see Robert G. Walker, "Jonathan Boucher: Champion of the Minority," *William and Mary Quarterly*, ser. 3, 2 (1945): 3-14. Michael Clark believes that the case for Boucher's toleration has been overstressed. His real purpose, in Clark's opinion, was to persuade the Maryland Catholics to be loyal to Britain and to rebuff the Patriots if the neutrality he preferred became impossible. Clark refers to the Zimmer-Kelly article in the *Journal of American History* which states that the sermons were in part reconstructions and in part newly written in England. However, he based his article, "Jonathan Boucher and the Toleration of Roman Catholics in Maryland" (*MHM* 71 [1976]: 194-203), on an incorrect premise: "They do not suggest that any alterations were made in the sermon 'On the Toleration of Papists,'" (p. 194). Boucher's motive during reconstruction in 1797 would have been different.
30. Boucher explained the liberal attitude he had expressed in America in letters to James in the wake of the Stamp Act and Townshend Acts as follows: "Contented to swim with the stream, . . . I embraced those doctrines which are most flattering to human pride, and most natural to a youthful mind." He quoted Xenophon: "'I thought it a noble thing both to be free myself and to leave liberty to my children.' And mistaking the imposter Licentiousness, the enemy of law, for that constitutional liberty, the child of law, and its surest defense, I joined a giddy and dangerous multitude in declaiming, as loud as the loudest in behalf of liberty and against tyranny. I, too, bowed at the altar of liberty, and sacrificed to this idol of our groves" (*A View*, p. 590). Boucher subscribed to a publication of lectures on civil and religious liberty, and allowed his name to be included with those "Given in to the Author, who have not forbidden their Names to be published" (Rev. David Williamson, ed., *Lectures on Civil and Religious Liberty: with Reflections on the Constitutions of France and England; and on the Violent Writers, Who Have Distinguished Themselves in the Controversy About their Comparative Goodness: and Particularly Mr. Burke and Mr. Paine* . . . [London: J. Johnson, St. Paul's Church Yard; T. Evans, Pater-Noster-Row; T. Cadell, Strand; and J. Stockdale, Piccadilly, n.d.], Cumbria County Library, Carlisle).
31. Without obedience, the whole fabric could be destroyed. Paraphrasing Epaminondas, the Greek who was praised for his leadership, Boucher pointed out that Epaminondas had deflected that praise, saying that it was not solely his own effort, but depended on his people who made his success possible because they "obeyed well" (ibid., p. 311).
32. Passive resistance was a major theme of Boucher's sermon, "On Civil Liberty, Passive Obedience, and Non-Resistance" *A View*, pp. 495-560. He did not think it a servile and degrading principle, nor did he think that he had at any time subscribed to the principle of unlimited obedience, of which he was often accused.
33. Boucher drew upon a variety of sources. Indeed he seems to have ignored only the Puritan revolutionaries and their Whig liberal successors.
34. Boucher's brand of conservatism is still found in America. "If legitimate authority above us all is removed, society breaks up, for all we have left is contending groups that tear each other to pieces. Respect for legiti-

mate and constituted authority is the cement of society" (The Right Reverend Richard S. Emrich, "The Decline of Authority," *The Detroit News*, 22 May 1966).

35. Quoted in Paul Duke, "Jonathan Boucher, Tory Parson, Teacher and Political Theorist" (Ph.D. diss., University of Washington, 1956), p. 58.
36. Ibid., p. 107.
37. Rev. John James carried on correspondence on the same subject with Richard Radcliffe, also a Queen's College man. Radcliffe wrote: "Nothing, however, in my humble opinion, is more absurd and ridiculous than to keep a boy six or seven years at a Grammar School, and then condemn him to the sea or the counter." Without competence in a language and constant use of Greek and Latin, "in a few years" a boy "will know no more of them than my dog does" (Evans, *Letters*, p. 19).
38. Ford, *Letters*, p. 10.
39. Ibid., p. 9.
40. "The Parish of Bromfield," in Hutchinson, *History*, 2: 313. Boucher was describing education in the free school at Bromfield where he first formally studied Latin.
41. The Quebec Act was passed by Parliament in 1774 to improve the administration of the old French North American empire which was acquired at the Treaty of Paris of 1763. The original arrangements had proved less than satisfactory. In addition to liberalizing the oath of loyalty requirements of the French people in Canada, the Quebec Act incensed the colonists because it extended the southern boundary of Quebec Province down to the Ohio River.
42. Thomas Sanderson commented that this description more justly referred to the northern and eastern extremities of the county, areas of great poverty (Rev. R. J. Lothian, *The Life and Literary Remains of Thomas Sanderson* [Carlisle: B. Scott and John Richardson, 1829], p. 273). Sanderson wrote a highly complimentary poem on Boucher's loyalty to England and his public spirit, entitled "Epistle to the Reverend Jonathan Boucher, M. A. on his Arrival in Cumberland from America" (ibid., pp. 48-59).
43. *An Address to the Inhabitants of the Parish of Epsom With a Plan for a Soup-Establishment* (Southwark: Philanthropic Reform, St. George's Fields, J. Richardson, 1800). The *Address* is dated 27 December 1799.
44. "The Parish of Bromfield," in Hutchinson, *History*, 2: 323-24.

CHAPTER THIRTEEN

1. Boucher's introduction to the *Glossary*, p. lxiii (first published in full in Joseph Hunter and Joseph Stevenson, eds., *Boucher's Glossary of Archaic and Provincial Words: A Supplement to the Dictionaries of the English Language, Particularly those of Dr. Johnson and Dr. Webster* [London: Black, Young & Young, 1833]; hereafter "Introduction").
2. Ibid., p. lxiii. Quotations until otherwise noted are from this source.
3. Jefferson to Boucher, 23 February 1798, Jefferson Letters.
4. Jonathan Boucher, *Proposals for Printing by Subscription in Two Volumes, Quarto: Linguae Anglicanae Veteris Thesaurus; or, A Glossary of the Ancient English Language, in Two Parts: . . .* (London: Luke Han-

sard, Great Turnstile, Lincoln's Inn Fields, 1801-2), p. 13 (hereafter *Proposals*).

5. Boucher, "Introduction," p. xx. Quotations until otherwise noted are from this source.

6. Jefferson to Boucher, 23 February 1798, Jefferson Letters.

7. Boucher to unknown correspondent, 2 January 1802, Letters of English Clergymen, Ferdinand Dreer Collection, Historical Society of Pennsylvania.

8. Jonathan Boucher, *Preparing for the Press: A Provincial Glossary*, stitched into *Sermon Preached at Carlisle*, pp. 21-24.

9. Jefferson to Boucher, 17 February 1801, Jefferson Letters.

10. Boucher to unknown correspondent, 30 July 1801, Letters of English Clergymen. The correspondent might be Rev. Francis Leighton of Shrewsbury, or the Reverend Blakeway of the same town, both of whom rendered assistance in critical revision and correction of the manuscript. Others who helped were the duke of Somerset and Sir Frederick Morton Eden.

11. Jefferson to Boucher, 20 December 1802, Jefferson Letters.

12. Boucher also aided in a publication, *Beauties of England and Wales*, and in 1803 he read and criticized the manuscript of Charles Daubeny's *Guide to the Church* (Jefferson to Boucher, 20 December 1802, Jefferson Letters: Daubeny to Boucher, 11 July 1803, Boucher Manuscripts). Daubeny also told Boucher of the prospect of a stall for Boucher at Durham.

13. Jefferson to Boucher, 15 November 1798, Jefferson Letters. These are not the same sermons as those delivered at Carlisle and Guildford; Jefferson indicated that he already had copies of those and had lent them to a clerical friend. Apparently the nonpolitical sermons were never published.

14. Boucher, "Introduction," p. lxiii.

15. Boucher to unknown correspondent, 20 June 1803, Simon Gratz Collection of Letters of the American Clergy, Historical Society of Pennsylvania.

16. Advertisement, *A Supplement to Dr. Johnson's Dictionary of the English Language: or, A Glossary of Obsolete and Provincial Words. By the Late Rev. Jonathan Boucher, A.M., Vicar of Epsom, in the County of Surry* [sic]. *Part the First.* (London: Longman, Hurst, Rees, and Orme, Paternoster Row, 1807). This is a much shortened version of the first advertisement, and makes clear that the people on the list of 800 subscribers of 1801-2, who anticipated a complete work, were not automatically assumed to be interested in the partial work which Boucher's family attempted to have published in 1807.

17. Boucher, "Introduction," p. lxiv.

18. Charles Dickens, "As the Crow Flies: Due South, Epsom to Box Hill," *All the Year Round*, n. s., vol. 2, no. 40 (4 September 1869), p. 321.

19. The six stanzas appeared under the caption "Written on a fine Autumnal Evening in 1803 at Epsom in Surrey, after hearing a sermon preached by the Rev. Jonathan Boucher, late vicar of that parish, who was then in a declining state of health," and were signed "W.B." (*Gentleman's Magazine* 95 [July-December 1804]: 760). His letter to the editor explaining the circumstances of his having known the Boucher family appeared in the same issue (p. 740).

20. Jefferson to Boucher, 18 April 1804, Jefferson Letters.

21. The reference to the cause of death is from Bouch, "Jonathan Boucher," p. 137.

22. The last entry on the Bromfield memorial is that of Elizabeth, Boucher's

third wife, who died 12 October 1846, aged eighty-five, at Seagrave Rectory, Leicestershire, the home of her first child, Mary Ann James Gutch, her husband the Reverend Robert Gutch, rector of Seagrave, and their ten children.

23. The provincial section of Boucher's work had been completed from *A* to *Thirlage* and the archaeological part from *A* to *Gib*. Boucher family friends arranged to publish the work from the letter *A* through *Aynd*. With the urging of the poet Southey that the Royal Society of Literature should purchase the manuscript and attempt to complete it, it received some attention which may have led to the publication by Hunter and Stevens in 1833.

24. I am grateful to John Syrad of Epsom, who furnished valuable information from church records and photographs of the Boucher memorial in Saint Martin's Church, and to the vicar of Saint Martin's Church, Epsom.

◡ *Bibliography* ◡

WRITINGS BY AND ATTRIBUTED TO BOUCHER

[A Cumberland Man.] "Address to the Inhabitants of the County of Cumberland." Whitehaven: 1792. In Sir Frederick Morton Eden, *The State of the Poor.*

An Address to the Inhabitants of the Parish of Epsom, with a Plan for a Soup-Establishment. Southwark: Philanthropic Reform, St. George's Fields, J. Richardson, 1800.

[Camillo Querno, Poet Laureate.] *The American Times: A Satire in Three Parts in which Are Delineated the Characters of the Leaders of the American Rebellion. Amongst the Principals are: Franklin, Laurens, Adams, Hancock, Jay, Duer, Duane, Wilson, Pulaski, Witherspoon, Reed, M'Kean, Washington, Roberdeau, Morris, Chase, etc.* In John Andre, *The Cow Chace.* New York: James Rivington, 1780.

[Unsigned.] "Biographia Cumbriensis." In William Hutchinson, *History of the County of Cumberland, and some places adjacent, from the earliest accounts to the recent time: Comprehending the local history of the county, its antiquities, the origin, the genealogy and the present state of the principal families, with biographical notes; its mines, minerals, and plants, with other curiosities, either of nature or of art. . . .* 2 vols. Carlisle: F. Jollie, 1793-97. Reprinted in two volumes, East Ardsley, Wakefield, Yorkshire: E. P. Publishing, Ltd., in collaboration with the Cumbria County Library, 1974. Boucher's personal copy has been expanded by interleaving into seven sections.

[Unsigned.] "A Character in Real Life in the Manner of Swift on Stella." 6 September 1776. Boucher Manuscripts.

[Unsigned.] "A Chapter on the Secret History of Hutchinson's Cumberland." n.d. Interleaved in Boucher's copy of Hutchinson's *History.*

Glossary of Archaic and Provincial Words, edited by the Reverend Joseph Hunter, F. S. A., with Large Additions Principally from Early Manuscript Authorities by Joseph Stevenson, Esq. Forming a Supplement to the Dictionaries of the English Language, Particularly those of Dr. Johnson and Dr. Webster. Parts 1-2; A-Blade. London: Black, Young & Young, Covent Garden, 1833.

[Unsigned.] Letter. *Virginia Gazette,* 25 July 1766.

[Unsigned.] "On a Picture of Mrs. Peale." *Maryland Gazette,* 18 April 1771.

[Unsigned.] Parish Histories. In William Hutchinson, *History . . . of Cumberland.* (Boucher wrote the Bromfield, Caldbeck, and Sebergham histories, according to the editor of the reprint of Hutchinson's book. However, internal evidence and the marginal indications in Boucher's own copy of the *History* suggest that he also wrote the histories of Saint Bees, Penrith, and Wigton.)

"Pastoral." In Boucher's *Glossary,* preface.

"Petition of Their Old Church." *Maryland Gazette,* 5 September 1771.

[Unsigned.] "Preparing for the Press: A Provincial Glossary." In Jonathan Boucher, *A Sermon Preached at the Assizes Held at the City of Carlisle, August 12, 1798.*

Proposals for Printing by Subscription, in Two volumes, Quarto, Linguae Anglicanae Veteris Thesaurus; or A Glossary of the Ancient English Language, in Two Parts: The First Comprising Provincialisms, or Such old Words as still exist in the various Dialects of the Provinces; And The Second, Such Archaisms, Or Old Words, As, Being Lost Even to the Provinces, Are Now To Be Found Only in Old English and Scotish [sic] Writers: Intended to be a Supplement to Dr. Johnson's Dictionary; And, in Conjunction With That Work, To Exhibit A Complete View of the Whole English Language. London: Luke Hansard, Great Turnstile, Lincoln's Inn Fields, 1801-2.

"Quaeries Addressed to the People of Maryland." In *Reminiscences,* pp. 128-30.

[Unsigned.] *Remarks on the Travels of the Marquis de Chastellux in North America.* London: G. & T. Wilkie in St. Paul's Churchyard, 1787.

Reminiscences of an American Loyalist, 1738-1789. Being the Autobiography of the Reverend Jonathan Boucher, Rector of Annapolis in Maryland and Afterwards Vicar of Epsom, Surrey, England. Edited by Jonathan Bouchier. Boston: Houghton Mifflin Co., 1925. Reprinted Port Washington, New York: Kennikat Press, 1967.

A Sermon Preached at the Assizes Held at the City of Carlisle, August 12, 1798. Carlisle: Printed for the Author by the Executors of the late W. Halhead, 1798.

A Sermon Preached at the Assizes Held at Guildford, July the 30th, 1798 Before the Right Honourable Lord Chief Justice Kenyon and the Honourable Sir Francis, Bart. London: J. Plymsell, 1978.

"Song for the Homony Club." Homony Club Folio, Historical Society of Pennsylvania, pp. 144-45.

[Unsigned.] "To Miss Hallam." *Maryland Gazette,* 6 September 1770.

[Unsigned.] "To Miss Hallam." *Maryland Gazette,* 10 October 1771.

"To the Hon[ora]ble the Deputies in Congress from the Southern Provinces." In *Reminiscences,* pp. 130-36. (Boucher indicated that this piece was published in New York by James Rivington's *Gazette,* 1775. However, the pamphlet has not been found, nor has a charge for it been located in Rivington's account books. He apparently did not print it in his *Gazette.*

"To the Printer of the *Maryland Gazette.*" Series of seven letters attacking and counterattacking critics (primarily Samuel Chase and William Paca) on the issue of clerical salaries and the establishment of the church. Boucher to Paca and Chase, 31 December 1772; 4 February; 15, 29 April 1773. Boucher to Paca, 4, 18 March; 1 April 1773.

[Unsigned.] Untitled verses on Scottish manners and dress. In a letter to Sir Frederick Morton Eden from Carlisle, 16 October 1798. Boucher Manuscripts.

[Unsigned.] "Verses to an old Hawthorne Tree." Interleaved in Boucher's copy of Hutchinson's *History*.

A *View of the Causes and Consequences of the American Revolution; in Thirteen Discourses, Preached in North America between the Years 1763 and 1775: with an Historical Preface*. London: C. G. and J. Robinson, Paternoster Row, 1797. Reproduced from the original edition of 1797 and published, New York: Russell & Russell, 1967.

MANUSCRIPT COLLECTIONS

ANNAPOLIS, MARYLAND. HALL OF RECORDS

The Archives of Maryland include the originals of the official colonial records: laws, proceedings of the executive council and the assembly, proprietary papers, wills and inventories, church records, court records, and county records. References to and actions against Boucher are scattered throughout volumes designated as the "Rainbow Series," but primarily in the Red, Brown, and Blue Books. The Brown Books and the Prince George's County Court records were most helpful in tracing Boucher's problems in Maryland through the actions taken against him or his estate. The records of the Land Office were particularly valuable for knowledge of his western land holdings.

Cotton Manuscripts. Includes the Eden Papers, correspondence to, from, and regarding Robert Eden.

ANN ARBOR, MICHIGAN. UNIVERSITY OF MICHIGAN

William Clements Library. Stopford-Sackville Collection. Contains Boucher's letter to Lord Germain.

Graduate Library. Letter, Bihop Samuel Seabury to Boucher.

AUSTIN, TEXAS

Archives and Historical Collections of the Protestant Episcopal Church. The Francis L. Hawks and General Convention Collection of Early Episcopal Church Manuscripts, 1650-1850. Includes correspondence between Boucher and Bishop John Skinner, a letter from Boucher to William Smith, Philadelphia, and letters of Myles Cooper to William Smith and Samuel Peters.

BALTIMORE, MARYLAND. MARYLAND HISTORICAL SOCIETY

Maryland Diocesan Archives, on deposit in the Maryland Historical Society. Records of the clergy of Maryland, 1695-1773. Also includes miscellaneous minor Boucher items.

Addison Papers, Manuscript Collection 3. References to Boucher.

Callister Papers. Consists of about 800 documents, including Henry Callister's correspondence from 1742 to 1766, enlightening on social and economic conditions of life below that of the gentry. Also contains letters on the subject of the established church.

Calvert Papers, Manuscript Collection 174. Large collection of colonial period correspondence, proprietary commissions, instructions, accounts, and miscellany.

Coffing Account Book, Manuscript Collection 249. Includes charges to the account of Boucher, sometimes misspelled *Voucher*.

Dulany Papers, Manuscript Collection 1265. Includes a poem dedicated to Boucher and other Homony Club members and a letter from S. Wirt to an unknown friend with references to Boucher.

Fisher Transcripts, Manuscript Collection 360.1. Typescript copies of some of the letters in the Boucher Manuscripts at Lewes, England; three letters to Boucher from Rev. Thomas B. Chandler; and three letters to George Ellis.

Gilmor Papers, Manuscript Collection 387 and 387.1. Covers the period of Governor Horatio Sharpe's administration and includes rare handbills and some papers of the Homony Club, including lines by Boucher rhyming his last name with *voucher*.

Kennedy Papers, Manuscript Collection 1336. Edward Pinkney's Notes on the life of his father, William Pinkney. Has references to Boucher.

Scharf Papers, Manuscript Collection 1999. Includes numerous papers regarding Boucher's accounts and debts. (Originals now at the Annapolis Hall of Records for microfilming.)

BOSTON, MASSACHUSETTS
Massachusetts Historical Society. General Theological Seminary Papers. Includes correspondence between Samuel Seabury and Boucher.

CARLISLE, ENGLAND
Cumbria County Library. Includes miscellaneous documents, articles, copies of portraits of Boucher and Boucher family history, his motto, arms and crest, and his own copy of Hutchinson's *History* with R. L. Ferguson's "Explicatio."

Cumbria County Records Office, Castle Carlisle. Survey of Boucher family estate, 1813, survey maps of Cumberland, etc.

KINGSTON-UPON-THAMES, ENGLAND
Surrey Record Office. Duplicate land tax returns for Epsom, 1780-1831; Surrey Quarter Sessions and Clerk of the Peace records. Includes information on Boucher's Clay Hill and Epsom Parish holdings.

LEWES, ENGLAND. EAST SUSSEX RECORD OFFICE
Boucher Manuscripts. Includes several series ·of letters dating from 1759 to 1799. The bulk of the letters are to Rev. John James, and run from 1759 to 1784. Most of these letters were printed in whole or in part in the *Maryland Historical Magazine*, vols. 7-10 (1912-15). Other letters are from Boucher to John James, Jr., Rev. Joseph Tickell, Sir Frederick Morton Eden, Lord Germain (still listed incorrectly as William Knox [?]), William Eden, Elizabeth Hodgson, and Dr. Douglas, bishop of Salisbury. Also included are letters to Boucher from James Maury, Myles Cooper, William Stevens, Sir Frederick Morton Eden, and Rev. Charles Daubeny.

Locker-Lampson Collection. Correspondence relating primarily to Frederick Locker-Lampson, but including the letter of William Cobbett to Jonathan Boucher of August 1798 (vol. 2, p. 14, ii).

LONDON, ENGLAND
British Library. Egerton Manuscripts. Including Boucher letters to the bishop of Salisbury, copies of the advertisement and prospectus for Boucher's glossary, and his proposal for a soup establishment.

Lambeth Palace. Fulham Papers, American Colonial Section. Includes letters of recommendation to ordination for various individuals by Boucher, Boucher's letter to the bishop of London protesting the delay in his own ordination, a list of Maryland counties and parishes prepared by Boucher in 1775, and the "Memorial Representing the Present Case of the Church in Maryland." Also miscellaneous documents.

MANUSCRIPTS AND ARCHIVES DIVISION,
NEW YORK PUBLIC LIBRARY
NEW YORK, NEW YORK

Astor, Lenox and Tilden Foundations. American Loyalist Transcripts, 60 vols. Vol. 36 was particularly useful for the claims and memorials of Boucher and other Marylanders.

Bancroft Collection. Miscellaneous letters and documents, 1765-1783.

Webster Papers. One letter regarding Boucher's lexical work.

NEW HAVEN, CONNECTICUT

Sterling Memorial Library, Yale University. Benjamin Franklin Collection.

OXFORD, ENGLAND

Oxford University. Bodleian Library. Advertisement for Boucher's glossary and a catalog of Boucher's English library.

Montagu Manuscripts. William Upcott Collection. Non-Juror Papers. Cartwright letters to Boucher and Boucher letters to unknown correspondents.

PHILADELPHIA, PENNSYLVANIA
HISTORICAL SOCIETY OF PENNSYLVANIA

Cadwalader Collection. Letter from Boucher to the printer of the *Maryland Gazette*, 2 October 1783; covering letter to Gen. John Cadwalader.

Ferdinand Dreer Collection of Letters of English Clergymen. Includes three letters from Boucher to unknown correspondents.

Simon Gratz Collection of Letters. Includes Boucher letter to George Washington.

Homony Club Folio.

SAINT PAUL, MINNESOTA

Macalester College Library. Records of William Eddis.

SAN MARINO, CALIFORNIA

Huntington Library. Letters of Boucher to Edward Jerningham regarding an epitaph for Eleanor Addison Boucher and a poem for Boucher's eldest son, James.

SOUTHAMPTON, ENGLAND

University of Southampton. Letters of Joseph Jefferson of Basingstoke to Boucher, 1797-1804.

WASHINGTON, D. C. LIBRARY OF CONGRESS

Allen Papers. Accession 5223. Synodalia: Records of clerical meetings in Maryland between 1695 and 1773. Also Maryland Personal Miscellaneous Documents. Address to Robert Eden, Governor of Maryland 5 October 1771, signed by Boucher and twenty other ministers of the Established Church.

Bray Manuscript Collection. One letter of Boucher to Rev. John Waring, SPG.

Papers on Maryland's Church of England. Transcripts and photostats of Fulham Palace material; list of parishes and incumbencies, 1738-78.

Society for the Propagation of the Gospel in Foreign Parts. Miscellaneous papers in connection with Boucher's post as undersecretary to the SPG; two letters from Boucher and a salary receipt for £80.

BOOKS AND ARTICLES

Addison, James Thayer. *The Episcopal Church in the United States: 1789-1931.* New York: Scribner's, 1951.

Allan, Anne Alden. "Patriots and Loyalists: The Choice of Political Allegiances by the Members of Maryland's Proprietary Elite." *Journal of Southern History* 38 (1972): 283-92.

Allen, Bennett. *An Address to the Vestrymen Church-Wardens and Parishioners of the Parish of All-Saints, in Frederick County: Wherein the Author's Conduct is Explained, and his Character Vindicated From the Aspersions Thrown Upon it in the Maryland Gazette: With a Preface.* Philadelphia: William Goddard [?], 1768.

Allen, The Reverend Ethan. *Clergy in Maryland of the Protestant Episcopal Church since the Independence of 1783.* Baltimore: J. S. Waters, 1860.

_____. "Notes on Maryland Parishes." *Maryland Historical Magazine* 9 (1940): 315-26.

American Archives: A Documentary History of the English Colonies in America from the King's Message to Parliament of March 7, 1774 to the Declaration of Independence by the United States. Edited by St. Clair Clarke and Peter Force. Series 4. 9 vols. Washington, D. C., 1833-37.

Ammerman, David. "Annapolis and the First Continental Congress: A Note on the Committee System in Revolutionary America." *Maryland Historical Magazine* 66 (1971): 169-80.

_____. *In the Common Cause: American Response to the Coercive Acts of 1774.* Charlottesville: University Press of Virginia, 1974.

Anderson, James Sims M. *History of the Church of England in the Colonies and Dependencies of the British Empire.* 3 vols. London: Rivington's, 1856.

Andrews, Matthew Page. *History of Maryland: Province and State.* Garden City, New York: Doubleday, Doran and Co., 1929.

Archives of Maryland. 72 vols. Baltimore: Maryland Historical Society, 1883-1972.

Ashe, Samuel A. "Memories of Annapolis," *Southern Atlantic Quarterly* 18 (1919): 197-210.

Association of the Freemen of Maryland, 26 July 1775. The Long Premeditated and Now Avowed Design of the British Government to Raise a Revenue from the Property of the Colonists Without Their Consent . . . . Annapolis: Frederick Green, 1775.

Bacon-Foster, Corra. "Early Chapters in the Development of the Potomac Route to the West." *Records of the Columbia Historical Society* 15 (1912): 96-322.

Barker, Charles Albro. *Background of the Revolution in Maryland.* New Haven: Yale University Press, 1940.

_____. "Maryland Before the Revolution: Society and Thought." *American Historical Review* 46 (1940): 1-20.

Beirne, Rosamond. "Portrait of a Colonial Governor: Robert Eden." *Maryland Historical Magazine* 45 (1950): 153-75.

Benjamin, Marcus. "Maryland During the Revolution." *Maryland Historical Magazine* 24 (1929): 324-42.

Bernhard, Winfred. *Fisher Ames, Federalist and Statesman: 1758-1808.* Chapel

Hill: University of North Carolina Press, 1965.

Billington, Ray Allen. *Westward Expansion*. New York: Macmillan Co., 1949.

Bolton, Sidney Charles. "The Anglican Church in Maryland Politics." Master's thesis, University of Wisconsin, 1968.

Bouch, C. M. Lowther. "Jonathan Boucher." *Transactions of the Cumberland and Westmorland Antiquarian and Archaeological Society*, n.s., 27 (1927): 117-51.

Boucher, Jonathan. "Letters to George Washington." *New England Historical and Genealogical Register* 52 (1898), 53 (1899), 54 (1900).

Bouchier, Jonathan. "Reminiscences of an American Loyalist." *Notes and Queries*, ser. 5, 5 (1876): 501-3; 6 (1876): 21-23, 81-83, 141-43, 161-62. "The Reverend Jonathan Boucher." *Notes and Queries*, ser. 5, 1 (1874): 102-4.

Bowie, Effie G. *Across the Years in Prince George's County: A Genealogical and Biographical History of Some Prince George's County, Maryland and Allied Families*. Richmond, Virginia: Garrett & Massie, 1947.

Bowman, Larry. "The Virginia County Committees of Safety, 1774-1776." *Virginia Magazine of History and Biography* 19 (1971): 322-37.

Bridenbaugh, Carl. *Mitre and Sceptre: Transatlantic Faiths, Ideas, Personalities, and Politics*. New York: Oxford University Press, 1962.

Brown, Alan. "William Eden and the American Revolution." Ph.D. dissertation, University of Michigan, 1953.

Brown, Richard D. *Revolutionary Politics in Massachusetts: The Boston Committee of Correspondence and the Towns, 1772-1774*. Cambridge, Mass.: Harvard University Press, 1970.

Brown, Wallace. *The Good Americans: The Loyalists in the American Revolution*. New York: William Morrow and Company, Inc., 1969.

____. *The King's Friends: The Composition and Motives of the American Loyalist Claimants*. Providence: Brown University Press, 1966.

Brumbaugh, Gaius M. *Maryland Records: Colonial, Revolutionary, County and Church, from Original Sources*. 2 vols. Lancaster, Pa.: Lancaster Press, 1928.

Brydon, G. MacLaren. "Clergy of the Established Church in Virginia and the Revolution." *Virginia Magazine of History and Biography* 41 (1933): 11-23, 123-43, 231-43, 297-309.

____. *Virginia's Mother Church and the Political Conditions under Which It Grew*. 2 vols. Philadelphia: Church Historical Society, 1952.

Calhoon, Robert McCluer. *The Loyalists in Revolutionary America: 1760-1781*. New York: Harcourt Brace Jovanovich, Inc., 1973.

Callahan, North. *Royal Raiders: The Tories of the American Revolution*. New York: Bobbs-Merrill Co., 1963.

Chalmers, George. *An Introduction to the History of the Revolt of the American Colonies, Being a Comprehensive View of Its Origin, Derived from the State Papers Contained in the Public Record Office*. London: Baker and Galabin, 1782. (Vol. 1 was suppressed; vols. 1 and 2 were published in Boston by J. Munroe and Co., 1845.)

Chester, Joseph Lemuel. "George Washington and the Reverend Jonathan Boucher." *Notes and Queries*, ser. 5, 9 (1878): 50-51.

Clark, Michael D. "Jonathan Boucher and the Toleration of Roman Catholics in Maryland." *Maryland Historical Magazine* 71 (1976): 194-203.

____. "Jonathan Boucher: The Mirror of Reaction." *Huntington Library Quarterly* 33 (1969-70): 19-32.

Coke, Daniel Parker. *The Royal Commission on the Losses and Services of the American Loyalists, 1783-1785 being the Notes of Mr. Daniel Parker*

Coke, M. P., one of the Commissioners during that Period. Edited by Hugh Edward Egerton. Oxford: H. Hart, 1915.

A Constitutionalist [pseud.] A Reply to the Church of England Planter's First Letter Respecting the Clergy. Annapolis: Anne Catharine Green, 1770.

Cross, Arthur Lyon. The Anglican Episcopate and the American Colonies. New York: Longmans, Green and Co., 1902.

Crowl, Philip. Maryland During and After the Revolution. Baltimore: Johns Hopkins Press, 1943.

Daubeny, Charles. An Appendix to the Guide to the Church; in which the principles advanced in that work are more fully maintained; in answer to objections brought against them by Sir Richard Hill, Bart. in his letters addressed to the author, under the title of "An Apology for Brotherly Love." London: J. Hatchard; F. & C. Rivington, 1799.

_____. Guide to the Church in Several Discourses . . . . London: T. Cadell, Jun. & W. Davies, 1798.

Dickerson, Oliver M. Review of Reminiscences of an American Loyalist: 1738-1789. Mississippi Valley Review 12 (1925-26): 593.

Dixon, Richard Ferguson. "Forgotten Cumbrian Worthy: A Blencogo Man in the War of Independence." Cumberland News, 25 December 1926.

Duke, Paul. "Jonathan Boucher, Tory Parson, Teacher and Political Theorist." Ph.D. dissertation, University of Washington, 1956.

Dulany, Daniel. Considerations on the Propriety of Imposing Taxes in the British Colonies, For the Purpose of Raising a Revenue, by Act of Parliament. Annapolis: Jonas Green, 1765.

Eddis, William. Letters from America, Historical and Descriptive: 1769-1777. Edited by Aubrey C. Land. Cambridge, Mass.: Harvard University Press, 1969.

Eden, Sir Frederick Morton. The State of the Poor; or An History of the Labouring Classes in England from the Conquest to the Present Period; in which are Particularly Considered Their Domestic Economy, with Respect to Diet, Dress, Fuel, and Habitation; and the Various Plans which, from Time to Time, Have Been Proposed and Adopted for the Relief of the Poor, Together with Parochial Reports Relative to the Administration of Work Houses and Houses of Industry, the State of Friendly Societies; and Other Public Institutions . . . With a Large Appendix Containing a Comparative and Chronological Table of the Prices of Labour, of Provisions and of other Commodities . . . . 3 vols. London: J. Davis for B. & J. White, 1797. Facsimile ed. London: Frank Cass & Co. Ltd., 1966. Reprinted London: George Routledge & Sons, 1928, 1 vol., with the Boucher "Address" eliminated.

_____. The Vision: A Poem by the Late Sir Frederick Eden, Baronet, Addressed to the Late Reverend Jonathan Boucher. London: William Ainsworth, 1828.

Eden, Robert Allan. Some Historical Notes on the Eden Family. London: Blades, East and Blades, 1907.

Edgar, Lady Matilda. Colonial Governor in Maryland: Horatio Sharpe and his Times, 1753-1773. London: Longman's, Green, 1912.

Edwin-Cole, James. "A Genealogical Memoir of a Branch of the Family of Bourchier." The Herald and Genealogist 8 (1874): 367-76.

Einstein, Lewis D. Divided Loyalties: Americans in England during the War of Independence. Boston: Houghton, Mifflin Co., 1933.

Evans, Margaret, ed. Letters of Richard Radcliffe and John James of Queen's College, Oxford, 1755-1783. Oxford Historical Society Collection Publication No. 9. Oxford: Oxford University Press, 1888.

Evanson, Philip. "Jonathan Boucher: The Mind of an American Loyalist." *Maryland Historical Magazine* 58 (1963): 123-36.

Fall, Ralph Emmett. "Jonathan Boucher, Turbulent Tory." *Historical Magazine of the Protestant Episcopal Church* 36 (1967): 323-56.

Fitzpatrick, John Clement. *Writings of George Washington from the Original Manuscript Sources: 1745-1799.* 39 vols. Washington, D. C.: George Washington Centennial Commission, 1931-44.

Ford, Worthington Chauncey. *Letters of Jonathan Boucher to George Washington, with Other Letters to Washington and Letters of Washington to Boucher.* Brooklyn, New York: Historical Printing Club, D. Clapp & Son, 1899.

"Forgotten Cumbrian Worthy: A Blencogo Man in the War for Independence." *Cumberland News,* 12 December 1926.

Freeman, Douglas S., ed. *George Washington.* 7 vols. New York: Scribner's Sons, 1947-57.

Gassaway, John. "Confiscated British Property." *Maryland Historical Magazine* 8 (1913): 369-70.

Giddens, Paul H. "Maryland and the Stamp Act Controversy." *Maryland Historical Magazine* 27 (1932): 79-98.

_____. "Governor Horatio Sharpe and his Maryland Government." *Maryland Historical Magazine* 32 (1937): 156-74.

Goodwin, Edward L. *Colonial Church in Virginia.* Milwaukee: Morehouse Publishing Co., 1927.

Greene, Jack P., ed. *The Diary of Colonel Landon Carter of Sabine Hall, 1752-1778.* 2 vols. Charlottesville, Va.: University of Virginia Press, 1965.

Gruber, Ira D. *The Howe Brothers and the American Revolution.* Chapel Hill: University of North Carolina Press, 1972.

Gummere, Richard M. "Jonathan Boucher, Toryissimus." *The American Colonial Mind and the Classical Tradition: Essays in Comparative Culture.* Cambridge, Mass.: Harvard University Press, 1963.

Hamilton, Allan McLane. *The Intimate Life of Alexander Hamilton, Based Chiefly on Original Family Letters and other Documents, Many of Which Have Never Been Published.* New York: Scribner's Sons, 1912.

Haw, James Alfred. "Politics in Revolutionary Maryland, 1753-1788." Ph.D. dissertation, University of Virginia, 1972.

Hawkins, Ernest. *Historical Notices of the Missions of the Church of England in North American Colonies Previous to the Independence of the United States; Chiefly from the Documents of the Society for the Propagation of the Gospel in Foreign Parts.* London: B. Fellows, 1845.

Hawks, Francis L. *Contributions to the Ecclesiastical History of the United States of America.* 2 vols. New York: Harper Brothers, 1836-39.

Heatwole, Cornelius J. *History of Education in Virginia.* New York: Macmillan Co., 1916.

Hodgson, Sarah. *History of the Parish of Bromfield.* Cockermouth: *West Cumberland Times,* n.d.

Hoffman, Ronald. *A Spirit of Dissension: Economics, Politics and the Revolution in Maryland.* Baltimore: Johns Hopkins University Press, 1973.

Hofstadter, Richard. *The Idea of a Party System: The Rise of Legitimate Opposition in the United States, 1780-1840.* Berkeley: University of California Press, 1969.

Hooker, Richard. "The Anglican Church and the American Revolution." Ph.D. dissertation, University of Chicago, 1943.

Hutchinson, William. *History of the County of Cumberland, and some places adjacent, from the earliest accounts to the present Time: Comprehending the local history of the county, its antiquities, the origin, genealogy, and present state of the principal families with biographical notes, its mines, minerals and plants, with other curiosities, either of nature or of art . . . .* 2 vols. Carlisle, England: F. Jollie, 1793-97. Reprinted in 2 vols. as *History of the County of Cumberland* by E. P. Publishing, Ltd., in collaboration with the Cumbria County Library, 1974.

Inventory of the Church Archives of Maryland. Protestant Episcopal: Diocese of Maryland. Baltimore: Maryland Historical Records Survey, 1940.

Jones, Jerome Walker. "The Anglican Church in Colonial Virginia, 1690-1760." Ph.D. dissertation, Harvard University, 1959.

Karinen, Arthur E. "Numerical and Distributional Aspects of Maryland Population, 1631-1840." Ph.D. dissertation, University of Maryland, 1958.

Labaree, Leonard. "Nature of American Loyalism." *American Antiquarian Society Proceedings* 54 (1944): 15-58.

Land, Aubrey C. *The Dulanys of Maryland: A Biographical Study of Daniel Dulany, the Elder (1685-1753) and Daniel Dulany, the Younger (1722-1797).* Baltimore: Maryland Historical Society, 1955.

_____. "Genesis of a Colonial Fortune: Daniel Dulany of Maryland." *William and Mary Quarterly* 7 (1941): 255-69.

_____. "Sharpe's Confidential Report on Maryland." *Maryland Historical Magazine* 44 (1949): 123-29.

Laslett, Peter. "Sir Robert Filmer: The Man Versus the Whig Myth." *William and Mary Quarterly*, ser. 3, 5 (1948): 523-46.

Lemay, J. A. Leo. "Robert Bolling and the Bailment of Colonel Chiswell." *Early American Literature* 6 (1971): 99-142.

Locker-Lampson, Frederick. *My Confidences: An Autobiographical Sketch Addressed to My Descendants.* London: Smith, Elder & Co., 1896.

McConnell, S. D. *A History of the American Episcopal Church.* New York: Thomas Whittaker, 1890.

McGrath, Francis Sims. *Pillars of Maryland.* Richmond: Dietz Press, 1950.

McIntire, W. T. "Jonathan Boucher." *Cumberland News*, 3 January 1951.

McSherry, James. *History of Maryland; From its First Settlement in 1634 to the year 1848.* Baltimore: J. Murphy, 1849.

Manross, William W. *A History of the American Episcopal Church.* New York: Morehouse-Gorham Co., 1950.

Marcus, Benjamin. "Maryland During the Revolution." *Maryland Historical Magazine* 24 (1929): 325-42.

Marshall, R. W. "What Jonathan Boucher Preached." *Virginia Magazine of History and Biography* 46 (1938): 1-12.

Meade, William. *Old Churches, Ministers and Families of Virginia.* 2 vols. Philadelphia: J. B. Lippincott Co., 1906.

Middleton, Arthur D. "The Colonial Virginia Parson." *William and Mary Quarterly* 26 (1969): 425-40.

Neill, Edward D. "Life and Times of Jonathan Boucher, The Tory Clergyman, A.D. 1759-1775." In *Notes on Virginia Colonial Clergy*, pp. 29-34. Reprinted from the *Episcopal Recorder.* Philadelphia, 1877.

Nelson, William H. *The American Tory.* Oxford: Clarendon Press, 1961.

Norton, Mary Beth. *The British-Americans: The Loyalist Exiles in England, 1774-1789.* Boston: Little, Brown and Company, 1972.

"The Loyalist Critique of the Revolution." In *The Development of a Revolutionary Mentality.* Edited by Elizabeth E. Hamer. Washington, D. C.: Library of Congress, 1972.

Odell, Jonathan. *An Essay on the Elements, Accents, & Prosody of the English Language, Intended to have been Printed as an Introduction to Mr.*

Boucher's Supplement to Dr. Johnson's Dictionary. London: Printed for Lackington, Allen & Co., Temple of the Muses, Finsbury Square, 1806.

Overfield, Richard Arthur. "The Loyalists of Maryland During the American Revolution." Ph.D. dissertation, University of Maryland, 1968.

Parkhurst, John M. A. *A Hebrew and English Lexicon.* London: W. Faden, 1762.

Pascoe, Charles F. *Two Hundred Years of the SPG: An Historical Account of the Society for the Propagation of the Gospel in Foreign Parts, 1701-1900.* London: By the Society, 1901.

Pate, James E. "Jonathan Boucher, An American Loyalist." *Maryland Historical Magazine* 15 (1930): 305-19.

Pennington, E. L. "Some Observations Regarding the Colonial Clergy." *Historical Magazine of the Protestant Episcopal Church* 10 (1941): 23-68.

Perry, William Stevens. "The Alleged 'Toryism' of the Clergy of the United States at the Breakout of the War of the Revolution: An Historical Examination." *Historical Magazine of the Protestant Episcopal Church* 45 (1976): 133-44.

Perry, William Stevens, ed. *Historical Collections Relating to the American Colonial Church.* 5 vols. Hartford: Church Press Co., 1870-78.

Read, Allen Walker. "Boucher's Linguistic Pastoral of Colonial Maryland." *Dialect Notes* 6 (1933): 353-60.

Rightmyer, Nelson W. "The Anglican Church in Maryland." *Church History* 20 (1941): 187-98.

_____. "The Character of the Anglican Clergy of Colonial Maryland." *Maryland Historical Magazine* 44 (1949): 229-49.

_____. *Maryland's Established Church.* Baltimore: Church Historical Society, 1956.

Ryerson, Adolphus E. *The Loyalists of America and Their Times: From 1620-1816.* Toronto: W. Briggs, 1880.

Sabine, Lorenzo. *The American Loyalists; or Biographical Sketches of Adherents to the British Crown in the War of the Revolution.* 2 vols. Boston: Little, Brown, 1847.

_____. *An Historical Essay on the Loyalists of the American Revolution.* Springfield, Mass.: Walden Press, 1957.

Scharf, J. Thomas. *History of Maryland from the Earliest Period to the Present Day.* 3 vols. Baltimore: John B. Piet, 1879.

Scisco, Louis Dow. "Colonial Records of Anne Arundel." *Maryland Historical Magazine* 22 (1927): 62-67.

Scott, Andrew, ed. *Political Thought in America.* New York: Holt, Rinehart, 1959.

Seiler, William. "The Anglican Parish in Tidewater Virginia: 1607-1776." Ph.D. dissertation, University of Iowa, 1948.

Sharpe, Governor Horatio. *Correspondence of Governor Horatio Sharpe . . . : 1753-1771.* Baltimore: Maryland Historical Society, 1888-1911.

"Short Account of the Late Mr. Boucher." *Gentleman's Magazine* 94 (1804): 591-93.

Silver, John Archer. *The Provisional Government of Maryland (1774-1777).* Baltimore: Johns Hopkins Press, 1895.

Skaggs, David Curtis. "Maryland's Impulse Toward Social Revolution: 1750-1776." *Journal of American History* 54 (1968): 771-86.

Skinner, John. "Correspondence with Jonathan Boucher, 1786." *Historical Magazine of the Protestant Episcopal Church* 10 (1941): 163-75.

Smith, Paul H. *Loyalists and Redcoats: A Study in British Revolutionary Policy.* Chapel Hill: University of North Carolina Press, 1964.

Smith, Zuma Zeda. "Status of Churches in Maryland: 1763-1783." Ph.D. dissertation, University of Chicago, 1924.

Steiner, Bernard. *Life and Administration of Sir Robert Eden.* Johns Hopkins University Studies, no. 16. Baltimore: Johns Hopkins University Press, 1898.

———. "Unpublished from Lambeth Palace." *Maryland Historical Magazine* 12 (1917): 130-31.

Stevens, William Oliver. *Annapolis, Anne Arundel's Town.* New York: Dodd, Mead and Co., 1937.

Sweet, Mary C. "Massachusetts and Maryland in the Revolution." *Magazine of History* 20 (1915): 222-41.

Sweet, William Warren. "The Role of the Anglicans in the American Revolution." *Huntington Library Quarterly* 9 (1947-48): 51-70.

Thomlinson, George C. "Account of St. Bees, Cumberland." *Gentleman's Magazine* 148 (1831): 301-3.

Thompson, Marcella Wycliff, ed. "Jonathan Boucher (1738-1804)." *Blackwood's Magazine* 231 (1932): 315-34.

Thornbury, Walter. "The Reverend Jonathan Boucher." *Notes and Queries,* ser. 3, 9 (1866): 75-76.

Thrax [pseud.] "The Reverend Jonathan Boucher." *Notes and Queries,* ser. 3, 9 (1866): 282-84.

Tyler, Moses Coit. *Literary History of the American Revolution: 1763-1783.* New York: Putnam's Sons, 1897.

———. "The Party of the Loyalists in the American Revolution." *American Historical Review* 1 (1895-96): 24-46.

"Washington's Cumbrian Friend." *Cumberland News,* 13 May 1977.

Van Horn, R. Lee. "Jonathan Boucher." In "Out of the Past," *The Prince George's Post,* 13 October 1960.

Van Tyne, Claude H. *Loyalists in the American Revolution.* New York: Macmillan Co., 1902.

Walker, Robert G. "Jonathan Boucher: Champion of the Minority." *William and Mary Quarterly,* ser. 3, 2 (1945): 3-14.

Washington, George. *Detroit to the Tidewater, A facsimile of an autograph letter signed by George Washington, dated Oct. 25, 1784.* Edited by James M. Babcock. Detroit: Detroit Public Library, 1962.

Wheeler, Joseph Towne. *The Maryland Press, 1770-1790.* Baltimore: Maryland Historical Society, 1938.

Weis, Frederick Lewis. *Colonial Churches and the Colonial Clergy of the Middle and Southern Colonies: 1607-1776.* Lancaster, Mass.: Society of the Descendants of the Colonial Clergy, 1950.

Zimmer, Anne Y. "The 'Paper War' in Maryland, 1770-73: The Paca-Chase Political Philosophy Tested." *Maryland Historical Magazine* 71 (1976): 177-93.

———, and Kelley, Alfred H. "Jonathan Boucher: Constitutional Conservative." *Journal of American History* 58 (1972): 899-902.

⌒ Index ⌒

A

Act of Establishment, 123-26, 340
Adams, John, 205, 272, 277, 279, 293
Addison, Ann, 114, 190
Addison, Eleanor (Nelly). *See* Boucher, Eleanor Addison (Nelly)
Addison, Rev. Henry: befriends Boucher, 69, 132; and Boucher's courtship of Judith Chase, 327, 329; and Boucher's courtship of Nelly, 115; and Boucher's intellectual development, 70, 93, 174; departs for England, 189; encourages Boucher to seek Maryland post, 68, 71, 76, 82-83, 112; and sons' education, 68, 135; mentioned, 73, 88, 143, 173, 186, 209, 220-21
Addison, John, 142, 358n.15
Addison, Thomas, 142
Allen, Benedict. *See* Allen, Rev. Bennet
Allen, Rev. Bennet, 71-77, 82, 220
American episcopate. *See* Boucher, Jonathan, resident bishop issue
American Revolution, 245, 269-70, 275-76, 285, 287, 301
Ames, Fisher, 278, 283, 286
Anglican church. *See* Church of England
Appendix to the Guide to the Church, An (Daubeny), 255
Articles of Association. *See* Continental Association
Assembly, Maryland. *See* Maryland House of Delegates

Association. *See* Continental Association

B

Bacon, Thomas, 71, 77
Baltimore, Lord: death of, 106, 120; and Rev. Bennet Allen 72-74; and Henry Hartford's inheritance, 106; and resident bishop issue, 92
Blair, John, 63-64
Boston Port Act, 140, 147
Boucher, Eleanor Addison (Nelly): acquaintance with George Washington, 134; Boucher's early interest in, 114; death of, 229; family estates of, 142, 145; health of, 115-16, 211, 223, 226, 228, 244; and life in England, 195, 208, 210, 215, 223; personality of, 116, 147, 184, 212, 224, 311
Boucher, Elizabeth Hodgson, 246-47, 345, 375n.22. *See also* James, Elizabeth Hodgson
Boucher, James (father), 17, 31-33
Boucher, James (son), 244, 264, 324, 367n.29
Boucher, Jane (Jinny): acquaintance with George Washington, 82, 134; annuity for, 213, 264, 311; death of, 245; goes to America, 45; relationship with Boucher's family, 47, 79, 184, 216, 232-33, 264, 327; remains in America, 190-91; mentioned, 32, 67, 114, 186, 240

389

C

ℱ

𝒢

ℋ

ℐ

𝒥

Anne Y. Zimmer is an associate professor in the Department of History, Wayne State University. Born in Detroit, she received her B.S., M.A., and Ph.D. from Wayne State. She has been awarded several scholarships and fellowships, and is active in many professional and cultural organizations. Her previous publications include articles on Jonathan Boucher and other eighteenth-century persons and topics.

The manuscript was edited by Sherwyn T. Carr. The book was designed by Mary Primeau. The typeface for the text is Caledonia, designed by W. A. Dwiggins about 1938, and the display face is LeGriffe.

The text is printed on Sebago cream white antique paper. The book is bound in Holliston's Kingston cloth over binder's boards. Manufactured in the United States of America.